Ensouling Language

On the Art of Nonfiction and the Writer's Life

Stephen Harrod Buhner

Inner Traditions
Rochester, Vermont • Toronto, Canada

Inner Traditions
One Park Street
Rochester, Vermont 05767
www.InnerTraditions.com

Text paper is SFI certified

Library of Congress Cataloging-in-Publication Data

Buhner, Stephen Harrod.
Ensouling language : on the art of nonfiction and the writer's life / Stephen Harrod Buhner.
p. cm.
Includes bibliographical references and index.
ISBN 978-1-59477-382-2 (pbk.)
1. Authorship. I. Title.
PN145.B745 2010
808'.02—dc22

2010016052

Printed and bound in the United States by Lake Book Manufacturing
The text paper is 100% SFI certified. The Sustainable Forestry Initiative® program promotes sustainable forest management.

10 9 8 7 6 5 4 3 2 1

Text design and layout by Priscilla Baker
This book was typeset in Garamond Premier Pro with Throhand used as a display typeface.

To send correspondence to the author of this book, mail a first-class letter to the author c/o Inner Traditions • Bear & Company, One Park Street, Rochester, VT 05767, and we will forward the communication.

For the ones who taught me:

John Dunning, Robert Bly, John Gardner,
and William Stafford

And for all those who come after

illigitimi non carborundum

Thanks are extended to the following publishers and authors for granting permission to reprint:

"For Freckle-Faced Gerald" from *The Essential Etheridge Knight,* by Etheridge Knight, copyright © 1986. Reprinted by permission of the University of Pittsburgh Press.

Robert Bly, for permission to reprint from *American Poetry: Wildness and Domesticity,* Harper and Row, copyright © 1990 by Robert Bly, as well as his translations of two poems of Machado, one of Jiminez, and one of Rilke.

Samuel Delany, excerpts from *The Einstein Intersection,* copyright © 1967 by Samuel Delany and reprinted by permission of Wesleyan Press.

From *The Notebooks of Malte Laurids Brigge* by Ranier Maria Rilke, translated by M. D. Herter Norton. Copyright © 1949 by W. W. Norton & Company, Inc. Renewed © 1977 by M. D. Herter Norton Crena de Iongh. Used by permission of W. W. Norton & Company, Inc.

On Becoming a Novelist by John Gardner. Copyright © 1983 by the Estate of John Gardner. Reprinted by permission of Georges Borchardt, Inc., for the Estate of John Gardner.

William Stafford, "A Ritual to Read to Each Other" from *The Way It Is: New and Selected Poems*. Copyright © 1960, 1998 by William Stafford and the Estate of William Stafford. Reprinted with the permission of Graywolf Press, Minneapolis, Minnesota, www.graywolfpress.org.

Laura María Agustín, *Sex at the Margins,* copyright © 2007 by Laura María Agustín. Reprinted by permission of Zed Books, London & New York, www.zedbooks.co.uk.

From *The Art of Fiction* by John Gardner, copyright © 1984 by the Estate of John Gardner. Used by permission of Alfred A. Knopf, a division of Random House, Inc.

From *One Way to Spell Man* by Wallace Stegner. Originally published in *Saturday Review,* August 1958, copyright © 1958, 1982 by Wallace Stegner. Reprinted by permission of Brandt & Hochman Literary Agents, Inc. All Rights Reserved.

From *Habitations of the Word,* Cornell University Press, Copyright © 1985 by William Gass. Reprinted with the permission of the author.

Contents

IV—*On Technique*

The First Draft, Revision, Clarity, and Refinement

The Appendices—*On the Business of Writing*

We must ask ourselves:
Who benefits when the gods disappear from the world.

James Hillman

Before Buying This Book

The still small voice of reason is what I keep trying to protect in myself and cherish in others. Don't tell me what forensic speakers have forced on you. Relax, forget them. Tell me quietly, here in this room, what you really think.

William Stafford

I am a barbarian; it is only polite to tell you that up front. You should keep that well in mind before you decide to buy this book. And, though I have been dressing myself since my early twenties, I am not really house-broken, not really civilized. That especially applies to my writing—and my opinions, observations, and advice about the craft.

I disapprove of most of what passes for professional nonfiction (and literary fiction) in American culture. You'll also find I disagree with a great many things that are considered necessary for writers to learn, especially in writing schools. I don't think writers should be too civilized, that they should be too much of the cities (which is what the word civilized means). I think that they must, of necessity, live in the crucial but commonly overlooked transition zone that lies between human habitat and the wildness of the world, the place where wild plants exchange genome with their more domesticated cousins.[1] I believe writers must travel into wilderness and bring back what they find, envelop it in words, and release it into the world. I believe that is their ecological function and without that renewal human culture deteriorates. I believe in the sacredness and the necessity of the art.

You should also be aware that I think the three worst books on writing ever published are Strunk and White's *The Elements of Style, Writing Down the Bones,* and *The Chicago Manual of Style,* followed by most of the others. Thus, I am also a heretic. I believe, too, that most MFA programs, rather than teaching passionate human beings how to write, teach them how to be like everyone else, that they, in fact, teach genius to be mediocre, teach the gifted to fit in, actively constrain talent in corrals made of outdated rules, grammatical fascism, envy, and general ignorance. Thus, I am also rude and insensitive, in the end not much a fan of crossing-the-aisle gesturing.

Regrettably, due more to failures of character than any legitimate rationale, nonfiction, the subject of this book, is rarely recognized as a major literary form, a form that can take on the same luminosity that occurs in great poetry or fiction. And I am not talking here about those semifraudulent forms of nonfiction known as narrative nonfiction and the memoir. Those two types of nonfiction, the ones most commonly taught in writing schools, are the most susceptible to absorption into the dead-end literary styles that make up most products of the New York publishing scene: modernism, postmodernism, poststructuralism, postmodernmetafiction, postmodernrealism, posttraumaticstressism, and all the rest of that nonsense.

I am talking about *nonfiction:* how-to books, self-help books, groundbreaking investigative reporting, nature books, plant identification books, environmental books, new age books, spirituality books, academic books, technical books, leading-edge research texts, and books by independent scholars. What is called narrative nonfiction (biographies, rugby players who eat their dead, death on Mount Everest, escaped plague viruses, i.e., gossip) or currently thought to be memoirs (i.e., adult survivors of abusive parents) are only a tiny part of the vast world of nonfiction. As Raul Hilberg, the holocaust historian has observed, "historiography is also an art form"[2] but is never recognized as such by either writing schools or the critics. "If one thinks," he says, "about the critical commentary devoted to literary or artistic works, replete with dissections of their structure, style, and ideas, one cannot help noticing that this bountiful attention is not lavished on historical sources, which are commonly deemed lifeless. Yet each source has a definite configuration, a characteristic style, and a highly selective content."[3]

Alternate forms of nonfiction are rarely recognized by critics and writing schools as legitimate literary expressions, nevertheless they make up the majority of books written and sold in the United States. They are the poor relations of what is called creative or literary nonfiction, what might be called genre nonfiction just as mysteries, science fiction, and fantasy are considered genre fiction. They are often poorly written just as genre fiction once was (and oftentimes still is).

Genre fiction developed its modern form in the pulp magazine market in the early to late-middle of the twentieth century. Three people were instrumental in changing it from pulp writing to something else: Raymond Chandler in mystery fiction, John Campbell (as an editor) in science fiction, and J. R. R. Tolkein in fantasy. (Stephen King did the same thing somewhat later for horror fiction.) I believe it is time for genre nonfiction to undergo the same transformation—and to gain a similar recognition for its literary potential.

Because nonfiction is such a huge market, the writing schools and the literary world are trying to subsume it. It's for the money, of course, but that's rarely mentioned. Still, they are primarily interested only in what they call narrative nonfiction or memoirs—respectable nonfiction, nonfiction that seems like fiction, nonfiction that is well dressed, nonfiction without cow shit on its boots. A book on plumbing is about as welcome among works of literary nonfiction as a plumber with grease on his hands is at a book release party for a member of the literati. Genre nonfiction is still considered pulp writing and is very much looked down upon by most mainstream writers, publishers, and writing schools. (We be lowbrow, make no mistake.)

As Leah Price comments in the *London Review of Books:*

> *Those works which we group under the rubric of "literature" have never made up more than a fraction of the world's printed matter. That discrepancy makes it hard not to suspect that the distribution of book historians' attention is skewed by agendas imported from other disciplines. What gets over-represented is not just literature, but a particular genre: the novel. . . . Realist fiction's well-known obsession with the material world fits almost too perfectly with book history's own anti-idealism; so does the unabashed worldliness of the*

> *drama. Both crowd out any attention to lyric. . . . It can be argued that [a true history of the book] challenges the mind-body dualism that has come to shape the assumptions about literariness held by popular and scholarly audiences alike. . . . At a particular time and place, [Bourdieu] argues, art came to define itself through its contradistinction to economic life.*[4]

In other words, if you believe in lyricism in language and story, if you believe in the transcendent nature of the word, and write from that orientation, you aren't realistic, you're idealistic (in the pejorative sense of the word). And if you work with your body and your hands, and then write about that work in any practical sense (especially if you make money doing it), what you write just ain't literary.

The general public doesn't care, of course; they are just interested in what they are interested in, just as they didn't care about literary pretensions in the 1920s, '30s, and '40s. They read genre fiction then because that is what they were interested in then and they read genre nonfiction now because that is what they are interested in now. Genre nonfiction, like genre fiction, often has a lot more to do with real people's lives and their needs than do the alternatives.

Times have changed and instead of the pulps, which depended on the huge magazine readership that existed before television, we now have small presses (i.e., *independent* presses). Genre nonfiction, rather than being formatted for the needs of magazines, is usually book length and most of it is being published by those same *small* presses (even though some of them publish a hundred books a year). These presses, notoriously not discussed in most books on writing or publishing (e.g., Jason Epstein's egregious *Book Business: Publishing Past, Present, and Future*), are the places where many young writers can explore the craft of writing and serve their apprenticeship, just as Chandler and others did in the pulps. They are easier to break into than the New York houses and generally offer a greater range of exploration in writing than the New York publishers will ever be able to. They are the places genre nonfiction has been slowly explored and developed since the 1960s, ever since the hippies broke the New York publishers monopoly on distribution by forming their own distribution companies.

Genre nonfiction is *the* great undeveloped region of nonfiction, just as mysteries, science fiction, and fantasy once were in the fictional world. A great many writers, disgusted with the irrelevance of the New York publishing scene, are doing some of the best writing in the world in this undeveloped and generally unrecognized area. It is the most vital and vibrant area of publishing and writing that now exists outside the Internet. It is the one area of writing in which one can work outside the tired and dead-end forms that dominate most of the corporate publishing world.

Genre nonfiction can be raised to a sophisticated literary form, just as genre fiction has been, and supporting that is one of the primary intentions of this book. So, while this book, at its core, is about the art of writing and can be applied to any form of writing (including fiction and narrative and memoir nonfiction), it's focus is on genre nonfiction. And though you will find it useful if you only want to write one book, or even if you have published a number of them, this book has primarily been written for people who are called to the craft, for those who have felt the luminous power of language, who have fallen in love with it, and who are compelled by some deep part of themselves to take on this lineage as their own.

This book has not been written for the literati, the illiterati (critics), or the alliterati (graduates of MFA programs). It is for all the children who stayed up late, covers over their heads, flashlight on, reading when they were supposed to be sleeping. It is for every child who read a great line, and when the meaning of it penetrated them, felt the hairs rise on their arms. It is for every child who has felt touched by the greatness of this craft and then, when they were, heard someplace deep inside a tiny voice speaking, saying something like, "I wish I could write like that; I wish I could write something that would make other people feel like I just felt. I want to do that too."

You can and what is more, you must.

The Touch of a Golden Thread

Beginnings are such delicate times.

Frank Herbert

I was, indeed, then in the dark and struggled on, unconscious of what I was seeking so earnestly; but I had a feeling of the right, a divining-rod that showed me where gold was to be found.

Goethe

What anyone who speaks for art must be prepared to assert is the validity of nonscientific experience and the seriousness of unverifiable insight.

Wallace Stegner

CHAPTER ONE

The Bookman

I remember the day a name changed my life.

I'd driven down the mountain, hugging the twisting canyon walls of Flagstaff Road—carefully avoiding the five-hundred-foot drop into the ravine below—into Boulder, Colorado, then down 12th Street, past its huge nineteenth-century homes, onto Pearl Street, finally angle-parking in at Trident, a used bookstore and coffee shop—one that had existed long before Barnes-and-Noble took that dark, espresso poetry, cleaned it up, made it brighter, and expressed it, half suburbia, half yuppie, with only a hint still remaining of shadowed, university revolutionaries and poets in the wooden background, into half the world's consciousness.

I stopped a minute on the sidewalk to look at the books comfortably standing, covers slightly akimbo, on the scattered, staggered-level, blue-cloth-draped platforms behind the plateglass windows of the store, then grabbed the brass handle on the dark door and pulled it open. The smell of old books swirled over me blending subtly with the aromas of French roast coffee and cinnamon and years of human beings hunched over tables and textbooks and broken hearts, finding solace as millions have done before them in words of the long dead who had themselves once felt this sun's light and breathed this same air.

I wandered the book-lined canyons, lingering in the safety of nineteenth-century literature, sunning myself in the warmth of ancient philosophers, stopping briefly near poets who called me in brilliant, diamond-edged language, and grazed gladly among the shelves of science fiction, until I drifted into the half-dream state all old bookstores—and most libraries—can evoke. Time slowed and in some sort of half-waking, half-sleeping state I felt myself pulled to the special bookcase that towered behind the checkout counter. Some special gravity found only in such unique mind states, folded the space around one particular book, shifted light waves, until it was all I could see. I stretched, gathered the book off the shelf, took it in my hands, and opened the front cover of *I Sing the Body Electric*. There, in his trademark blue-felt-tip scrawl, covering half the page, was Ray Bradbury's signature. I reached out and touched the page—and felt a thrill go through me. Ten dollars seemed absurdly cheap and I gladly paid the money.

As I write these words, I stop, reach over, and take the book from the case in front of me. It's still as fresh and new as the day I found it. I touch the page once more and again I feel that thrill run through my body. Then I slowly flip the pages and find the lines Walt Whitman wrote so long ago, the lines that Bradbury took for his title:

> *I sing the body electric;*
> *The armies of those I love engirth me, and I engirth them;*
> *They will not let me off till I go with them, respond to them,*
> *and discorrupt them,*
> *and charge them full with the charge of the soul.*

There are times, I swear there are times, when something grabs hold of us and takes us places we would never have gone otherwise. Some magic thing took hold of me that day and only in the rearview mirror of middle age can I see its ghostly hand on my shoulder.

A few days later I traveled down the mountain again, parking farther up Pearl Street at the rambling, heavy-beamed Stage House II. The building is two stories tall, the books not only on scores of shelves along the downstairs walls but also upstairs along the balcony running three sides of the enormous store, and in the aisles and on every conceivable surface—stacked staggering, drunken, leaning against all odds into some force of gravity that only used bookstore owners know.

There, disguised as an old book, half-hidden among the scruffy remains of abandoned magazines and travel guides, was a novel by H. G. Wells. I opened it at random and caught glimpses of strange landscapes and nineteenth-century lives. I turned from the time-distorted language, flipped to the front of the book, and found that it, too, was signed. I reached out, tentatively this time, letting my fingers rest lightly upon that place Wells had touched so long ago. Something seemed to flow into me from the page, some living essence, as if I had dipped my hand in a flowing stream and for a moment some strange current was catching at my fingers. It pulled on me, took my hand, and murmured to some deep part of me, "Come, come and follow me." With difficulty I pulled my fingers off the page, stared at it a moment, then closed the book and set it back on the shelf. I stood bemused, feeling the pull, wanting to follow it, yet not understanding what it wanted, why I was so strongly affected by these unknown currents.

With an effort, I broke the spell and wandered upstairs. The section along the west wall was filled with books on poetry, mysteries, science fiction, and fantasy. Letting my eyes go soft focused, the titles and bright spines flowed into me like some kind of food. One book stood out and I reached out slowly and took it off the shelf. It was a first edition of *Earthlight* by Arthur C. Clarke, published, I later discovered, in an absurdly small hardcover print run in 1955 when Ballantine was just a small press few had heard of. The book was nearly perfect, the dust jacket like new. I felt drawn to it, some part of me wanted that book even though I didn't know the title well, didn't particularly desire to read it. I glanced through it, flipping the pages slowly. Reluctantly, I put it back on the shelf, and in a kind of dream, drove home.

The next week I received a catalogue of rare and out-of-print science fiction and fantasy from Lloyd Currey in Elizabethtown, New York. There were hundreds of signed, and unsigned books, by so many of the writers I loved. Flipping the pages, I noticed scores by Arthur Clarke, found *Earthlight* and glanced at the price, 600 (1985) dollars. My brain went black; I seemed to remember an entirely different price on the one at the bookstore. I drove back down the mountain, slipped into the store and up the stairs to the science fiction section, pulled the book off the shelf. I snuck the price catalogue out of my pocket, hurriedly found the page, stared at it. $600. Looked at the price lightly penciled on the front free endpaper of the book. $60. Must be a typo in the catalogue I kept thinking. I went outside, called Currey on the phone. After a few rings, he answered in that grumpy voice I would come to know so well, "L. W. Currey."

"Uh, hi. Ummm. Do you have a first edition of *Earthlight* by Arthur C. Clarke?"

"Yes."

"How much is it?"

"$600."

"Uh, thanks," I said and hung up, then stood a minute, thinking.

Went back in the store. Snuck upstairs. Picked up the book. Stood uncertain, trembling. Took a deep breath, carried it downstairs, picking up the Wells on the way. I placed the books on the counter, feeling like a thief, trying to keep my eyes calm, trying not to blush or look away. The clerk walked over.

"Help you?"

"Uh, I'm interested in these books but they are a little much for me. Can you offer a discount?"

The guy behind the counter, balding, glasses perched low on the end of his nose, glanced keenly at my face, opened the books, took a look at the prices. "$100 and $60." He paused to think for a minute. "Yeah, sure. Twenty percent off."

I mumbled something, took out my checkbook, began to write. Tried hard to keep my hands from shaking.

I felt a hand grabbing my shoulder all the way to the car.

The rare book game is an addiction, an endless Easter egg hunt, an exciting adventure, and a constant swimming in the transcendent world of language, printing, storytelling, storytellers, and the human solace and wisdom that can be found in books. If you are ever touched by it, it pulls you in, and, for a time, you can think of, do, nothing else.

I was not immune. I began to haunt used and rare bookstores.

Back then, Book Row in Denver was a collection of adjoining stores on Colfax Avenue a few miles east of the capital building. In the midst of bad restaurants, street prostitutes, drug dealers, Salvation Army stores, antique shops, and decrepit clothing outlets was one block on the south side of the street dedicated to used books. The stores began with Michael Grano's and Steve Wilson's Kugleman and Bent and ended with John

Dunning's Old Algonquin bookstore. In between these bookends was a collection of stores that traveled the spectrum from nice, if spare, to heaped collections of rotting, rain-soaked books in a store I never found open in seven years of regular trips to the Row.

Rumor had it, romantic it seemed to me then, that Grano and Wilson, one or both of them, had been motorcycle-riding, leather-clothed wild men, possibly heroin addicts. Wilson had once been a dedicated alcoholic (they said) who still had a first edition (in dust jacket) of the Alcoholics Anonymous handbook. Grano was charming, loquacious, and possessed a seemingly inexhaustible knowledge of books, their first edition points, value, and marketability. Wilson was towering, black-bearded, wild-eyed, less talkative—both of them showing the wear and tear of years spent too close to the bone. Because they were always short of cash for the store rent, my ready checkbook and raw enthusiasm for rare and unusual first editions were very welcome.

The day I first arrived in their shop they had just bought the entire collection of an early, Denver-based, science fiction publisher. Grano pulled out some gems: one of only three copies of Merritt's *The Black Wheel* bound with *The Fox Woman and the Blue Pagoda* and the original cover art for Frank Belknapp Long's *The Horror from the Hills*. I bought them all. Then I made my way down to the Old Algonquin where I could see John Dunning through the plateglass window, his back to the street, huge frame oozing over the stool, elbows on counter, head on hands, eyes scanning *AB Bookman's Weekly*. Back in those days, of course, he wasn't on the bestseller lists, wasn't selling a half-million copies a year, was just a writer down in the trenches like all of us. Getting up at 3 a.m. to write, eating breakfast at 6, scouting antique stores, the Salvation Army, and early-opening bookstores before unlocking the doors to his store at 10. He worked till 5, closed the shop, scouted books again on the way home, ate dinner, and went to bed. Repeated it the next day.

He had some great books and that first visit I bought a lot of them. Sitting on the shelf is one I still have. *The Complete Stories and Poems of Edgar Allen Poe* in two volumes, the Alfred A. Knopf edition of 1946, both volumes fine in jackets—a beautiful set. His tiny writing, penciled at the top of the front free endpaper, notes: "two volume set, 1st thus." On page 72 is Poe's immortal "The Raven," which, ten years later, John turned into one of the best mysteries ever written: *The Bookman's Wake.* But back then, of course, he was in his long, ten-year dry spell and had almost given up on writing. He spent his days learning the rare book game, sitting, along with the rest of us, at the feet of Grano and Wilson, just trying to keep a roof over his family's head and food on the table.

That first day in his shop he pulled himself off the stool, towered over my near-six-foot frame, shook my hand, and said, "As you can tell, I rarely miss a meal." Then he patted his stomach and grinned.

As the years went by we became friends and he told me stories—of his years at *The Denver Post,* how he started out sweeping the floor and ended up being the *Post's* lead investigative reporter, of even earlier times when he worked the racetrack circuit as a walker, and, of course, all about being a writer and what it's really like for most of us who decide to do this strange thing of weaving meaning-filled words together into a living fabric filled with dreams.

I remember one year when a bunch of us—Grano, Wilson, John, and some others whose faces and names have been lost in the wasteland of middle age—were on the road someplace, perhaps in Los Angeles at its great antiquarian book fair. We were at dinner, each of us telling stories of the rare book game, and into a pause John cleared his throat and said, "Here's a great one." And then he paused, making sure he had our attention.

"I was in L.A., scouting books, and wandered into a great store. The owner was one of the *old* bookmen, been around forever, and I struck up a conversation. We talked about the trade awhile and then he started telling me about this one book he'd sold recently.

"An old guy, tall and thin, with a shock of white hair above an incredibly lined, ancient face came into the shop one day.

"The bell above the door tinkles as the old guy enters the store, then he stands there a minute, blinking his eyes, letting them adjust to the gloom of the shop. He begins to glance around, sees the owner there, walks over to the glass counter, and pauses uncertainly.

"The owner smiles at him and says, 'Hi. Can I help you?'

"And the old guy says, 'Yes, I hope so,' and clears his throat, a bit nervous.

" 'Well, you see,' he says glancing at the bookman's face a bit timidly, 'there is this book I am looking for. My mother used to read it to me when I was young. I haven't thought about it in many years, but at this point in my life it is beginning to take on great importance to me. I want to read it again, once more, before I die.'

"The old bookman looks at him, waits a minute, and seeing that the old guy isn't going to say anything else, asks him, 'Well, what book is it?' And the old guy tells him.

"'Oh,' the bookman says, 'I know that book. And though I do get it from time to time, I don't have one now. It's not an expensive book but it is a little uncommon.'

"At this the old man's expression falls and the bookman sees this and says, 'Would you like me to do a book search for you?'

"The guy looks up hopefully, nods his head. 'Oh, yes,' he says.

"So, the bookman takes his name and address and phone number and the guy leaves."

Now most people, when they hear that a bookstore is going to do a book search for them have an image, difficult to avoid, of a fleet of little cars out back of the store with guys in black suits and ties, just waiting to search out hard-to-find books. When an order comes in, the thinking goes, they spread out over the country looking for just your book. The truth is much more pedestrian. What actually happened (in those days before the Internet) is that all those requests for book searches were thrown in a drawer. When enough of them accumulated the store owner would take out an ad in *AB Bookman's,* a used and rare book magazine that listed books wanted and books for sale. Used book store owners around the country, a few collectors, and some of the more solvent book scouts subscribed to the magazine, read it when business was slow and, if they had one of the books listed, would send out a postcard saying they had the book, its condition and cost, and that they would hold it awhile if the advertiser was interested.

"So," John goes on, "The bookman eventually takes out an ad in *Bookman's.* A couple of weeks, maybe a month, goes by and he gets this postcard, from Iowa or someplace, from a book scout, saying that he has a copy of the book. Pretty nice copy, previous owner's inscription on the first page, and not too expensive."

Now, as all of us at the table knew, book scouts are the only form of life, besides cockroaches, that can survive a direct nuclear attack. They are often marginal people, many times homeless, who generally got started as scouts when passing a garage sale one day. "Hardback Books, 50 cents" the sign says and they happen to have three dollars. So, they pick out six nice-looking books and take them down to the used bookstore, which buys them for twelve dollars, and they're hooked for life. Oddly enough, these guys often get very good at it and although they travel alone, they sometimes show up in large numbers at Salvation Army stores and garage sales, fighting each other over books they think they can sell. And once or perhaps twice a year they find a great book. A first of *Gone With the Wind* or an early Stephen King, perhaps a first edition *Salem's Lot* in the very rare first-state dust jacket, books worth many thousands of dollars. But usually it's just three dollars into twelve dollars.

"So," John continues, "the old bookman calls this guy and says, 'We've managed to locate a copy of the book you wanted.' He tells him the price and says, 'Would you like me to order it for you?' And the old guy says, 'yes.'

"Then, in a couple of weeks, the book arrives. The bookman calls the guy and says, 'Your book is here.' And the old guy tells him he'll be right over.

"Now this bookman has a great sense of style and he cleans off the glass counter top and sets the book just so in the middle of the glass and pretty soon he hears a car pull up in front of the store, the car door slams, and the shop door opens. The little bell tinkles and the bookman looks over to see the old guy standing like before, eyes blinking, getting used to the gloom of the store.

"Well, the old guy, once his eyes have adjusted, turns to the bookman and starts over. Then he sees the book there on the counter and stops in his tracks. Slowly, as if in a dream, he walks over and reaches out for the book. His hands are trembling a little and just before he touches the book, he looks up at the bookman and his eyes are a bit moist. He looks back down again, picks up the book, and slowly opens it."

Here John pauses, picks up his water glass, and drinks thirstily.

"And . . . ," one of us finally says.

"Well," says John, "there, on the first page, is his mother's name."

John stretched and grinned. "God," he said. "I love this life. There are times that will break your heart, but then something like this happens . . ."

And then we all shuffled in our seats and cleared our throats and tried to pretend that we hadn't felt goose bumps when we heard the story, hadn't been as moved as we were, and the evening ran on and we went back to sell at the convention and Grano and Wilson disappeared into the bowels of Denver and John went on to the bestseller lists and I ended up in southwestern New Mexico, writing about that moment in time, a moment that touched me and pulled me even deeper into a world that people have known as long as they have known language.

I bought and sold rare books and manuscripts for five years in Denver and Boulder before I began writing myself but I've never lost my love for a book signed by someone whose work has deeply touched me.

The wall in front of me is covered by the writers I love and who have given me the gift of their thoughts and their company. Across from me is a signed photograph of John Gardner, black motorcycle jacket half-zipped, white-blond hair down to his shoulders, and that stare and set of mouth that seems to be saying, "Did you sell out yet?" (Usually, but not always, I can tell him, "No, not yet.") Just below him is George Bernard Shaw, scowling, and in fading yet still-insistent ink is his signature with the comment: "Yours out of all patience." (When I start to sell out, when I start to write only for the money, for some reason my eyes always see that one first.) Over there is an original manuscript leaf from Mark Twain's *The Gilded Age,* written in ink in Twain's hand, and most wonderfully, his ink-smudged thumb prints on the edges of the page. Just under that are some heavily corrected manuscript pages from George Bird Grinnell's writings about the antelope herds in Yellowstone Park, written years before he got Glacier Park protected as wilderness. Here are some of Robert Bly's first tentative translations of Kabir, typed on an old manual typewriter, corrected in his illegible scrawl. There, Walt Whitman stands, peering intently, white beard flowing, aged as old oak, with his card inscribed "from the author." Edward Abbey and R. Crumb stare out at me from Moab Park in Utah, Crumb in his trademark hat, holding his infamous notebook, looking like a refugee from the 1950s. Abbey is desert taking on human form, face a craggy expression of stone and sand and sun, of silent places and wilderness, of the battering that all writers suffer if they don't quit. And Ambrose Bierce too, young and handsome, eyes reflecting the horrors of Civil War, not yet the bitter man who would go seeking Pancho Villa.

From them comes some odd, strange current of life force. It spills from the walls, flows into this room, onto this desk, and then back into the past, carrying part of me with it. And it flows into the future, surging outward, from the living touch of their pen to paper, flowing through this moment in time, passing through me, (and now you) during this life, on its way.

All of us writers, living and dead, are caught up in that current, part of some great movement, some strange craft whose magic captured us one day when we weren't consciously looking and pulled us into a world that we might never have found on our own.

Now I look over and see Barry Lopez gazing out at me from a stand of trees and I read the signed typescript . . .

> *Those that we revere as our great teachers, from a certain distance, were faithful. They did not break faith with their beliefs, they remained dedicated to something outside the self. As far as we know, they never became the enemies of their souls or memories.*

And as I read it I wonder, as I sometimes do: Will I have the courage to do the same? It is a question that must be answered each day of a writer's life. For there are none of us that are exempt from the pressures that go with writing, none who are not subjected to the siren call of money, or New York, or success, or of our work (or ourselves) being liked, or even the sometimes-years-long hope of finally being published . . . someday . . . someday . . . please someday.

CHAPTER TWO

The Secret All Beginning Writers Want to Know

Though learning to write takes time and a great deal of practice, writing up to the world's ordinary standards is fairly easy. As a matter of fact, most of the books one finds in drugstores, supermarkets, and even small-town public libraries are not well written at all; a smart chimp with a good creative-writing teacher and a real love of sitting around banging a typewriter could have written books vastly more entertaining and elegant. . . . For the serious young writer who wants to get published, it is encouraging to know that most of the professional writers out there are push-overs.

John Gardner

The people I've known who wanted to become writers, knowing what it meant, did become writers. . . . True artists, whatever smiling faces they may show you, are obsessive, driven people.

John Gardner

Anything will give up its secrets if you love it enough.

George Washington Carver

There are two secrets all beginning writers want to know, though most of them don't realize there are two. The one discussed most often is: "How do I get published?" It's an important question but there is a lot more to it than "send out proposals."

Although it cannot be seen with the eye, there is a wall between the writer and the nonwriter. It is perhaps three feet thick, composed of the psychic equivalent of plexiglass. Sometimes it feels so physical—for those of us who have not yet been published—that you can almost put your hand out and touch it, run your fingers over its surface. All beginning writers know of its existence. They know they are on the wrong side and they want desperately to be on the other side of that wall: "I have a book I'm writing. How do I get it published?"

The answer is very simple really, though there is a price to pay for using it. And that price makes its execution very hard indeed.

1. *The first and most important thing is to recognize the existence of the wall.*

This one is easy, most of us destined to be writers feel it every day of our unpublished lives.

2. *The second is the desire, more than anything else, to be on the other side of that wall.*

This is an indication of your call to the craft; there are easier ways to make tens of dollars. The desire must be of the category: *more than anything else.* Though, of course, this does not mean giving up the qualities of character that the kind of writer I am talking about in this book must have. "More than anything else" means more than being safe, more than working solely for money, more than social respect or cultural acceptance, more than not being afraid, more than not being rude (all writers are rude), more than being lazy, more than not engaging in self-reflection, more than not thinking. More than all those things. And still more.

3. *The third thing you must do is to apply pressure on the wall. And this pressure must be unrelenting, that is, you can never let up.*

The pressure is created by blending the passion of your unmet desire with your directed will. This combined force must be channeled into the never-ever-stopping writing that you send out for publication. Mere writing, without the power of your will behind it, is insufficient to break through the wall. Desire without this angry determination is not enough. You must combine the two into a potent, directed force that allows of no defeat. It is what some martial arts adepts call *indomitable will.* True artists really are obsessive, driven people. They have to be to succeed. They must be capable, continually, of *focused insistence.*

We press against the universe around us in our quest to find success as a writer, complaining endlessly but never stopping. The constant pressure eventually causes an opening, though it is impossible to predict where that opening will occur. The path we take as writers comes from following these fate-determined openings. And that path shapes our experience and later descriptions of the writing life. All the many descriptions you have read of that life are necessarily a description of the destiny that awaited that particular writer. If they won the writing lottery (Stephen King) their life story will appear one way. If they labored in obscurity for a decade (John Gardner) or longer (John Dunning) the story they tell will be entirely different. Nevertheless, all of them put pressure on the wall and they did not stop.

If you keep the pressure up long enough, eventually the wall will begin to crack. *Eventually, always, an opening, will appear.* However, you cannot control where or when it occurs. As William Stafford observed, "Dawn comes, and it comes for all, but not on demand."

4. *Fourth: when an opening appears, you must force your way through it.*

Please understand that many people do not like the appearance of the crack that opens (you may not yourself), are uncertain about that tiny, claustrophobic opening, do not like its sharp edges, and back off. ("We like your book *History of the Windsor Knot* and would like to publish it but would like some changes. Can you rewrite it without the necktie?") Regrettably, going into the opening is essential.

You must force your way through. It's a painful process, the edges of the opening are *sharp* and a lot of your skin—your old life even—is scraped off during the journey. You begin then to understand an important truth: *To become a writer you must shed your skin.* The process itself demands it. Those who refuse to do so fail of ever writing anything meaningful, perhaps fail of ever being published. It is not a failure of talent but of courage.

It takes great courage to take the first trembling steps as a writer in open view of publishers and editors, most of whom do not understand what it means to be a writer, courage to become defenseless inside the work, to write what is *in* you to write, rather than what society or acclaim or empty bank accounts tell you to write.

You must follow the path that opens to you and you must never stop. And it will demand that you shed your skin, over and over and over again. Your skin *must* be shed for that skin is not the skin of a writer; it is the skin of whatever you were before.

It takes more than one book to make it through that wall.

5. *And fifth, trust that the things you feel, that insist they be said, are there inside you, pushing on you, for a reason, Trust that there are people out there that need to hear those things, just as much as you need to say them. Understand that, as Antonio Machado said, "My feeling is not only mine, but* ours." *Trust the thing that leads you on and the writing to which it takes you.*

Although it's hard to believe in yourself in this way in the beginning, it is crucial. For the things you have to say, that are unique to you, are held someplace deep inside the feelings you have that have led you to the craft and that continue to lead you on. If you follow those feelings, trust the sense of the right that is in you, the voice that is insisting on taking written form, you will be original in your work. You will be speaking from the territory in which *you* live, in which your deepest feelings reside. And in touching the deepest feelings inside you, you will also touch everyone and anyone who encounters your work. (This doesn't mean, however, that they will like your work, merely that they will rarely be indifferent.)

If you do trust yourself in this way, you will find—in the future, when it matters most—that you were faithful to who you really are and, as a result, you never became the enemy of your soul or memories. Then, when people buy your books, if you have trusted yourself, trusted that thing inside you, you will experience one of the greatest joys I have ever known: making a living by being who you genuinely are at the deepest core of your being.

Doing these things will take you through the wall. Eventually. And when you finally emerge on the other side you will find that it is true, as you have always known it would be, that you are different than you were before. You will find that in some important way you have changed.

There are obstacles, of course. You must understand at the outset that almost no one will encourage you in becoming a writer or in making the journey through the wall (and this will include many writers). Almost no one will understand what you are doing or why. Almost no one will understand what you will lose in the journey or what you will gain. It is a process of transformation, a learning to live from a certain truth of soul rather than the more common truth of culture. Because most people live from the truth of culture, they *can't,* by orientation, understand what you are doing or why. You will find that this shift in orientation on your part is a bit *unsettling* to those who are not shifting along with you. Something mythic is entering your life, something beyond culture. So, you will hardly ever be able to talk with others about what is happening to you as you undergo this rite of passage, as you are subsumed into this lineage, as you learn to *inhabit the word*. And to make it harder, in the beginning you will receive a lot of unasked for discouragement.

Generally, the discouragement will look like this . . .

1. Everyone you know and meet will suddenly reveal to you that they are a writer, too, although even in your nascent state you can look at them and generally tell they are not. You know how the wall feels and how its absence feels (and how the touch of the mythic feels as well) and that sensitivity of feeling tells you that these people are not writers (even though they may be typists of words). Nevertheless, they will talk earnestly about themselves and their writing and what they will eventually do when they are famous. Sometimes they will confide to you that they are saving all their letters so that a collected volume can be issued posthumously. You will usually be unable to share any of your own

hopes, dreams, aspirations, or difficulties during this "sharing."

2. For some reason, no one really understands why, a large number of people will make it their job to quash the tiny flame of hope you have lit within yourself. A great many people will inform you that what you want to write about is uninteresting, will not sell, and that you will never make enough money to support yourself as a writer. Family, many acquisition editors, and close friends generally fall into this category, although they can sometimes respond absent-mindedly with "that's nice honey" or, when guests are visiting, "tell them about your little project."
3. Editors, publishers, agents (and sometimes writing teachers—in or out of MFA programs) will many times be rude, uncomplimentary, and cold about your submissions or your work. Half to two-thirds will simply send you a form rejection letter. One-eighth will never respond at all. Another eighth will go out of their way to tell you that you are the lowest, most miserable excuse for a writer they have ever had the displeasure of encountering. They will tell you to never give up your day job. They will explain in a variety of ways why your particular interests will never sell even if you are the last writer on Earth and all other books have been burned up in a nuclear war and none of the survivors will have anything to read unless you write it. Perhaps one-eighth will actually respond with something approaching human feelings. Very rarely you will receive an incredibly kind, handwritten rejection to a submission. You should save these; you will need them when things are bad.
4. Real writers whom you approach socially will generally be disinclined to talk to you or respond at all because: a) everyone they know and have met has said they are a writer, too, and they are really tired of hearing it; b) They have been asked for advice since they sold their first book and having eagerly given it they were then told by too many I-am-going-to-be-a-writer-too's that their advice is wrong, or the advice was not taken, or it wasn't believed, or they were blamed for it later, or it turned out (usually the case) that the person was not really serious about being a writer—their foray into the writing field was only some sort of personal growth exploration and the writer wasted a lot of her time, which she

> does not have enough of anyway, trying to help them. So most writers will tell you how hard it is and that you probably won't make money or they will smile and say, "that's nice, honey" with an abstracted look on their face and will change the subject, or leave as soon as they can reasonably do so.

But if you persevere, you will eventually find someone who believes in you and will offer useful advice (much of which will irritate you). More, that person will pass into you the living essence of this lineage that writers carry, that you have been touched by in the books you have read, whose presence you have felt stirring inside you since the day you were born, this thing that will not let you rest. It is something that, in the midst of words, is passed in silence—from one generation of writers to the next. In that moment of transference, you will be immersed in dark waters, the touch of a living writer's hand on your brow. You will never know how or where or when you will meet that person. But you will, eventually, meet.

It always happens sideways, when you are doing something else. It's rarely recognized for what it is when it begins to happen. The deep you has cried out and the universe has responded; it is then that your real apprenticeship begins. And that apprenticeship, ultimately, has little to do with techniques of the craft; it has to do with something else entirely.

In that moment of transference, the real secret that all beginning writers want to know begins to be revealed, slow as that revelation will be. It is the answer to a question that all of us who are driven to be writers have wanted to know from the first conscious stirrings of the craft inside us: "How can I be a writer, too?" In that moment *something* begins to be transferred from the older writer to the younger, some *invisible* that is at the heart of the craft, some *feeling sense* or *state of mind* that is essential to the work. And it is that *something* that is at the core of what it means to be a writer, someone who desires to be more than a typist of words. It has nothing to do with technique and it never has.

The answer, though, is rarely as direct or comprehensive as the young writer wishes it to be, in part because he does not really understand what it is he is asking. He is feeling his way toward the question, asking it as best he can, but it is coming from someplace deeper in the self than his conscious mind. And even though many writers intuitively understand what is being asked, the question is rarely answered directly, for, oddly enough, most writers don't understand how they do what they do. They don't really understand *how* to answer the question, at least not in words.

Most writers *feel* their way into the craft, one slow step at a time, just as the young writer is feeling his way into the question. Writers know what they do, they just can't tell you how they do it. And many of them, though they won't say so, are also a bit afraid of talking too much about what it is that they do do. They don't want to disturb the balance they have found by inquiring into it too deeply or by talking out loud about it too much. We are, at core, a superstitious bunch.

So, the question, if it is answered at all, is almost always answered wrongly, much to the frustration of the young writer. The answers given usually have more to do with techniques of writing, or how to prepare proposals, or how to approach publishers, or how to deal with the depression of nonsuccess. Much easier questions on the whole. *Show don't tell,* they are told, or *Cut the adjectives* or *Don't give up.* But the question answered is not the question being asked; it has never been the question asked. The question is more accurately something like this: "Something more than you comes through you and onto the page. I can *feel* it. How do you do it? Can you tell me how I can do it, too?"

That is the question and it is the most important question of all. It is the real secret that all beginning writers want to know.

The ancient Greeks knew writers entered a real, imaginal realm when they wrote and that they encountered the mythic there. They knew there was something more than the merely human involved. Writers, artists of all kinds, enter a particular kind of dreaming state as they create and something from *out there,* from some other place, comes into and through them. Writers inhabit an older world, or perhaps it is more accurate to say that their dreaming is a bridge between two worlds, or perhaps even that their dreaming allows them access to an ancient, imaginal realm filled with myth and that their writing is an account of what they find there—perhaps it is all three. Writers begin in this normal everyday world in which we live when we think we are awake, and they move, as a way of life, into another, one that is, as Homer intimately understood, filled with powers all of us have been told no longer exist.

In our time the recognition of that world has fallen out of favor in the fluorescent glare of reductionist literalisms (making it even harder to answer the question). Cultural injunctions may embarrass people into not speaking of that other world but they can never be prohibited from feeling the impact of it. And it is this that all new writers want to know. "How do I do *that*? How do I enter that dreaming state? How do I let those things flow through me and into what I write? How do I journey into that ancient world so I can experience it for myself? How do I become a writer, too?"

The rest of this book is an answer to that question.

For those of us who are meant to be writers, this is a mythic journey and a mythic profession. We learn how to intentionally dream and by dreaming enter mythic realms in order to write what we write. For our work to approach art, we must learn how to let the mythic flow through us and onto the page. Unimpeded. And we must respond, when we are called to do so, to the new generations of writers who follow us. For in each generation the truths, archetypes, and mythic images that flow through us, through this lineage we carry, must be renewed by emerging generations, in new language for a new time. The work we do is only loaned for a time, the lineage we carry must be passed on.

If you persevere you will meet a living writer who will pass it on to you. It will happen sideways, as it did for me with John Dunning. And I will tell you now what he told me then: "You must want to be a writer very much to become one, but you *can* become one and you can be good."

Inhabiting the Word

I watched a woman being interviewed. She sat in a wheelchair because she was elderly and feeble. She said that she was dead for she had lost her heart. The psychiatrist asked her to place her hand over her breast to feel her heart beating: it must be there if she could feel its beat. "That," she said, "is not my real heart."

JAMES HILLMAN

You must find the living pulse of the spirit.

ANTONIO MACHADO

He learned his art the only way an artist ever learns, by probing the secrets of his own vast heart.

JOHN DUNNING

You don't become a better chair maker. The chair becomes better.

BEN MIKAELSEN

CHAPTER THREE

On the Art of Nonfiction

The average critic never recognizes an achievement when it happens. He explains it after it has become respectable. . . . I have been fortunate to escape what has been called "that form of snobbery which can accept the Literature of Entertainment in the Past, but only the Literature of Enlightenment in the Present."

RAYMOND CHANDLER

There are no vital and significant forms of art; there is only art, and precious little of that.

RAYMOND CHANDLER

How to study the outer world without losing inward richness—that is the issue Rilke and Ponge lived. If we look only at our problems, Machado said, the inner world dissolves; if we look only at the world, it begins to dissolve. If we want to create art, we have to stitch together the inner world and the outer world.

ROBERT BLY

Many people think that nonfiction is easier to write than fiction. They're wrong but it is easy to understand why they think so. Mostly, it's because the majority of nonfiction writers take the easy way out and produce poor work. It isn't so much a failure of the form but a misunderstanding of the nature of the form. Perhaps too, it's a failure of character combined with poor habits of mind—laziness and the statistical mentality as the forces governing their nonfictional crafting; dissociated mentation never makes good reading.

It is true that poor nonfiction is easier to craft than good nonfiction. That poverty of execution, however, is often projected onto the genre itself as innate to it. The thinking goes, perhaps, something like this: it's just an argument they are making in nonfiction, a discussion. It's not a story. And besides there is already something there to work with, you don't have to create it, whole cloth, from nothing. A man's life, the event or events that resulted in the car crash, the research that led to the new discovery, are already there, just waiting to be written. So the nonfictional form is really not much different than a governmental form you have to fill out, just a bit longer and with no real creativity involved.

Fiction, many proponents of the writing craft think, is substantially different, and not only because it is writer-created from the first word, generated somehow out of the depths of the writer's imagination. There is also the belief that fiction involves a unique kind of analogical thinking, that fiction writers think their way through and into a kind of deep truth (or truths) that can only be revealed and expressed through the sideways, never-to-be-exactly-grasped, experience of analogical thinking and the fictional dreaming it generates. And in this process, the assumption goes, deeper archetypes, transformed myth, symbol, and theme, (perhaps story itself), emerge that can only be found and experienced through that specific kind of analogical thinking, exploring, and creating.

If the kind of nonfiction being discussed is how-to or self-help most people believe it is an even easier form to produce, even less generated out of analogical thought. A book on plumbing is pretty simple (they think), you got the house, you got the rooms, you got the people. So, there are a certain number of sinks, toilets, bathtubs, and showers and all the inflow and outflow lines they connect to. There are a few different types of pipe and a few different ways to join them together. Such writing (it is supposed) is no more difficult or challenging than making up a grocery list. *A* to *B* to *C*. And yeah, that kind of book can be, and often is, written in just that simplistic a manner. And yeah, they are often as boring as hell. As William Stafford's mother once said about some acquaintances, "They are so boring you get tired of them even when they're not around."

But they don't have to be.

There is something more to the heart of any craft, trade, or human endeavor than the mechanics of it. Why this truth is so often overlooked is hard to fathom but it seems we have forgotten something essential about our humanness the past sixty years or so. And although a lot of things could be considered (and will be as this book goes on) at the simplest level, there is always ethos and eros in any endeavor in which a human being attains a degree of mastery. And eros and ethos make anything they are part of a great deal more than a grocery list.

Most people who become good at a craft do so, in part, because they love the thing they are doing. They invest some eros energy in the work. They put love energy into what they do. It flows from them into the materials and how the materials are worked. And all craftsmen, if they are good, invest ethos as well. They want to do well, to produce work that they can be proud of. So, invisible things go into the work—whether that of a writer, a plumber, or a cook—and those invisible things begin to move the work into the realm of art. Always.

Most good craftsmen are artists, they cannot help but be so. And it doesn't matter the field. A how-to book on writing and a how-to book on plumbing should have at their core a similarity of essence. Both should concern themselves with the invisibles of the craft first and its techniques second. There should be at the core a certain kind of relationship, first with the craft and secondly with the materials of the craft. If the right relationship is established at the beginning, everything that follows flows out of that relationship. There is a kind of coherence, an integrity, that emerges. It begins at the deepest core of the craft and percolates outward, layer by layer. Ultimately, the creating, whether plumbing or baking, begins to take on a luminous quality, something more than the sum of the parts coalesces into being. And the outcomes of the craft, and the degree of mastery that is achieved, are much greater if that core element is present than if it is absent. If you do not love the craft, do not understand that every craft is a conversation between you and the living material with which you are working, a conversation with the essence of the craft itself, that core will never be found, never be understood. What you get then is reductionist writing (or plumbing or baking), mechanical determinism of some sort, a kind of writing that is not only boring but one that dries up the soul.

As well, nonfiction is not as nonfictional as it seems when you sit down and really look at it. There is no such thing as a completely objective report of reality; everything is shaded by the person encountering it, shaded by unexamined beliefs, biases, orientations, assumptions, fears, hopes, and dreams. Nonfictional writing about what a human being encounters in the world is also shaped by how much of what is encountered is perceived—and how much is not. It's also affected by orientation: if you talk about *this,* you are making a choice to not talk about *that.* No human report is value free; it is shaped by where the focus of mind goes, what is emphasized and not emphasized, the *meanings* that are discovered and expressed and that are particular to the person and the moment. Every how-to thing is, in some sense, a metaphor for human life, a way for a human being to see and experience reality, a conversation between the human and the focus of their craft: wood, or pipe, or politics, or the body, or the mind. A writing does not have to be autobiographical to explore the nature of identity.

When a nonfictional writer begins to move below the surface of a thing, begins the act of dreaming that writing is, begins to work with deep meanings directly instead of the surfaces of meaning, she begins to encounter the same analogical thinking that is at the core of fiction. The book-to-be begins to take on its own life, determine where it wants to go. Strange serendipity occurs. Over and over again. Odd thoughts, sometimes mistakes even, emerge of their own accord and begin to reveal truths and approaches that the writer did not remotely have in mind when she began to write. Golden threads, unusual intuitions, moments of duende catch her attention. She senses something but can only guess (at this point in the writing) at the meaning. But it pulls on her so she begins to explore it, to follow where it leads. She begins to think analogically. The writer dreams and some other part of her writes the book and the journey begins to take on the same mythic dimensions as those which occur in fiction. When this happens to us as nonfictional writers we enter the same world that Homer knew and Shakespeare explored, the same world in which Frank Herbert traveled and J. R. R. Tolkein lived. The art and the craft of fiction and nonfiction are identical. As Michael Dirda observes, "What is fiction after all, if not a kind of creative nonfiction."[1] There are just slight differences in some of the techniques used. Each form restricts behavior.

Character development and plot, for example, are less important in most nonfictional works than they are in fiction. But the gradual emergence and development of central idea or gestalt, which generally replaces plot in a nonfictional how-to or self-help work, often belongs to nonfiction alone. Such development possesses its own movements, its own unique stages and moments. It is one of the aspects of nonfiction as art that has been, so far, relatively undeveloped.

To play with this a little, characters interact and respond in fiction, developing, through their behaviors and interactions and thoughts, plot line. In a work of nonfiction, a central idea runs through the book like a thread of meaning around which the whole book revolves, just as a fictional work resolves around the plotline. Concepts, each of which are an essential element of the central idea, are introduced one by one and like characters they interact with each other, deepening in this instance not plotline but central idea. Plot waxes and wanes in intensity as it moves closer to point of resolution, so does central idea. When writing nonfiction, just as when writing fiction, you can slow the pace of the work or speed it up, increase intensity or decrease it.

At the culmination of a fictional piece, all primary characters (unless they've been killed off—though their ghosts often show up in some form) converge with plot line during the final conflict resolution of the work. In nonfiction, concepts and central idea converge similarly in a moment of duende as the whole central idea comes flowering into existence as a complete gestalt.

Then there is the slow movement toward the end of the book. In fiction, this final movement after climax is often very brief or, in some instances, may be as long as a chapter or two. In nonfiction, there often tends to be a longer resting in the afterglow, a slower movement toward the final pages of the book. This final, lengthier movement in nonfiction allows a deeper integration of the invisibles that come flowering into being at the climax of the material.

With nonfiction, we are working with a specific and distinct perception of reality, focused through whatever thing is the focus of the book—baking, or cabinetmaking, or writing. The readers are led into that reality, that point of view, that perception of reality, step by step, taking them, if it is good nonfiction, into a true experience, inside themselves, of the heart of the thing that is at the core of the book. They learn to see the world through cabinetmaker eyes or baker eyes. And when they turn their gaze on the craft they are wishing to understand, the essence of the thing is there. They only need to apply it over time to develop mastery of the *tools* of the craft; it takes time to make any art form one's own. But the living heart of the thing is already inside them, they have already eaten the real that underlies the form.

So, as the nonfictional book develops there are, to differing degrees, shocks of understanding, moments of penetrating, directly experiential insights, which are themselves moments of duende as the poet García Lorca describes them. The whole of them, together, make up the internalization of the central idea or gestalt that will, eventually, emerge in a unique moment of insight, a much greater moment of duende. Or as Robert Heinlein once put it, "Suddenly, what they were saying burst on me and I raced through the rest of the book. Glorious!" The development of this idea-line (as it might be termed) can be as subtle and sophisticated as any plotline in fiction and the subconcepts that are introduced similarly to characters can have as much complexity and living reality to them as the people populating a novel.

Like characters in fiction, these concepts become more deeply known through their behaviors. In a sense, a form of *show, don't tell* occurs. The concepts are described, much as a character is described at its initial emergence in a book. But it is behavior that lets the reader know what and who that character is underneath its visual surface. It is behavior that reveals crucial invisibles. The concepts that are introduced in nonfiction also have behavior. For the nonfictional work to become art, the concepts must be allowed to come alive, to demonstrate their living reality within the book itself. The concept is described, then it begins to act in some form so that the reader has an experience of the invisibles that lie at its heart.

And because this process is identical to that of fiction, though different in form, the good nonfiction writer, like any fiction writer, only discovers what is true by writing it. They may begin with some concrete thing—how to build a house for instance—but suddenly discover unexpected meanings in building a house as they write the book. They may discover that when we build a house we build ourselves, that when we remodel a house we end up restructuring deep parts of our own psyche, that there is some mirroring process that goes on in our psychological selves as we work our way through the house, room by room. Or they may discover that a man laboring in a field over a dry stone wall uses gravity as a building material just as coherently as a man uses mortar in a brick wall. Suddenly a whole world of perception, hitherto unsuspected, opens to the interior gaze. Invisibles begin to emerge into awareness, perception of reality begins to escape the clutches of the statistical mentality.

By the same process of analogical thinking common to good fiction, the nonfictional writer creates something that is more than the sum of the parts, something that touches on the depths of the human and the human relationship to the universe around her. Truths about the nature of existence emerge that could never have been predicted, not even if the writer knows the craft she is describing as well as she knows the shape and feel of her lover's hands. We all enter the dream not really knowing where we're going. As Tom Stoppard remarked about *his* work, "After 40 years, the problem remains, each time. You can't start writing until you know what you are doing, and you don't know what you are doing until you start writing. I still have to resist the false intuition that I need to know as much as possible in advance. The essential thing is to know as little as possible. Ideally, when things fall out well, you shouldn't feel clever, you should feel lucky."[2]

How-to books that approach art, that become art, focus on essence first, technique second. They enter into territories of spirit, experience, and theme that most fiction writers insist belong to them alone. They are crafted out of analogical thinking and they focus on invisibles. There are a lot more of them than supposed, mostly unrecognized. James Krenov's *The Fine Art of Cabinetmaking* is one.

> *Getting into this matter of listening to wood, of composing, weaving together an intention with what you and your chosen wood have to say, is an experience difficult to describe. To me, it is the essence of working with wood.*
>
> *A painter or sculptor visits a certain place and sees and feels something there he wants to interpret: a person, a scene, the way the light falls. A time and a place. A sense of life. Something similar happens*

> *with the cabinet maker—he who is more than a maker of cabinets. He has an idea, maybe a sketch. A boxlike object with a few gentle curves whose meaning he only guesses. Or a more sculptural piece where he imagines the play of light on shapes; serious or with humor, difficult or easy. And there before him is the wood he has chosen. Wood—and with it a mood.*
>
> *Then within this mood, all these other aspects: the shadings, accents, tensions—that which corresponds to the painter's inspiration and later on, often much later, all those bevels, roundings, shapes within shapes which will clarify and enhance what has been an intention and a hope.*[3]

Krenov discusses in detail the core that must belong to the craft, the essence from which all else will come. But he doesn't leave it at that as many nonfictional works on aesthetics do. He gets his hands dirty. He works, step by patient step, to teach the movements of the craft so that the attentive reader can begin to *see* as Krenov sees, can actually begin to do what Krenov himself has done. Krenov begins with the initial feeling impulse where all art has its beginning then moves on to the chosen piece of wood, to the conversation that occurs between craftsman and living material, then to the initial design that arises out of that conversation. Then he explores, in depth, each of the tools used to shape the wood (and his conversations with them as well), then the shaping itself and the slow step-by-step emergence of the piece, and finally how to sand, polish, and finish it. And during all this he keeps in mind, in the forefront of his understanding, how that piece will live over time—how the wood will breathe and move in different seasons, different humidity, different climates, different centuries. And he senses as well the conversations it will have with owners to come, in times far distant from his own, most of whom will remain unknown to him. He isn't just articulate, giving us glimpses of a philosophy that goes no further than the drawing room door. He rolls up his shirt sleeves and gets down in the dirt and *makes,* engages in the difficult co-creative conversation a living material demands, lives through his body and life the rigorous give-and-take of *shaping.* Readers of Krenov's book, as with any good how-to book, catch glimpses of deeper parts of themselves. The truths in Krenov's exploration of a man's relationship with wood and its shaping mirrors deeper truths of the nature of identity and just how a human being should approach living a life, approach the world in which that life is lived.

All those who shape, all who make, touch in the daily movements of their lives this core of craft, this conversation with the living material of their work. They all know, and daily utilize, a keen feeling perception and deep, intuitive sensing in their engagement with the work, the material, and the final form that emerges. They are well aware of the invisibles that are the core and essence of their craft. Most of them, however, do not have the skill of introspection, the skill of looking at the tiny movements of the self as it engages in each tiny step of the craft. Fewer still can put their self-awareness and understanding into words that make any kind of sense to someone seeking to understand what it is they do. They can demonstrate what they do; they can rarely explain the subtle elements of how they do it. Even fewer have an innate talent for writing.

Unfortunately, most books on writing nonfiction cannot help them. Most books on the nonfictional craft are about as exciting as a grocery list or terminally boring neighbors—and they suffer the same limitations. And, oddly, since they are how-to books themselves, they often denigrate how-to books and focus on what are considered more literary forms of nonfiction: memoirs of abusive childhoods and plane crashes and cannibalism in the Andes. Often badly written, even when by accomplished fiction writers, books on writing nonfiction commonly leave out the core of the craft; they avoid essence and focus on technique. A fatal error. Regrettably this error is endemic to Western cultures: we have come to equate form with essence, schooling with education, training in technique with the generation of art. It's no wonder most how-to books on writing more closely resemble bad engineering texts than useful instruction manuals on the art.

Nonfiction, especially how-to and self-help, does not have to be boring or poorly written. It can and should be a living, vital form of writing, as powerful and with the same impact as great fiction. Of the 400,000+ books published or distributed in 2007 in the United States, most were nonfiction, and most of those how-to or self-help.[4] There is no reason that the art of writing should neglect the largest segment of the nonfiction field. Well, no reputable reason. Raymond Chandler responded to exactly this issue when he discussed the emergence of the mystery as a legitimate literary form. Dorothy Sayers had written that mysteries could never "attain the loftiest level of literary achievement" because they were a "literature of escape" and not a "literature of expression." Chandler replied:

> *I do not know what the loftiest level of literary achievement is: neither did Aeschylus or Shakespeare; neither does Miss Sayers. Other things being equal, which they never are, a more powerful theme will provoke a more powerful performance. Yet some very dull books have been written about God, and some very fine ones about how to make a living and stay fairly honest. It is always a matter of who writes the stuff, and what he has in him to write it with. As for literature of expression and literature of escape, this is critics' jargon, a use of abstract words as if they had absolute meanings. Everything written with vitality expresses that vitality; there are no dull subjects, only dull minds. All men who read escape from something else into what lies behind the printed page; the quality of the dream may be argued, but its release has become a functional necessity. . . .* **all** *reading for pleasure is escape, whether it be Greek, mathematics, astronomy, Benedetto Croce, or* The Diary of the Forgotten Man. *To say otherwise is to be an intellectual snob, and a juvenile at the art of living.*[5]

All nonfiction facilitates the reader's movement into the same dreaming state that John Gardner described as belonging to fiction (that is, the fictional dream) to greater or lesser extents. All writing, no matter the form, allows people to escape into something outside of and beyond "the deadly rhythm of their private thoughts" (as Chandler put it). And if the writing is good, whether fiction or nonfiction, it allows movement into the mythic realms that the dreamer inside of us innately understands. The question is not whether it is literature but rather, how powerful the dreaming. And the nonfictional dream can be, and often is, just as powerful as, if not more powerful than, the fictional: "We hold these truths to be self-evident, that all men are created equal, that they are endowed by their Creator with certain unalienable rights, that among these are Life, Liberty, and the pursuit of Happiness."

The important thing, as Chandler observed, is not the form but what is *inside* the form. So, when we move from how-to books to self-help (a subcategory of how-to) we find that they, too, become art and are often great literature. We find that, if they are genuine, they too deal with the nature of identity, the real, and the human relationship to the world in which we live. James Hillman's book *The Soul's Code* is an example.

> *There is more in a human life than our theories of it allow. Sooner or later something seems to call us onto a particular path. You may remember this "something" as a signal moment in childhood when an urge out of nowhere, a fascination, a peculiar turn of events struck like an annunciation: This is what I must do, this is what I've got to have. This is who I am.*
>
> *This book is about that call.*
>
> *If not this vivid or sure, the call may have been more like gentle pushings in the stream in which you drifted unknowningly to a particular spot on the bank. Looking back, you may have a sense that fate had a hand in it.*
>
> *This book is about that sense of fate.*
>
> *These kinds of annunciations and recollections determine biography as strongly as memories of abusive horror; but these more enigmatic moments tend to be shelved. Our theories favor traumas setting us the task of working them through. Despite early injury and all the slings and arrows of outrageous fortune, we bear from the start the image of a definite individual character with some enduring traits.*
>
> *This book is about that power of character.*
>
> *Because the "traumatic" view of early years so controls psychological theory of personality and its development, the focus of our rememberings and the language of our personal storytelling have already been infiltrated by the toxins of these theories. Our lives may be determined less by our childhood than by the way we have learned to imagine our childhoods. We are, this book shall maintain, less damaged by the traumas of childhood than by the traumatic way we remember childhood as a time of unnecessary and externally caused calamities that wrongly shaped us.*
>
> *So this book wants to repair some of that damage by showing*

> *what else was there, is there, in your nature. It wants to resurrect the unaccountable twists that turned your boat around in the eddies and shallows of meaninglessness, bringing you back to feelings of destiny. For that is what is lost in so many lives, and what must be recovered: a sense of personal calling, that there is a reason I am alive.*[6]

So, I am going to go through the art of nonfiction from the beginning, working inward toward the core of the craft, into the journey into dreaming, into those states of mind necessary for the craft to be real. Then I will move outward and look at the process that leads to the completion of the first rough draft of a manuscript. After that, I will work back inward once more, exploring the revision process by first focusing on the larger whole and then, by increasing the magnification, explore the nature and structure of more subtle elements. Finally I will talk about the business of writing and what you can expect when you begin to approach and work with publishers, editors, and the business world that surrounds books.

I will quote from different sources throughout that process and without much discrimination, that is, I will include poets, fiction writers, nonfiction writers, and any old kind of book or writing that catches my attention by being good. You will find that I have been deeply affected by some particular kinds of poets: Robert Bly, William Stafford, García Lorca, Antonio Machado, and Dale Pendell, for instance, but I love them for what they do with language and meaning; I could care less that they are poets. It should not be assumed from the thread that emerges that all poets have similar capacities; most are dreadful, including many who are highly regarded. They are as dull and irrelevant as the poorest nonfiction, as the most pretentious literary fiction. It is not what they do but what they are that matters.

Good poets are almost always the first to travel into new wilderness. They are skilled at scenting the wind and they catch the emergence of tiny fragrances that duller sensibilities miss. Chandler commented that by the time Dashiel Hammett arrived on the scene "A rather revolutionary debunking of both the language and material of fiction had been going on for some time. It probably started with poetry; almost everything does."[7] A similar debunking has been going on since the late 1950s.

Like that earlier period, poets were the first to catch a glimpse of new territories, understand the debunking that needed to occur. But the focus has shifted. While still on language, it is not so much on fiction (though dead-end literary fiction is still getting a deserved bashing by anyone with subtle sensibilities) but has expanded into the nonfictional—in many ways into all writing, no matter the genre.

Some of the poets of the 1950s, '60s, and '70s, in their debunking, broke trail into new territory; their writings contain hints of newly discovered wildnesses, descriptions of the terrain and roadmarks they've found, and suggestions for a different kind of journey. (And as always the majority of people are just now noticing something's been going on.) But most of all, their poems contain the particular fragrance they've been following. And that fragrance is intimately entangled in the art of nonfiction as I have been describing it. So, I will explore that fragrance, use some of the trail that they have broken and perhaps, just perhaps, push it along a bit farther. So, the first thing to understand, the most important thing that all of us have found who have journeyed into this wildness, is that if you wish to move nonfiction from the flat, thudding, grocery list writing that pervades the field, you must begin with something deeper in the self than the statistical mentality can offer.

CHAPTER FOUR

You Must Begin with Something Deeper in the Self

Some people who are terrified of grandiosity spend their vital energy defending themselves from the godlike furnace that is cooking inside them. They are the flat people. Side by side with the light poetry we have the flat poetry of the universities, flatter than any poetry ever known in the world before.

ROBERT BLY

American fundamentalism is against the journey to dark places; capitalism is against the descent to soul; realism is against the leap to spirit; populism and social thought are against the solitary wildness.

ROBERT BLY

The spirit won't stand waiting for years until the mechanics of learning are mastered. It must be enlisted from the first or it will fly away to other things.

ROBERT FROST

When you find you do have a response—trust it. It has a meaning.

WILLIAM STAFFORD

The key to the kind of writing I'm talking about in this book is feeling, not thinking. The art of nonfiction has nothing to do with the reductionistic behaviors necessary to get some words on a page while following the rules of grammar. It is not a matter of technique but of essence, of feeling. "You must understand," as Milton Erickson once said when training others to generate deep trance states, "this is a communication, not a technique." To write what is true, you must abandon the statistical mentality as a point of beginning. You must begin with something deeper in the self. You must begin with the part of you that feels. And that abandonment of the statistical mentality, that reliance on feeling, in and of itself, will bring you into conflict with the culture in which you live. For here is a truth that all writers eventually encounter: *You must not extend awareness further than society wants it to go.*

Do you know what I mean here? Does this touch something inside you?

There is a reason psychotropic drugs are illegal in the United States, a reason a million people a year are arrested for using them. There is a reason why every field of study and art has been reduced to some form of mechanicalist technique or orientation; that we are taught the exterior world lacks consciousness; that poets and writers, in the writing schools that exist on every college campus in every state in the nation, are so very thoroughly domesticated, that they are endlessly told the lie that a writer's main tool is words, that they are not companioned into landscapes that lie outside the rational.

You must not extend awareness further than society wants it to go.

If you wish to be more than a typist of words, you have no choice, you must extend awareness further than society wants it to go. You must travel in the mythic and living landscapes that lie outside of and beyond the statistical mentality. You must enter dark waters. At minimum that means understanding that the primary thing a writer works with is not words but meanings; the most important things with which a writer works are invisible to the eye. They cannot be seen, they can only be felt. And so you must feel. Keenly.

Our interior responses to the touch of meaning upon us gives us clues to the nature of those meanings. We know when energy from the deep psyche has filled a line, when something luminous has entered a word, when writing has shifted from form to essence—no longer water safely channeled through irrigation ditches for domesticated crops it becomes instead swirling, dark waters seamed with deep and dangerous currents, waters in which the massive back of an immense, shadowed creature sometimes rises near the surface. We know it because we feel it.

The kind of writing that I am discussing in this book has its origination in the part of us that works with deep meanings, that was made to work with deep meanings. It does not come from what is usually called our conscious minds. Robert Bly comments that . . .

> *Most of the poetry written since the rationalists and pragmatists took over language resembles a trip on land. On land one is surrounded on all sides by recognizable objects. But when one enters the sea, the back is turned to recognizable objects and the face to something else.*[1]

And it is this "something else" that is crucial to face. To write inhabited words, to live an inhabited life, it is crucial to leave the certainty of dry land, to step into something liquid and moist, to immerse the self in the deep interior life that flows beneath the shallow surface of reason. And the key to this, to finding that deep interior life, is feeling.

The analytical part of a writer, his conscious capacities for shaping language, come into play later in the process of writing. That is when a writer uses learned technique to edit what has been created. But the real work happens someplace else inside the human than the analytical portions of the brain. The creation of the work happens in the part of us that works with deep meanings, with the part of us that dreams, what too many writers call the "basement," the "unconscious," or perhaps "Milwaukee." It occurs in waters in which rationalists don't normally swim. And it is in these deeper waters that your words take on a certain fragrance that they can attain no other way. There they brush against deep parts of the psyche, that of the human—and of the world. When they do they are infused with a kind of fragrance, they take on a certain feel, a certain vibration. A luminosity begins to emerge from someplace inside them.

But to get that deep in the psyche, to the part that dreams, to the part that is meant to touch and work with mythic and deep meanings, it is first necessary to work with the human capacity for feeling, with *your* capacity for feeling. Feeling is the key to deep meaning.

When you read, the kinds of things that most draw you do so because they generate a certain kind of feeling. (Even if the emotional aspect of that feeling is emptiness and lack of feeling, the existential despair contained in too much contemporary literary work, it is still a kind of feeling.) What you feel as you read is intimately connected to the meanings that permeate the text, the meanings with which the writer has filled the words. And those meanings are what draw us here rather than there, to this book rather than that. The meanings that touch us, that move us, that call us, do so because they touch some part of our deep self, some part of our soul reason for being. And if we follow that touch, follow our feeling, we begin to move deeper into the mythic world that all writers access when they write. Our lives begin to be filled with meaning and, most importantly, so does our writing.

All writers have to develop an exquisite sensitivity to the subtleties of their interior responses when feeling the meanings that touch them. At the least, that is necessary because all writers check their work by *feeling* it. That is, first they write and then they pause a minute to check what they have written. In that moment of pause they do something specific, something on which the whole art of the craft depends. Some nonphysical part of them reaches out and touches the work, *feels* it, to see if what they have done is right, is congruent. It senses the meanings in the work, reaches out to see if, when those meanings come inside them, they produce the interior responses that should be produced for the work to be true and real writing.

Writers will always analyze the form they have created to the level of their skill to do so but the final appeal is always to something deeper in the self, the final determinant is how the piece feels. And this is a great deal more important than technique. If a work is filled with meaning, even though the technique is poor, it will still possess luminosity and the capacity to move the reader, where a highly polished work filled with subtle technique, if it does not possess this kind of livingness, will remain only an empty suit of very-well-made clothes.

Meaning-filled writing that is technique challenged may be raw ore but there is still something precious at its core. The writer, with much practice and diligent patience, eventually learns to cut, shape, and polish that precious thing so that it becomes diamond, or emerald, or ruby. This is a process that all writers go through. We all start from where we are and develop in skill from that place. (It is a never-ending process. None of us *ever* reach the destination.) A lack of polished technique is not something to be ashamed of; raw ore is never shameful. Sometimes, often, there is a greater beauty in raw ore than in the most polished work. *Remember this:* language and technique are there to serve you in fulfilling the work you feel you must do. You are not there to serve the rules of language that some grammarian has given you as law. Any writer who forgets that loses the only thing that truly matters to the craft.

So, writers use some invisible part of themselves to feel what they have done, to determine just how well their work is holding the precious thing that has set them writing to begin with. Some invisible part of the writer runs its fingers over the words, feels into them, individually and as a whole. And it is only when that deeper part, the part that is exceptionally sensitive to untruth—to bullshit—says the work is true, that the work really is right, that it really is done. The writer knows in that moment that the work is filled with the meanings that are supposed to be in there and that the form supports and strengthens those meanings to the level of his skill to do so at this moment in time. He can let go of it then, let it out into the world, let it find the people it is supposed to find. Then he can turn away from it, go on to the next thing. It was feeling that brought you to writing, you know. Something in the books you read touched you, something in you wants to create writing that will touch others similarly, some deep feeling has driven you on. It is feeling that is at the root of why we do this, not thinking. And that is the most important thing. If you want to create work that will touch people the way you were touched, you have to become elegant in your capacity to feel, you must educate that part of you and give it experience. You must learn to play with it consciously—as a reader and a writer. As a writer you must consciously shape the feeling impacts of your work through intentionally shaping the meanings for which words are only the containers. So . . . let's play with it a little.

Here. Taste the fragrance of this line . . .

A human body just dead looks very like one still alive, yet something invisible has left it.

Just sit with that line a minute and let yourself feel how that feels as it begins to move inside you.

Notice what happens inside you as the meaning of that line envelops you, as you drop slowly down below the surface of the words.

Consciously slow your interior thinking, linger on the sentence and its words and just let the *meaning* of the thing work inside.

Now, let's look at the interior movements that occur . . .

As you read, there is the first impact of the line and perhaps a slight interior avoidance of the initial subject: death. Then as you get used to what you are encountering, there is a relaxation and a moving deeper. A sense of the living meaning of the line begins to occur. A particular kind of feeling goes along with that, and as you move deeper inside the line, perhaps an image also appears: someone just barely dead perhaps, lying in a bed, the sheet pulled up, covering the chest. And then a comparison: time runs backward and just before death, we see the person still alive, still in that same bed, moving slightly, perhaps murmuring to someone near him. And then the film slowly runs forward, tipping slightly over that invisible line between one state and the next. Moving from one tiny millisecond in time to another, from the last flickering movements of life to the tiny instant in time when the person is dead. There is that moment when something that had been present is present no longer. It's gone.

Do you get a sense of that invisible thing that has left the body? Something that cannot be put into words yet still has substance to it, something that is a great deal more important than the grouping of physical parts that remains?

Notice now that this is a feeling thing, you literally can *feel* the difference in the two states, feel the thing that has left the body even though it really isn't present in any of the words in the sentence. Do you have a sense of it? A feeling of it?

Now let's take it a little further . . .

> *In writing, as in life, it is the invisibles that make all the difference.*

Do you get what I mean here? Just as the most important thing in life is that invisible thing, the most important thing in writing is that very same invisible thing. Writing can be either alive or dead . . . well, alright, there are some people who do actually sew all the necessary parts together and inject them with an energy source (usually the drama triangle) in order to animate them. Even then, however, the writing is not really alive, it just takes on a semblance of life. So, perhaps there are three states: alive, dead, and fake-semblance-of-life writing.

Life, the thing that writers work so hard to capture in language, is an invisible thing. The penetrating point of Mary Shelley's *Frankenstein,* a point that neither science nor writing schools have taken to heart, is that you can sew all of the, supposedly important, pieces together and it still does not make it a human being, still does not make it writing.

Here, taste the lines again, together, as one piece, as they belong.

> *A human body just dead looks very like one still alive, yet something invisible has left it. In writing, as in life, it is the invisibles that make all the difference.*

Nice, isn't it. There is a good feeling to it, some luminosity inside it that can be felt. There is some invisible thing inside those lines that comes out, that touches you as the meaning moves inside you, that produces a certain kind of feeling. The lines possess a certain rightness; there is almost a hum as if some invisible string has been struck. The lines themselves demonstrate what they are talking about. So you get a layering of impacts, both form and essence reverberating the meaning back and forth between them, mirroring its nature in different ways.

Sound is involved here as well. The *sounds* the words and sentences make as they are read, and the accompanying backbeat, that is, the patterning of how they are read (which is mostly controlled by the syllabication and punctuation), creates an auditory analog of the experience. There is deep meaning, deep truth, in the sentences, and the form, on multiple levels, is congruent with that meaning. The words are filled with meaning and the way they are arranged, the way they associate with each other, enhances and shapes that meaning, that truth, into the purest expression it can take in language (at least that this writer's skill can produce at this moment in time). The form of the sentences carries echoes of the deep meaning that the words themselves were meant to hold while at the same time becoming invisible to the eye. In a sense, nothing is left but the meaning of the thing and, for an instant, because of this, it penetrates deep into the unconscious. And at that moment of penetration, we experience a shift in perception. We've moved from one reality orientation to another and it's an experiential, feeling thing that happens. Thinking about it comes later.

Readers don't normally notice all this consciously, they just *feel* it. They drop into a dream state and no incongruency in the lines awakens them from that dream state. The reverberation the lines create as they move inside the readers is echoed someplace deep inside them, perhaps in what might be called the truth receiver. Some new insight about the nature of things has occurred for the conscious mind, but the deep self, where the truth receiver resides, where the part that dreams and works with deep meanings lives, experiences something else. Some sort of truth that it knows is real is reflected back to it; some sort of chord is struck and that vibration sets up a resonance. And that part of the self begins to resonate in harmony with the truths in the sentence. As a result the reader feels more real, more in touch with truth, more whole in herself. (And this is exactly what I mean when I talk about the necessity and importance of moral nonfiction. Moral nonfiction is writing that sets up this kind of resonance; it has nothing to do with the twisted darkness that contemporary users of the word "moral" mean when they use that word for political ends.)

Writers work with invisible things, things that are more than the sum of their parts, things that reductionist approaches to writing cannot see, things that can and must primarily be felt. Words are shaped to hold the meanings the writer is bringing into the world but the words themselves must disappear as completely as possible. Words are only potentialities. They are nothing in themselves. This invisible thing, so crucial to inhabited writing, is put into words by something the writer does and the true test of the craft is how it feels.

Now . . . try this line:

The writer piles up meaning behind the word like water behind a dam.

Spend a minute with it and again, notice what happens inside you as you eat the sentence, as its meaning moves deeper inside you.

There is the initial impact of the sentence, the moment when it's just words, just sounds. Then a part of you begins to work with it, to ingest it, to eat the meanings in it. As that occurs you begin to move from one state of consciousness into another, all sense of the room you are in fades and for a moment you are enveloped by an invisible thing.

Perhaps an image appears, of a dam with water behind it. There is the concrete of the dam and perhaps the unique smell and slight taste in the mouth that occurs when you are around concrete that is wet from water or when the air is very humid. Then awareness shifts, focuses on the water behind the dam. Perhaps a scene you once saw emerges in a burst of visual remembering. There is the dam and the water. You see the blue of the water and perhaps the sky and maybe some trees around the edges of the reservoir. But the focus doesn't stay there, awareness shifts again. Now it is on the water itself. There is a sense, a feeling, of the depth of the water, of the weight of it pressing against the dam. In that moment you have the sense, the feeling, of an invisible thing. Weight is an invisible thing, pressure is an invisible thing. Yet, somehow, we have the feel of it, the sense of it, captured for a moment in our experience.

Then that sense of weight and depth that you have, the feeling of it pressing up against the dam, transfers to a different object, the word a writer writes. There is meaning piling up behind that word. And a sense comes of depth and pressure inside the word, something living, something that is longing to escape its confinement, something pressing. You can *feel* it. That meaning, piled up behind the words, is a living force. It can be felt when there is the slightest touch of a human mind upon an inhabited word. (And just to break state a little, I want to point out that what you are experiencing right now is analogical thinking and the state it creates in both reader and writer.)

The writer piles up meaning behind the word like water behind a dam.

Every reader is always reaching for meaning, always reaching out to nonphysically touch what you have put into the word. Some deep part of us is *always* looking for meaning—that's its job. And the exchange of meaning between writer and reader can be exceptionally intimate. It is one of the joys of reading; people expect it (though many times they do not get it if the writing is poor). It is crucial to remember that there is always a reaching toward intimacy whenever a reader picks up a book and begins to read. Whether a work is nonfiction or fiction, its readers want to hear a story, to be held in the intimate embrace of the story that has been created. And if nonfiction, it does not matter if it is self-help, how-to, investigative reporting, memoir, scientific text, or narrative nonfiction. All those, in fact, are forms of story and should be treated as such. Even if it is a book on how to do your own plumbing, the reader wants to hear a story. And information about plumbing, conveyed by a writer who understands that how-to books are a specific form of story, is taken in and understood much more easily than if it is presented as an expanded grocery list.

The writer carefully fills his words with meaning, like the delicate pouring of water into an empty glass. If care is taken, the liquid will slightly overfill the glass, the excess held in place by the surface tension of the water. It takes but the slightest touch to break that surface tension and then the water, the meaning in an inhabited word, spills out, runs to the thing that touches it. As the reader's conscious mind touches the first words, the reading remains superficial, yet in a tiny space of time something begins to happen, they begin to enter a different state of mind and being. A part of the reader opens and the meanings that the writer so carefully poured into his words begin to spill out, to fill the reader. The contents of a full container moving into a receptive one, intentionally empty. The reader allows access to her deep self, and some living essence comes in through the words she takes in. She begins to listen to a story but meanings enter with the words and they in turn hold things within them that are as necessary as food, as necessary as love. For inside the meanings there are other invisibles, archetype, and myth, symbol and theme, and the intimate touch of another human being.

By understanding that your work is with invisibles, by consciously working to inhabit words, by filling your words with meaning, with waters from the deep psyche, the words come alive. *They are soaked in life force,* in *your* life force. The livingness inside the words, and all that gives rise to it, enters the reader as she takes the story inside her.

And the essence of the process, the most important thing to it, the element crucial to it happening, is feeling—your capacity to feel. Your passions: the things you care about and the things you hate, and your exquisite sensitivity to the invisibles that surround you, that touch you every minute of every day, all this goes into the writing. The love you have of the touch of meaning upon you goes into it, as does your love of working with words as containers for meaning. *Eros* enters the work. The experiences you have had of being touched by great writing, of your own desires to touch in turn, enters the work. The deep truths that have moved you, that are and have been crucial, central experiences to every human being in every time and culture on this planet, enter the work as well. And, as a result, the words come alive, become inhabited.

As you read, as anyone reads, you can feel the difference between inhabited words and those that are uninhabited, between ensouled and unensouled writing. You can feel whether words are soaked in life force. You can tell if meaning is piled up behind the words like water behind a dam.

So, let's play with it a little more. To get a sense of what I am talking about, read the following excerpts. As you do, pay close attention to how you feel as the meaning of these pieces flows into you.

Here is the first one:

> *Without guidance, adolescents create their own rituals and values with their own dress, symbols, language, beliefs, and blessings. Because they are created by the adolescents themselves, they do not contain good advice, values, or perspective about the future.*[2]

Notice how you feel now.

Stay with the impact of this piece a minute and allow the experience to deepen. Pay attention to the subtle movements that are occurring inside you. As the impact of the thing deepens, ask yourself how you feel. What emotional state are you in? How is it different than how you were feeling before you read those sentences?

Split the beat of the fly's wing into a thousand discrete movements, analyze the tiniest movements and touches that occur. Now that you have taken those meanings inside you, how do you feel about yourself? How do you feel about your life? How do you feel about the world around you? About people? What is your level of joy? Hope? How strong do you feel in yourself? How is your vitality level? Do you have more or less energy now than you did before you read those sentences?

The meanings within a piece of writing act much like a lens that is placed between a reader's perceiving self and reality—they are cognitive spectacles. Once you eat a piece of writing or soak in its meanings, for a time, you will see the world through those invisible meanings. The meanings embedded in the piece shift perception and alter, at very deep levels, how you define and experience reality. (This is why great writing makes such a strong impact; it allows the direct experience of deep truths about ourselves and our world and by so doing moves us to become what we can be, not the little that we have been told we are.) So, pay attention to how this piece shifts your perceptions. How does the world look when you look through the lens of this piece? Do you like it? Or not?

No? Well then . . . try this one:

> *When we fight for the soul and its life, we receive as reward not fame, not wages, not friends but what is already in the soul, a freshness that no one can destroy. This soul truth, which young people pick up from somewhere, sustains them. It assures the young man or woman that if not rich, he or she is still in touch with truth; that his inheritance comes not from his immediate parents but from his equals thousands of generations ago; that the door to the soul is unlocked; that he does not need to please the doorkeeper, but that the door in front of him is his, intended for him, and that the doorkeeper obeys when spoken to.*[3]

Now how do you feel?

It's different isn't it?

Stay with it and let the meaning of this writing slowly drop down inside you. Let it infuse you. Pay attention to what happens as it moves slowly through your interior world, as who you are becomes entangled in its meanings.

How do you feel about yourself now? How do you feel about your life? How do you feel about the world around you? About people? What is your level of joy? Hope? How strong do you feel in yourself? How is your energy level? Greater or less than before reading the piece? I want to make a point about these two writings, they are about the same thing—that is, the wisdom of actions chosen by adolescents who are seeking deeper truths about being human beings—but the meanings in them, and as a result how they feel, are very different.

It is crucial, if you wish to really take on this work as your profession, if you really wish to inhabit the word, to engage in this kind of perceptual sensing and analysis with every piece of writing you read, with every piece of writing you write. It is a kind of sensitivity that all writers must have and most likely do have to some extent before they even begin to write. It is part of why they are called to the craft. In focusing your attention on how these things impact you, in working with your feeling response consciously, instead of letting it remain only a vague sense, you give experience to the part of you that is sensitive to meanings. You educate it. This leads to your being able to consciously shape meanings into language, to very subtle and sophisticated capacities as a writer. It allows you to consciously grasp the meanings in language that touch you from outside sources, often with great subtlety. But it all starts with this basic thing—feeling—and paying attention to how everything you encounter feels to you.

If you paid close attention to how you felt as the meanings of those pieces penetrated you, you will have noticed that something entirely different happened within you in response to each piece. One distanced you from your feeling sense, one made you *feel* more. In one you experienced a greater sense of your potential as a human being and with the other it was diminished. One made you feel more capable of encountering and dealing with life, one less. One enhanced your trust in yourself, one weakened it. Notice, too, which one was more musical to your ear, which one less. In which did you feel yourself moving into a different state than the ordinary and which one brought that ordinariness up in all its emptiness?

The first piece was less pleasant was it not? The second more uplifting? The second piece is inhabited word, the first is not. The second piece is moral nonfiction, the first is not. It is the second piece in which I believe, the second that transcends its medium and becomes great, the second that carries within it something more than the sum of the parts. It is the kind of writing this book is about.

Here are two more pieces to compare. Again, they are about the same thing. And, again, pay close attention to how you feel as the meanings penetrate you. How does your sense of the world and yourself alter?

First this one:

> *Within that part of the physical environment which was actually inhabited by humans were many places where mythic beings had left evidence of their presence. There was, for instance, a certain cliff by the seashore where Wohpekemeu had lain on his back, singing and slapping himself on the chest. When the tide was out, one could still see the marks that Wohpekemeu's feet had made as he kicked them about against the vertical face of the cliff. Not far from there, the Indians also showed Waterman an offshore rock that was known by a Yurok word meaning "refuse," as this was the place where Chickenhawk had thrown the guts of an enemy he had killed. The number of similar examples in Waterman suggests that any natural configuration might come to have mythic relevance in Yurok thought. . . . We learn, for example, from one Yurok narrative that Wohpekemeu used to fish at a place near the village of Kenek, just below the mouth of Tuley Creek but any fisherman could see why this is a good spot. Just above there is a very strong rapid, and this is the first real barrier that salmon and other species encounter on moving upstream from the mouth of the river.*[4]

Again, stay with the experience of this a minute. *How do you feel?* If you turn your gaze on your life, on any problems that you are struggling with, on the exterior world, how do those things appear through the lens of the meanings that are now inside you, the meanings that you have ingested from this writing?

Now try this one:

> *It is only when we are aware of the earth and of the earth as poetry that we truly live. Ages and people which sever the earth from the poetic spirit, or do not care, or stop their ears with knowledge as with dust, find their veins grown hollow and their hearts an emptiness echoing to questioning. For the earth is ever more than the earth, more than the upper and lower field, the tree and the hill. Here is mystery banded about the forehead with green, here are gods ascending, here is benignancy and the corn in the sun, here terror and night, here life, here death, here fire, here the wave coursing in the sea. It is this earth which is the true inheritance of man, his link with his human past, the source of his religion, ritual and song, the kingdom without whose splendor he lapses from his mysterious estate of man to a baser world which is without the other virtue and the other integrity of the animal. True humanity is no inherent right but an achievement; and only through the earth may we be as one with all who have been and all who are yet to be, sharers and partakers of the mystery of living, reaching to the full of human peace and the full of human joy.*[5]

Now how do you feel? Just let yourself stay with that feeling for a minute. Let it deepen and become a lens through which you can view the world.

If you now turn your gaze on your life, on any problems with which you are struggling, on the exterior world, how do these things appear through the lens of the meanings that are now inside you? It's different than after the last piece, isn't it?

There's a lot of insight in this if you really determine what you feel as you eat the meanings in this writing. More if you can determine just why these meanings create those feelings. And even more if you can determine how these meanings shape your worldview, your view of yourself, your perceptions of reality.

However, what is most important right now is that you could *feel* the impact of those meanings inside you. You did not have to know how it occurred, or even why, you experienced it directly. You felt those meanings and you needed no degrees, no training in grammar, punctuation, or writing to do so.

Young writers are called to the craft in part because they *feel* so deeply.

It is crucial they be encouraged in following the feelings they have, for those feelings are the most important clue to where they must go, the path they are to travel. It is a clue to the kinds of writings that most move them, to the kinds of writers in whose company they belong. It is a clue to where in the field they are meant to work, what they are meant to say, and the mythic elements they are meant to encounter and shape.

Initially, in any confused life, the writings that touch a young reader, that make him want to be a writer, emerge, seemingly out of nowhere. There is a magic and mystery to just how the right books enter a young writer's life. They are found on a park bench or the color of a dust jacket catches the eye in a bookstore. You sit waiting at a friend's house, in boredom pick up a book just to pass the time, and find a world your sense of purpose needed you to find. The books we find, that we need to read to become ourselves, cannot be programmed in. The books we need to find are rarely found through being force fed "good literature." The young can be flogged all day long in school with Herman Melville's *Moby Dick* (They made a *book* outta that?), Nathaniel Hawthorne, Joyce Carol Oates, Thomas Pynchon, Virginia Woolf, Philip Roth, Samuel Beckett and all the rest of the "important" writers, but if their path lies elsewhere, these works are nothing and will remain nothing. If they do not speak to the deep self in the young writer, they are useless. For every student who has found wonder through being forced to read *Moby Dick* or Pynchon's *V,* a thousand others have been turned off to reading for the rest of their lives.

Both writing and the desire to be a writer begin with an impulse. It's not a mental act but comes from someplace deep in the self, some feeling place. So, to be a writer, you must keep your sense of feeling and never ever let anyone convince you that it is an impediment to the craft. Never let anyone, as they do with physicians in *their* training, batter you into a loss of your capacity for empathy, for deep feeling, for following where your feeling leads you. For the writer's path lies, always, on "the road of feeling."

CHAPTER FIVE

"The Road of Feeling"

A person suffers if he or she is constantly being forced into the statistical mentality and away from the road of feeling.

Robert Bly

Under the influence of objectivism and abstraction, not only does our poetry become mediocre but our criticism also. When the senses die, the sense within us that delights in poetry dies also. And it is this sense of delight that tells us whether a given group of words contains genuine poetry or not. A great poet and a great critic are like the mule who can smell fresh water ten miles away. There is a sense that tells us where the water of poetry is, abroad or at home, West or East, even under the earth. When this sense is dead, critics have to decide whether certain books are poetry by the presence of forms, or of "important statements," or of wit, or even of length.

Robert Bly

A poet is somebody who feels, and who expresses his feelings through words. This may sound easy. It isn't. A lot of people think or believe or know they feel—but that's thinking or believing or knowing; not feeling. And poetry is feeling—not knowing or believing or thinking. Almost anybody can learn to think or believe or know, but not a single human being can be taught to feel. Why? Because whenever you think or you believe or you know, you're a

> *lot of other people but the moment you feel, you're nobody-but-yourself.*
>
> E. E. CUMMINGS

The English language is weak when it comes to subtle discussions of our interior worlds, confusion is easy. The indigenous cultures of Alaska, I have heard, have over twenty words for the different kinds of frozen precipitation they experience, most of the rest of us have about three: snow, sleet, and hail perhaps. We have about the same level of perceptual sensitivity in our language when it comes to subtleties in the area of feeling, emotions, and feelings. In technical areas, we can easily use the lens of analytical reductionism to view certain aspects of the world outside us, use the mind to make distinctions in what we find there, and so end up with great subtleties in the industrial or scientific description of matter—of concrete, for instance, or of cellular differentiations. We have no such elegance with our interior lives; our language in that area is stunted, undeveloped, thick-fingered. So, let's drag it out from under the rug and poke at it a while.

All of us have some sense of what is meant when someone says, "I love broccoli" or "I love my dog" or "I love my children." We automatically adjust our definition of "love" depending on context. Even though most of us, if forced to do so, could not easily define love, we sense that the love of children is of a different category than the love of broccoli. We tend to work with our experience of what we call "love"—an experience that everyone knows is real and important and as essential as food—unconsciously. We know love when we feel it or when we encounter it, though most of us can't really say what is going on when love is happening. We know that when people say "I love broccoli" they really mean they like it very much. It tastes good to them, it makes them feel good to eat it, it is highly enjoyable, and most likely, even though this is odd to me, they like the smell. With a dog, love is a very different matter. When "love" is used here people mean, and we know they mean, that there is some kind of exchange of energy, an interactive sharing of some sort that is not present with cooked broccoli. And this kind of love is complex; it possesses layers and subtleties that love of broccoli does not. "Love" of dog automatically includes some sort of interactive sharing, a sharing that contains emotions, the exchange and meeting of needs, a trust, a healthy dependency that goes in both directions, some sort of bonding, and again, some sort of energy exchange—some invisible thing goes from the dog to the person, from the person to the dog.

When we get to child, "love" means something else again. It's similar to that which exists between a person and a dog but there is a difference of degree. Some other element (or elements) has entered into the equation. Still, to begin with, I can use the same description of love that I used with a dog. It is a love that . . .

> *contains emotions, the exchange and meeting of needs, a trust, a healthy dependency that goes in both directions, some sort of bonding, and again, some sort of energy exchange—some invisible thing goes from the child to the person, from the person to the child.*

But, again, there are other elements. Bonding with a child is generally much deeper. It also has survival elements entangled in it. There is a deep biological drive to protect the child, to ensure her safety, to see her safely into the future. We see ourselves in the child. The child, in a way, is ourselves going into the future—there is some sort of immortality in it. But there is also some kind of deep selflessness, a giving of the deepest parts of ourselves to the child, freely and without reservation. We know, even though we can't easily define it, that this kind of love goes much deeper in the self than the love that occurs with a dog or broccoli. We know it involves some primal unconscious part of the self, that the bond between parent and child has an unreasoning element to it that is exceptionally deep. And you can feel the depth to which each love goes if you imagine losing the object of that love: my broccoli died, my dog died, my child died.

Nevertheless, we use the same word for all three kinds of love. If we were sophisticated with our interior lives, we would have, at minimum, three words to describe these three types of love (and as well, other words to indicate degree, to allow subtle shadings in each kind of love). There's a tremendous lack of awareness, of refinement of perception, in our culture and language when it comes to feeling, to emotion, to feelings. We have put emphasis in a place that older cultures did not (on technoscientific minutiae in the exterior world) and have lost some of our language and perceptual skill in the process. And when a people no longer possess words for subtle experiences, even crucially important ones such as love, elements of those experiences, perhaps whole ranges of experience, move into the unconscious to greater or lesser degrees. In a sense, they get lost. "What we cannot speak about," Wittgenstein observed, "we pass over in silence." As a result, a lot of people spend a lot of time being very confused about what it means to be a human being. Writers are not exempt (nor are scientists, physicians, or any other member of a Western industrialized culture). Ancient and indigenous cultures, in a manner similar to Alaskan tribes' perception of snow, looked in this area with quite different eyes; they had a much more refined vocabulary.

One of the tasks that lies before us as writers is this reclamation of ourselves, this ecological restoration of our interior world, this restoration of our capacity to feel. That, and the reclaiming of our ability discuss that capacity in all its complexity and subtlety.

To begin with, here are some distinctions to make what I am describing more tangible, for there are very clear differences between feeling, emotion, and feelings. As well, each of them possesses interior subtleties and shadings depending on how they are being applied and in what context.

FEELING

Normally, when people use the word feeling, they mean one of three things, a kinesthetic perception, an emotional perception, or an environmental perception.

Kinesthetic perception means bodily perception or physical sensation, as in "I touched the stove; it was hot." Emotional perception describes an interior state, as in someone asking you how you feel and your responding by saying "I feel happy" (or sad or mad or depressed). Environmental perception is when you and a friend go into a restaurant and the two of you stop and look at each other and say: "This place feels kind of weird. Let's leave." All of us are aware of these different meanings to the word "feeling." They rise in complexity, from simple to more complex in just that order. They are accepted in our society, in contemporary Western cultures, in importance, decreasingly in that order. That is, the first is strongly accepted, the second less so, the third not so much at all.

Physical sensation is considered to be an essential skill in navigating the physical world. It doesn't give too much trouble, unless sex is involved, and so is pretty acceptable. The second kind of feeling perception, where emotions are involved, is viewed more as an inescapable part of life in the United States. It is generally considered to be the source of a great deal of trouble because it leads people to do all sorts of disruptive things. They fall in love and out of love, explode in anger or cry uncontrollably at the most inopportune times. This kind of feeling interferes with work schedules and school and leads people to make all kinds of decisions that the society and the corporations that employ them would rather they not make, and so they are controlled with drugs such as Prozac more and more all the time.

Now the last kind of feeling, the one that occurs when you go into a restaurant that feels so uncomfortable you decide to leave, is a pretty common experience although almost no one talks of it. It's the kind of feeling that is usually the domain of artists and other people who don't fit into the boxes of life all that well. It is the most atrophied kind of feeling in the Western world, which is a problem, because it's this kind of feeling on which the craft of writing depends.

Nevertheless, it is common to all people, no matter how atrophied it is. In essence, this third kind of feeling is a nonphysical form of kinesthetic touching. It is used by the part of us that works with the touch of meaning upon us. It is this kind of feeling I am talking about when I use the phrase *How does it feel?* Everyone uses this capacity for nonphysical touch to some extent.

For instance, all of us have had the experience of coming home to an empty house when we expected someone to be there. We walk in and something feels funny. An empty house feels empty and while our minds may be saying that we are making it up, a deeper part of us is telling us that no, nobody's home. Emptiness has a *feel* to it.

As well, we have all had the experience of our mate or friend or someone in our family being mad at us but not saying so. It *feels* different than if they are not mad, even if they are not saying anything, even if they are pretending, with all their might, that nothing is wrong. And, of course, sooner or later we have to say something ("Are you upset?"), at the very least just to avoid the part of the argument that will be concerned with our lack of sensitivity in not noticing. When those we love are mad at us, it *feels* different than if they are not.

Now, let's take a more complex example. While it's normally an unconscious process, all of us routinely scan any new room we enter with this nonphysical part of ourselves. It goes something like this . . .

Perhaps you are going to a workshop or conference. You walk to the open door of the room where the teaching is to take place. You step just inside, out of the way of other people, and begin scanning the room. First you feel how the entire room feels, in essence, you check for the meanings in the room. Part of this is simply a "how safe is it" scan. Every animal that's been hit on the back of the head at a watering hole has learned to do it. Another aspect to it is that the deep parts of you look over the room to determine just what they are going to have to deal with. Is the crowd of people friendly? Is the room friendly? Is the room emotionally warm? Or cold? Is it a nurturing environment? Or not? A room with medieval torture weapons on the wall will feel much different from one with pastoral landscapes. Then there is another element: where is the most fun place to sit? (Which people do you definitely *not* want to sit by?) Where would you feel best sitting for the duration of the conference? So, you look at the various parts of the room and in your imagination try sitting in that chair, then that one, then *that* one, until you find one that feels the best to you in that moment in time. And there you sit. All of us do this.

What I mean by the word *feeling* in this book is that specific kind of nonphysical touching. All writers develop some degree of skill in using that type of feeling. The more conscious it is for you, that is, the more you use it, educate it, and give it experience the more elegant your use of it can become. I consider it the primary skill that a writer must develop and use. Its use is the only thing that will allow a writer's writing to come alive. It's the only thing that allows a writer to work with meanings directly. Only it will allow the shaping of meaning in such a manner as to produce inhabited words. Only it allows access to the imaginal. So, again, let's look at what happens when it is used with writing.

If I give you a line, such as this one by Rilke . . .

A man who can praise comes toward us like ore out of the silences of rock.

. . . and I ask you, "How does it feel?" Something specific happens. You don't need any training to do it, nevertheless, when I ask you "how does it feel?" some nonphysical part of you reaches out and touches that line. And at that moment of touch a very real, very specific phenomenon occurs. You can feel something in the line, perhaps several somethings. There is an emotional tone or flavor to it, an "intimation of mood or feeling" as Goethe called it. You have an exact sense of it even though you might not be able to put into words just exactly what it is. Though we have come up with names for all the thousands of colors that can be created from subtle blendings of the basic or primary colors, we have no such sophistication with the thousands upon thousands of emotional tones that exist and are perceived when this kind of touching occurs. We are still at snow, sleet, and hail. Nevertheless, there is a specific emotional tone or flavor to it, and feeling that is where all sense of the meaning of the line begins. And this feeling is the first step in unlocking its meanings. If you stay with it, if you keep feeling into that emotional tone or flavor, your touching begins to lead you deeper into the meanings that Rilke captured in that sentence. As Robert Frost commented: "Like a piece of ice on a hot stove the poem must ride on its own melting."[1] Rilke's line starts out in solid form but as it moves deeper inside you it begins to melt; you become entangled in its meanings and those meanings float on the poem's own melting within you. As you become more deeply entangled in the line, it becomes clear that it possesses some great truth or truths that, when touched by your awareness, come reverberating up out of it. They touch the truth receiver someplace deep inside you and capture its attention. There are so many layerings of meaning in the line it could take a lifetime to tease them out. The meal is rich, the line heavy with deep psyche, luminous and alive. There is, in fact, a highly complex series of interior responses to your nonphysical touching of the line. And what is more, they stay with you, altering your internal world, provoking responses throughout the many parts of yourself. The meaning piled up behind the words has moved into you as an experience.

That is what I mean by the word *feeling* when I use it in this book. Emotions, however, are something else.

EMOTIONS

Emotions are things like mad, sad, glad, scared, and so on. They generally occur as a response to either an interior or exterior event of some kind. So, for instance, if I ask you to look out the window and notice how the man with the tattoos and cruel expression, sitting in the dark car, in front of your house, feels to you, without much hesitation you might say scary. However, if you slow the process down a bit, you will notice some specific steps occur before "scary" emerges, however quickly, into your awareness.

When I ask you how he feels, you, automatically, reach out with that nonphysical part of you and touch him with it. There is a moment of contact where all that is happening is your engaging in that capacity for nonphysical touching. Next, another part of you interprets what occurred in that moment of touch.

Some invisible substance flows from you to the man and *feels* who and what he is with it. Then the *meaning* of the phenomenon, the man sitting in his car, moves inside you. A part of you then analyzes that meaning and determines safety level, just as you do when you enter a conference room. The analysis comes up "dangerous." And then you feel scared. The emotion is a response to the analysis of a nonphysical touching or *feeling* of the exterior world. The whole process takes place in just a fraction of a moment. It's very quick.

That is an example of an emotional response to an exterior event. Here is an interior one. If I ask you how you feel right now, what occurs is that you use that nonphysical touching to feel inside yourself. You touch your interior world, just as you did that man in the car, and an emotion or series of emotions arise in response to that touching. So, you say mad, or happy, or sad, or irritated. If you go further, if you think about that emotion, you can often say why you are irritated, "because you keep asking these stupid questions." So, emotions are responses to things, inside or outside of us.

Feelings are something else again.

FEELINGS

If you think of the current political climate in the United States, you might actually use the word *feelings* as in "I have strong feelings about it." *Feelings* is a much more comprehensive phenomenon than either feeling or emotions. It includes an object of attention of some sort, a nonphysical touching of that object, all the emotions that arise in response to that touching, and all the thoughts, experiences, and memories that you have about that particular thing (or any similar things in your past experience) that you have touched. As examples: I have feelings about my ex-wife, I have feelings about liars, I have feelings about cluster bombs, I have feelings about food.

To go into it more deeply: When you read the bookman story that is Chapter One of this book, first you engaged in *feeling* the story, then you experienced emotions that arose in response to your *feeling* the story, and then, over a slightly longer period of time, you had *feelings* about the story. Again, these feelings are more complex in nature and extent than feeling or emotion. They are, in essence, a complex grouping or gestalt of responses. Some of those responses were *physiological.* Your physiology altered as the meanings moved inside you: your breathing patterns changed, eye focus and muscle holding patterns altered, hormonal cascade shifted.

Some of those responses were *psychological:* how you felt about yourself, your future, your degree of hope or hopelessness, your sense of possibility, of wholeness. Some of those responses were *emotional:* a series of emotions occurred as the meanings touched you—fear, joy, wonder, hope, a mild grief at times, a longing perhaps. Then as the meanings worked deeper inside you, *memories* were generated. Things out of your past began to emerge and all of these things had emotions attached to them, flowing through them. In other words, associative emotional experiences and memories occurred. And, as the associative emotional experiences and memories occurred, a great many thoughts emerged as well. Altogether, all these things make up what we generally call *feelings* about something.

And even more deeply . . .

Everyone has had the experience of meeting a good friend for lunch at a crowded restaurant. You remember how it goes. Say it's a cold blustery day. You park the car and walk to the restaurant. You pull open the door and there's that particular swirl of experiences common to restaurants that flow out with the opening door: smells of delicious food, the moistness and warmth of air from a people-filled room, sounds of people talking, noises of plates and waitstaff hurrying across wooden floors.

You walk in, step out of the way of the door, and stop a minute. Your eyes adjust to the difference in light, your ears to the sounds coming to you, your nose to the rich aromas that surround you. You notice the soft light coming in the windows, the fire in the fireplace. The slight, murmuring conversation of people eating good food. Your conscious mind pauses and some deeper part of you takes stock of your new surroundings just as you did at the workshop or conference. You begin to feel into the place. You sense how it *feels* in that restaurant, check out how nurturing it is, begin adjusting to the meanings in the place. Once that analysis is complete, you adapt, adjust to what that deep part of you now understands about the place you are in. Your breathing patterns change, becoming deeper and more even, your muscles loosen. You relax into where you are. This only takes a few moments, then you begin to look around for your friend. You look at this table, then that, scanning the room for your companion. Remember how that *is*. You look at a particular table, at that person sitting there. Is that him? No. So, you move on, scanning this table, then that. No, not him. No, not him. Then you do see him, sitting at the table near the fireplace. He looks up and sees you. Your eyes meet. In that moment something flashes between the two of you. Some sort of energy leaves through your eyes and touches him; some sort of recognition, filled with feeling, comes out of his eyes and touches you. You can *feel* it. And a part of you feels good and warm and loved, excited to be there.

Then you begin crossing the room, carefully edging between tables to get to him. He stands up as you come toward him, placing his napkin on the table, then you arrive and the two of you touch each other—perhaps with a handshake or a hand on the arm or a hug.

Remember again how it was when you looked at that first table where your friend was *not* sitting. Slow the experience down and just be with it a moment. You look at the table, at the person sitting there, and some deep part of you is, at the same time, *feeling* that person nonphysically, touching the stranger at the table. Visual pattern recognition is not the whole of what happens, you are feeling outwardly as well. And when it penetrates your conscious mind that it is not your friend sitting there, that deep part of you feels something in particular, perhaps a sense of wrongness, a disappointment, a kind of emotional letdown. So, you abandon that table and your eyes begin to search again. There. Another table. Another person. And again and again. Then, eventually, the deep, sensing part of you has a different experience. It's him and instead of a wrongness, there is a sense of completion, a sense of a completed connection of some sort. And with that sense of completed contact there is a kind of joy or rightness. The deep part of you that is engaging in comparative analysis tells you by this feeling of joy or rightness that this is the person you are looking for. Then you switch from comparative analysis and move into the experience itself and something flows between the two poles that are you and him. A rush of emotions comes; the emotions you have about your friend, about spending time with him, about any needs that you might get filled by being with someone who loves you and whom you love. Then all the *feelings* you have about him, the relationship between the two of you, other relationships you have had, and so on begin to occur. Associative emotional experiences and memories, and a great many thoughts, emerge. And all of this only takes a few moments. We have such tremendous capacity for subtle complexities of perception and analysis. We are so much more than we have been taught. We perceive and understand a great deal more than we realize.

Feeling is one thing, emotions another, and feelings still something else. The more awareness you have of these distinctions, the greater the potential impact of your craft, for if you are aware, you can create with intention, you can touch with subtlety, you can shift the awareness of your readers by working with the depths of them in ways that their conscious minds will rarely notice directly.

But to begin with, you must be willing to feel, to allow emotions to arise in response to your feeling, to have strong and deep feelings. These things can all be described as aspects of a passionate life. They belong to the human who fully engages the world, senses alive, to those who have reclaimed the response of the heart to what is presented to the senses. It generates writing that "burns the blood like powdered glass."

CHAPTER SIX

"It Burns the Blood Like Powdered Glass"

[During wild association] The poet enters the poem excited, with the emotions alive; he is angry or ecstatic, or disgusted. There are a lot of exclamation marks, visible or invisible. Almost all the poems in Lorca's Poet in New York *are written with the poet profoundly moved, flying. Powerful feeling makes the mind move, fast, and evidently the presence of swift motion makes the emotions still more alive, just as chanting awakens many emotions the chanter was hardly aware of at the moment he began chanting.*

What is the opposite of wild association then? Tame association? Approved association? Sluggish association? Whatever we want to call it, we know what it is—that slow plodding association that pesters us in so many poetry magazines, and in our own work when it is no good. . . . Poetry is killed for students in high school by teachers who only understand this dull kind of association.

Robert Bly

Those songs that speak of love without having within their lines an ache or a sigh are not love songs at all but rather Hate Songs disguised as love songs, and are not to be trusted. These songs deny us our humanness and our God-given right to be sad and the air-waves are littered with them. The love song must resonate with the susurration of sorrow, the tintinnabulation of grief. The writer who refuses to explore the darker regions of the heart will never be able to write convincingly about the wonder, the magic and the joy of love . . . just as goodness cannot be trusted unless it has breathed the same air as evil.

NICK CAVE

To help us seek the duende there are neither maps nor discipline. All one knows is that it burns the blood like powdered glass, that it exhausts, that is rejects all the sweet geometry one has learned, that it breaks with all styles. . . . Whoever beholds it is baptized with dark water. . . . The duende, then, is a power, not a work, not a thought.

FEDERICO GARCÍA LORCA

The dispassionate writing so common in newspapers, so common among contemporary writers of the many kinds of nonfiction, is devoid of courage. It is failure of character raised to professional stature. Cowardice as technique. Taught in too many writing schools its only real function is to enervate the profession, the culture, and the vitality of democracy, to get people to shut up and behave nicely. It results in ineffectual responses to totalitarian impulses in government, support of preemptive attacks on weaker nations, failure to investigate malfeasance of the powerful, and a refusal to speak truth to power. It kills any possibility of powerful writing, teaches young writers to be flat, does not encourage their blood being burned by powdered glass. Its function is domestication. Its impact on writing and language, on the craft itself, is inescapable. Dispassionate writing means writing devoid of passion, unemotional writing, writing devoid of feeling. It is writing that does not upset, does not emotionally challenge, pretends to a false objectivity (there is not, never has been, and never will be any such thing as objectivity).[1] It drives passionate, powerful writing to the margins, drives it underground. It should be resisted by every means possible. I despise it.

As I told you in the beginning, I am a barbarian. I am not civilized, not dispassionate, not interested in absence of feeling, emotions, or feelings.

I believe in writing that burns the blood, in which you feel forest wolves tensing behind you, writing filled with wilderness, writing that forces the margins, writing that challenges, that insists, that bleeds when it's cut, writing that uplifts the best in us and defies the worst, writing that's not afraid to breathe the same air as evil, writing that unashamedly believes in the good, that is undefended, writing that has death in it, writing with the same power that fills ancient redwoods, writing filled with darkness, writing with untamed wildness flowing through it, writing carrying an eagle's call, floating in the high cold winds of a mountain pass, writing that is not civilized, not contained, not channeled in irrigation ditches of tired grammatical form and civilized demeanor, writing that grabs readers by the neck and shakes them, writing that stirs the deepest parts of the soul, that allows the mythic to flow again into consciousness, writing that undoes, that unmakes, that touches on chaos, writing in which the old gods live, writing that touches on the deepest parts of the human and finds no definite line between us and other life forms on this planet, writing that surges, strains, demands, forces, rages, writing in language as liquid and mercurial as life itself, writing that is nonlinear, filled with luminosity, deep psyche, writing that DOES NOT SHUT THE FUCK UP. And certainly writing that does not fail to use the word fuck when it is called for, and it will always be called for. Eventually.

The old states of consciousness, reasserted under conservative governance the past thirty years, have shown again the bankruptcy of their position, perception, and orientation. The bankruptcy of the country is both literal and metaphorical, secular and spiritual. And these old states of consciousness are embedded in all forms of literature, all forms of writing. The New York literary style is the polished language of a bankrupt view of life, a dead-end consciousness, that can never be reclaimed. It has exhausted its potential. Renewal must come from outside, from the energy that new generations bring, must come from the turning over process that that new generational energy contains. Modern writing cannot be made to live again through the imposition of old forms. A door must be opened so dark wells of energy can flow up from the deep psyche and soak the words in life force.

You will find nothing in here to support the decision to write flatly, to be dispassionate, to attempt objectivity, to remove feeling, emotions, or feelings from your work. This chapter is concerned with finding the deepest wells of energy that are in you. Tapping them will ensure that your work is filled with energy and the kinds of meaning that only the touch of the deep self can bring. As William Stafford once put it . . .

> *In your life—the center of it, not the part for earning a living, or the part that gains you notice and credit, or even the part that leads others to like you—but in the central self are feelings so important and personal that the rest of the world cannot glimpse who you are and what is happening, deep in there, where it is you alone.*[2]

Literature, he says, is writing that comes out of that central place, no matter its form. Thus, it is necessary for your writing to be powered by your deepest passions and feelings. Here are some exercises that can help you clarify those deep feelings and help you pour meaning powerfully into words.

First, this one. It is composed of four parts: everything you love, everything you hate, your heroes, the books that have deeply moved you.

First Exercise

1. Make a list of everything you love. Everything.
2. Make a list of everything you hate. Everything.
3. Make a list of your heroes. All of them.
4. Make a list of the books that have deeply moved you, that you read again and again, that you hold inside yourself in some special light.

I want to encourage you in this exercise to, for a moment, give yourself permission to say anything that comes to you. Most of us censor ourselves far too much of the time, but for the duration of this exercise, please give yourself permission to say anything, to really write the truth of what is in you. Here are some comments on how to do the four parts of this exercise, approaches that can increase your clarity in the doing of them.

On Love

Almost everyone can make a list of everything they love. For, as you know, in this culture we are encouraged to have nice feelings and love is generally considered a nice feeling (though when you really get deep inside it, it has its own power, its own darkness, its own shadow). So this part of the exercise does not generally extend awareness further than the society wants it to go. Still, think about it deeply.

All of us have a tendency to assume that some of the things we most love are included in the list when they are not. You might love dogs, for instance, and decide to put that on the list. But when you think of your love of dogs, you are really seeing, experiencing, thinking of something more than dogs. Most likely you are remembering how it feels to share closeness with a dog, even with a particular kind of dog. A nice dog. A friendly dog. It is very rare that people actually love a mean dog that is going to bite them. So, what you might really be loving is not dogs *per se* but friendly dogs or perhaps dogs that will share that special closeness. To begin with, just list everything that comes to mind that you love. Then take a minute to go below the surface of each of those things to make sure that you are not assuming something that you have not actually written.

On Hate

Some people have a lot of trouble making a list of everything they hate. Nevertheless, it's very important. Whether you call it irritation, anger, rage, or hate, there are certain things you just feel strongly about in this way. Owning those kinds of emotions, however, often extends awareness further than society wants it to go. I have seen people try to get out of this in many ways. "Things I dislike" was one of them. "Things I don't love" was another. Neither one works.

A good writer always hates and I imagine you do, too. I don't know anyone who has waited patiently for a parking space to be vacated and who, when just about to angle into it, has been cut off by another driver zipping into it (all the while ignoring your existence), who does not hate. At least for a minute or two. So, let yourself really think about what you hate, what makes you really mad, what you believe is just plain wrong and bad in the world.

Now write all those things down; they are important.

On Heroes

Some people have trouble with this one as well. Usually it is people middle-aged and older who have had so much experience with people, that they know, in a deeply experiential way, that people are just people. They no longer believe in heroes, you see. One other group also has trouble with this: people who have been filled with a strange form of misplaced egalitarianism in which they feel it is wrong to elevate any one person over all others. "We are all heroes" they insist. Yeah, right.

So, here are some ways to think of it. Use any of them that make sense to you (the concept of heroes works best for me). When you were in darkness, who helped you believe again? Who has inspired you? Who do you admire? Who have you wanted to be or to be like? When you did admire people when you were young and knew no better, who were they? (Just pretend you are sixteen again.) If you did have heroes, who would they be? If someone were really mean and insisted that you write down your heroes, even though you don't have any, who would they be?

Now, write all of them down.

On the Books That Have Moved You

Most writers read a lot and have done so since they were young—often between fifty and two hundred books a year and perhaps as many as three or four thousand articles as well. There isn't a writer alive who has not been called to this work by books and the writers they have read. List every book you can think of that means or meant a great deal to you, that you find yourself reading over and over again, the ones that hold a special place inside you.

If you have been infected by the foolish thinking that says *these* kinds of books are good and *those* are not, if you feel like you are doing something wrong by saying you like Ian Fleming and find Herman Melville terminally boring, ignore it. Write down the books that *you* love, that have moved you, that have made you want to do this work, that have called you to the craft. Remember, the first step in freedom is to tell Mrs. Grundy to go to hell. Give yourself permission to love the books that you really do love; the rest of them probably suck anyway.

It's better if you stop now and do this exercise without reading further but most people don't. So, I would exhort you, after you read the rest of this, to give yourself permission to really do the exercise as if you had not read further, to do it for real, without knowing why I am asking you to do it. Sometimes knowing the purpose of the thing causes people to alter their answers, just a smidgen, toward what they think is better. Please understand, however, that in this *you must trust that who you are in your deep self genuinely has value and is important in the world.* Who you really are and what you really feel about these things really are good and necessary things. You really are needed for what you bring.

ON THE MEANING OF THE EXERCISE

I have led this exercise in workshops many times over the years. People's answers are astonishing in their variety. One of the interesting things about it is that most people think everyone else's list will be the same as theirs. Even in the rare instances where there are overlaps, the lists are strikingly different. These things that you have listed, they are the motivators of your life, the power sources that drive the engine. They are the things that, in so many ways, make you uniquely you. They are the things that give indications of where your soul work resides, of just what should be motivating your writing, of the meanings that you should be working with in your writing, of the community of people, of writers, with whom you belong.

About Love

Everything that you love is everything you stand for, everything that you will fight to protect. If you look at your list closely and think about it, two things will become apparent. First, there will be commonalities to the things that you have listed. Recognizing this will allow you to move the loves into one or more groupings. Secondly, areas of expression, work, or play that are the most fun for you are revealed.

When closely examined, you might find that your love list, for example, is oriented around three common themes: deep intimacy, writing, wild places. The list, since it deals with instances of these occurrences, might show that you like these most when they occur in small intimate settings, when they are attended by deep feeling, when they occur in ecologically undisturbed areas. A partial listing might look something like this:

> *Old trees, wise people, people who truly live their life, books that make me believe, my son, my dog, my best friend, sitting with a teacher I love and respect, high mountains, helping someone who needs me, wild water, flowers nodding in sunlight, early morning light flowing in the bedroom window, the lines in a good man's face, someone who stands up for what he believes in, people who oppose the powerful, great writers, the touch of a lover, walking in woods, seeing otters play, seeing ravens play, writing a great line, reading a great line, ancient rocks, healthy ecosystems, wild animals, lightning, wild thunderstorms, the sweet intimacy of sex, real love, hugs with people I care about, incredibly well prepared food, a fine film, seeing the world through another person's eyes, the touch of deep meaning, duende, the imaginal world, playing with shifts in consciousness, the crazy coyoteness of wild desert,* and so on.

This part of the exercise tells you what *must* be a part of your writing and of your work as a writer. Working in the public school system with twelve-year-old children, teaching them English while writing on weekends, would probably not fulfill the person who made this list.

About Hate

Once upon a time I was giving a talk on writing and in the group was a very old, very kind, and sincere woman. During a question-and-answer period she raised her hand and said, "I've lived a very interesting life. I really did travel with my parents in a covered wagon when I was small, and I have experienced a lot of truly wonderful things. I have thought for a long time that my life would make an interesting book and I have tried to write one several times but . . ."

And here I interrupted, "you keep running out of steam about page 60."

She looked at me in surprise and said, "why, yes."

"I know the answer," I said, "if you would like to hear it."

"Oh, yes," she said.

"Well," I continued, "the only way to make it through the choppy headwaters of the book's interior is to hate."

"Oh, no," she said. "I could never do that. How about if I love?"

"Well, love is nice," I replied. "But writing is too hard for love alone. Love is crucial for many reasons but it is not enough to get you through the book. And whether you call it hate, or rage, or anger, or irritation, it is all some form of the same thing. You must have this hate, this rage to be a writer for this is one of the hardest professions on the planet and without rage you will never survive it. You will always run out of steam about page 60."

She was a kindly woman and she shook her head at my foolishness and didn't say anything. But she never did write that book.

Everything you hate is everything you stand against. It is everything that you oppose, that you write to change, that you want to be a part of changing, that you must participate in changing in order to respect yourself. They are the things that if you do not speak against them, you will be complicit in promoting, merely by your silence. Your rage against these things is what will make it possible to face the blank page, day after day after day.

A partial list of things that someone hates might look like this:

> *Torture, imprisoning innocent people, liars, people who misuse power, large corporations, the poor being controlled by the rich, the "war on drugs," lobbyists, clear cutting, treating Nature as if it is just a bunch of resources, assuming that nothing is intelligent except people, stupidity in people, being afraid, physical pain, lack of compassion in healers, cruelty in the guise of kindness, duplicity of all kinds, laws that are passed "for your own good," reductionism, the arrogance of scientists and physicians, hospitals that take someone's life savings for treating them—all the while telling people they exist to alleviate suffering,* and so on.

If this were your list, then every book you write should exist in part (as Edward Abbey put it in one of his dedications) *to hate injustice, to defy the powerful, and to speak for the voiceless.* These kinds of things indicate that focusing your work on technical writing about cellular division or writing instruction manuals for electronics is not the right approach.

If you write about what you deeply love and what you deeply hate, then there is never a lack of motivation to write. And every day you do write, what you most deeply believe is made manifest. Your writing is filled with deep meaning because you are only writing about what you deeply believe and feel strongly about. Every day you get to work with the things that mean the most to you of all the things in the world. And what is great about it is that *you* get to define those things, no one else. You stand for that which you love and you oppose that which would attempt to do it harm. There is no greater thing that anyone can do.

On Your Heroes

They are *your* heroes and they are your heroes for a reason. They touch something inside you. They raise a response from the deepest part of your self. They do so because in some manner you are like them. They have allowed a part of themselves to come alive in the world that has a counterpart in you. You are, in fact, very much like them in some basic, essential manner. They are *your* community, the nation to which you belong, the people among whom you are meant to be. In the reflection of their lives you see an image of who you are meant to be, who you really are.

All the people who are our heroes were once themselves just like us—just a kid from a trailer park. They, themselves, were touched by others who had gone before them, those who'd traveled on ahead. They, themselves, had heroes, men and women whose lives called out to something buried deep within them, urging it into the light.

Most of us have difficulty in letting these great, hidden parts of ourselves emerge, usually because of fear or a belief in our limitations. Our heroes are mirrors of who we are meant to be, who we deeply are, or are people who represent repressed parts of ourselves that want out and must necessarily come out for us to be fulfilled. This is why we are drawn to them and not to others equally impressive.

If you look at the list you have made carefully you will also find that those who you respect as your great teachers, as your heroes, generally engage in work that can be grouped into a few categories. That is, they have focused their work into areas that are themselves meaningful to you. These people show you not only qualities of self and character that are to emerge but where your true chance of greatness lies. They show you the fields in which you will find the most joy, the most meaning, the fields in which you are most strongly called to contribute. It is among these people that you belong.

A list of heroes might look like this:

> *Edward Abbey, Barry Lopez, Alice Walker, John Gardner, Gandhi, Robert Bly, William Stafford, Eleanor Roosevelt, George Bernard Shaw, George Bird Grinnell, Helen Keller, Mark Twain, Dale Pendell, John Dunning, Henry David Thoreau, Goethe, Masanobu Fukuoka, Bill Mollison, Jane Goodall, Walt Whitman, Barbara McClintock, Frank Herbert, Charles Bowden, Buckminster Fuller, Black Elk, Luther Burbank, John Muir, James Lovelock, Lyn Margulis, Gregory Bateson, Vaclav Havel, Manuel Cordova Rios, Margaret Mead, David Hoffmann, Isabelle Allende, Mary Midgley,* and so on.

The people in that list fall, roughly, into several groups. They are all people of great courage. Nearly all of them are or were concerned with speaking truth to power; nearly all of them fought against the oppression of the weak by the powerful. Many of them work or worked to protect the wildness of the world, to protect Nature. All of them believe or believed in the essential dignity of the human being. Most of them generated unique contributions that positively affected the world. Most of them are or were outside conventional reality frameworks. Nearly all of them speak or spoke for the livingness of the world. All of them are writers, most of them as a major expression of their work (as opposed to actors or musicians or engineers, for example).

If this were your list you would probably not be happy as a musician, a politician, or an engineer. You would probably not be happy writing conventional education texts, books on mining technology, mysteries, or how to make money in the stock market.

On the Books That You Love

According to Bowker's *Books in Print,* over 400,000 books were published or distributed in the United States in 2007; Amazon.com lists at least

7,500,000 books on their site (perhaps as many as 10,000,000—many of Amazon's older, out of print books have no ranking because no one has ever bought one of them). The important question is: out of that incredible number of books, which ones draw you to them? Which ones do you read over and over again?

These books, like your heroes, draw you to them for a particular reason. The ones you cherish, that you read over and over again, that you buy in first edition and keep pristine on the shelf, affect you in the way they do for a reason. And that reason tells you a lot about what you are meant to write, about where your area of focus actually is. (If you aren't reading *Moby Dick* and other, similar works every year, that kind of work is not your cup of caffeinated beverage.)

Here is what the poet William Stafford has to say about the kinds of books that draw a person:

> *You are unable to read up to a standard greater than the standard of yourself. You may feel a good deal of gusto about a great poem, but that's because you are worthy of it. You just cannot feel that gusto if you're not worthy. So, if you really do feel that a certain poem is* **that** *good, you are just about there yourself. I mean, you are that kind of person. . . . [You cannot] realize how good something is until you are worthy of it. I mean, you're that kind of person. . . . If a person reads a poem and feels its greatness, that's not a reflection on him, it's a* **confirmation** *of his ability.*[3]

In other words, it is *only* because that thing already exists within you that you have that deep feeling response to it, it is part of who you are. And that work of fiction, nonfiction, or poetry moves you *only* because the depth of meaning that it contains within it is *already* in you. The feeling that you get when you read a great book is the greatness within you vibrating in response to the impact of the deep meanings held within the book.

A list of loved books might look like this:

> *Dune, The Art of the Impossible, Healing Gaia, The Stories of Eva Luna, The Autobiography of Mark Twain, The Club Dumas,*

The Fencing Master, The Flanders Panel, The Bookman's Wake, The Winged Life, The Kabir Book, The Soul's Code, News of the Universe, On Moral Fiction, Light Action in the Caribbean, Black Elk Speaks, The Hidden City, Wizard of the Upper Amazon, Shamanic Voices, Babel-17, Lord of the Rings, Pharmako/Poeia, The Dresden Files, When Food is Love, Traveling in Dreams, The Permaculture Design Manual, Soldier of the Mist, Writing the Australian Crawl, Games People Play, Voltaire's Bastards, A Little Book on the Human Shadow, Sex at the Margins, The Natural Way of Farming, Walden, The Fractal Geometry of Nature, Earth in Mind, The Fine Art of Cabinetmaking, The Reality Overload, and so on.

Like the other elements of this exercise, these books can be grouped together in various categories and, even if fiction, they will be found to have certain things in common. They will address certain issues (the necessity of undamaged Nature, for example), explore similar truths (the essential dignity of the human being irrespective of birth or station, for instance), explore solutions to the problems of our times, encourage the best in the individual to emerge, and so on. At the simplest, they all possess duende.

Second Exercise

Here is an exercise that can help in piling up meaning behind the word like water behind a dam, in creating writing that is soaked in life force.

This works best if you just do the first part of the exercise without looking at the rest of it. With this exercise the tendency to alter the first part if you know the second part is high; it is better if you just do this first part first.

So . . . think of five words that mean a great deal to you, that generate memories and feelings of all you hold important, that *feel* luminous to you, that in some manner touch on the deep psyche in you, words that hold within them the essence of what you consider important in your life.

I have encouraged people to do this exercise for many years in many settings and, like the earlier exercise, it is a continuing source of interest to me how different the lists are from person to person. But of course they inevitably will be, for this exercise touches on what is most important to the individual who does it. It opens a channel to the meanings that are held deep inside us and allows them expression in the world through the words that are chosen.

A list someone makes might look something like this:

Earth
Stone
Green
Leaves
Plants

Or it might look like this:

Love
Happiness
Child
Wandering
Hope

It doesn't matter except in that each of these words *matter* to you. You can even think of it this way: If you were forced to sum up, in one word each, the five most important things to you in this life, what would they be? Really think about it and let yourself feel each of those things. Weigh them against other things until you have, at this moment in time, the five most important. The words, because they represent the most important things in your life, should almost shimmer with meaning when you say them.

Now, take a fresh sheet of paper and write them down.

You didn't cheat and read this sentence before you wrote them down did you? (I did.) Now that you have your five words, here is what to do with them.

Write five poems, each of which uses all five of the words. You can use as many other words as you want, nevertheless each poem *must* contain all five of the words you have chosen.

Take as much time as you need . . . there's no hurry.

When you are done, read the poems in sequence. Notice how they change. Often, the first one is a bit stilted. As you spent more time with the exercise, however, the work deepened, you began to drop down into what you were doing, down below the surface of the word, began to work with the substance of meaning itself. You began to *feel* your way through the writing rather than thinking about it mentally. The poems often become more coherent, possessed of more interior richness, better flow, more luminosity.

What is striking to me over the years I have offered this exercise in classes, is how good the poems are. Anyone can write poetry . . . if they choose words that have deep meaning to them. Poetry is something that is inherent in every human being. It is inherent because it deals with meaning and all human beings work with the substance of meaning every day. It's just that few people make it the focus of their life; they rarely place the whole of their attention on it. When it comes to poetry, nearly everyone has been confused into thinking it has something to do with technique, or rhyming, or form. It has nothing to do with those things but everything to do with working directly with the essence of meaning itself. *It is a communication, not a technique.*

In the West we have been convinced through constant messages in all mediums that form is more important than essence, that technique matters more than meaning. The result is mediocre writing, flat writing. Because the mediocre in writing is so continually praised, too many end up doubting their own critical perceptions. Too many think that they cannot write because their work does not look (or feel) like all those other people's. Here is part of the secret; *it's not supposed to.*

The writing that you do must spring from the life you inhabit. It must originate in what has meaning to *you.* As Stafford comments: "To curry favor by saying what you do not mean, or what you do not feel, is as damaging in poetry as it is in politics or business or other parts of life. You can become a lost soul in literature just as surely as you can in any activity where you abandon yourself to the decisions of others. Technique used for itself will rot your soul."[4] The craft must always spring from who you are and the meanings that are important to you. The only thing that you ultimately have to give is your experience of your own life, your essential *individuality.*

For any writer, poetry is good exercise for the craft, no matter what kind of writing you do. Poems are perhaps the most condensed form of language that exists. Writing with all the fat removed. Writing boiled down to essentials. Decoctions of meaning. It is one of the best ways to practice inhabited writing, writing that piles up meaning behind the word like water behind a dam.

It is your passions and your deep feelings that are the key to your writing ensouled communication, to inhabited language. As García Lorca put it, you "must awaken the duende in the remotest mansions of the blood."[5] This can only occur if you reclaim your capacity to feel deeply and keenly. Then, some force, some powerful energy comes out of you and into the words. The words themselves arise out of the deepest passions that stir your blood. And that makes an incredible difference in what your work becomes and how it feels. William Gass makes a powerful observation on this when he says . . .

> *[Rilke's] work has taught me what real art ought to be; how it can matter to a life through its lifetime; how commitment can course like blood through the body of your words until the writing stirs, rises, opens its eyes.*[6]

Your writing will only mean something to the readers who buy your work if it means something to you. Your passions, your commitment, must course like blood through the body of your words. Then, truly, the writing will stir, rise, open its eyes. And the more you fill your writing with the meanings that come from deepest in yourself, the more it will impact your readers. That is why, if the work is good, you will always feel afraid as you write it. For you are exposing some deep part of yourself to outside view. You are allowing yourself to be naked inside the work. And one of the difficulties with this is that you know it, you feel it.

Letting an undefended work go out and into the world allows others access to your deepest self. You are engaging in an act of intimacy with the reader by revealing, without trying to hide or protect, your deepest feelings, beliefs, and experiences. You are naked inside the work.

Any work, to be good at all, must come from the deepest wells inside the self and contain the deepest meanings you hold dear. As John Gardner puts it:

> *Nothing can be made to be of interest to the reader that was not first of vital concern to the writer. Each writer's prejudices, tastes, background, and experience tend to limit the kinds of characters, actions, and settings he can honestly care about, since by the nature of our mortality we care about what we know and might possibly lose (or have already lost), dislike that which threatens what we care about, and feel indifferent toward that which has no visible bearing on our safety or the safety of the people and things we love.*[7]

This exercise is one way to get there.

As Earth leaves,
we remain,
stones,
not plants,
not green,
just tiny pebbles
scattered
on an empty street[8]

CHAPTER SEVEN

The Skill of Duende

> *The New Critical ideas do not apply at all. Readers go on applying them anyway, in fear of the content they might have to face if they faced the poem as they face a human being.*
>
> ROBERT BLY

> *We all walk in mysteries. We do not know what is stirring in the atmosphere that surrounds us, nor how it is connected with our own spirit. So much is certain—that at times we can put out feelers of our soul beyond its bodily limits; and a presentiment, an actual insight is accorded to it.*
>
> GOETHE

> *[Duende] needs the trembling of the moment and then a long silence.*
>
> FEDERICO GARCÍA LORCA

There are moments in life when we experience something out of the ordinary. Moments when we feel the trembling and then a long silence. Something shakes us out of our daily world into something new and we feel an ecstasy. We get caught up in something outside of and greater than the self. We feel a moment of what García Lorca called duende. We get entangled in a direct experience of meaning without having to go through the medium of language. We have an experience like this . . .

The reporter had been assigned the story by his editor. Human interest story. Kids, dolphins. You know, are they intelligent, aren't they cute. But this guy really wasn't interested in the story and resented having to do it. He was someone to whom the concept of intelligence in dolphins was a joke.

Bored, his disdain under the lightest of social controls, he accompanied the scientists to the long glass wall of the lab where the dolphins waited, as they did every morning, to say hello. He watched the scientists go through their morning ritual, watched the dolphin family respond. Made nice noises over the six-week-old baby dolphin, took a short tour around the lab, went through a desultory question-and-answer session, drank the obligatory bad coffee that scientists can never seem to remedy, and then spent the rest of the time leaning against the glass wall of the dolphin tank, chain-smoking cigarettes.

Now, for whatever reason, the young dolphin was fascinated by this guy and instead of swimming off with his family, he just kept floating there looking at the reporter in the curious way that the young of many species have about something new. The man, with his back to the glass, ignored it as long as possible, but the young dolphin seemed to possess inexhaustible patience. He just kept hanging there. Staring. After awhile the reporter began to get twitchy, then mad. So, he took a deep drag on his cigarette, turned, and blew smoke at the glass, directly in the dolphin's face. The dolphin back-pedaled in surprise, looked at the man for a moment, then swam rapidly off. The reporter, at peace, leaned back against the glass, and continued to smoke.

But in a minute or two the young dolphin returned, swam up close to the glass, and waited for the man to notice him. And, of course, eventually the reporter did. In irritation he turned and glared at the young dolphin, and at that moment, the young dolphin blew a cloud of smoke directly in the journalist's face.

And the whole room stopped.

It took awhile for everyone to figure out what had happened, for of course dolphins don't smoke (and anyway, even if they did, it wouldn't work under water). The dolphin, who was still nursing, had gone to his mother, taken some milk, and come back and puffed it in the man's face. A very sophisticated response, especially in a six-week-old infant of a species considered to be inferior in intelligence to humans.

But something else happened in that moment, something that caught up everyone in the room. It was not simply a series of mechanical behaviors that occurred, *A* then *B* then *C*. Some living essence came out of the dolphin and touched the man. A *communication* occurred. Some deep meaning came reverberating up and out of that moment of touch and swept away the statistical mentality. For a moment in time every human in the room swam in deeper waters. They stopped thinking, caught up in *feeling* the meaning that had entered the room. Time seemed to stop and each human there was caught up in contemplation of an invisible thing, something that captured their whole awareness, the attention of the deep self.

A person who observed the interaction said he had never seen cynicism and skepticism evaporate in a human being so quickly. In that one tiny moment of time, the journalist's separation from the other life forms with which he shares this planet ended. He was touched by a living, aware, caring, intelligence from the world and he could not deny it. Some door in him opened and the whole aware universe came flooding in and he was never the same again. For him, the long loneliness of the human species ended.[1]

Now, there is something more in this interaction then a demonstration of dolphin intelligence. Some invisible thing entered your experience as you sat reading this story. And it is that invisible thing, and your capacity to feel it, that is of the essence here. I want to stress it is an experience—it is not an idea or simply a mental recognition of a certain state of reality, it is an experience and that experience is attended by a particular kind of feeling. When the meaning of that story penetrated you, this experience I am talking about was, for a moment, present inside you and so was the feeling that goes along with it.

The thing that happened in that room with the baby dolphin, when time seemed to stop and some strange force caught everyone in its grasp, is a moment of what the Spanish poet Federico García Lorca called duende. It is a moment in which a particular kind of experience occurs, one that lies beyond mechanicalism, beyond reductionist approaches, beyond the linear mind and the statistical mentality. It is integral to the kind of writing that this book is about.

So . . . let's play with it a little.

Here is another piece of writing that describes (and evokes) a moment of duende. It is from Robert Bly's *Hearing Gary Snyder Read:*

> *He speaks softly before the student audience, confident that he has much to say, and it is exactly what they need to know. He makes a few remarks about [his poem] Rip Rap to start with. On certain mountainsides in the far west where one might want to build trails, an obsidian rock sheath is found, glassy, impossible for horses' hoofs to get a grip on. So smaller rocks have to be laid on it, but carefully. So he thought that words might be used that way, one slipped under the end of another, laid down on the glassy surface of some insight that one couldn't stand on otherwise.*[2]

There is something that happens when that last line moves inside you, isn't there? As it reverberates down inside you, as its meaning penetrates, when you are finally held in the gestalt of understanding, there's this sort-of interior trembling, then a kind of silence. You find yourself standing on the glassy surface of a particular kind of seeing, a particular kind of understanding. You begin in this world but you end up someplace else, someplace where dolphin children blow smoke in reporters' faces.

Bly's piece starts with a simple description. We are there in the room with him. Some images come, some sounds. A sense of the room emerges, and the student audience perhaps, restless in their seats. Then Gary Snyder standing in front of them with a certain look on his face. We are entering the dreaming state that writing evokes. And as Gary Snyder begins to speak, more images emerge, of horses and men and a mountainside. We see the slippery obsidian sheath beneath their feet. We get a sense of just how hard it is to take a horse across that slope. Then we get a sense of what we have to do to make a trail on that slick surface.

We start in a room with students shuffling in seats and a poet standing ready to speak. Then we find ourselves on a mountainside in the west with men and horses and a difficult trail. These descriptions of the world that surrounds us come first, capturing the attention, firmly anchoring awareness and perception in one kind of reality. Then there is a movement into something else. The reality framework of the piece shifts entirely, leaving one paradigm, one reality orientation, and ending up in another, the two connected by the slenderest of threads. What the self sees, what it perceives, when that shift occurs is very different than what it saw before. Some new insight into the nature of things occurs. The world the conscious mind lives within expands tremendously and in an unexpected direction. For a moment the statistical mentality catches glimpses of something far outside its normal boundaries and perceptions. And there is just a little bit, or perhaps a lot, of a kind of awe at this unexpected glimpse of a reality unsuspected, a reality that surrounds us every day of our lives. There is the trembling of the moment and then the silence. Duende.

Bly refers to this shift from one state of perception to another as taking a long floating leap.

> *In ancient times, in the "time of inspiration", the poet flew from one world to another, "riding on dragons", as the Chinese said. . . . They dragged behind them long trails of dragon smoke. . . . This dragon smoke means that a leap has taken place in the poem. In many ancient works of art we notice a long floating leap at the center of the work. That leap can be described as a leap from the conscious to the unconscious and back again, a leap from the known part of the mind to the unknown part and back to the known.*[3]

You could even say it's a leap from a known part of the world to the unknown. And the reader, immersed in the words, takes the leap as well. Caught up in the movement of the writing, the reader takes on a momentum that has its own, ever-increasing, inertia. Reaching the edge of a precipice and not even realizing it is there, the reader continues on, taking a long, floating leap. Then there is the landing on the other side, the arrival in an entirely different terrain. There is a momentary shock at the impact, a slight emergence out of the dreaming, then a looking around with new eyes. The reality one is in is different; some new insight is accorded the self. It lasts but a moment perhaps, with especially powerful duende as long as a minute or two, then there is a pulling back, as if some sort of elastic band is contracting. The reader is swiftly drawn back into the old world, the old perspectives. Yet, something of that other world comes along, some new view, some piece of a reality the reader did not suspect existed. Some new kind of perception or understanding, perhaps a new piece of consciousness, human or nonhuman, is now a part of perception and the tapestry of personal life.

The moment just after the long floating leap, when the reader lands on the other side of the abyss, awakens and looks around with new vision, seeing from the unworn sides of the eyes, that is the experience Lorca called duende.

The writer Brook Zern describes it as a moment that:

> *dilates the mind's eye, so that the intensity becomes almost unendurable. . . . There is a quality of first-timedness, of reality so heightened and exaggerated that it becomes unreal, and this is characterized by a remarkable time-distortion effect.*[4]

If, during a living performance, you have ever experienced a powerful moment of duende you know what he means. There is not only a quality of first-timedness but of a moment where it seems the self has moved outside of time. It feels as if time stops. There is a feeling of familiarity, too, as if this timeless place has always been known, just forgotten for some reason that has itself been forgotten. Not only is there a time-distortion effect, as Zern notes, but both a visual and auditory distortion. The eyes become soft focused and luminous, colors are more vivid. The room may even seem to visually shimmer as if waves of heat were rising off sun-baked sidewalks, affecting the view. But this is a different kind of energy that is rising now. It is not heat. In spite of the visual distortion, everything has a freshness to it, as if one were seeing the world for the first time, as if one were newly born. And there is a silence as deep as the farthest reaches of space. Like a blanket it covers everything and stuffs up the senses. Paradoxically, there is a loudness to it that is almost unendurable. The inner voice has stilled, simultaneously, in everyone in the room. And in that stilling one becomes aware of just how much the self has been immersed in noise since language was first learned and internalized. A certain kind of meaning has become the central focus of awareness. This invisible thing, held in the work, in containers made of living language, has burst into awareness and the self, the entire audience, is caught up in wonder and in contemplation of it. The senses are alive, the entire surface of the body awake. There is no movement, no sound, no time, yet the self is feeling, and experiencing, deeply. There is a sense of recovered personhood. The thing that the writer or poet is describing is understood, but not with the brain; mental activity is almost nonexistent. It is instead understood with the whole self. Experientially. One has entered an entirely different reality and now breathes its fragrance, becomes entangled in its meanings, *feels* it with every part of the self.

Lorca said that whoever experiences duende is *baptized with dark water.* Do you get a sense of what that means here?

Time seems to stop, there is a silence that falls on everything, so complete that you really could hear a pin drop. The thinking mind stops, feeling is exceptionally enhanced, the meaning from the thing being experienced is palpable, filling the room, filling the self so there is no room for anything else. The whole self is caught up in contemplation of the thing experienced. Some transcendent thing, some soul force, has moved from somewhere out there to in here. You are completely immersed in something, what Lorca called *dark water.*

But with Lorca's word *baptized* something else enters the equation. It touches on some other truth that occurs in moments of duende. There is a sacredness to it, a feeling of the holy. And there is also a doer, the one who baptizes. Some sacred thing, perhaps the living reality of the imaginal world itself, has reached down and touched your brow with the dark waters of meaning. The author or performer is only the conduit for this. He opens a tiny door inside himself, as the Lakota holy man Black Elk described it, and something flows through him. From up out of the ground or down from the heavens, out of the imaginal realm it flows, filled with mythic substance, and it comes into the world, baptizing not only the audience but the performer. All are caught up together in that moment of duende, sharers and partakers in the mystery of being. There is some fragrance that attends to them now, some infusion of the sacred into their deep selves; they are made holy. *Baptized with dark water.*

Generating this experience is the core of art, of any writing that is genuine or real. No writer, no matter how well regarded, how well schooled, how much published is good at the craft if they fail to generate moments of duende in their work.

Evoking a moment of duende in a living performance, when delivering a work before an audience, is much easier, as Lorca noted, than generating it in a writing. During a performance you have help, something besides composed language to work with. You have your stance, the movements of your body and hands, the touch of your eyes on their eyes, the soft touch of your voice on their ears. You can modulate the words with great subtly, using tone, pacing, emphasis, degree of softness or loudness of sound. And most importantly, silences. Moments when you stop and let the meanings reverberate inside the listeners. The trembling and the long silence. Still, it can be done, must be done, in writing as well as in living performances.

Whether performing or writing, you deliver a symphony of meanings, put together just as expertly as a symphony of music. The work is *composed*. Like a musical symphony it possesses movements. There are moments of soft touch where the most delicate of sounds weave themselves into the listeners' fabric. Each member of the audience is pulled along on currents of meaning that begin softly, rise in intensity, soften again, and build toward moments of crescendo, moments of powerful duende. These moments of duende are intentional, a part of the symphony you are creating, just as are the differences in tones, meanings, patternings of sound, and silences you are using in what you are creating. Meaning is piled up, not only behind the word like water behind a dam, but inside and behind the whole piece. The artist, in the living performance or in the writing, lays up the meanings in layers, building on each preceding piece, piling it on, this piece leading to that, until the thing itself is full. Then it is released into the room like an arrow taking flight, filled with energy from the deep self. The long floating leap occurs, carrying the listener or reader (and performer or writer) along with it. Together they burst through into a different state than the ordinary. They stand in the midst of a living reality, all experiencing it together. Bypassing the rational mind, the linear world of cause and effect, they are together caught up as one in experiential contemplation of a particular kind and moment of meaning.

Moments of duende fulfill a basic need in human beings. At their emergence, people are held in the embrace of some deep and exceptionally *real* meaning. Some ensouled force is present, moving into and through the room, and all partake of it. Together. It is a living communion, as far beyond the pale imitation of communion in churches as the stars are from our sun. It is a food that all people need to become human. In moments of powerful duende you can see the audience fill with it, become satiated. It is an invisible thing but one of the most important experiences we can share together.

Few artists now express this in their work. Perhaps they fear the grandiose, fear the intimacy of this kind of moment, fear the surrender that such work demands. Or perhaps they have believed what they were told, that if they bring this kind of joy and belief into their work they are somehow shamefully naive or innocent in their beliefs, idealistic, not sophisticated in their writing or performing. Perhaps they fear shaming by critics or their contemporaries. Perhaps they have internalized some of the voices from the world around them, voices that have become that small voice inside that tells too many of us our deepest hopes and dreams and feelings are without merit, only holdovers from a naive childhood.

Without duende, however, writers fail the most essential aspect of their craft. They remain caught in the dead end of the New York literary style or the futility of mechanical reductionism. Duende is the antithesis. It is a restoration of the holy to everyday life. As Lorca describes it, "The duende's arrival always means a radical change in forms. It brings to old planes unknown feelings of freshness, with the quality of something newly created, like a miracle, and it produces an almost religious enthusiasm."[5]

The job of the writer is to travel into wilderness and bring back meaning in buckets made of words, to give it as drink to the thirsty, to slake the thirst of those who have lived isolated for too long inside their own houses, to give them the living experience of wild water. Duende.

It is easier, as I have said, to create moments of duende in a living performance, nevertheless they can be created in any written work in which a writer feels deeply and keenly, by any writer who pays attention to how things *feel* at the limits of their capacity to do so and then seeks to craft a work that embodies it.

Moments of duende are an integral element of the art, just as is the use of punctuation, and they can be intentionally generated in any form of the work. They can be woven into any writing that is genuine, no matter its topic. I have seen it, experienced it, in books as various as how to build mortarless stone walls, books on dieting, theoretical mathematics, natural farming, William Stafford's prose about writing, Machado's poetry, the dynamics of fractals, the early novels of Arturo Perez-Reverte, Bly's commentaries, or John Dunning's *The Bookman's Wake.* You can get a feel for it again in this piece by Antonio Machado, a master of duende.

People possess four things
that are no good at sea:
rudder, anchor, oars
and the fear of going down.[6]

Even in this short of a piece, there's that same progression, isn't there? You start in one world and suddenly find yourself in another, one concerned more with invisibles than the wood of oars and rudder, the dense metal of anchor. And there is a specific feeling associated with it, one that marks the emergence of just this experience we are talking about. Lorca had this experience over and over again, when listening to great poets and writers, watching supreme bullfighters, hearing the work of great musicians. He felt it a crucial element of art and wanted to put some salt on its tail, to make the concept real enough that all artists could begin to work with it consciously. He began to reclaim the invisible, to bring a particular experience back to a Western culture that had abandoned it, along with the words needed to describe it.

Lorca worked to articulate a moment of direct perception of meaning, a moment that bypasses the conscious mind and linear thinking, an experiential feeling place that emerges, as he says, "without explainable causes and effects." He seized on the Spanish word *duende,* a subtle term, full of interesting meaning.

You have sensed the subtlety of it; it's like a spirit that moves in language, a current of meaning that catches hold of the attention of the deep self, carrying it out of rational perspectives into an entirely different state of being. In its loosest translation a work that possesses duende means that it has soul or soul force. The exact meaning of the word (in Old Spanish—similar to Old English or ancient Greek) is "lord" or "owner" of a house. Slang usage: it means "charm" or "personal magnetism." Charisma. In contemporary, conversational Spanish it means "ghost" or "spirit" or "daimon." It is the "true" owner of the house, the spirit that gives it a living reality, that possesses it. When applied to writing, it means "inhabited word." The word is inhabited by a living meaning or spirit or soul force. Word possessed by spirit. And that soul force or spirit passes through the artist and into the word, is shaped by his skill, and enters the listener, catching up writer and listener alike in a moment of duende.

Duende, like anything else, can be expressed at different times in a performance or a writing with differing degrees of intensity. It is possible to create tiny moments of duende, educating the listeners or readers in the experience of duende as you go along. They get used to it, come to expect it. Their deep selves know, of course, what you are doing, begin to get excited, begin to look for those tiny moments of duende. You engage in a subtle and developing communication with a part of the reader or listener that he or she does not consciously realize is there. The piece builds and eventually the reader or listener bursts through into a moment of duende that is much stronger than that which has gone before. Then it slowly fades, the reader and listener move back into daily reality but . . . bringing something new back with them.

It is an intentional thing, part of the craft. It doesn't happen by accident. But to find the moment of duende and then to capture it in an art form, in a written work in this instance, you must work even more keenly with feeling. For duende is both a feeling thing and a specific place where that capacity for nonphysical touch takes you. When you arrive, you burst through into a place that knows neither cause nor effect, neither the statistical mentality nor linear thinking. It is a place that babies understand and a place that the part of you that was once that young still understands. It is a place beyond and before words, where meaning is perceived directly, where there is no sign in place of the thing. To find it, and to recreate it in language, you must learn to follow golden threads.

CHAPTER EIGHT

Following Golden Threads

If every detail can by careful handling, through association, sound, tone, language, lead us in, then we live in a sacred universe.

ROBERT BLY

I feel ready to follow even the most trivial hunch.

WILLIAM STAFFORD

How many nights now
has the stream told you:
"This is the way
to deal with obstacles."

DALE PENDELL

The term *golden thread* was coined by William Blake (though he called it a *golden string*) but developed as a theme in writing by the poet William Stafford, someone whose poetry I like very much.

Here is an example of his work, his poem "A Ritual to Read to Each Other":

If you don't know what kind of person I am
and I don't know what kind of person you are
a pattern that others made may prevail in the world
and following the wrong god home we may miss our star.

For there is many a small betrayal in the mind,
a shrug that lets the fragile sequence break
sending with shouts the horrible errors of childhood
storming out to play through the broken dike.

And as elephants parade holding each elephant's tail,
but if one wanders, the circus won't find the park,
I call it cruel and maybe the root of all cruelty
to know what occurs but not recognize the fact.

And so I appeal to a voice, to something shadowy,
a remote important region in all who talk:
though we could fool each other, we should consider—
lest the parade of our mutual life get lost in the dark.

For it is important that awake people be awake,
or a breaking line may discourage them back to sleep;
the signals we give—yes or no, or maybe—
should be clear; the darkness around us is deep.[1]

That's a phenomenal poem, isn't it? It stirs things. It holds a mirror to the deep self and we catch glimpses of shadowy images moving in the background. Meanings that could take years to unlock flow into us. There is a sound as well, almost a hum, as if an invisible chord has been struck. It possesses what Lorca called "black sounds."

Lorca said that duende was accompanied not just by baptism in dark water but also by the caress of black sounds. That baptismal water is dark, not because of its color but because of its depth. And just as water may become dark when you travel deep within it, so, too, does sound. That's an interesting concept, isn't it, depth of sound? This poem is filled with such depths; there's some of those black sounds in this poem, aren't there? And accompanying them, a particular kind of feeling, something that permeates the poem—and ourselves now that we have read it.

We know, because William Stafford described his process so well, that that poem arose out of an invisible thing, a meaning that he encountered one day. It arose from what he called the touch of a golden string or thread and that thread had a particular feeling to it. We know, too, that the final form of the poem holds within it that same feeling, condensed to its essence to the extent of Stafford's skill to do so. To know the feeling of what touched him we only have to feel the finished poem ourselves, as we have done. That feeling is now part of us, in our awareness as it was once in his.

At the touch of that feeling, of the golden thread, Stafford abandoned whatever had been occupying him, turned toward what he was feeling, and focused his full attention on it. James Hillman uses the Latin word *notitia* to describe that focusing, that aware intentfulness toward a meaning that has touched us. Our word *notice* (to get to know, awareness, knowledge) comes from it. It is the attentive noticing of the soul. And from that noticing, as Hillman describes it, comes "the capacity to form true notions of things." William Stafford was a master of it. Meaning touches him; he feels its touch and focuses on it with his whole attention. Then he begins to follow it, to work to capture it in language that will hold the essence of it in living form.

To the alert person, a golden thread may emerge from any ordinary thing and open a doorway into the imaginal, and through it, the mythic. Because no one can know when or where or from what it will emerge, the writer remains attentive to everything that is encountered, always paying close attention to how everything, even the tiniest little thing, feels. Light pours through a window in a particular way, a person moves their body slightly, you enter a summer field and experience it as a property of mind. Something inside those things brushes against you. Meaning of some sort, not yet understood, touches someplace deep. Ripples flow up from the depths of the unconscious and touch your conscious mind. A particular feeling envelops you and you stop and focus your whole attention on what is right in front of you. *Notitia.* The touch of a golden thread.

You can begin to follow it then, if you wish, by simply writing down, as concretely as you can what you are experiencing, what you are feeling, what you are seeing, hearing, sensing. Bly describes this, brilliantly, as "following the tiny impulses through the meadow of language."[2] It must be done slowly. Carefully. Feeling your way. Tiny movement by tiny movement. It is the feeling equivalent of catching the hint of an elusive scent. You lift your nose to the slight breeze, a delicate touching. Seeking. Ah, there. Your feet move of their own accord as you trail what you have sensed through the meadow in front of you. You twist and turn slightly, following where the scent leads, adjusting your movements to the rise and fall of the land through which you walk. Following the scent home. Finding the core that gives rise to it. Following tiny impulses through the meadow of language.

It begins with the simplest of things: A tiny, odd feeling in a social interaction or elephants walking, holding each other's tail. Anything can become a door into deeper worlds. Stafford comments that "the artist is not so much a person endowed with the luck of vivid, eventful days, as a person for whom any immediate encounter leads by little degrees to the implications always present for anyone anywhere."[3] Golden threads touch all of us, every day, but most often only artists and children take the time to follow them.

The initial touch of a golden thread is *always* attended by a specific kind of feeling. Experience will bring trust in that touch and the feeling that accompanies it, familiar recognition at its emergence. You feel the touch of the thing, it captures your attention, then you work to encapsulate it in language. Working to describe it, of course, causes you to step back slightly from the experience itself. You write a line, perhaps several, then you stop and begin to compare what you have written to the feeling that has demanded your attention.

You look at the lines, focus on them with the whole of you, ask yourself "How does it feel?" and a certain emotional tone emerges. Then you step back inside the thread itself and feel *it*. Then you compare that feeling to the feeling of your written words. You are going for congruency, for identity.

You can get an experience of how this works from a simple exercise. Say you are sitting at a table. Place something on the table in front of you, perhaps a cup or a pen. Look at it intently, at its placing, its orientation with the other things on the table, its relation to you in space. Anchor that location in your memory and experience. Now . . . move it six or seven inches, to a different location on the tabletop.

The goal is to move it back to the exact spot it was in originally. But . . . do it this way: first, move it halfway back and then ask yourself, is this in the same spot? Notice the feeling that arises within you when you ask yourself that question. There will be some sort of uncomfortable feeling, a lack of rightness. Some part of you will say *no,* but it sends the negation as a particular kind of feeling. It's not in words. Yet, you know at a deep level something is wrong. This isn't it. You feel twitchy. It's wrong. Now, move it a bit closer to the original spot and ask yourself again if this is the right spot. No, it's not. That part of you is still telling you that something is not right.

Now, finally, move it back to the location in which it began and ask yourself, is it the same? The feeling that comes now is specific. There is a sense of rightness, a kind of *yes* occurs. In place of an uncomfortable feeling, there is instead a good one, a kind of internal joy or sense of rightness.

This is a skill that every one of us uses every day one way or another. We have an innate capacity to determine the congruency between two things by comparison. Some nonphysical part of ourselves reaches out and feels for congruency and lets us know, through a specific kind of feeling, if congruency exists or not.

When a writer compares a written line to the experience the line is intended to describe an identical process takes place. You write the line. Then, you touch it and compare it to the golden thread you are following. If it is not right, there is a sense of wrongness, an uncomfortable feeling. So, you change the line. You feel into the meanings that are held in the words. You feel how the words sit with each other. You listen to and feel the sound patterns of each individual word and the sentences they create together. And you make slight adjustments, shifting meaning by altering the container. Micromolecular adjustments. The tiniest of shifts. Now, how does it feel? If you are closer to congruency, the sense of wrongness lessens, the discomfort's not so great. Yet, you can still tell something is not quite right. So, you adjust it again. Eventually, a sense of rightness occurs. A yes comes from the deep self. Ah. This one is done.

This is, in part, what Robert Bly was referring to when he talks about the truth receiver inside each of us. When we work with this kind of comparative analysis between golden threads and how the words we have written feel we are working with the truth receiver. Bly talks about it like this:

> *Other poems, equally marvelous, awaken the truth receiver somewhere inside the body mind. We go into a different trance in which we expect truth, or perhaps, come out of our ordinary trance, in which we are inured to lies. How much sadness we feel because we have given up expecting truth. Every moment of our lives we exchange comfort or discomfort for statements we know are lies, or mostly lies, in gather-*

ings with our parents, or at speeches, or watching a movie. How abandoned our truth receiver is: a bag-man, who spends the day without hope.[4]

Or as William Gass puts it: "We've grown accustomed to the slum our consciousness has become."[5]

Writing in this way means writing up to the standards of the truth receiver inside us. In many respects, it is the truth receiver that is most sensitive to the touch of golden threads. It is the truth receiver that catches our attention when a golden thread is encountered. And it is the truth receiver that insists we follow that thread and seek its origin, its home. Then when we write, we follow the truth receiver's lead, its sense of rightness, and in so doing we write morally. We work at the deepest levels possible to us to make the two things one, to make what we have written and the golden thread we are following the same thing.

It takes work and practice at the craft to make the two things as close to identical as possible. (They will never be exactly the same but they can be so incredibly close that almost no one can perceive any of the so-very-tiny deviations. This is all mastery is, an increasingly small deviation from perfection. Only those working at the same level of perceiving can consciously perceive those so-very-tiny differences between word and phenomenon.)

The work of bringing the two to identity may not be completed quickly; shaping and polishing may take hours, or months, or years for some pieces. But in the initial shaping, the line you have written and the experience that has captured your attention approach a congruency. They get close enough for the deep you to give a *yes,* even if a provisional one. Some sort of polishing usually has to occur later. That is when the first draft slowly becomes the final draft, where you work to make the two things identical at the tiniest levels of which you are capable, where all the implications in the word are teased out and developed so that the experience itself flowers in those who read it. Nevertheless, we have a *yes* and for now we have captured that thing sufficiently for a rough draft.

What happens next is interesting. You are sitting in completeness with that line and, of its own accord, the attention of the self suddenly shifts, moves in some new, never-to-be-predicted, direction. The part of you that is intimate with meanings flows along the line of meaning that touched you, heading toward its depths. The golden thread moves and the deep you moves with it. The feeling of the thread is the same but there's more to it now, it has deepened in some way, become richer. More meanings inside the thread begin to reveal themselves. New thoughts, feelings, sensations, images, emerge—spontaneously—into awareness. And now you begin the process of capturing *them* in language. Stafford comments: "If I let the process go on, things will occur to me that were not at all in my mind when I started. These things, odd or trivial as they may be, are somehow connected."[6] The lines that take up residence in your heart, as William Gass might put it, "father or nurture other lines, sentences, further feelings and thoughts of significance."[7] And they do so automatically.

The writer is feeling his way along the string that has emerged into his awareness. He is using that capacity for nonphysical touch to follow a particular meaning that has touched him and captured his attention, trusting it to lead him where it needs to go to be itself, to emerge complete and whole in language. "Any little impulse is accepted and enhanced," Stafford remarks. Over time you learn to trust the process, the experience, for, as Stafford continues, "only the golden string knows where it is going, and the role for a writer or reader is one of following, not imposing."[8]

There is a kind of devotion in this, a returning, as Bly calls it, "like a swallow to the barn of yielding, to the little spark of light given off by the end of the thread."[9] Basho, the great Japanese poet, describes that spark and how new lines naturally emerge when you follow it . . .

Your poetry issues of its own accord when you
And the object become one—
when you have plunged deep enough into the object
to see something like a hidden glimmering there.[10]

(Ezra Pound, with his concept of the antididactic, "luminous detail," was reaching toward the same truth.) True writers follow; they are servants of the process, not its masters. They follow the thread where it leads and write down what they find on the journey. They are, in a sense, transcribers, and good writers know it. Being too purposeful, Stafford observed, may break the thread. One must be careful not to pull too hard.

And what *is* that pulling too hard? Trying to control where the thread is going, directing it where the statistical mentality wants it to go, forcing it away from its nature and into the desires and needs of the writer. This may be conscious on the part of the writer who has too much investment in the psychological, the social, or in reductionisms of one sort or another. It may be unconscious in the writer who has not developed the skill of rigorous self-examination and introspection or in the writer who is still too afraid, who does not trust the dreamer inside him enough to let go of control. Ultimately, those limitations must be abandoned. To become good at the craft demands a yielding to the thread and the process of following.

Practice at the craft develops the skill of following the thread without pulling too hard. In the beginning all of us pull too hard. The thread breaks, we wander off and don't find the park. But over time, as the skill is refined, the threads can be followed wherever they lead. The meanings of which they are composed are captured in language in such a way that the words themselves are an experiential map of the territory. They take the attentive listener deep inside particular kinds of meanings. The meanings slip over the self like a lens and you see aspects of reality that can only be glimpsed, as Thoreau described it, with the unworn sides of the eye.

Every golden thread, if followed, generates somewhere within it, often toward its end, a long floating leap into a moment or experience of duende. By focusing so completely on the feeling of the thing and getting it as fully as possible into language, the words become imbued with life force, filled with meaning. The longer the thread is followed, the more meaning that piles up, not only behind the words but behind the sentences and paragraphs. A powerful forward movement takes hold, an inescapable inertia toward some destination occurs in the writing. You reach the end of the linear world, a chasm appears, and you take a long floating leap up, out, over, landing for a moment on the other side. Duende.

A golden thread may lead only a short (writing) distance, as in this poem by Machado:

It is good knowing that glasses
are to drink from;
the bad thing
is to not know what thirst is for.[11]

And nevertheless possess a long floating leap into the unconscious and tremendous duende. A golden thread always leads to such a leap if it is followed; it always generates an experience of duende somewhere in the piece. And those moments of duende may be strong or mild, they may be connected together in an interwoven duende conversation, or they can stand individually. Golden threads always lead to a shift in perception, a traveling from one state of mind to another.

In a fiction work, such as Conrad's *Heart of Darkness,* Bly comments that "Conrad takes us inside a human mind, but when we get there it turns out we are deep inside a continent."[12] In a nonfiction work such as the *Declaration of Independence* we may start inside an act of defiance and end up deep inside the essential dignity and rights of human beings. In a self-help book on dieting we may begin by seeking a way to be thin and end up finding a way to companion ourselves in this life.

> *If you really wanted to know what a friend wanted for dinner, you would ask, then wait for the answer. You wouldn't demand that she eat what you tell her to eat and then call her a fat pig after all that food went to her hips. If you did, you would not have that friend for very long. But this is exactly what we do to ourselves several times a day, around each meal, for years and years. It takes time, trust, compassion, and a willingness first to ask, second to wait, and third to listen to the answer* **without judgment** *and without argument. We need to become our own best friends so that we can perform the holy and sacred act of breaking bread with ourselves.*[13]

This paragraph, from *It's Not About Food* by Carol Normandi and Laurelee Roark, begins by focusing on how we treat and interact with others but it ends in a surprising place. It is a social given that we should treat others with a certain kind of respect and kindness; Normandi and Roark illustrate that beautifully by describing a powerful act of unkindness. But suddenly we find that they are talking about us individually, not someone else. Suddenly, the unkindnesses we do to ourselves are revealed for what they are. A bright light comes on when we least expect it, revealing shadowy toxins within our culture and ourselves. Why should it be acceptable to treat ourselves in ways we would never treat others?

But the way they have done it is remarkable. They focus outside, in the social realm, talking about other people. It's not personal so we go along with it, no self-protection or defensiveness in place. Then wham, suddenly we are looking in a mirror and we catch a glimpse of things we normally hide: the unkindnesses we have done to ourselves, our belief that it is legitimate to treat ourselves unkindly but not others. A shift has occurred, from the social to the psychological, from out there to in here. We were looking at them but now we see ourselves. Enough in and of itself. But a further, quite remarkable experience emerges from how they develop the material. Two things that we normally keep quite separate come together and merge: the social training we have received in how we are to treat others is suddenly somehow attached to how we treat ourselves, the two inextricably intertwined. We, perhaps for the first time, feel an ingrained sense of sociability toward ourselves. It happens at a gut level, much deeper than words.

They have taken us to a very important place, again, enough in and of itself. Nevertheless, they don't stop there. They stay in the psychological and secular realms just a bit longer to draw us along toward where the piece is really going: *We need to become our own best friends* . . . and then they do this . . . *so that we can perform the holy and sacred act of breaking bread with ourselves.* Suddenly we find ourselves someplace else entirely.

The development is beautiful. We start *out there* with a friend. Then we treat her cruelly. The act brings up a great many feelings about that kind of cruelty and it activates not only our empathic sense but our social training. Then suddenly it turns out it was really ourselves we were treating that way, not somebody out there. We are horrified at what we have done. And somehow, at that moment, our empathic sense and our social training connect to ourselves, perhaps for the first time in our lives. Then the authors bring the process to wholeness by saying *We need to become our own best friends.* The circle is complete. It goes from our friend out there to being our friend in here, from using all the tools we have to be caring of friendships out there to using them in here with ourselves. It's nicely developed, a well-rounded piece. At its completion, we are holding ourselves in a new way and it releases a lot of repressed energy from someplace deep inside.

They could have stopped right there and it would still have been a great piece of work but they don't . . . they keep going. All that freed-up energy attaches to the momentum we have gotten from the rest of the material and it carries us on even faster. We reach the line . . . *so that we can perform the holy and sacred act of breaking bread with ourselves* . . . and suddenly we find ourselves taking a long floating leap. We land and find we are someplace else, in some other reality, one that has a great deal more to it than the social or the psychological or the secular. The long trembling moment and then the silence. Duende.

Something else is in the room with us now. We find ourselves baptized with a truth that our culture has forgotten, something abandoned in the haste for modernism and the statistical mentality. The truth receiver inside us takes it in and somehow we are more ourselves, filled with a kind of food that satisfies the deepest parts of who we are. Some soul force has entered and given the starved part of us a food that all of us need to be whole and fully human. You see, it can happen anywhere, in any kind of book, in self-help or how-to. What matters is not the form but what the person is doing inside the form.

It's in exactly this way that golden threads lead to duende and golden threads can occur *anyplace,* in any field of endeavor. Simply: they are only the presence of a deep meaning that resonates with the perceiver. They capture the attention of an ordinary human being and, if followed, and articulated, they end up speaking about the experience of all people. They end up revealing truths that can only be found after such long floating leaps are taken. And that leap is inherent in the golden thread itself, though, of course, when we begin to follow the thread, we don't know it.

If you pay close attention to that paragraph by Normandi and Roark, you can tell perhaps how it came to be written. You can sense the emergence of the thread they followed (and also how it felt).

They were talking to themselves, perhaps, telling themselves how bad they were for being (fat or ugly or lazy or not smart enough or not good enough or not loveable enough or . . .) and then maybe their daughter comes into the room and they shift what they are doing, begin telling her how much they love her. And somehow, for some reason that day, those two things touch in their awareness for the first time. A certain kind of feeling occurs. They can tell something important is happening. They may even have had a sudden burst of seeing, of insight, as the two things combined. And so they begin to tease it into language;

they try to capture the thing they have felt. They begin writing their way to the truth of it.

They describe talking to a friend and then treating her like they treat themselves. They're really in the experience, describing it as best they can. There is a lot of energy there, they care deeply about what they are saying. They want to capture what has happened in language so that when we read it we'll have that same experience. And so, they begin to go step by step, following tiny impulses through the meadow of language. Slowly, they get to the denouement: *becoming our own best friend . . .* then, from someplace unexpected comes: *so that we can perform the holy and sacred act of breaking bread with ourselves.* The other lines were groping after that truth but the writers, like all writers, didn't know it. They just kept following the thread and when they got close enough some other part of the self took over and, trailing dragon smoke, wrote the line.

Such writing begins with noticing something that touches us and captures our attention. We begin to follow it to find out where it wants to go. Paying close attention in this process to what is. . . not what we think is, is crucial. Most often we see only what is in our minds, not what is in our eyes. Mostly we feel only what we have been taught to feel, not what we truly feel. With the attentive noticing of the soul, we step away from our programming and what we think we know. We feel something and then we stop and genuinely *look,* identifying what has caught our attention. Then we begin to really see it, noticing whatever it is as if for the first time. The senses begin to bring us tidings of invisible things, all of them filled with meaning. To do this work, to become this kind of writer, we have to genuinely see whatever it is that we have felt, then follow wherever that feeling takes us. James Krenov, in *The Fine Art of Cabinetmaking,* describes it like this:

> *I wonder if people notice that with all the technical skill, love, and care put into them, many of his bowls still lack something? They are not all of them alive. It is sad, almost tragic. . . . Because of ignorance, as well as prejudice, we exclude so much. We need to see better. To see—in the way that Yanagi meant, which is to sense and notice (in that order) even before we know. That seemingly odd bevel, that uneven curvature of line, the surface flat yet somehow*

> *alive—these we see only when we have first sensed the meaning of their conversation. The craftsman works, looking and looking again, from one revelation to another—often by way of mistakes, listening to the material, coming upon unexpected signals. Good things and bad things: knots that should not be where they are, fascinating colors that appear as if out of nowhere. It takes effort. But it gives something more in return.*[14]

That perfectly describes what Stafford and Bly are talking about, doesn't it? *The craftsman works, looking and looking again, from one revelation to another—often by way of mistakes, listening to the material, coming upon unexpected signals.* But always following that feeling, following tiny feeling impulses from one revelation to another.

Golden threads always start with an experience, a moment being lived. They are not something that belong only to those who write. It's just that some of us work to write them down after we have lived them. It's possible to follow golden threads behaviorally, not just linguistically. It is a skill that belongs to living an inhabited life. Something touches you and you begin to follow it, to find out where it leads. It signals that something important is happening; it captures the attention of the deep self.

The signed Ray Bradbury with which I began this book was a golden thread. The Wells and the Arthur Clarke; they were part of that same golden thread. The story that John Dunning told is part of it, too. Writing about them came later, after they had become the fabric of a lived life. The initial golden thread, the feeling that took me to the special bookcase in the bookstore, led me to the signature on the Bradbury book and a moment of duende. And that moment led to another and to another and to another, eventually to this moment now and the place where I sit, writing these words. (And now to you where you sit reading them.) A golden thread led me to the miraculous that lies hidden in the commonplace. Such things make up the threads of my life and, perhaps, if we paid attention, of all of our lives.

It begins with the lightest of touches really. The golden thread has already emerged and is in play before it gathers enough energy to capture the attention of the conscious mind in a moment of notitia. The deep self perceives such threads, of course, usually long before they come to the attention of the conscious mind, and it begins movements in response. You wake up and for no particular reason feel like driving into town to a particular bookstore to look around. James Hillman described those movements in *The Soul's Code* as *gentle pushings in the stream in which you drifted unknowningly to a particular spot on the bank.*

We are moved by golden threads not only in our writing but in the lives we live that lead us to be writers. What we begin to write down afterward are only movements of the golden threads in which we have immersed ourselves when we take on this life and this craft. The things we write down are only specific examples of a general phenomenon that has subsumed us into itself, only specific articulations of the larger thread in which we live. For me and for most writers they happen experientially first—we live them then we write them. A new thread, to be woven into the fabric of our life, begins to emerge but we don't notice it yet, we just think we are living any old day at all. Nevertheless, something urges us to go this way instead of that and for some reason we do. Later, we begin to try and capture it in language. Like this . . .

I was visiting the British herbalist David Hoffmann near Sebastopol, California, once upon a time, and while there, I happened to mention that I was writing a book on ancient fermentation and the uses of plants in fermentation.

David listens, then stops a minute, and pulls a book out of his bookcase and says, "Here, have you seen this?"

It's by some guy named Dale Pendell, a book called *Pharmako/Poeia*. People try to give me books all the time, I hate it. The cover is nice though.

"No, I haven't," I say. "Why?"

"Well, he's got some great stuff in there on fermentation."

"Really?" I say and take the book and David goes off to do something and I sit down and begin to read. Four hours later, when David returns and awakens me from the page, I stretch and put the book down on the table, tell him, "This is a great book, thanks."

"Well," David says, "I know him. Would you like to meet him?"

"Well, yeah. I would. Do you think he would mind?"

"No. Let me give him a call."

David goes into the other room and I can hear him dialing, then talking on the phone. After awhile, he hangs up, returns. "We are on for tomorrow," he says. "That okay?"

"Shit, yes."

The next morning is particularly California. One of those days that Californians try to convince people they have every day. Warm but not too warm. Sunny but not too bright. The breeze a gentle caress, a lover's careful embrace. It seems to promise that all the ills of humankind can be solved if only we liked each other more, were a little kinder, maybe had some sort of harmonic convergence.

David comes into the kitchen wearing, as usual, cream linen slacks and leather sandals with socks. His blue, shimmering silk shirt is half unbuttoned down his chest, the jade Green Man pendant gleaming softly against his skin. He has the kind of British accent that makes almost everything he says seem meaningful. His speech is musical, soft on the ear, without the nasal tones of the American approach.

"Ready to go?" he asks and I nod and get my stuff and we walk outside.

"Oh, by the way. My car is broken, can we take yours?"

"Sure," I say, and an odd tingle ripples its way down my spine. I shake it off.

My car is sitting on gravel under a huge eucalyptus and we crunch our way over and get in.

"Oh, I've got a couple of errands to run. That okay?" I look at him and he is exceptionally cute and endearing.

"Er, mmm, okay," I say, letting go of my picture of the day, and starting the car I begin following his directions. We drive for a few miles in the midst of farm fields and eucalyptus-lined roads, begin to experience the first tentacled extrusions of new suburbia—roads that go nowhere, for sale signs on vacant lots, cut trees lying abandoned in death, an occasional new house—some of Sartre's bleaker thoughts made manifest. Sebastopol is pretty though.

"Pull in at the co-op," David says and I do. "Just be a minute," and he walks off toward the back of the store.

I linger just inside the front doors. Notice the espresso counter, two young women behind it, talking. Walk over diffidently.

"Er, could I have a breve?" I ask. The younger one nods, keeps on talking, her hands moving automatically in coffee gestures ingrained by long practice.

"Well, I have had a lotta bodywork," she is saying as she tamps the coffee grounds into the port. "But you were right. When that guy put his hands on me it was amazing. I've never felt anything like it and my neck and back don't hurt anymore. Not at all."

"I told you so. He's great."

The store is busy and a line is building up behind me and soon both of them are at work, churning out lattes.

"That'll be $4.50," the younger one says sliding it toward me on the counter.

I take the cup, burn my hand, pick up an insulation sleeve and carefully slip it on. I stand demurely by the door, sipping it, notice David threading his way back toward me. The day is still nice outside.

We get in the car and I put the cup carefully in the holder on the dash and ease back into traffic, begin to follow his directions deeper into town.

The next stop is the record store. One of those independent stores where the interior is painted so white it has the faintest of bluish tinges. But, like most such stores, painted long ago. Black marks from what-the-hell-were-theys and dings from this-and-thats cover the lower halves of the walls, the marks and white paint blending together to produce a post-structuralist's experience of life. Abstract jazz and existential despair as decor. The floor is the cheapest linoleum, the bins cobbled together from plywood and stained that terrible dark walnut brown color from the '70s. In them are the exact records you would expect and standing in front of the bins the exact people that have to be there, flipping slowly through record after record, glazed expressions on their faces. Everyone looks like they belong in exactly that store. I stand by the door, sipping my breve. I keep breathing but it's a conscious decision.

David looks around, says: "Hey, I've got to talk to this guy but you might like to look at those while you wait." He points off toward the back of the store, gestures to some pictures high up on the wall. I nod, wander over, squeeze around the end of the bins and look at them. Pictures of the Beatles, together and separately. Eric Clapton, Jimi Hendrix. All from the '60s. The frames are cheap, black, and go perfectly with the walls. The pictures however are very good, taken by someone with a very good eye. All of them are black and white.

"Yeah," this guy at one of the bins behind me is saying. "I did go to that bodyworker and he was great. Never felt anything like it."

"Told you," another voice replies and that funny feeling tingles its way down my spine again. I'm never coming back to California, I think to myself.

A bit later David wanders over. He nods at the pictures. "Good aren't they?"

"Yes," I say, "they are."

"My dad took them. He was the Beatles official photographer. I grew up with those guys. That one," he says pointing, "gave me my first drugs."

"No shit," I say, peering more closely at the photograph. "Were they good?"

He laughs and we wander out of the store, get back in the car and begin to drive. I, pumping him for more stories. Him, not giving me much.

A couple of stops later we finally start up into the hills, heading for Dale's place. After a lot of this-ways and that-ways, we turn onto a tiny dirt road that meanders up a steep hill through a beautiful grove of California oaks. The road hasn't been graded in centuries; the deep ruts demonstrate how water found a way to deal with obstacles. The car jerks from one side of the road to the other as first one set of tires is sucked into the ruts, then the other. The whole time we're getting slammed around inside the car as if we're on a carnival ride. I can almost hear the tiny clicking sounds the roller coaster makes as it pulls you slowly to the top. You know, the moment when you begin to have those thoughts telling you a real, real bad decision has just been made.

We pass by a red, wooden house on stilts, set back in the trees on our left, a spidery staircase up one side. "Jack London's cook's house," says David. "That's where Dale lives. But we're going up to the main house. Keep going."

I glance at him sideways, he doesn't seem to notice, and I keep on, finally pulling into a fairly flat, gravel parking area. I stop the car, unclench my hands from the wheel, and pull on the brake. We both get out and stretch.

Just then a door in front of us opens and this guy walks out holding a very large glass beaker in his hands. It's filled with a vibrant green liquid. The guy is tall and thin, mid-fifties, touches of gray in his hair, with remarkable upswept eyebrows. He walks over, looks at both of us. "Want some absinthe?" he asks, "It's almost ready."

David introduces us, then shakes his head. "You guys go ahead. I don't like alcohol, besides there's something I need to do. I'll see you later." And he walks off.

"I want some," I say, visions of Anais Nin and Paris and the 1920s in my mind. Dale looks at me, grins, and says, "Let's go." And we begin to walk down the rutted road talking about this and that.

We get to Jack London's cook's house, glomp our way up the stairs. There's a sign above the door: I stop and read it, "Demons welcome here," and look at Dale.

"Turns out they already had the address," he says, and laughs. Then we go in. I sit at the table and he wanders into the back where I catch glimpses of him holding tiny tincture droppers over the beaker, putting a few drops of this and then that into it. He comes back, puts two glasses on the table, each with some of that beautiful green liquid in them. Then he gets these strange kind of real flat forks, though he calls them absinthe spoons, and balances them over the glasses. He puts a sugar cube on each one and begins to pour water very slowly over the cubes. He pours until each glass is filled, each sugar cube dissolved. "Drink up," he says, taking away the spoons.

I lift the glass cautiously to my lips, taste a tiny bit. My face brightens. "It's good," I say, and we sit there companionably, talking and drinking.

"Want another?" he asks. I look at my glass, surprised to see it's empty.

"Yes. Yes I do," I say, and Dale makes a couple more.

We are about halfway into them when we start doing spontaneous readings. Dale recites one of his poems and it reminds me of something and I say it and that sets Dale off again. In the middle of this, we hear someone coming up the steps and David walks in. We keep right on going. David looks at Dale talking, looks at me responding. Looks at Dale again as he begins to speak, looks at our glasses of absinthe, then up at Dale again. "Gimme some?" he says. He still looks cute and endearing, Dale pours him a glass and he begins to try and catch up.

It's about then that I begin to hear the odd thumping. *Ba bump, ba bump, ba bump.* It's coming from the outside stairs. I turn my head slightly so I can see out the window. A man is slowly rising into view, walking up the stairs, but the sound of his footsteps is odd. The head rises, then the chest, then the arms, flailing oddly. He looks, I finally realize, like a marionette, as if strings were hooked to his wrists, his shoulders, his knees, the strings being operated by someone not too good at it. *Ba bump, ba bump, ba bump.*

The door opens and he comes in, marionettes his way to the table, sits down next to me. I am pretty high by now and the light has tremendous luminosity, the colors of everything are very vivid. It's as if I am seeing through some kind of lens that makes whatever I look at more vivid and clear. The grain in the wood of the table is exceptionally vibrant. It's almost as if I can see deep inside the wood itself. I find myself getting caught up in its flow, sensing movements of meaning within it. I run my hand along the top of the table, the texture is marvelous. I notice then that language and sound are particularly luminous and as a matter of fact they sound almost the way the wood feels and looks. Time has slowed and I am finding it really enjoyable to immerse myself in language; just hearing it is orgasmic. I can feel the tiny movements of meaning as I shape them into the words I drop shimmering into the room. I see how they penetrate the listeners, see their physiology shift in response. Why, I wonder, did they ever make this illegal?

I turn my head as the man sits down beside me. He leans close, looking deep in my eyes. His are startling, a brilliant, shimmering, and liquid blue. He is totally present, like a newborn infant. He looks very much like, I think to myself, he has had a left-brain stroke, shutting down the linear hemisphere of his brain, and can now only use his right hemisphere, the holistic part. And here I am, caught up in the moment with him, myself in a similar state of mind. Time slows more and I continue to look at him. He moistens his lips and leans a bit closer.

"I died, you know," he says, looking at me meaningfully.

"Oh god," I think. "Not now." I have no desire to engage in word salad with someone from northern California—yet I can't pull myself away.

"And then the angel came," he continues.

I seem to be stuck in some kind of horrible time warp where space is not quite right and I can't seem to get my body to do anything but sit there. The whole time this is going on I am face to face with the guy, eye to eye, both of us in this just-like-a-newborn-infant reality and I can't do anything but be there and take it in.

He takes a breath, clearly gathering energy for another run at me. I try to gather my resources, can't seem to find anything useful.

"The car went out of control down the hill and I broke my neck. In just the same place Christopher Reeve did. I died on the operating table. That's when the angel came and told me what to do to be able to walk again, to use my arms again. And I did it and I think I am getting around pretty good, don't you?"

He looks at me intently and I find myself nodding yes, because given all that, he certainly is getting around pretty good.

"Yes," he continues. "I have been an osteopath for over thirty years but now when I put my hands on their bodies something comes through me and goes into them—they just change. Their whole body shifts and I can see them letting go of things that have troubled them, often for years. It's like a darkness inside them. I see it there and something goes through me, then through my hands, then into them and they just . . . change." He looks at me earnestly, wanting me to understand.

The fabric of the day comes over me and I remember the women at the espresso stand and the people in the record store and I look again at the man in front of me and for a minute things shift and suddenly plain are the invisible currents that carry us this way then that way when all the while we think we are living ordinary lives.

He is watching me closely the whole time and he sees the slight shifting in my face. He waits a minute, feeling the shift, tasting it, savoring the flavor then comparing it to something inside him. Then he says again, "I died, you know," and here he pauses, "but this is a new life, everything is different. Do you understand what I mean?"

And I, caught up in the moment, nod and say "yes, yes I do." And suddenly I hear the voice of the poet Juan Ramon Jiminez reverberating inside me.

I have a feeling that my boat
has struck, down there in the depths,
against a great thing.

And nothing
happens! Nothing . . . Silence . . . Waves . . .

—Nothing happens? Or has everything happened,
and are we standing now, quietly, in the new life?[15]

And then I turned back to the conversation and continued to drink my absinthe and the world moved on and some place in the deeps of me that moment in time came to rest on some ground of being inside. And there it worked with who I was and who I am and who I will be. And from time to time over the years it has risen up like the shadowed back of some great thing from out of those depths and lets me see once again into a world that is a great deal more than any of us suspect it to be.

Writers, of necessity, must learn to follow golden threads. More difficult, and much more challenging, is to trust enough to follow them wherever they lead, for, as Stafford remarked, only the thread knows where it is going. And golden threads, as every writer discovers, don't care much for human cultural conventions or restrictions. If followed as a habit of mind, as a way of life, as a primary skill of the craft, they always lead into places outside of and beyond the rational. They lead, inevitably, into the imaginal realm and ultimately into contact with the mythic.

And that imaginal world, contrary to modern mechanicalistic perspectives, already is, and has long been, inhabited . . . among other things by archetype, and story, and theme—the living realities of the mythic world. The inhabitants of that realm are not reductionist, two-dimensional concepts, devoid of *logos,* but living phemonema that engage in communicatory interactions with the part of us that is meant to engage them—the part of us that dreams.

There are no passports issued by reductionist cultures for travel to the imaginal (an MFA degree is not such a passport). No overt permissions will be granted by an industrial community for its exploration. (Though, of course, once you are safely dead, as Van Gogh discovered, your art may sell for millions.) In following golden threads into such mythic territory, you truly do extend awareness much further than your culture wishes it to go.

Most reductionists continually insist that the imaginal realm—the mythic itself—is only shadows of a superstition still lingering from a primitive past. That belief has been deeply ingrained in most of us. It shows itself as a kind of *agnostic* reflex, as Henry Corbin called it; we tend to automatically discount as real both the imaginal and the mythic when we encounter them, in ourselves or in the world. We discount them in favor of what we have been told is reason, convinced is logic. But the world is and has always been a great deal more complex than linear approaches recognize. *The universe,* as Frank Herbert once said, *is always one step beyond logic.* And beyond logic is where we are going now. (If you are a diehard literalist you might as well stop here; the journey will be, as Robert Bly once observed, increasingly bad for your health.) For if you continue to follow golden threads (and that is what we're doing now) you will inevitably find the dreamer and the ancient realm only the dreamer can know.

III

Dreaming and the Journey to the Imaginal

To be able to induce at will the activity of that higher imagination, that intuition, that artistic level of the unconscious—that is where the artist's magic lies, and is his only true "secret."

DOROTHEA BRANDE

On a good day, I wake out of a dream and don't remember the dream—but it comes to life on the page.

JOHN DUNNING

The dark horse is stabled in the child. So the poet, the rhetorician, the philosopher, who thinks of a page as merely a page, and not as a field for the voice; who considers print to be simply print, and does not notice the notes it forms; whose style is disheveled and overcharged with energy or overrun with feeling, or whose frigid and compulsive orderings make the mouth dry; the author who is satisfied to see his words, as though at a distance like sheep on a hillside, and not as concepts coasting like clouds across his consciousness; such a writer will never enter, touch, or move the soul; never fill us with the feeling that he's seen the Forms, whether or not there are any; never give us that ride up the hill of Heaven as Plato has, or the sense that in accepting his words we are accepting a vision.

William Gass

The dreamer falling is about to hit the earth, and the energy slips him sideways and flows away with him over the sea, and turns the sword into a transparent substance that can hurt no one, and allows a single hair to stir the sea.

Robert Bly

For double the vision my Eyes do see,
and a double vision is always with me.
With my inward Eye 'tis an old man grey;
With outward a Thistle across the Way.

William Blake

CHAPTER NINE

"A Certain Adjustment of Consciousness"

I think the reason for a certain lameness in the novelists is that fiction in the West has traditionally been written in an ordinary state of consciousness. We imagine the novelist to be, like Thomas Mann, satisfied with bourgeois life and a steady laborer (he knocks out a certain number of words every day). Creative writing courses have, willy-nilly, supported the view that an ordinary state of consciousness is all right for serious writing.

Robert Bly

One learns that it is possible by a certain adjustment of consciousness to participate in art—it's a natural activity for one not corrupted by mechanical ways.

William Stafford

An invisible wall seems to fall away, and the writer moves easily and surely from one kind of reality into another. . . . Every writer has experienced at least moments of this strange, magical state. . . . These queer moments, sometimes thrilling, sometimes just strange, moments setting off an altered state, a brief sense of escape from ordinary time and space . . . are the soul of art.

John Gardner

When you sit down and begin to write, you are, finally, totally, completely, utterly, on your own. No one can accompany you where you are going now, there are no guides who can be in that territory with you. No matter how much you have read about, thought about, or studied writing, when the moment comes to begin writing, everything changes. No longer is it an academic exercise. You are about to find out at a deep, experiential level that map and territory are not the same thing. Any maps you have of the territory, once you are inside it, usually will prove inaccurate, only partly useful, or completely wrong. For no matter what kind of guidance you have had, it is you who are taking the journey now. And like all of us before you, you must find your own way into and through that territory. And the only way to do that is to feel your way through the work, step by step by step, one slow feeling step at a time.

The territory you are entering, I want to make clear, is real. You alter consciousness in a particular way and that alteration generates a special kind of dreaming. And as that dreaming deepens, you will ever more fully enter the imaginal, encountering there a mythic landscape that is as real as this other world often seems to be. It is from this shift that all genuine writing comes. Once you begin to alter consciousness in this way, a particular kind of communication will emerge, in many respects, of its own accord. And from that place, the deepest expressions of what writing is come into being. When we encounter them later, in a different state of mind, we call it writing, or a story, or a book.

I want to tell you now—*anyone* can do it. The ability to shift consciousness in this way is in all of us, built into our structure as human beings. As Stafford says, "it's a *natural activity* for one not corrupted by mechanical ways." I will tell you how to do it; I will tell you as much as I know.

So, let's play with it, explore what the experience of that shift in consciousness feels like from its earliest stages to its full-blown expressions.

To start, let's look at the nature of the experience itself. Here, at length, is John Gardner describing what happens as that alteration in consciousness takes place. (It makes no difference that Gardner is speaking about fiction, for the nonfiction writer the experience is identical.)

> *When the juices are flowing, or the writer is "hot," an invisible wall seems to fall away, and the writer moves easily and surely from one*

kind of reality into another. In his noninspired state, the writer feels all the world to be mechanical, made up of numbered separate parts: he does not see wholes but particulars, not spirit but matter; or to put it another way, in this state the writer keeps looking at the words he's written on the page and seeing only words on a page, not the living dream they're meant to trigger. In the writing state—the state of inspiration—the fictive dream springs up fully alive: the writer forgets the words he has written on the page and sees, instead, his characters moving around their rooms, hunting through cupboards, glancing irritably through their mail, setting mouse-traps, loading pistols. The dream is as alive and compelling as one's dreams at night, and when the writer writes down on paper what he has imagined, the words, however inadequate, do not distract his mind from the fictive dream but provide him with a fix on it, so that when the dream flags he can reread what he's written and find the dream starting up again. **This and nothing else is the desperately sought and tragically fragile writer's process: in his imagination, he sees made-up people doing things—sees them clearly—and in the act of wondering what they will do next he sees what they will do next, and all this he writes down in the best most accurate words he can find, understanding even as he writes that he may have to find better words later, and that a change in words may mean a sharpening or deepening of the vision, the fictive dream or vision becoming more and more lucid, until reality, by comparison, seems cold, tedious, and dead.** *This is the process he must learn to set off at will and to guard against hostile mental forces.*

Every writer has experienced at least moments of this strange, magical state. Reading student fiction one can spot at once where the power turns on and where it turns off, where the writer wrote from "inspiration," or deep flowering vision, and where he had to struggle along on mere intellect. One can write whole novels without once tapping the mysterious center of things, the secret room where dreams prowl. One can easily make up characters, plot, setting, and then fill in the book like a paint-by-numbers picture. But most stories and novels have at least moments of the real thing, some exactly right gesture or startlingly apt metaphor, some brief passage describing wallpaper or the movement of a cat, a passage that somehow shines or throbs as nothing around it does, some fictional moment that, as we say, "comes alive." It is this experience of seeing something one has written come alive—literally, not metaphorically, a character or scene daemonically entering the world by its own strange power, so that the writer feels not the creator but only the instrument, or conjuror, the priest who stumbled onto the magic spell—it is this experience of tapping some magic source that makes the writer an addict. . . .

The poison or miraculous ointment—it can be either one or both—comes at first in small doses. The usual experience of young writers is that during the process of writing the first draft they feel that all they write is alive, full of interest, but then when they look at the writing the next day they find most of it dull and lifeless. Then comes one small moment qualitatively different from the rest: one small dose of the real thing. The more numerous those moments, the more powerful the resulting addiction. The magic moment, notice, has nothing to do with **theme** *or, in the usual sense,* **symbolism**. *It has nothing to do, in fact, with the normal subject matter of literature courses. It is simply a psychological hot spot, a pulsation on an otherwise dead planet, a "real toad in an imaginary garden." These queer moments, sometimes thrilling, sometimes just strange, moments setting off an altered state, a brief sense of escape from ordinary time and space . . . are the soul of art, the reason people pursue it. And young writers sufficiently worried about achieving this state to know when they've done it and feel dissatisfied when they haven't are already on the way to calling it up at will, though they may never come to understand how they do it. The more often one finds the magic key, whatever it is, the more easily the soul's groping fingers come to land on it. . . . One knows by experience the "feel" of the state one is after.*[1]

As I finish reading Gardner's account, another quotation comes to me, something Joseph Chilton Pearce once said about young men and women who are trying to communicate what and who they are meant to be in this life: *They gesture toward the heart when trying to express any of this, a significant clue to the whole affair.*[2]

All of us do that with things that are important to us, things so deep in us we have trouble finding the words to describe them. We *know* what we want to express but we don't know how to capture it in language. So, we move our hands, our body, our face. We *gesture.* And those gestures, which originate in some deeper part of ourselves, hold clues to what we're trying to say. Gardner speaks well of what happens when the writing trance occurs, more succinctly than anyone I know, but the *gestures* he makes in language as he speaks are where significant, and important, clues to the whole affair reside.

He speaks of a *movement* "from one kind of reality into another," into "an altered state, a brief sense of escape from ordinary time and space," the attainment of "a strange, magical state."

This is the state that all writers inhabit when they write. Stephen King calls it "the zone," Goethe a "somnambulistic state," Dorothea Brande the "artistic coma," William Stafford the "creative trance." Others call it the writing trance, or the writing dream, or sometimes just "the groove." It is only when the writer is in that state, to a greater or lesser extent, that writing moves from the thudding grocery-list-prose of most nonfiction to something alive. And this is crucial, not only because it moves the writing into art but because of what it does to the readers when they read. Writing that emerges out of that state produces a shift in consciousness in the reader, and this is, in fact, why readers' read. "We read a few words at the beginning of the book or the particular story," as Gardner says, "and suddenly we find ourselves seeing not words on a page but a train moving through Russia, an old Italian crying, or a farmhouse battered by rain."[3] We enter a dream world, we forget ourselves, and our conscious mind sleeps.

Each of us has had the experience of being awakened suddenly from such a dream—by the insistent ringing of the telephone or a sharp knock at the door. It startles us awake as if from a deep sleep and it takes a few minutes for us to recall ourselves, for our conscious minds to begin functioning again. Yet even as we answer the phone or the door, the meanings, experiences, or people we were dreaming about linger in the mind like a wonderful taste on the tongue or delicate strains of music shimmering in the ear, more real yet than the salesman at the door or our friend on the telephone.

We enter a dream when we read because writing itself is a special kind of dreaming. It is dreaming developed into a particular kind of art. It is because writing begins as a dream in an altered state of consciousness that it ends as a dream in the reader's mind. It is only because we dream as we write that the reader, later, can dream at all. As Gardner says, "The organized and intelligent fictional dream that will eventually fill the reader's mind *begins as a largely mysterious dream in the writer's mind.*"[4]

As writers, we enter the same dream that our readers dream later when they read what we have written but we get there a different way. We do not sit down, pick up a book, and begin to dream. We sit down in front of a blank page and allow a dream to flow through us and onto the page. We intentionally shift consciousness into a specific state of mind, and from that state of mind, writing occurs. This is the real secret that all beginning writers want to know: how to induce that state at will. It is rarely, if ever, taught in MFA programs. As Gardner says, this skill "has nothing to do, in fact, with the normal subject matter of literature courses." But it is this skill upon which the whole of the art depends.

There is something fundamental that happens, something concrete. To write, your consciousness has to *shift*. You have to *move* from one reality into another, from one kind of perception into another. You are *changing* state of mind. It is this intentional act at the core of the craft that makes artists different from bankers or grocery clerks. Artists, at will, move from one reality into another and it is out of that other reality that their art comes.

Gardner gives us clues to the nature of that reality.

There is a wall. On one side (that is, in the "wrong" reality) all the world seems "*mechanical, made up of numbered separate parts.*" (This echoes Stafford doesn't it: "It's a natural activity for one not corrupted by *mechanical* ways.") Here, the writer "*does not see wholes but particulars, not spirit but matter.*" There is something in that nonwriting state of consciousness that is innately connected to mechanicalism, to seeing things as parts rather than wholes, seeing matter but not the spirit inside it, a focus on form rather than essence.

In contrast, when the shift in consciousness occurs, things do not seem mechanical. They are "*fully alive,*" the writing is "*alive and compelling,*" there is a "*living dream,*" the words "*come alive.*" And Gardner says this is "*literally,* not metaphorically" true. There is a "*flowering* vision."

A character or scene enters the world "*by its own strange power.*" There is the "*movement* of a cat, a passage that somehow *shines* or *throbs.*" There is "a *pulsation*" (on an otherwise dead planet). The writing "*springs up.*" The "juices are *flowing,*" the writer is "*hot.*" He talks about the *soul* of art, the groping of the *soul's fingers*. The *feel* of the state you are after. In contrast, in the "wrong" reality, things are "*cold, tedious, and dead.*" There is a "*dead planet.*" The words one has written in this state are "*dull and lifeless.*" One has to guard against "*hostile mental forces.*" You have "*to struggle along on mere intellect.*" Writing becomes a "*paint-by-numbers picture.*"

Brenda Ueland, in her book *If You Want To Write,* captures this paint-by-numbers approach when she says . . .

> *In music, in playing the piano, sometimes you are playing at a thing and sometimes you are playing in it. When you are playing at it you crescendo and diminish, following all the signs. "Now it is time to get louder," you read on the score. And so you make it louder and louder. "Look out! Here is a pianissimo!" So you dutifully do that. But this is intellectual and external. Only when you are playing in a thing do people listen and hear you and are moved. It is because you are moved, because a queer and wonderful experience has taken place and the music—Mozart or Bach of whatever it is—suddenly is yourself, your voice and your eloquence.*[5]

She's talking about this same transition, from one state of consciousness into another, isn't she? Mentation, simply following writing rules, has nothing to do with writing. It's too mechanical. It results in paint-by-numbers writing, not art. Robert Frost is talking about the same thing when he says, "A poem may be worked over once it is in being, but may not be worried into being."[6] Or as Robert Grudin says as he reaches for the same truth: "The creative process might be simplified if we stopped searching for ideas and simply made room for them to visit. . . . Mystery reveals itself to those who maintain an openness of character."[7] We begin to see here that the brain is insufficient to the task, not the right approach, not the right master.

In one reality, the world appears mechanical, dead, full of parts that have no relation to one another, things are static and possess no movement. There is a certain tedium or boredom, an uninterestingness, a lack of excitement. Things are cold. There is intellect alone, unconnected to the world, hostile mental forces, dead words on a page. In this state you are *outside* rather than *inside* the writing. There is mentation but no feeling. There is no life, no *inspiration*. In the other reality, in the writing state of mind, you are *inside* what you are writing. Things are alive rather than mechanical, full of wholes rather than parts, full of spirit and soul rather than empty matter, there is movement, heat, life, growth. There is feeling rather than mentation. There is *inspiration*.

The journey through the wall that exists between the young writer and the accomplished writer, is, in fact, a movement from one form of cognition into another, from one reality into another. We have to shed our old skin because it has been contaminated by mechanical ways—that is, by a reductive, mechanical view of the universe, the world as a system of interchangeable, nonliving, unintelligent parts—except for the human (of course), which is alive, intelligent, and the apex of creation. That perspective has become an inflexible lens through which most of Western culture sees and experiences reality. It kills access to the imaginal world. For the imaginal world, accessed through a special form of imagination, is where true writing originates, and by its very nature it is not reductive, not mechanical.

That is what makes it so hard to move through the wall between the wanting-to-be-a-writer and the writer. Our consciousness has been affected, perhaps even infected, by a certain kind of thinking, by certain assumptions about the nature of the world, and of reality, that are antithetical to art. And most of these assumptions, beliefs, and perceptions are deep in our unconscious. It takes time to undo that kind of programming and it's often painful to do so. We have to alter fundamental assumptions that affect how we perceive the world around us. This has potent psychological impacts, on our sense of self-identity, certainly on our cultural identity, and most definitely on our conceptual sense of the reality in which we are embedded.

To intentionally shift state, we have to experientially understand that the reality in which we have been raised is not fundamental but is contingent on our interior orientation, on our belief matrix, on our programming. It is not immutable. We have to come to terms with a lie. *Consciousness* is not fixed but mutable. Reality is not fixed but mutable, not single-dimensioned but many-layered, complex, and very different than we have been led to believe. Perception and cognition—and the creative act that writing is—depend on orientation of consciousness. And that reorientation of consciousness necessarily moves us from a mechanical frame of reference into one where *everything* is alive. That alone allows us to access the imaginal, and through it touch the mythic itself.

It is this *experiential* reeducation of the self that makes the journey through the wall so difficult. We must learn to become comfortable in a state of mind and a perceptual reality that is very different than the one inhabited by most of Western culture. As Gardner says, "One knows by *experience* the 'feel' of the state one is after." To gain that experience, every writer actually has to shift cognition. Must, as a habit of mind, intentionally shift consciousness and discover for themselves what its parameters are, what its nature is.

The more we engage this other state the more we understand it has a particular *feel* to it. After awhile, after lengthy experience, we learn how to induce the state simply by remembering the feeling of it and duplicating that feeling in our experience, right now. We *feel* our way back into it. So, this feeling aspect of it is crucial. It is perhaps the first thing upon which the whole process rests. But enhanced visual perception, working with the *image,* as Gardner makes clear, also plays a significant role. It's integral to the dreaming.

He says that the writer *sees* "his characters moving around their rooms, hunting through cupboards, glancing irritably through their mail, setting mousetraps, loading pistols." These detailed visual descriptions, he insists, provide the writer "*with a fix*" on the dream. They somehow anchor the writer in the altered state of consciousness itself. Simply by reading detailed visual descriptions of his imaginary world, the writer finds "*the dream starting up again.*" He *sees* people doing things, "*sees them clearly*" as Gardner says. The writer wonders what they will do next, then "*he sees what they will do next.*" And "*all this he writes down in the best most accurate words he can find.*" Later, as he refines the material, captures it even more accurately in words, this causes a "*sharpening or deepening of the vision, the fictive dream or vision becoming more and more lucid.*"

Feeling and *attentive visual perception* then, when blended together in a particular manner, are integral to the writing state of mind, they are essential to that state of mind, essential to the reality we, as writers, access.

To enter the trance, to begin to shift consciousness into the state so necessary for writing, we have to move out of thinking and into feeling. We have to be *in* the experience, feeling it intently. We can't remain outside it, thinking *about* it. Ueland gives a great example of how descriptive writing feels when written from outside the experience, then from inside . . .

> *I have sometimes collaborated with people who were not writers. (Incidentally, the better-educated these non-writers were, the worse they wrote.) To help me they would write out their material, their memories of presidents, generals, and so on. But it was usually very bleak and thin,—like this: "The great statesman's wife, Mrs. K, was a splendid hostess and entertained lavishly all the interesting personages who were in Washington that year." So my collaborator would write it down.*
>
> *"How did she look? What was she like?" I would ask.*
>
> *My collaborator's face would at once brighten with intelligent, excited, witty interest and she would volubly and eagerly pour out:*
>
> *"She was violent, fascinating. She'd explode at a second's boredom. She had arched black eyebrows and a red face, because of high blood pressure. She walked in a rubber union suit to keep her weight down. She was generous and not a snob at all, but she couldn't stand stupidity. She'd burst like a boiler. Her husband used to hang back and turn off all the electric lights. 'That's right, Eddie,' she'd call over her shoulder. 'Turn them all out. That's right, you might save a couple of cents.' He was afraid of her and did not like to be at home."*[8]

You can see here that when the speaker is in the material it comes alive. She forgets herself; she begins to really see and feel what Mrs. K is like and what she describes comes out of that seeing and feeling. When it does it affects us immediately. We begin to have a living experience of the woman being described and we begin, as readers, to enter a dreaming state ourselves. We really see that woman, hear her voice, have a feeling for what she is like. But that aliveness begins the moment the woman forgets herself and moves inside her own experience and then shares it without censoring her describing.

It is in this sense, again, that all writers have to become naked inside the work. We have to reveal our real feelings and observations without thinking about or worrying about what others will think. We have to not mind that we are being watched. We have to *unconceal* our real feelings and reveal them to any who wish to see them in our work. (And this will always include the unkind, those offended by what we are saying, and those who strongly disagree.)

For our writing to come alive, for the writing trance to occur, we have to feel the reality of what we are describing and our descriptions have to be described accurately, they have to be visually acute. (You can see how, to some extent, this is automatic. When the woman forgot herself, when she began to feel deeply, she naturally began to describe visually.) Somehow, by doing this, the state itself is anchored to the page and deep inside *us*. It gives us a *fix* on it so that we can find it again simply by reading our visually acute descriptions. There is then, something in those visually acute descriptions, in how they are done, that generates or recreates the feeling state that writing consciousness is dependent upon.

However, visual descriptions alone won't do it; they must be created in a certain way. For them to work, feeling and seeing have to combine together into one coherent whole. What you have then is feeling/seeing or seeing/feeling—a sensory experiencing that blends two sensory mediums into one single sensory experience. Feeling then, automatically resides inside the visually explicit descriptions. There is something more in the image than a simple visual description, feeling is inextricably interwoven with it. It is this blending of the two sensory mediums that allows the writer and the reader to dream.

Robert Bly captures the importance of this blending of feeling and seeing when he says: *If we want to create art we have to stitch together the inner world and the outer world*. That is, what we are feeling (the inner world) and what we are seeing (the outer world) have to, in some way, merge together into one, unified whole. The key to blending the inner and outer in just this way is to be found in what William Gass calls "*the secret kinesis of things*."

CHAPTER TEN

"The Secret Kinesis of Things"

Words befell Emerson often. . . . In his head his heart heard the language of the other side.

William Gass

[Machado] knew that a secret "you" was present in the feelings evoked by a landscape.

Robert Bly

A man has not seen a thing if he has not felt it.

Henry David Thoreau

Where I am, it's still dark and raining. We've got a fine night for it. There's something I want to show you, something I want you to touch. It's in a room not far from here—in fact, it's as close as the next page.

Stephen King

The inspiration for Stafford's understanding of golden threads came, as I've said, from one of Blake's poems. This one . . .

I give you the end of a golden string
Only wind it into a ball,
It will lead you in at Heaven's gate
Built in Jerusalem's wall.[1]

Stafford came to understand that if you minutely focus your perception in a particular way on something, that thing, and it can be anything at all, will reveal the presence of a golden thread within it. And that thread, if followed, will take the perceiver deep into dreaming, eventually into the imaginal realm, ultimately into contact with the mythic world itself. It will shift consciousness from a mechanical orientation to one where everything is alive. This is what Bly was reaching for when he commented that: If every detail can by careful handling, through association, sound, tone, language, lead us in, then we live in a sacred universe.[2]

But what does it mean to "minutely focus perception in a particular way?" What does "careful handling" mean?

At root, it means an extension of the capacity for nonphysical touch outward, *into* the world (the focusing part) and then writing down, in a specific way, what is perceived (the careful handling part). Rather than focusing nonphysical touch on words as we have been doing, focus is shifted onto the world, onto the things that surround us every minute of every day. It is when we do this that we find *the secret kinesis of things.*

So, let's play with it so you can get a sense of what I mean . . .

Let your eyes wander around the room you're in until something catches your attention—desk, pen, cup; it doesn't matter what it is. It is just, for whatever reason at this moment in time, interesting to you. It appeals in some way.

Now. Look at it carefully, note its shape, notice its color. Really *look* at it; let your visual sensing take it in. Let your eyes touch the thing as if they were fingers capable of extreme sensitivity of touch. Immerse yourself in *seeing* the thing that has caught your attention. Now, ask yourself, "*How does it feel?*"

In the tiny moment of time that follows that question, there will be a burst of feeling, an "intimation of mood or feeling" as Goethe once described it. Your nonphysical touching has just *felt* a part of the exterior world. There's a specific and unique feeling experience that occurs whenever this question is asked about something that is acutely observed. What stands revealed is a dimension to things beyond height, width, and breadth. There is a feeling dimension to them. *The secret kinesis of things.*

Now, let your eyes be captured by something else, again focus on how it looks, its shape and colors, and when you are really noticing it, ask yourself *How does it feel?* There will be, again, that immediate emergence of an "intimation of mood or feeling." The thing has a *feeling tone* to it. Even if you might not be able to say exactly what that feeling tone is, it's very distinct, isn't it? And this particular feeling tone will be unique to the thing itself. It's different than the one possessed by the last thing you felt. In fact, everything you touch in this way will have a slightly, or sometimes very, different feeling or kinesis to it.

Now, do it again with something else. Only this time after you ask *How does it feel?* just after the unique feeling tone emerges, savor it for awhile as if you are smelling a unique but delicate perfume or tasting a unique and subtle flavor. Immerse yourself in what you are now feeling.

Now . . . shift your attention to yourself. Notice how *you* are feeling.

Interesting, isn't it? The state you are now in is different than how you were before this exercise began.

If you really have immersed yourself in this exercise, you will find that your physiology has shifted. Your breathing will have slowed and deepened, your body become more relaxed. Eye focus will be different, too, more soft focused; peripheral vision has been activated. You are seeing with Thoreau's "unworn sides of the eye." Colors will likely be a bit more luminous, sounds more resonant, body sensations more sensitive. Things will feel more *alive.* State of mind has shifted as well. Your thoughts will be slower and deeper. Perceptual focus is enhanced. You will feel a bit *dreamier.* Even though there are some important differences, the state feels a bit like that which occurs in daydreaming, doesn't it?

Now, do it again—look at something, observe it in detail, and then ask yourself "How does it feel?" At the emergence of the feeling tone, again savor it for awhile, then pay attention to your state. Pay attention to how *you* feel. Now compare that feeling to the feeling you had just a moment ago, when you last focused on yourself. There's a similarity, isn't there? There is a particular feeling that accompanies this kind of perception.

This is what it feels like as you begin to enter the dreaming state that writing comes out of. And this is all it takes to generate its first stages, looking at something carefully and asking how it feels. (The fiction writer does the same thing when he looks at the things he is seeing in his imagination; he feels how they feel and then he captures those feelings in language.) The particular feeling you have in your body when you do this can be remembered, if you wish, and recreated anytime. This is what Gardner was reaching toward when he said *One knows by experience the "feel" of the state one is after.* Habituating yourself to this feeling, deeply anchoring it in your experience, gaining familiarity with it, will allow you to drop down into the initial stages of the dreaming state over and over again. At will.

This state, as every writer learns over time, can be deepened considerably. It must be if you wish to fully enter the dreaming state that generates genuine writing. This first step, you might say, is where you get your foot in the door of "the secret room where dreams prowl." This particular feeling is the key to the deeper state that Gardner was talking about.

You can, if you wish, extend it a bit further now . . .

Do the exercise again and while you're in that state, slowly take your eyes off the thing you are looking at and slowly look around at everything else you can see. (Keep breathing from this more relaxed state, let your eyes remain soft focused.) Let your eyes slowly pan the room and allow that feeling part of you to feel everything in the room as a wash of feeling flowing into you from what you are seeing. Instead of feeling the secret kinesis of one thing, you are feeling the secret kinesis of many things at once. At this moment you are *feeling* the world around you (with the part of you that can nonphysically touch) as a continual act similar to the way you *see* or *hear* the world around you as a continual act.

This form of perception is a natural one for all people. But for most people in Western cultures, the skill hasn't been developed (often it has been actively discouraged). The same isn't true for our other forms of sensory perceiving.

When we were born we experienced a continual flow of visual and auditory sense impressions but we had no interpretations for them. It was by experience that we learned to understand what we were seeing and what we were hearing. By intentionally working with the secret kinesis of things, intentionally activating this form of sensing as a regular part of our perceiving, we learn to understand and work with *these* sensory impressions just as we once did visual and auditory impressions. We reclaim a form of perception that was once common to all people and cultures and which is innate in every infant born into this world. Engaging again with this kind of nonphysical touching is what James Hillman describes as "recovering the response of the heart to what is presented to the senses."

Continually sensing in this way is crucial to entering the writing trance; it is this skill that is at the core of the secret that all beginning writers want to know.

When this form of perception is initiated, the conscious mind begins to move into the background, the statistical mentality begins to be left behind, mechanicalism begins to be abandoned. (Those hostile mental forces Gardner spoke of begin to move out of the way.) By focusing intently through the senses and then asking *How does it feel?* you move out of analytical thinking, out of the brain, and begin to move toward the dreamer and analogical thinking, a thinking that is intimately interwoven with feeling.

So, there are two initial, essential steps to this. The first is seeing what is right in front of you, the second is asking *How does it feel?* (As a caveat, nonphysical kinesthetic touching of the world, rather then seeing, can come first as a general sensory perceiving. Then, at the touch of a golden thread, of something out of the ordinary, or of anything that catches your attention, seeing is activated and is focused on that thing. Feeling first, then seeing, rather than seeing first, then feeling. Either approach will work. For most people who have habituated this kind of perception, there tends to be a complex intermingling of the two. Which one is primary depends on circumstances and the unique personality of the writer. Both sensory mediums, however, must be used.) Then, for the writer, there is a third step—and this is where the writing trance begins to emerge as a distinct state.

First you see, *then* you feel what you are seeing. *Then* . . . you begin to describe in words what you are seeing and feeling. Then you see again, and feel again, and then, again, you write. When you do this, become totally immersed in it; when your perceptions continually focus through what you are doing, both feeling and seeing begin to, automatically, combine into a unique synaesthesis of sensory perception. They begin to flow together into one, combined, sensory organ.

This is what John Felstiner, in his magnificent book *Can Poetry Save the Earth?,* is insisting upon when he explores the necessity for *attentiveness to live detail. Live detail* describes that particular kind of synaesthesis.

It is *live detail* that shifts consciousness in the readers who encounter it—and in the wirters who write it. Goethe felt that this merging of sensory mediums created, in fact, a new organ of perception: *Every new object, clearly seen,* he said, *opens up a new organ of perception in us.*

Close visual description by a good writer is *always* combined with the perceptions they've gathered through feeling what they are seeing, the two inseparably intertwined. For instance, when you write a visually descriptive passage, say, of driving up to a house on a dark, rainy night . . .

> *I turned into the driveway. It was a long dirt road that wound through the trees. The rain was beating down steadily, a ruthless drumbeat. In a moment I saw lights appear through the trees. A house rose up out of the mist, an old frame building with a wide front porch. It looked homey and warm, like home is supposed to look to a tired and heart-sick traveler.*[3]

. . . you end up, inevitably, describing how the place feels. "Homey" and "warm" are not visual descriptions (even though the writer used the word *looked* when he wrote the passage), they are feeling descriptions, part of the house's secret kinesis. And it is the presence of that secret kinesis in the writing that activates the feeling sense of the reader. This is what brings the scene alive. At that moment, you see not words on a page but "a house rising up out of the mist, an old frame building with a wide front porch."

This passage, from John Dunning's *The Bookman's Wake,* is a perfect example of the blending of the visual and feeling senses as a single sensory medium. That simple description: "looked homey and warm" evokes both feeling and seeing simultaneously as a unified perception. You literally feel what you are seeing.

From fairly minor clues, the blending of the two senses automatically generates a complex gestalt in the reader of both kinesthetic and visual perceptions of the house. The passage doesn't deliver a great deal of visual description of the house, does it? But it doesn't need to, the scene is vivid. In my mind, I can see the siding on the house, see the beginning-to-peel white paint, see the well-worn screen door with a bit of screen curling up from one of its corners. I can see the way the house is snuggling down under its weight, shifting this way and that to make itself more comfortable in the earth. And at the same time as that visual vividness emerges, I *feel* what the place feels like. And that feeling is as comprehensive as the images I see. I feel not only *homey and warm* but also relaxation, safety, envelopment in caring arms, a place of refuge where I don't have to be anything in particular, just myself, however that is. There is a kindness and caring that flows out of the house and into me. This blending of the two sensory mediums automatically generates associative emotional and visual experiences, which effectively generate a great deal of both visual and feeling vividness in the scene.

That is part of the power of writing. Whenever these two sensory mediums are blended in just the right way, only a tiny part of what is being perceived through the writer's imagination needs to be written. When it touches the reader, is taken inside her, a complex of associational feeling and seeing is automatically generated. But what really brings the writing alive, the trigger for all this, the core of it, is the feeling dimension of the house, the secret kinesis within it. Without that, the writing might still be visually descriptive but the scene would feel cold and lifeless. (And that's the exact problem with most nonfiction; it almost always presents as a dissociated mentation, devoid of feeling.)

And the feeling that is described in that scene? It belongs to the house. It's not a projection but a reality, something inherent in the thing itself. Though Dunning may have *imagined* that particular house, he had already experienced houses that felt like that. The part of him that dreams, during the analogical thinking through of the book, pulled on those memories to bring the scene alive, to make it true.

All of us, in our day-to-day lives, have experienced the secret kinesis of houses; it is one of the things that enables that scene to come alive within us. All of us have spent time in warm houses and all of us have spent time in cold ones.

All of us have been in houses that will never be homes. Houses where some coldness of spirit resides and which, if you stay in them too long, begins to seep into your own spirit and drag it down. Houses in which the lines are wrong, the rooms too small. Houses so clean that anyone entering them feels unkempt. Houses in which you cannot conceive of putting your feet up, or smiling, or feeling love.

And all of us have had the experience of walking into a house where a very different experience occurs. Houses that have windows that look out on happy gardens and where happy sunlight looks right back in. Houses where we feel some kind of spirit reach out and gather us to its breast. Houses in which a part of ourselves suddenly relaxes and breathes deeply. Houses filled with warmth of spirit, of joy, of happiness. Houses in which we feel the touch of an aged relative on our brow telling us that we are loved and wanted and welcome. Houses that are homes. It does not matter whether, when we walk into such a house, someone is there or not. We walk in and we *feel* the truth of the place. We experience its secret kinesis. That feeling is just as much a part of the house as the plumbing, the wood in the walls, the shingles, the carpet. It is felt (consciously or not) by all who enter. It draws certain people to it and repels others.

This secret kinesis of a house (or any thing) is a golden thread that leads deep into its heart. How that place feels is really an articulation of the meanings that infuse it. And those meanings, multiple in nature, contribute significantly to the story being told. Once the secret kinesis of a thing is revealed *through the feelings engendered in the readers* as they read, it tells the readers at an unconscious level just what kind of territory they are entering. They begin to engage with the deeper meanings in the scene, which quite commonly turn out to be necessary, as in Dunning's book, for the plot to work. Furthermore, layered within that secret kinesis, within the feeling of that place or thing, are the imaginal and mythic dimensions that must enter a work for it to become more than mere words on a page. Without this secret kinesis of things, neither the imaginal world nor the mythic can ever be found.

For writing to be alive, the visual and the kinesthetic have to be interwoven into one unified whole—images have to become filled with feeling. When the reader then reads a visual description of something they feel, *at the same time,* the secret kinesis within the thing being described. As the writer writes, because she has blended these sensory mediums together inside herself, this feeling perception somehow, automatically, enters the visual description that is being written. *Feeling* is inextricably interwoven with visual description. And it is this that activates the reader's own kinesthetic memories of the world; it creates an associational reverberation within the reader that comes out of their own feeling experiences.

Everyone has and uses this capacity for nonphysical touching of the world. *Everyone* knows about the feeling dimension of things; it's just that very few people talk about it. It doesn't fit into our cultural paradigm so it's become unconscious for most of us. Nevertheless, if it's left out of your writing the writing becomes flat and lifeless, untrue to life, and the reader knows it. They *feel* something essential is missing. So, the writer has to learn to, intentionally, put that feeling dimension into their work, step by step by step.

Gardner suggests a brilliant exercise to get an experience of this blending of both the visual and feeling senses in your writing. Though it applies primarily to fiction, you can see from it just how powerfully it automatically blends the two sensory forms.

> *Describe a barn as seen by a man whose son has just been killed in a war. Do not mention the son, or war, or death. Do not mention the man who does the seeing. . . . [if done well the result] should be a powerful and disturbing image, a faithful description of some apparently real barn but one from which the reader gets a sense of the father's emotion; though exactly what that emotion is he may not be able to pin down.*[4]

In this exercise a fictional barn is imagined as being seen by a fictional person in a particular state of mind. What a writer, during this exercise, does, just as Dunning did with the house he described, is to pull on memories of the secret kinesis of buildings (or barns) he has already experienced. He literally pulls from memory, from deep within his unconscious, his feeling experiences of buildings that have that kind of secret kinesis within them. And that reality, built from the author's experiences of the secret kinesis of the world, is layered into the writing so that it becomes a true description. (Without this use of the secret kinesis of the world a writing may be factual but it will never be true.)

You can sense from Gardner's exercise the powerful impact that occurs from capturing these kinds of invisibles in language, how tiny shifts in consciousness affect the structure of language and thus the dream the readers enter. In nonfiction, such subtleties, resident in the things themselves, are captured similarly and just as powerfully. All forms of writing—if they are to be art—depend on this synaesthesia of perception.

If the visual element is left out the work tends to become foggy, muddled, neither lucid nor vivid. This can often be seen in writers who have an undeveloped visual sense, who write confessional poetry, or who write in emotional reaction against overly mental cultural paradigms or repressions they have encountered.

If the feeling dimension of things is not written into the book, if the secret kinesis is left out, the writing immediately becomes mechanical and lifeless. And this is where young writers (and most nonfiction writers) commonly fail, why their writing is dead and lifeless. They remain in the realm of the lifeless idea and never move into the world of feeling. Rather than a writing that is filled with both seeing and feeling, many nonfiction writers write what is essentially a nonkinesthetic, verbal discourse. There is no feeling and very little visual in it. It is primarily didactic. The interior impact, then, on readers is an experience of dissociation; lifeless idea denying the body, denying the feeling sense, and, at its worst, denying the visual sense as well. There is no feeling connection to either ourselves or the world out there. As Robert Grudin comments, the belief in dissociated idea as a legitimate writing style in nonfiction is a wrong step:

> *We do not create, or even learn, by conscious concentration alone. The mind is not an instrument distinct from the "body" it inhabits and from that body's surrounding environment. It communicates freely and profoundly with the noncerebral anatomy, via both the nervous system and the cardiovascular system. It can receive powerful stimuli from outside events, both great and small. Its various structures of language make it an organic part of culture, of history. The mind feeds on all these sources, yet transcends them in its ability to modulate and focus their input. Original thought is the product not of the brain, but of the full self. And "self," as I understand it is not confined by our skins.*[5]

Most nonfiction writers can write about emotions but not the feeling of things, often because no one ever told them of its importance. The skill of nonphysical touching in them remains unconscious and undeveloped.

Such writers stand back and describe, they do not feel what they are writing (even if they are highly emotional about it), they are not *in* the experience. This lack of ability in blending the feeling dimension into nonfiction is (historically) fairly new and comes out of what Annie Le Brun calls *the assault on the imaginal realm,* what John Ralston Saul calls *the dictatorship of reason in the West.* It comes from a worldview, now prevalent, that was very uncommon a century ago. Nonfiction writers then, as an integral habit of mind, folded both the feeling and visual senses into their writing. It's just what they did when they wrote. In fact, writing submitted without it would likely have been rejected for publication.

To get a sense of what I mean, here's an average newspaper article from the nineteenth century. Titled "An 'Innocent' Interviewed: Mark Twain Pays a Visit to St. Louis," it's from the *St. Louis Dispatch,* May 12, 1882:

> *He has not been seen here since 1864, so that most people do not know how he looks. Imagine a middle-sized stout man in a common suit of gray, with coat cut sack-style. A careless, wide-brimmed hat is thrown recklessly over his hair, which is full and long and rather gray. A countenance which shows good living, a pair of gray eyes, and a face entirely smooth, save a rakish gray mustache that gives a light devil-may-care appearance to the man. He certainly does not look at "all funny" as the clerks put it, and would be mistaken for a serious, matter-of-fact gentleman who would not waste his time on anecdotes and would look down on a joke with lofty contempt. The most curious thing about him is a reckless, rolling gait, which he probably caught when as a cub pilot, he swaggered on the upper deck of the Mary Amandalane on the lower Mississippi. The aforesaid gait has stuck to him so persistently that it would make a sensitive man seasick to sit and look at Mark meander across the corridor of even so solid a hotel as the Southern. He also has a remarkable drawling way of speaking, which he most dislikes to see mimicked in print, and which adds quite a charm to his conversation.*[6]

If you should take the time to read the book from which this quote comes (Gary Scharnhorst's *Mark Twain, The Complete Interviews,*

University of Alabama Press, 2006) you would find that the vast majority of the 258 interviews within it are just as visually alive and full of the feeling sense.

There was no television then; writers had to make their writing come alive in the reader's mind, as if what they were describing were happening live on a stage in front of the reader. And they did. They understood the secret kinesis of things; it was part of their world view—the assault on the imaginal, on people's experience of the secret kinesis of things, was not so great. People in the nineteenth century took the secret kinesis of things for granted. The *agnostic* impulse had not yet been so deeply implanted in us or as Paul Ricoeur (and Geoffery Hartman) describe it, "the hermeneutics of suspicion" had not yet become commonplace.[7]

A visual description then, in the writer's hands, becomes infused with feeling. Simply by reading the visual description you have written, the reader *feels* the secret kinesis of the thing described. Visual sensing, inside the writer (and subsequently inside the writing), has taken on kinesthetic dimensions. And simultaneously, feeling has taken on a visual dimension. Simply by reading a line filled with feeling, a visual image or series of images unfolds within the reader. This ability to sense the secret kinesis of things can be extended further; it must be if we are to fully enter the "secret room where dreams prowl." If we wish to deeply engage the mythic, to work fully in the imaginal realm, we must extend our feeling sense even further, into an experience of what the ancient Greeks called aisthesis.

CHAPTER ELEVEN

Aisthesis

Descartes' ideas act so as to withdraw consciousness from the non-human area, isolating the human being in his own house, until, seen from the window, rocks, sky, trees, crows seem empty of divine energy.

ROBERT BLY

Stevens and Frost, both geniuses, walk gingerly in this area . . . the area where meeting a mandolin or a moose is meeting consciousness.

ROBERT BLY

I am certain there can be no comprehension of the present without the past, just as I am certain the past is not past. And there can be no comprehension of the present without all the tribes, human, animal, floral, and stones, river and dry wash, at the table taking part in the talk.

CHARLES BOWDEN

This "mysterious power which everyone senses and no philosopher explains" is, in sum, the spirit of the earth, the same duende that scorched the heart of Nietzsche, who searched in vain for its external forms on the Rialto Bridge and in the music of Bizet, without knowing that the duende he was pursuing had leaped straight from the Greek mysteries to the dancers of Cadiz or the beheaded, Dionysian scream of Silverio's siguiriya.

FEDERICO GARCÍA LORCA

We began engaging the secret kinesis of things by extending our feeling sense into objects in a room but what happens if we extend our awareness in a new direction? What happens if we leave the human world entirely and enter the wildness of the world? What happens if we use this capacity for nonphysical touching out there? What happens when we look closely at some part of the natural world us and ask ourselves, "How does it feel?"

Try it yourself now and find out.

For instance, you might go into your yard or take a walk in a park. Let yourself wander, just looking at this and that, until something catches your attention—a large tree perhaps. Stop and let yourself really look at it and then, when you are really immersed in seeing it, ask yourself, "how does it feel?"

In that tiny moment of time a unique feeling tone will emerge into your awareness, just as it did before. But, if you pay close attention, you will notice that there is a difference. There is a livingness to it, which the pen or cup or desk did not have (or perhaps did not have as much). And that livingness itself has a particular feeling to it. There is a secret kinesis to the natural world and it is perhaps the most important secret kinesis of all.

Basho was speaking of this when he wrote:

Go to the pine
if you want to learn about the pine,
or to the bamboo
if you want to learn about the bamboo.
And in doing so,
you must leave
your subjective preoccupation with yourself.
Otherwise you impose yourself on the object
and do not learn.[1]

And Thoreau when he said:

It is only when we forget all our learning that we begin to know. I do not get nearer by a hair's breadth to any natural object so long as I presume that I have an introduction to it from some learned man. To conceive of it with a total apprehension I must for the thousandth time approach it as something totally strange. If you would make acquaintance with the ferns you must forget your botany. You must get rid of what is commonly called **knowledge** *of them. Not a single scientific term or distinction is the least to the purpose, for you would fain perceive something, and you must approach the object totally unprejudiced. You must be aware that* **no thing** *is what you have taken it to be. [To perceive something truly] You have got to be in a different state from the common.*[2]

And the German poet Norbert Mayer when he wrote:

Just now
a rock took fright
when it saw me
it escaped
by playing dead.[3]

Isn't that last one marvelous? Mayer not only makes a commentary, as Thoreau and Basho do, but he does it directly in the orientation of the poem itself. It reveals its commentary through what you experience; it doesn't verbalize the point. Simply by reading it you are pulled *into* the experience that both Thoreau and Basho are speaking of. Some sort of energy flows up and out of the poem and into the reader who becomes entangled in it. In that moment of entanglement, perception shifts in a particular direction—into the *experience* of the secret kinesis in the things of the world and a sense of the *livingness* that that secret kinesis contains.

So, after the tree, go to something else, perhaps a blade of grass or a small flowering plant or even a stone, and do it again. Focus on it and ask yourself, *How does it feel?* Again, an intimation of mood or feeling will emerge, one that is different than the tree. Yet, it, too, will possess that *livingness,* that unique difference, however slight it is, in feeling, from the manmade things you perceived earlier.

Interesting, isn't it?

Now, just stay in that state of perception and let your eyes pan over everything. Simply feel the world around you and let the feeling tones of everything that you see wash over you. Nonphysically touch the world as a general mode of perception just as you do with your eyes when you see and your ears when you hear. There is something much more *living* about this, isn't there, than when you apply it solely to the human world?

Something new enters experience when we reach out with that non-physical part of us and touch the wildness of the world. It is a great deal more complex than what occurs in cities or houses or books. Importantly, hidden within the secret kinesis of the world, within the feeling of any particular wild place or thing, are the mythic dimensions that belong to the world in general and that thing or place in particular. And these mythic dimensions are a great deal older than the human.

When you travel farther along the road of feeling, going from "how does this language feel?" to "how does this table feel?" to "how does this river feel?" you begin to find that there is a great deal more to the world than we have been taught. You begin to notice that a complexity of perceptual feeling arises from touching the wildness of the world and that that feeling possesses dynamics that are more complex than those that come from focusing solely on the human world or any of its elements. You begin to experientially engage the first faint stirrings of the imaginal, begin to feel subtle expressions of the mythic that are held in *images.*

Writers who develop depth, complexity, and livingness in their work, of necessity, have to have the sensibility to feel *all* the things with which they come into contact, to feel the invisibles that infuse everything they encounter.

All of us decide on a form of some sort when we begin to write. We may be writing a book on plumbing or a mystery or a memoir or a book on dieting. That form is a doorway that constricts the flow of meaning that goes through us into the book. It compresses the flow of meaning from the world into a particular shape. Nevertheless, all the things we write about through that particular shape still touch some place on the natural world, not just the human world. And our kinesthetic sensing of the world will always be an essential aspect of whatever we are writing in some way. Plumbing touches the real world (although many people would rather not think about just where it does so). All mysteries, too, touch the real world—not just the human. A gray day, stormy and overcast, will create certain moods in the reader because those moods are part of the secret kinesis of that kind of weather. Certain landscapes create certain moods as well, and for the same reason.

By extending this perceptual sensing outward to the world itself writers begin to consciously explore the invisible nature of everything they come into contact with. Their internal database of their nonphysical touching of the world expands because they are now consciously exploring the feeling dimension of the world around themselves. And when the thousands of feeling tones they experience from the thousands of things they have touched in the wildness of the world enters their writing, it lends it greater depth and power. This kind of sensing is essential to the descriptions of the world that infuse the work, essential if those descriptions are to come alive, essential if the readers are to dream when they read. The part of the writer that dreams uses that database of experiential touching to build true worlds even if, in the case of fiction writers, they are not factual. The readers feel the difference. They can tell they are entering true worlds for someplace inside themselves where they, too, have felt the touch of such meanings upon them.

Many writers do, in fact, work with this extension of the secret kinesis of things into the world (even if they don't do it consciously) but it can be taken a great deal further (and it must be if the deep mythic is to be found). If you practice this sort of touching, something interesting will eventually occur. It's often subtle but if you pay close attention you will notice that, quite often, there is some sort of *response*. Sooner or later, often when you least expect it, something will look back. Sooner or later something will touch you in return. And though it's usually subtle, it doesn't have to be . . .

We are riding in a small boat and suddenly a whale rises to the surface right beside us, rolls to the side and eye-to-eye we suddenly are not looking at but really *seeing* each other. Do you know what I mean here? Can you feel what that would be like? Or we are leaning against a glass wall and a dolphin breathes smoke in our face. Or we are walking along in the woods, our thoughts a million miles away, and suddenly we come upon a great tree or magnificent stone outcropping and we are caught up in something that has nothing to do with our human world. We suddenly feel something coming into us from what we have encountered, something that is not of the human world. We are pulled out of ourselves into a world that is a great deal more ancient than human civilization. We discover that trees have been doing something more for the past 700 million years than simply pining away for our emergence. We feel the touch of life, of a particular kind of nonhuman awareness, upon us.

When that happens we take a long floating leap, land someplace else, and look around with new eyes.

These moments of touch with the nonhuman world are what the ancient Greeks—the Athenians—called aisthesis. To get to aisthesis, those moments when we are touched in return, our nonphysical touching must go deeper than merely feeling the world. It must go to the place where touching travels both ways. And this, very definitely, extends awareness a great deal further than our society wants it to go. It involves a living exchange between the human and the nonhuman world, eventually, with the world itself. By engaging in that exchange, we break a very powerful cultural injunction that is present in many Western cultures. We abandon the view of life that does not allow us to extend interiority to dolphins or trees or stones.

Being unable to extend interiority and consciousness outward, as Bly comments, keeps human beings isolated in their own house and, in extreme cases, we simply look out at a world with which we have no possibility of contact. We are cut off from the imaginal and our perceptual capacities are kept in a box. If that box is very tiny, as it is with strict reductionists such as Richard Dawkins, the mind can see very little of the world outside the box; there is only the human on a ball of resources hurtling around the sun. All things in the universe—from that orientation—center around the human, for there is no exterior consciousness. To such scientists the sun may no longer revolve around the earth but most certainly it still revolves around human beings.

Most people's boxes are bigger than Dawkins's so they know there is some sort of life and awareness in the world that is not solely concerned with the human. Many gardeners know it, most horsemen do, and dolphin researchers are very aware of it. But artists of necessity must be able to enlarge their perceptual box very far indeed; that is, in fact, what we are meant to do. As Gardner says, *The writer must learn to step outside himself, see and feel things from every human—and inhuman—point of view.*[4]

If we are to enter the imaginal realm and infuse our work with the deep mythic, if we are to experience not only the human but the nonhuman, and from *its* point of view—which we must do if our work is to escape two-dimensionality, for the world inside the book to be more than a cardboard cutout background to the story we are telling—if we are to create work that truly is art, we must extend our perceptual touching deep into the world itself and allow ourselves to be sensed, then touched, in turn.

This extension of our feeling sense and the experience it generates is, however, not so strange as it might sound upon first hearing. We do still possess remnants of aisthesis that are culturally acceptable, though they are generally limited to the domesticated. And though few of us speak of it, all of us have had varieties of the experience, for it is extremely natural to us; it is part of our natural range of sensing. This can be most easily understood when remembering what it is like when we encounter puppies.

Remember how that kind of moment *is*. . . . You're just hanging out, doing nothing in particular, perhaps resting in a comfortable armchair, maybe daydreaming a bit, when something catches your eye. A little puppy, about six weeks old, is wandering into the room from the hall. He hasn't seen you yet; he doesn't know anyone else is in the room. He's concentrating on the floor, smelling it intently. His tail is slowly waving back and forth as he follows some scent that only puppies know. His back legs are walking a bit faster than his front legs, as puppies's legs often do, so he's walking a bit crooked.

He looks incredibly cute and endearing and you begin to smile at the *puppiness* of him. You can't stand it any longer so you sit up and say, "Here boy. Here," and perhaps you whistle slightly and pat your leg.

The puppy looks up and sees you, the floor completely forgotten. His whole body begins to wag. "It's *you,*" he seems to be saying. "I have been looking all over for you."

In that moment something comes out of each of you and flashes across the room and touches the other. At that moment of touch both of you feel something unique, something we have no word for in our language. Yet it is one of the most wonderful experiences we can have. Our hearts open, we breathe more deeply, we relax more fully. There is a spontaneous joy that arises, naturally emerging out of the caring, though invisible, touch of another living, aware being upon us. And immediately after that invisible touching, the puppy bounds over to you and you begin to pet him and the two of you want nothing more than to physically touch for awhile, to be close.

Everyone who loves puppies, who loves this kind of sharing with puppies, knows there is something real happening here. Some invisible thing is exchanged, something basic to our natures to exchange, something that feels exceptionally good to share. This is an experience all people know, one of the most rewarding we can have, yet we have no word for it in our language.

The ancient Greeks did not suffer that kind of enfeeblement; their explorations and subsequent descriptions of their interior worlds were sophisticated and well developed. It is this exact exchange they called *aisthesis.* For the ancient Greeks, the organ of aisthesis, that is, the part of us that is capable of accessing this experience, is the human heart—aisthesis comes directly out of our capacity to feel. The ancient Greeks insisted this experience could be shared with any part of the world, even the world itself, insisted there could be an invisible, sensorial touching between the human and the nonhuman in such moments. And during those moments, understandings, perceptions, and insights that can be obtained no other way flow into us.

We learn through aisthesis that there is some sort of essential similarity in the world *out there* to our world *in here;* some sort of shared identity. This is what Thoreau was talking about when he said *This earth which is spread out like a map around me is but the lining of my inmost soul exposed.* The human, during such moments, is no longer isolated in her own house but reinhabits her interbeing with the world.

Aisthesis literally means "to breathe in." The Greeks noticed that at those moments of nonphysical touch there is, automatically, a deepening of breathing. There is an immediate *inspiration,* a breathing in of something coming to us from the world, some kind of soul essence that can only be found *in* the world. For the ancient Greeks, the source of inspiration that all humans need and that all artists seek is the world itself. This extension of the capacity for nonphysical touch *into* the world, this engagement with the secret kinesis of the life with which we are surrounded, literally is the source of our inspiration.

Remember Gardner's gestures in language. In the writing state one is *inspired,* things are *alive.* In the nonwriting state there is no inspiration, things are dead and lifeless. When we exchange touch in this way, things *are* alive. Naturally. We *are* inspired. Naturally. There is movement rather than a static state, there are wholes rather than parts, spirit rather than matter. Something must flow into us from the world for us to be inspired, for us to be whole, for us to create the art that is in us to create.

Some of this awareness is still encoded in our word *aesthetic* whose root *is* the word *aisthesis*. Inspiration and true aesthetics in art come from a life that embraces aisthesis, that allows this kind of sharing with the wildness of the world. Duende itself depends on it. It resides in the moment of intimate sharing with the world that aisthesis describes. Lorca understood this when he said that:

> *This "mysterious power which everyone senses and no philosopher explains" is, in sum, the spirit of the earth, the same duende that scorched the heart of Nietzsche, who searched in vain for its external forms on the Rialto Bridge and in the music of Bizet, without knowing that the duende he was pursuing had leaped straight from the Greek mysteries to the dancers of Cadiz or the beheaded, Dionysian scream of Silverio's siguiriya.*[5]

The natural world is filled with phenomena that will forever be outside and beyond the human world. We are expressed out of Earth's ecological matrix but remain only a subset of a much larger, living, system. A complete understanding of that larger system (and of the invisibles that infuse it) is impossible for the linear mind; it will forever be beyond its full comprehension. The only way we can access that deeper world is to think analogically—a thinking that is generated out of our capacity to feel. And this is crucial, for it is out of our touching the complexity of the natural world that our accessing of the mythic is possible.

The earth is, and always has been, a depth repository of the mythic. Without this secret kinesis of the world, and without the aisthesis that comes from it, the deep mythic that lies in the world, behind and within every form—every image—we encounter, can never be found. Emerson was long conscious of this, conscious of the deepening split between spirit and matter. It is why he said, "We too must write Bibles, to unite again the heavens and the earthly world."[6] He knew the truth, that a dreamer too controlled by the conscious mind, or severely curtailed by reductionistic descriptions of the world, can only write thinly. Such writing will always remain weak on symbol, theme, and the great truths that have concerned people since people have been. It is not, and never can be, fully real.

To make full alliance with the part of ourselves that dreams we must enter *its* world. And that world is much older than the world our conscious minds occupy during our ordinary lives. The part of us that dreams when we write is the same part of us that dreams when we sleep. And the dreams we have when we sleep have little to do with rationalism or reductionism or a mechanistic universe. That is why artists of all kinds have so much trouble fitting into the boxes of life; they use the part that dreams to create their art. They enter another kind of reality, every day of their lives. And that reality is filled with the ancient stuff of dreams.

We leap up into other psyches when we fully enter that writing state of mind and seeds from some other country attach to our clothes. When we return they return with us, hitchhikers from a mythic world. They drop from our clothing into our writing and a certain kind of life takes root. It spreads its leaves and our readers enter a forest where they become entangled in fragrances they could not have known otherwise. Thus does the mythic world, and all its elements, enter our writing, for in the seed is not only the tree but also the shade and the scent and new seeds that themselves lodge in the clothing of those who read our work. And something more besides . . . something that touches us in turn, something that brings tremendous energy with it, filled with meaning.

When we begin to be touched in turn, that is the moment we begin to enter the imaginal realm. When we fully enter it, we find ourselves in the midst of a living conversation, a conversation as ancient in our experience as the first storyteller. We can understand then what Rilke meant when he said *There is no place that is not looking at you,* for that is the moment when we find the world that Homer and Rilke found before us . . .

To praise is the whole thing! A man who can praise
comes toward us like ore out of the silences
of rock. His heart, that dies, presses out
for others a wine that is fresh forever.

When the god's image takes hold of him,
his voice never collapses in the dust.
Everything turns to vineyards, everything turns to grapes,
made ready for harvest by his powerful south.

The mold in the catacomb of the king
does not suggest that his praising is lies, nor
the fact that the gods cast shadows.

He is one of the servants that does not go away,
who still holds through the doors
of the tomb trays of shining fruit.

RAINER MARIA RILKE[7]

CHAPTER TWELVE

Synaesthetic Writing and the Beginnings of Analogical Thought

Most of us put words on a page the way kids throw snow at a wall.

WILLIAM GASS

It is the journey to the truth which convinces the traveler that he has arrived. To be dropped on the top of Mount Everest by helicopter is not to gain the glory of the peak.

WILLIAM GASS

Barfield maintains that every true image—every image that moves us—or moves the memory—contains a concealed analogical sequence. "Analogy" holds the word "logic" in it. He believes that the imagination calls on logic to help create the true image and so to recover the forgotten relationship.

ROBERT BLY

Every thing that is a thing is out there and there it stands waiting under your eye till some day you notice it.

ROBERT FROST

Anyone can, of course, find the secret kinesis of things. You don't have to be a writer to do it. But you are a writer and so that secret kinesis has to enter what you write in order for it to come alive. It takes practice; the same sort of practice that musicians who love music do every day.

Musicians do it not out of some "should" but because of love of the craft, because they are driven, because they are stubbornly insistent on mastering their art. And writers do it for the same reasons. As Wallace Stegner comments:

> *Except for amateurs and dilettantes, writing is not a part time occupation, nor is it the automatic spilling over of genius. It is the hardest kind of work, the making of something from nothing. No one but a dedicated, disciplined, even bullheaded individual is going to go on, day after day, sweating for five or six hours to make a page that may have to be thrown away tomorrow.*[1]

Underneath that bullheadedness is the love of something, a love so deep that it causes a person to abandon truth of culture for a life that is a great deal more uncertain, a love that itself generates an unending stubbornness. Writers love the thing they do, sometimes more than life itself. They love the invisibles behind words just as musicians love the invisibles behind musical notes. They love the process of gathering those invisibles into words and they are driven to capture those invisibles well; they cannot rest from the work until the line is right, until nothing feels "off" to their imaginative sensing.

There is nothing more beautiful for me, more transcendently fulfilling, than working on a line (or a work) that is coming alive, nothing more beautiful than engaging in the shaping of such a line and experiencing that moment when it comes to fullness, when it rests there on the page, resonate, condensed to its essence, and filled with life. It is a song sung between the writer and the living meanings that infuse the world, a harmony where the voice of the human and the other-than-human join together, and the moment when something more than either comes into being.

There is, as Gardner commented, an addiction to that process, that song, that singing—to those moments when that blending of voices produces something alive, something that takes on its own life and destiny. For those of us destined to be writers it is mostly at these moments that true fulfillment of soul and purpose occurs, when truly, we have done what we have come here to do.

All writers love these kinds of moments; it is, in part, why they have given themselves to the craft. Mark Twain was talking about aspects of this when he said:

> *To get the right word in the right place is a rare achievement. To condense the diffused light of a page of thought into the luminous flash of a single sentence, is worthy to rank as a prize composition just by itself. . . . Anybody can have ideas—the difficulty is to express them without squandering a quire of paper on an idea that ought to have been reduced to one glittering paragraph.*[2]

"To condense the diffused light of a page of thought into the luminous flash of a single sentence." Isn't that a beautiful phrase? It demonstrates, by its very shape and feel, the thing that Twain is describing.

To condense in this way takes a great deal of work. Few of us can sing this kind of song without practice. As John Dunning patiently, accurately, and irritatingly explained to me more times than I wish to remember, "Every writer has a million words of bullshit inside them and the only way to get them out is to write them out."

So, let's take everything we've been doing a bit further and play with it in a particular kind of exercise. Let's begin to extend the capacity for synaesthesia of perception into the writing process and begin to play with the analogical thinking that emerges when we do that.

Again, synaesthetic sensory perceiving occurs when you blend two sensory mediums into one unified medium. In this case, feeling and seeing. These two mediums will automatically begin blending together when you focus intently on how something feels and looks and then work to describe what you are feeling and seeing—over and over and over. (It is the repetition of the process that creates the synaesthesia.) As that progresses as a habit of mind, analogical thinking will, of its own accord, begin to occur.

The Exercise . . .

. . . involves looking around your house (or an art gallery or . . .) until you find two pieces of pottery, or woodworking, or furniture (or . . .) to work with. (I have also done this with two houses that are built similarly but which feel very different.) You are going to be describing them in language.

To find the first one, just look closely at each thing you encounter, as you have been doing, and then ask yourself, "How does it feel?" You are looking for one that, for whatever reason, feels good or that has more feeling interest to you than the others. (Conversely, you can just let your eyes go soft focused and engage in a general feeling perception of everything in the house or gallery. Walk until something catches your attention, until something pulls you toward it. This is one way to find the golden thread in a thing. Once you have found it, begin to look at it more closely.)

For the second piece, you want to find something similar (for example a second pottery bowl) but it should not feel quite as good. The technique used by the different craftsmen for each piece should be similar in skill level, but one of the pieces will strongly draw you, the other one not so much. This is the distinction Krenov was talking about when he said . . .

> *I wonder if people notice that with all the technical skill, love, and care put into them, many of his bowls still lack something? They are not all of them alive.*

You want to find pieces that are similar in skill but one of them feels better, more alive, the other less so.

The point of this exercise is to practice synaesthetic perception and then to write from that perceiving state. If you do it well enough, anyone reading your descriptions will *feel* the secret kinesis in those pieces—it will become part of their own sensory experience just as it is part of yours. Too, your kinesthetic perceptions, folded invisibly into the writing, will allow, through a most interesting sideways process, the deeper mythic elements of the thing you are describing to enter the writing. For the visual description, filled with the secret kinesis of the thing being described, is, as Gardner puts it, *the only way the barn—or the writer's experience of barns combined with whatever lies deepest in his feelings can be tricked into mumbling its secrets.*[3] Remember, really looking at what is in front of you, seeing it keenly, is essential. Developing the capacity for minutely descriptive seeing is a priority. Here's Gardner again:

> *The good writer sees things sharply, vividly, accurately, and selectively (that is, he chooses what's important), not necessarily because his power of observation is by nature more acute than that of other people (though by practice it becomes so), but because he cares about seeing things clearly and getting them down effectively. Partly he cares because he knows that careless seeing can undermine his project.*[4]

"Careless seeing," I love that phrase. Careless means "without care," "without attentiveness." There is a lack of emotional involvement in the action being taken. You're not attentive because you just don't care, you're not emotionally involved, not connected in your feeling sense with what you are doing. Seeing without feeling may in some circumstances be acceptable (though I think it questionable) but for a writer it is deadly. You must care about the act of seeing. You must care about what you are seeing. That is why, in part, the first thing you are going to describe should be of interest to you in some way. It is a mark of emotional involvement with the piece, a sign of caring.

To get the most out of this, use the snowball approach, don't worry about how messy the writing is. In fact, make it a point to make the writing as messy as possible. Throw words at the page the way kids throw snow at a wall and see how much sticks. (Most writers do their initial draft like this, by the way.)

I, like many writers who are beginning a new work, find it a bit challenging to move into the state of mind necessary to write. I tend to have a lot of inertia built up from my normal, daily state of mind, and I find it difficult to just switch tracks into the state of mind necessary for writing. (Part of me is always scared of doing so because of the underlying nature of the journey I am about to take and what that journey will entail psychologically.) So, I build up a great deal of feeling first, a reservoir of motive force. (For some reason a lot of writers need to do this to be able to write.)

Every writer comes up with some way of doing this that is unique to them. Some drink a lot of coffee and pace, thinking furiously the whole time, as Alfred Bester used to do, then race to the typewriter and get it all down as fast as possible. I tend to think of all the things that make me angry, that really piss me off, that I'm writing in opposition to, then build up that energy strongly enough that I can overcome the inertia and begin writing. If worse comes to worst (and it does for all of us) I fall back to thinking of myself on my death bed remembering back to the time I was defeated by a blank piece of paper.

When that energy is built up, as rapidly as possible I write down everything that I notice, think, feel, observe, see about the thing I am trying to describe or write about. I throw snow at the wall. I just write whatever comes to me without any censoring. Anything that occurs, no matter what it is, I write. And I write until I am written out.

> *Remember: The initial writing, the first draft, is supposed to be messy, supposed to be, as Anne Lamott says, shitty. Just let whatever is in there come out.*

So, with this particular exercise, just sit down with the first thing you're working to describe and begin to write whatever comes to you about it. Write a visual description of some part of the thing you're focused on. Then ask yourself *How does it feel?* and write whatever that feeling is. Then visually examine it again and write down *that* description, then feel it again and write *that.* If you get stuck, can't seem to get the energy to get going, get mad about whatever makes you mad, use that energy to write, and write whatever comes to you. Then, when the writing begins to flow, focus on the thing you are working with and begin the descriptive process.

If, as you do this, you feel into the second thing you are going to describe later and from time-to-time compare its feeling tone to the feeling tone of the first piece, this comparative process will bring into relief the secret kinesis of the piece you like and are working to describe. This will help you capture those invisible differences in language.

When you are done, when you are written out, rest awhile, perhaps until the next day or even the next week. Then read what you have written over again and see how it feels. As you read it, begin to feel into what you have written just as you did earlier in this book with lines such as *The writer piles up meaning behind the word like water behind a dam. Feel* how the writing feels. Much of it, as it is with *all* of us during the first draft, will be plodding and mechanical. That doesn't matter. What you are looking for is a "psychological hot spot" in the writing, a "pulsation on an otherwise dead planet." There will be, there always is, at least one place in the writing where it seems to come alive in a way the rest of the material doesn't. It's at that point you forgot yourself enough to drop down inside the thing itself, to really write from what you were feeling and seeing—at that point the two sensory mediums began to combine into one, at that point you began to capture some of your synaesthetic perceiving in language.

Ignore everything except for that hot spot (if there are several, choose the one that feels most alive) and begin the exercise again, this time with more precision. In that one spot the writing came alive so begin to build on that, trying to make the entire written description alive in just the same way. Try to get the whole piece you are writing to take on the feeling that is in that one section.

Essentially, you take the part that is alive and use it as the center of the piece itself. Just reading it will take you to some extent into the writing state of mind. Just reading it will also, to some extent, bring the thing you are describing alive. So, use that line or paragraph as a *fix* on the reality frame you are working with. Use this section as your starting point and take a run at the longer description again. Again, look at the bowl or whatever you have chosen, and work to describe it in words. Then feel it again, working to capture that complex of emotional tones in words. We are still throwing snow at the wall here, but at this stage you are using that one line that pulsates as a point of orientation. The writing is just a bit more precise this time around because you have a written fix on the underlying experience you are working with. Again, write until you are written out. Again, from time to time compare the two pieces of furniture or art that you are working with. Then, again, rest awhile.

You are using new muscles in this process. The part of you that nonphysically touches will get tired. It takes time to build up these muscles just as it does physical muscles. Eventually you will be able to do this kind of focused work for long hours every day. Feeling tired from this kind of exertion is normal.

When you are rested, look over what you have written. You will usually find that the livingness you sensed in the section you are using as your fix has extended itself into this new material, though its luminescence may be spread out over the page; it may be considerably diluted. So, the next step is to condense it.

Go back to the original section that pulsated. Take some time to really sit with it, to feel deep within it. Focus your perception on it as you did lines like *A man who can praise comes toward us like ore out of the silences of rock.* As you read your own writing through your feeling sense, begin working to refine those original pulsating lines so that the feeling in them becomes as strong as you can make it, until it begins to condense, as that line by Rilke does. Feel it, then rewrite the material until that pulsation is stronger. Feel it again, then revise it again. What you are doing here is deepening the fix, working *to condense the diffused light of a page of thought into the luminous flash of a single sentence,* in other words, working to concentrate the feeling of that original pulsating section until the material begins to shimmer with it. You are working to fill a line with deep psyche, to pile up meaning behind the word like water behind a dam, to soak your words in life force. Simply rereading that section, when you are done, will take you deep into a living experience of what it is describing.

I keep going over and over such a place until I can feel the deep psyche vibrating in the lines, until every time I read them, they come alive and I feel the living reality of the thing I am describing, until I go into the dreaming state automatically when I read, until I click into a vivid, visual and feeling experience of the thing described.

> *"Now this bookman has a great sense of style and he cleans off the glass counter top and sets the book just so in the middle of the glass and pretty soon he hears a car pull up in front of the store, the car door slams, and the shop door opens. The little bell tinkles and the bookman looks over to see the old guy standing like before, eyes blinking, getting used to the gloom of the store.*
>
> *"Well, the old guy, once his eyes have adjusted, turns to the bookman and starts over. Then he sees the book there on the counter*

and stops in his tracks. Slowly, as if in a dream, he walks over and reaches out for the book. His hands are trembling a little and just before he touches the book, he looks up at the bookman and his eyes are a bit moist. He looks back down again, picks up the book, and slowly opens it."

You may have to go over such a section forty or fifty times, as I did this one, before it feels right to your sensing. Each pass through it, however, if you have kept your synaesthetic perception focused closely upon it, will get it closer to that sense of rightness that it needs to have for you to feel good about it.

When you have the initial section more refined, again use it as your primary fix and work outward from it through the new material that surrounds it, trying to condense it as well. As you do, if you run into sentences that are dead and lifeless, you might, at this point, work to reformulate some of them instead of just ignoring them.

Start reading at the place where you have condensed your writing and begin to build up inertia as you read. When you get to a dead spot, use the momentum of your reading to make adjustments to the lifeless words and sentences. See if you can alter them so they are more alive. If you get stuck, or run out of steam, back up to where the writing is alive and take a run at it again. If some of the lines just won't work, throw them out. Keep working at it, adjusting, adding new lines, revising, then focusing your feeling sense on them to see how they feel, then again adjusting them until they are as alive as you can make them. The point is to make the entire piece as vivid and alive and condensed as that original section you just reworked.

This is the beginnings of analogical thought. Analogical thinking naturally emerges when you direct your synaesthetic perception toward a goal, when you begin to think *through* your synaesthetic perceiving as you write. This is what writers are talking about when they say they are feeling their way through the book as they write it. Synaesthetic perception, directed toward a specific, written goal, becomes then a kind of thinking, a form of cognition.

Gardner considered the elements of this process as "the fundamental units of an ancient but still valid kind of thought."[5] What you are learning now is how to think in just that way. So, take the material you have written and keep working outward from that point of pulsation until the whole piece is alive as you can make it. Build up momentum over and over again from the places in the work that feel alive and try to write through the dull, unalive parts, actively working to revise them to be as alive as the core you are working from.

Every writer goes through this process, over and over again, with everything they write until, to the limit of which they are capable at that moment in time, every part of the work is as alive as they can make it. It's a craft like any other. Over time, with more practice, it gets easier.

Every time you make a pass through the text, working to expand that place of pulsation, the piece you are writing will come more alive. Subsequently, every pass you make through the material will demand more precision of writing, more precision of seeing and feeling. This is because the degree of "offness" will be smaller after every successful pass through the text; your revising then, with each pass, will have to focus at ever tinier levels of perception and correction. This demands tremendous focus and concentration. Gass comments that, "precise writing becomes difficult, and slow, precisely because it requires that we read it precisely—take it all in."[6]

You throw snow at a wall until you get a rough draft of a largish section of the book. Then you read back through it in just this way. The first run-through that you take to refine the material is a broad-brush approach. You work to expand those initial pulsations into larger sections, perhaps whole chapters. The important thing is to get a pulsation, an aliveness, moving throughout the text, irrespective of how condensed it is. Once you have, you begin to use more microscopic focus, begin the condensing process that is essential to get to that place Twain was talking about. You begin to narrow the brush strokes.

During that narrowing of focus, sections that are not right will feel, as I've said, funny or off in some way. Anything that feels a bit off has to be reworked, revised. You have to keep thinking through the writing to find the right way to revise every little thing that feels off, to figure out how to shift it so that the "off" feeling is eliminated. Sometimes it takes weeks or months to figure it out, so you keep going back to the section that feels off, over and over again. But you figure it out by thinking *through* the text over and over again until, in a moment of unconcealment, the section reveals to your internal gaze just what is wrong. Often the understanding will just pop up from deep in the self one day when you least expect it. Sometimes it will occur when you are sleeping and you will just wake up with a realization of what is wrong. Other times, during the hundredth working through of that section, you will just suddenly see what it is that you have been missing (often after you have taken some time off and done something completely unrelated to writing).

John Lancaster gives an example, from Ian Fleming's first book *Casino Royale,* of the movements toward perfection that occur during this kind of textual revisioning:

> *"Scent and smoke hit the taste buds with an acid thwack at three o'clock in the morning." That was his first try. "Scent and smoke and sweat can suddenly combine together and hit the taste buds with an acid shock at three o'clock in the morning." That was his second. He got it right the third time, with the sentence that became the opening line of his first book* Casino Royale: *"The scent and smoke of a casino are nauseating at three in the morning."*[7]

Everybody has to learn how to find the right words and they have to do it by feel. You can tell from this example just how much better Fleming's third sentence feels than the first two. Everybody has to practice the process somehow.

With this kind of exercise it is essential, as you work your way through the writing, to make feeling comparisons between your descriptive writing and the thing you are working to describe (something that Fleming did as he reworked those passages. He *knew* how that experience in casinos felt; he had been there himself). That is, look at the piece or art (if only in your imagination) and ask yourself how it *feels,* then look at what you have written and ask yourself how *that* feels, then compare the two. What you are going for is a description that feels just the same as the piece of art or furniture (or . . .) does. You are wanting the two things, the piece of art and the written description of it, to approach a congruency. An identity. When you get there, the writing will *feel* right, even if you can't say exactly why.

The combined feeling tones of the words, their sounds, and their interior meanings should, when you are done, blend together into a symphony of meaning that, when read, gives the reader an exact *experience* of the thing you are describing. (You are *not* going here for an exact, detailed visual description, even if you spend a great deal of time writing the visuals. You are going for a communicated *experience* that will, when read, automatically generate a detailed visual—as well as a detailed kinesthetic—in the readers mind, just as Dunning's description of that house did.) Your writing, if done well, literally becomes a cognitive lens through which the reader experiences a particular aspect of reality. And that will naturally generate associational responses in them.

SOME COMMENTS ON THE WORD

As you focus this way on your writing you will inevitably become aware of the third primary element of writing after feeling and seeing, that is, sound. As you immerse yourself in the process of feeling the secret kinesis of something while at the same time perceiving it through its visual aspects, synaesthetic perceiving is automatically generated. Then you begin working to capture your perceiving in words. You begin to let your perceiving flow into written form, allow words to wrap themselves around your synaesthetic perceptions, blending together with them, becoming living containers for them.

If your writing is approached through this kind of synaesthetic perception, you will find that words are very different than you have been led to believe. They are not fixed immutable objects but literally are living things, capable of movement, capable of altering shape. They possess tremendous plasticity. As you work with them through this mode of thinking they have a tendency to go fluid and mold themselves around the invisibles you are working to bring into audible form. (You will get your best results, by the way, if you approach each word as you would approach a living human being, just the same as you are approaching each thing you write about.)

This mutability of words rests on two important aspects. The first is the sound that accompanies each word. The second is the inherent meanings that lie underneath and behind every word, the living meanings for which words are the highly flexible exterior membranes.

Every word possesses a particular sound, or more accurately a sound range. You can find that sound range simply by pronouncing one word in several different ways. But notice that you can intentionally insert very different meanings inside any particular word and that shift of meaning immediately affects how the word sounds when it is said. (Shift of sound will, by itself, also shift meaning.) Or another way to approach this is to say that if you hold one particular meaning of a word in your mind when you say the word, it will create a different sounding to it than when you hold a different meaning in your mind. This gives you a clue to the sound range that words possess.

For instance: You come home. Your spouse is mad at you. "How are you honey?" you say. She says, *"Fine!"* and she says the word in the midst of feeling angry and upset. The sounding of the word will come out of that feeling experience. If she says "Fine" in the midst of feelings of happiness, the word sound will be entirely different. A specific sounding comes out of each of those feelings.

If you more closely examine the feeling tone or tones of anything you are describing, you will find that—as you feel them—there is a kind of sound that accompanies that feeling. Feeling tones naturally possesses particular sounds, a kind of hum perhaps. (This is one of the reasons I use the word *tone* to describe them.) Every word you ultimately choose to use should possess a sound tone that, as closely as possible, matches the sound inherent in the feeling tone of the thing being described. This creates a reverberation between form and essence that makes the writing much stronger. It's part of what creates the feeling of *deep psyche* in a line. (Most writers find their way to this similarity of sound tone and feeling tone intuitively rather than intellectually. They *feel* their way to it, naturally, as they write. But conscious knowledge of it enhances your capacity to revise the rough manuscript, to compose it.)

As you work with words more intently you will also find that every word intrinsically possesses a range of meanings and each of these meanings sets up very specific associational reverberations within those who hear or read them.

These meanings, I want to make clear, are not the same as the definitions found in dictionaries. What I am talking about here are living meanings not static definitions. You have to abandon what forensic speakers say and now, for yourself, discover the nature of words through your own experience. To do so, to experience the livingness of a word, you have to follow it home to its place in the *feeling* world, the invisible world, where the essential meanings that give rise to it live. When you do this, you begin to understand, intuitively, the associational reverberations contained within those meanings. You find the living essence that lies behind and underneath the word. As Gass says, "The reader or listener must return the word to its proper habitation; the word must be sent on the same pursuit as the soul, in search of *its* truth: the sincerity of its source."[8] And that proper habitation is in the imaginal realm, the place to which your synaesthetic perceiving is inevitably taking you.

By working so diligently to capture the invisibles of things in words we find that we naturally learn to follow the word home to where it lives. We discover the living reality that is underneath and behind words. That livingness then molds itself around our synaesthetic perceiving of the world, the two blending together into one, living, communicatory expression. These underlying aspects of the word are what Wallace Stegner was speaking of when he said . . .

> *It is precisely the patina of language that gives an artist in words his power and his subtlety. He would as soon think of cutting bread with a sunbeam as try to use language with the precision of mathematics. He is after a much more complex, much more subtle kind of precision, if it can be called precision at all. The right word may be located by its sound, or by some flicker of momentary association, quite as often as by its denotative accuracy; and it does not exist in itself, a single thing, a single meaning; it exists in total entanglement with other words, with truth by evocation and response. It assumes the view that emotions are a tone and a style, in adjustment to situation and character and mood. Words used poetically are a medium as fluid as watercolors, and some of the best effects may seem accidental even to the man who creates them. He does not have to know, with his conscious mind, exactly what he is doing. He is fishing in obscure depths, he is a dealer in mysteries, a witch doctor not always easy with the forces he evokes but acutely aware of them while they are present.*[9]

Every word has unconscious associations to it as does every grouping of words and sentences. That is a major reason writing will always remain an art, why it can never be a science. The conscious mind of the writer can never know all or even most of those unconscious associations but he does, when analogically working the text, feel those associations as they move like currents below the surface of the work. By feel he puts them together in a way that seems right to his kinesthetic sensing. When the words are later read by the book's readers those words generate similar associations and images inside them. This, too, helps bring the book alive.

If you are just beginning as a writer this may all seem incredibly difficult to work with, just as the elements of driving did when you were first learning to operate a car. Don't worry about it. If you just follow your feeling sense, eventually, you will naturally reach the place where you work more and more deeply with the underlying nature of the word itself. You will do so intuitively and naturally. Trust yourself . . . and trust the thing in you that's driving you on. There is a natural brilliance there that will take you wherever it is that as a writer you need to go.

All of us, when we write, come face to face with the word eventually. And we all begin similarly, as if words were some kind of lumber we're carting around the house. We try them in this part of the house, then that, trying to get them to fit. Eventually words become something more; they come alive. Eventually all of this will make sense, just as driving a car did. At first there are too many things to pay attention to, too much to hold in the mind. But, over time, you'll learn how to let some other part of you hold all the pieces as one coherent whole, just as you did with driving. So, for now, just focus on the feeling and don't worry about it. If you follow the feeling it will always take you home; it will always take you to the place where the word lives.

So, as you work to refine what you have written, just play with focusing your synaesthetic perceiving and analogical thinking on the words themselves. Work to shape them so that they hold the living reality of the invisibles inside the things you are describing. Once you get to a congruency between the writing and the thing itself you will know it, you will feel it. (Just as you did with that pen or cup you moved back to the position you shifted it from.) At that moment, your synaesthetic perception has produced a written description that is an exact analog to what you are describing. (It now possesses analogical symmetry.) And because your written description is filled with the secret kinesis of the object, it comes alive visually and kinesthetically on the page.

This, you will rapidly discover, demands tremendous precision (a capacity that develops over time). To accomplish it you have to immerse yourself in your sensing of the object, feeling it at the same time you are visually sensing it. You have to, at the same time, immerse yourself in the writing, seeing and feeling it the same way. Then you continually make tiny adjustments to the writing until the words and the thing you are describing become one thing.

Success in this is facilitated if you drop down inside the piece of art (or whatever it is that you are describing, even if it is in your imagination) as if it is an extension of your body, as if it is a part of you, as if it *is* you. Then describe this part of you in words. (The more you love the thing you are describing, the easier this is to do.) Then you drop down inside the words in exactly the same way, as if they are you. (And the more you love the words, the easier this is as well.)

Literally, look out at the world from these two points of view. When the writing and the thing approach an identity, what you see and what you feel when you look out at the world from either of these two vantage points should be the same. The world each of these cognitive spectacles reveals should be very similar.

When you are done with the first piece of art or furniture, do the second piece the same way.

The result, as I mentioned earlier, should be that when someone reads what you have written they have a sense of those things, they should come alive. The person should *feel* their reality at the same time that a vivid visual image appears on the screen of their inner vision. The reality your written piece generates in your (and your reader's) experience should be as real as this other reality you live in day to day.

You can tell how closely you have come to success by how deeply you go into the dreaming as you reread what you have written and by how vivid the feelings and images become when you do.

Practicing the craft in some way (and this exercise in some form is the core of that) is essential. For it educates the part of you that touches the world and gives it experience in doing so. It also develops your capacity to see what is in front of you and to sense the invisibles inside what you see. You gain experience in working directly with the invisibles of the world, learn how to pour them powerfully into language. You learn to use form to carry essence.

If you do this kind of exercise (whether or not you do it in exactly this way), you will also notice that, while you may have begun in one state of mind, as you got caught up in the process, you forgot yourself and became immersed in the writing. Sense of self disappeared. You moved, either lightly or deeply, into the writing trance. When you focus through your synaesthetic perceiving, headed toward a goal, you automatically drop into the writing trance and when you do, you begin, naturally, to think analogically.

CHAPTER THIRTEEN

Analogical Thinking

What of those passages that do follow us home?

WILLIAM GASS

Loving meaning the way Goethe speaks of means investigating the mythological implications of images in the way Goethe or Yeats actually did.

ROBERT BLY

It is the cognitive function of the Imagination that permits the establishment of a rigorous analogical knowledge, escaping the dilemma of current rationalism.

HENRY CORBIN

Analogical thinking occurs, as I have said, when you think through your synaesthetic perceiving, headed toward some goal, in this instance, creating a living description in language. Caught up in what you are doing, you literally become *immersed* in your synaesthetic sensing and in your describing of that sensing. All sense of self, and the world around you (except for what you are focused on), fades. As Wallace Stegner says, "The writer at work is submerged, and every intrusion that draws him to the surface costs him his concentration."[1] When there is submersion to the point where all sense of self fades you are *in* analogical thinking. Automatically. In essence, you are following a golden thread, focusing on it with your whole attention while at the same time working diligently to capture its essence in language. Nothing exists in your awareness but this perceptual exploration and describing. In the midst of your immersion you write. And when, as I mentioned earlier, you get something on paper that captures some of that essence you are going for . . .

> *What happens next is interesting. You are sitting in completeness with that line and, of its own accord, the attention of the self suddenly shifts, moves in some new, never-to-be-predicted, direction. The part of you that is intimate with meanings flows along the line of meaning that touched you, heading toward its depths. The golden thread moves and the deep you moves with it. The feeling of the thread is the same but there's more to it now, it has deepened in some way, become richer. More meanings inside the thread begin to reveal themselves. New thoughts, feelings, sensations, images, emerge—spontaneously—into awareness. And now you begin the process of capturing* them *in language. Stafford comments: "If I let the process go on, things will occur to me that were not at all in my mind when I started. These things, odd or trivial as they may be, are somehow connected." The lines that take up residence in your heart, as William Gass might put it, "father or nurture other lines, sentences, further feelings and thoughts of significance." And they do so automatically.*

Our capacity for nonphysical touching of the world opens up to us a different dimension of things beyond height, width, and depth. A feeling dimension. And this feeling dimension of things will lead, if followed with focus and diligence, very deeply into the meanings in the world. Artists take this natural human capacity and go much further with it than most do; they do it as a profession. They begin to follow the touch of meaning upon them, follow their sensate perception of a golden thread, into the depths of the thing itself, into the meanings that underlie its surface form, its image. Then they work to capture that in language. And as soon as they do, as soon as they get some aspect of that thread on paper, other aspects of those underlying meanings pop into awareness, associational reverberations filled with new perceptions occur, seemingly of their own accord. Some new aspect of the golden thread emerges and we begin to follow that, and then the next one, and the next. Bly comments that . . .

> *Something surprising happens often during the writing. It is as if the object itself, a stump or an orange, has links with the human psyche, and the unconscious provides material it would not give if asked directly. The unconscious passes into the object and returns.*[2]

The unpredictable insights and perceptions and material that Gass, Stafford, and Bly are speaking of emerge naturally from analogical thought. And every one of those new insights are somehow inherent in or innately connected to what is being synaesthetically perceived. Human beings find those connections *only* through their capacity for analogical thinking; in essence, we follow an invisible trail that wanders through the world by using a particular capacity of perception. And as we do it more often, as a habit of mind, we begin to be aware that we do not inhabit a world of disconnected objects, but are rather immersed in a much more fluid medium, what might be called a textual field, throughout which are scattered the condensed meanings we call objects. Underneath or within their apparently objective surfaces—their images—are other meanings that only analogical thinking can find. And between every object in that textual field exist threads of connection that can be perceived only through our analogical thought. We literally learn, as writers, to read the text of the world. We begin then to experientially understand what William Gass meant when he said: *All of us who live out in the world as well as within our own are aware that we inhabit a forest of symbols; we dwell in a context of texts.*[3]

Let's see if I can give you a more concrete sense of what I mean. . .

Have you ever had the experience of walking along a street and catching a glimpse of yourself in a shop window but, in one of those odd moments that sometimes occur, you don't realize it's you. So, for a few moments you really do see yourself as another person might. You don't know who that is you're looking at but for some reason you are caught up in looking at them. Then, suddenly, the *meaning* of what you are seeing coalesces inside you. With a start, you realize it's you that's reflected in the glass.

Or perhaps you've had the experience where you're looking at something but, for some reason, you can't figure out the perspective of what you're seeing. You can't figure out the scale. Is the thing near or far away, small or large? What *is* its relationship to the field around it? So, you keep looking at it, working at it, and suddenly you understand just what you've been looking at. The perspective of the thing suddenly clicks into place.

Or maybe you have looked at one of those books that were popular for a time (I forget what they're called). There's a picture of some sort, a lot of apparently random colors and shapes on the page, but it seems to make no sense. However, if you look at it in a certain way it turns out there really is a picture in there. So, you strain, your friends urging you on, trying this way of seeing, then that, then . . . suddenly, there it is.

The visual images we are looking at in such a book are composed of an apparently random grouping of irregularly sized color or black-and-white blotches. These are the sensory impulses that are reaching our eyes and then passing through them into the brain. The visual perceptions are coming in, but there is no meaning to them. Yet there *is* meaning; there is a picture, somehow, in there. If you keep looking at it, of a sudden, a recognizable picture emerges.

The same thing happens in the first two situations I described; visual images are coming in but what they mean is unclear. In the first example you know it's a person, you just don't know it's you. In the second, you are perceiving some sort of visual images from the world but you can't figure out their relationship to each other.

However, when you do finally understand what you're looking at, when you finally perceive the meaning inside it, you see it suddenly, immediately. As Henri Bortoft observes: *The effect is just as if the [image] had been switched on, like a light.* All of a sudden, click, it's just there.

Bortoft goes on to ask . . .

> *What happens in this instant of transition? There is evidently no change in the purely sensory experience, i.e. in the sensory stimulus to the organism. The pattern registered on the retina of the eye is the same whether the [image] is seen or not. There is no change in this pattern at the instant when the [image] is seen—the actual marks on the page are exactly the same after the event of recognition as they were before. So the difference cannot be explained as a difference in sensory experience.*[4]

What happens is that the *meaning* within the sensory impulses has been grasped. The part of the brain that deals with meaning has received the sensory impulses from the visual cortex and successfully analyzed and integrated the relationship of the visual elements to the whole and to each other. The thing that is more than the sum of the parts, the organized pattern that is there, suddenly bursts into awareness. The *meaning* is finally perceived and the image that is inside the sensory frame suddenly appears. Click. Like flipping a light switch.

The visual elements that make up the thing you are looking at, however are not the thing itself, not the meaning. The meaning is somehow *in* the picture, but it isn't the picture. It's not the series of visual impulses you have received. Nor is the meaning merely an element of the figure. If a person who cannot see the image in that apparently random grouping of black and white blotches makes an exact copy of them by hand, the image will not stand out any more clearly to them than it did before. Bortoft comments succinctly that: *What we are seeing is not in fact on the page, even though it appears to be there.*

This *meaning* is an added dimension to the patchwork blotches on the page. It's a dimension concerned with relationships and the tension between parts and that invisible something that comes into being when a grouping of parts suddenly unifies into one coordinated whole. It's an invisible yet vitally important dimension of everything we encounter. Bortoft says . . .

> *The error of empiricism rests on the fact that what it takes to be material objects are condensations of meaning. When we see a chair, for example, we are seeing a condensed meaning and not simply a physical body. Since meanings are not objects of sensory perception, seeing a chair is not the sensory experience we imagine it to be.*[5]

We live in, are immersed within, a world of meanings not objects. A person whose hippocampus is malfunctioning will receive the same sensory impulses from her visual sensing of a chair as we do, she just never has that moment of recognition, that coalition of understanding; she never knows the meaning of what she is seeing.

Because the condensation of meaning occurs almost immediately when we see a physical object, none of us notice the process happening. It's so automatic we miss ourselves doing it. But it has not always been so automatic; when we were babies it wasn't automatic at all. We experienced the same kind of sensory impulses then that we do now but we didn't understand the meanings in them. We learned how to understand the inherent meanings over time—and we learned it at the simplest level possible; we learned to stop at *chair* or *tree* and then go on with our lives. But the thing is, *chair* is only part of the complex of meanings that are embedded within the visual images we are receiving, and the most superficial one at that. The chair possesses not only *chair* as a meaning but also a feeling tone that is itself a key to the deeper meanings that it possesses, including its symbolic and mythic dimensions. If the chair is approached through our feeling sense, if we begin to develop our natural capacity for perceiving the secret kinesis of things, rather than leave it undeveloped in the unconscious, then those other meanings begin to emerge analogically through our practiced, synaesthetic perceiving. The invisible elements of the thing, including its mythic and symbolic dimensions, and its connections to other, apparently unrelated phenomena, become sensible to our synaesthetic perceiving. And as we think through our sensing, feel more deeply into the image itself, a similar pattern recognition experience occurs deep inside the self. Something new just pops into our awareness, like a light switch being flipped. We literally are feeling our way deep into the meanings that underlie the world of form. We are reading the text of the world through synaesthetic perception and analogical thinking.

We follow trails of feeling into the heart of the things we encounter and as we do, we begin to understand that nothing is isolated from anything else. Golden threads connect a myriad of apparently unrelated phenomena.

Gregory Bateson was the first person I read who talked about this in any depth. He took Bortoft's understanding of condensed meanings and extended it when he commented that all the things we see are not only condensed meanings but *transforms of messages*. He understood that all those condensed meanings *interact,* that there is some thread of connection between them. He called that thread *the pattern that connects* and he called our ability to perceive that thread *the sense of aesthetic unity*. Communicability is inherent within them and between them and, in fact, the condensation of meaning is itself a communication. Buckminster Fuller extended this further still: *Universe is a verb, not a noun. It is not a place but a scenario. You can get out of a place, you cannot get out of a scenario.*[6]

Most of us move through the natural world not realizing that the forms we encounter are not the apparent superficial objects we think they are;

they are condensations of meaning, wild poetry created from the dreaming of Earth. And those condensed meanings interact with each other, communicate, live, for they are, at core, not only wild poetry but interactive communications expressed out of the ecological matrix of this planet to fulfill certain ecological and communicatory functions. They are verbs, not nouns, endlessly involved in interactive scenarios at multiple levels of function, including the mythic—which is irremovably a part of the underlying, interactive matrix of the world. And we, through our analogical thinking, can read into the text of the world at any of those levels of meaning, and as writers, we must—it is integral to the art, to the essence of our function.

Writers, of necessity, learn to think analogically, for that is the only way that the deeper text of the world *can* be read. As Bly says, this form of perception not only sees deeper within things but it also "sees the hidden links between the 'ghosts of things' and the things themselves."[7] It is how we make the connections that are woven through the world visible to the conscious mind, which usually cannot see them. The new thoughts, perceptions, and understandings that emerge out of analogical thought occur as sudden epiphanies, moments of duende, intimations from who knows where. Like flipping a light switch, they are suddenly there. And there is no other way of getting to them except analogically. That is, at root, the power and beauty of what it means to be a writer. It is a way of thinking that is also a way of perceiving that is also a way of understanding; it gives us access to the underlying nature of the world. It is very different than scientific approaches, and a great deal older.

Goethe said that when he was in a state of analogical thinking . . .

> *My thinking is not separate from objects; the elements of the object, the perceptions of the object, flow into my thinking and are fully permeated by it; my perception itself is a thinking, and my thinking a perception.*[8]

"My perception itself is a thinking, and my thinking a perception." What a beautiful description of how the state feels. The perceptual sensing we use as writers is, as Gardner insisted, a unique and very specific "mode of thought." And it is a mode of thought that is innately connected to both the imaginal and mythic realms.

ANALOGICAL THOUGHT AND THE EMERGENCE OF THE MYTHIC

During analogical thinking, when you are so immersed you forget yourself, the dreamer inserts a lot of material into the writing. It does so when you aren't directly looking, while you are focused on other things. It does it sideways.

You are immersed in the writing, thinking analogically, focused on how it all feels, slowly finding your way, one slow feeling step at a time. Then, you reach a stopping place, you step out of that state of mind, flow back upward into consciousness, and begin to look things over. Suddenly, you notice a lot of unusual material has entered the work when you weren't paying attention.

As Gardner says . . .

> *No amount of* **intellectual** *study can determine for the writer what details he should include. If the description is to be effective, he must choose his boards, straw, pigeon manure, and ropes, the rhythms of his sentences, his angle of vision, by feeling and intuition. And one of the things he will discover, inevitably, is that the images . . . that come to him are not necessarily those we might expect. The hack mind leaps instantly to [clichéd] images. . . . But those may not be at all the kinds of images that drift into the mind that has emptied itself of all but the desire to "tell the truth"; that is, to get the feeling down in concrete details.*[9]

When the writer, in the dream, writes, the images that emerge will always surprise in their association. The things you include, you include because they feel right when you are in the dreaming. They emerge out of that pattern-recognition process that occurs in the unconscious when you are analogically thinking. They pop into awareness, they feel right, you include them. But it's not possible to understand their full, layered complexity until you step out of the dream. They may have felt right but once you begin to look everything over consciously you find that there is a lot more in the material than you understood as you wrote it. The dreamer inserted that complexity when you weren't looking. And the images that emerge? There is something in them, some living essence that is beyond the clichéd images that can be created by intellect alone.

The kind of descriptive exercise I outlined in the last chapter is much more than an exercise in painting a picture of the world in language. It's much more than an act of verisimilitude. It focuses the mind in the particular way that it must be for writing to occur but, at the same time, it allows the mythic to flow through the writer and onto the page. This allows the emergence of theme, archetype, and symbol into the writing as living expressions rather than mental constructs forced onto the page.

Gardner remarks . . .

> *Good description does far more: It is one of the writer's means of reaching down into his unconscious mind, finding clues to what questions his fiction must ask, and, with luck, hints about the answers. Good description is symbolic not because the writer plants symbols in it but because, by working in the proper way, he forces symbols still largely mysterious to him up into his conscious mind where, little by little as his fiction progresses, he can work with them and finally understand them.*[10]

By focusing consciousness through synaesthetic perception so intently—what Gardner calls "working in the proper way"—the writer steps aside enough that the dreamer can begin inserting its perceptions and understandings into the text. And those understandings and perceptions go deep into a very ancient world. As Gardner comments: *Somehow the endlessly recombining elements that make up works of fiction have their roots hooked, it seems, in the universe.*[11] They are connected as well in the matrices that underlie the universe.

They have their roots hooked so deeply because we are dreaming. The dreamer inside us lives partially in this world and partly in the imaginal world (where it has continual access to the mythic). When the conscious mind steps out of the way, whether when we sleep or when we write, some portal in the dreamer opens and the whole aware universe begins to flow into and through us. Archetypes and symbols, myth itself, then become entangled in the private substance of our words. Only after they emerge of their own accord can the conscious mind work with them intentionally. And while we can understand some of their complexity through our analogical thinking through of them, and our later conscious examination, their full nature will ultimately remain as mysterious to us as to any of our readers. We can only, if we are sensitive enough, learn to shape them, to enhance them, to develop them just as we would any element of the book.

Theme arises similarly out of the depths of the dreaming self. A writer can intentionally decide on a theme but the best ones emerge of their own accord as the work is being written. We start with an idea and that gets us going but once our dreaming self begins writing the book, different themes can and usually do emerge. A minor character in a novel suddenly insists on being the main character and, for some reason, he is limping, we don't know why, the deep self wrote him that way, and suddenly one day the novel, it is found, is oriented around that limping foot. The theme of the book, it turns out, is entangled in it. Or in a nonfictional work on adobe house building, you may begin writing about how houses can be made from soil but find yourself being drawn over and over again to the plants that are often mixed with clay to make adobe plasters. Suddenly those plants take on the same importance as the limping foot and the theme of the book emerges of its own accord, entangled in those plants and their extinction from wild landscapes.

Deconstructing a text, then, to explore its symbols (or its theme) makes as much sense as diagramming a sentence to find its meaning or dissecting a human being to find the livingness that is their unique self. It's impossible. A symbol, just like a word, is only a form, an aspect, of meaning. But like the true meanings that underlie and reside within words, the livingness of symbols cannot be seen directly with the eye; it can only be sensed through analogical thought. You *feel* them in the text, learn to sense the place they emerged, come to understand how they flow through the text, and then learn to shape them as an integral element of the book.

To be real, symbols have to emerge from the dreaming; they can't be inserted into the writing by the conscious mind. Deconstruction of text makes it seem as if they are found through the conscious mind; it misleads both writers and readers as to the nature of the craft. Ernest Hemingway was predictably adamant about it:

> *No good book has ever been written that has in it symbols arrived at beforehand and stuck in. That kind of symbol sticks out like raisins*

> *in bread.* [*In writing* The Old Man and the Sea] *I tried to make a real old man, a real boy, a real sea and a real fish and real sharks. But if I made them good and true enough they would mean many things.*[12]

The writing that comes out of synaesthetic perceiving and analogical thinking is the only way the things we write can become "good and true." It is the only way that symbols will emerge within our writing of their own accord. (Any symbol, like any element of writing, can become a cliché. That is what Hemingway meant when he said a symbol arrived at and stuck in sticks out like raisins in bread.)

The symbolic nature of things is inherent *within* them, another layer in the complexities that we know as objects are. If you write the thing true, with the feeling sense active, the symbolic aspect or aspects inherent in the phenomenon are released, activated. The symbolic is a living aspect of the thing you are working with—you can't make a symbol, you have to release the symbolic that is woven into the world through *how* you are thinking, through *how* you are approaching the things you are perceiving. It then takes on a life of its own within the world of the book. It interacts with that world, with everything else inside the book.

Symbols are living aspects of the world, an inherent layer to reality, woven into and through all things. They can retain that livingness only when they emerge out of our dreaming, out of the part of us that knows that stones talk and hide, that unseen golden threads move our lives, that there are powers far older than the human that still live and determine outcomes. They express themselves through the images that emerge of their own accord in our writing; they emerge as well through the images of anything we are describing visually.

Some images arise out of analogical thinking just as spontaneously as thoughts, insights, hidden correspondences, and relationships do. There is something inside the image that connects it to what we have been writing. Even if we don't know what that something is, we can tell the image is right because it feels right when we include it. And when we linguistically capture the image of something we are synaesthetically perceiving, a similar process occurs. Bly comments . . .

> *When a poet creates a true image, he is gaining knowledge; he is bringing up into consciousness a connection that has been forgotten, perhaps for centuries. . . . The power of the image is the power of seeing resemblances. That discipline is essential to the growth of intelligence, to everyone's intelligence, but especially to a poet's intelligence. Emerson, who was Thoreau's master, said, talking of true analogies:*
>
> *"It is easily seen that there is nothing lucky or capricious in these analogies, but that they are constant, and pervade nature. These are not the dreams of a few poets, here and there, but man is an analogist, and studies relations in all objects. He is placed in the center of beings, and a ray of relation passes from every other being to him."*
>
> *The question then we have to ask of an image when we write it is, Does this image retrieve a forgotten relationship or it is merely a silly juxtaposition, which is amusing but nothing more?*[13]

When Bly says: *When a poet creates a true image, he is gaining knowledge; he is bringing up into consciousness a connection that has been forgotten, perhaps for centuries,* he is talking about analogical thinking, revealing that the process, by its very nature, brings into consciousness connections that have always been there but which have been forgotten—perhaps, in some instances, connections that have never before been found.

When writers focus intently on the visual images of the objects surrounding them, they increase the amount and degree of their sensory inflow. They know (more often instinctively than consciously) that those sensory inputs are filled with a great deal more than *chair* and, through their synaesthetic perceiving, they feel their way more deeply into the meanings that are held within the image. Ezra Pound was working with this understanding when he said that an image "is that which presents an intellectual and emotional complex in an instant of time."[14] Writers are, in essence, seekers of meaning through a unique kind of cognition. The more sensory data from the image that flows into them, the more of the *text* that is embedded within it will flow into them. The more of the text they have access to, the more meaning they can distill out of it, the more rays of relation they can find and experience.

The meaning-filled text of the world is embedded deep within everything we *see,* within every image we encounter. And within that text, inside that image, as an element of it, is symbol, is myth, as integral elements.

When we enter the image, we find the imaginal (and the mythic) through using a particular kind of imagination.

To get a sense of the relationship between image, imagination, and the imaginal let's play again with one of the earlier exercises in this book. That is, just take a look at anything you wish in the room you are in now, and focus on it visually. Really *notice* it through your visual sensing and then ask yourself *How does it feel?* You will again experience that instantaneous burst of the feeling tone that is a part of that object. Just stay with it a minute and let the feeling develop.

Now, take a break. Take a deep breath, perhaps stretch a bit or move your body. Then . . . close you eyes and *remember* the thing you were just feeling. Remember how it looks in all the detail you are capable of and remember as well how it felt. Still with your eyes closed, keep seeing and feeling the thing. Now . . . reach out with your hand to the place where the image is. Now, open your eyes and look at where your hand is. It will most likely be out in front of you someplace, somewhere in the region of space in front of your chest.

Now, break state, that is, move a bit, stretch, or even get up and walk around, so you move out of the slight dreaming state you are in. Take a couple of deep breaths. Now . . . start thinking about something that you are troubled about, bills you have to pay, or a problem facing you, perhaps a government agency you are upset with. *Close your eyes* and see a visual image of it, of the people involved, and of you talking to them about it, and what you are going to do to attempt to solve the problem. Say all the things in that imaginary scene that you would say if you let yourself say whatever you wanted to. Let the scene unfold until it is clear. When it is, reach your hand out and put it in the place where *that* image is. Now open your eyes and look. Most likely your hand is up, either out in the region in front of your head or even higher—above it entirely.

This is an example of two different kinds of images—and two very different types of imagination. It is an example, as well, of two very different forms of thought, each of which works with images in very different ways.

The latter example is one that works through and with the brain. It works with the kind of imagination that most people define as something done in the brain, a mental fancy. It is the kind of imagining that is useless for writers.

However that first imagining, the remembering of the thing you were seeing and feeling, is an example of what Goethe called the exact sensorial imagination. The exact sensorial imagination is at the core of analogical thinking; it is another way of describing it. It is a thinking, a cognition, that occurs through both feeling and images. It is a thinking into the meaning dimensions of images through subtle perceptions of their feeling dimension. This is how the imaginal realm is accessed. And that imaginal realm is where the mythic, the world of the Forms that Plato spoke of, and the human can meet—the only place they *can* meet. It is a world that is entered through this particular kind of imagination. For most ancient cultures, this kind of imagining occurs not through or in the brain but through and in the heart.

Their understanding of the heart's capacity for sensory perception and cognition was far different than the kind of mushy sense of heart we now have in the West. To the ancient cultures, the heart was a sophisticated organ capable of both perception and a unique form of analytical thought, a thought that was oriented around images filled with feeling, a synaesthetic perceptual sensing that uses a specific form of imagination, what Goethe called the exact sensorial imagination—or, what I am calling here, analogical thought. Baudelaire was speaking of this capacity as well, when he said . . .

> *By* imagination, *I do not simply mean to convey the common notion implied by that much abused word, which is only* fancy, *but the constructive imagination which is a much higher function.*[15]

And the skill of that sensorial thinking, that imaginative faculty, can be developed through practice into a potent perceptual and analytical tool as elegant and specific as the brain (as many writers have proved). But, it is distinct from the kind of thinking the brain performs; it has a sensorial dimension to it—it is not mere mentation. (Again, this confusion is at the heart of the problems in most nonfiction. Most nonfictional writers are using dissociated mentation, not imaginal sensing.)

It is this kind of imagining that is central to the writer's art; it both works with and generates images that are filled with kinesthetic dimensions and those kinesthetic dimensions hold within them symbol and theme and a great deal more. It's how the imaginal is accessed, how we get to the place where we can touch the mythic.

That is what we, as writers, do. We access the imaginal through our capacity for analogical thought and we build, book by book, a body of our analogical exploration of the world. For us imagination is not something that happens in the brain but is rather, a different form of cognition, one inextricably interwoven with feeling, one filled with full sensate perceiving. It is the only way we can get to the meaning-filled text that underlies, that resides within, the world of form.

The earlier, white heat of writing that came from the built up energy you gathered is simply a way to get into this state of mind. It is a way to let go of your ordinary perceptual orientation and move into something different. As John Steinbeck commented: "The getting to work is purely a mechanical thing, as you well know—a conscious and self-imposed schoolroom. After that, other things happen, but the beginning is straight pushing."[16] Once you are in the analogical state, it is much easier to keep it going. Perceiving analogically is not only interesting; it's addictive; it's highly pleasurable. So, once in this state, you can often keep it going for hours. You write, write until you are written out, until whatever particular golden thread you have been following is exhausted. And then you stop.

What you then do, when you edit, is to focus that analogical thinking onto the writing itself.

Initially, you work to condense lines and paragraphs, perhaps whole chapters. But there is something else that happens later in the work, perhaps when you have just about completed the rough draft of the manuscript. It is one of the most beautiful, most magical moments that occurs in writing.

You have thrown snow at the wall, written and written and written, getting everything that occurs to you down on paper. You have followed this thread and that. Seemingly unrelated thoughts occurred. You put them in. You feel something important in ice cream cones and in they go. You sense something important in shoelaces and cement blocks. Those go in as well. When you are done, you have a huge mass of material. So, you step back and begin to look at what you have written.

The invisibles you have captured in words lie there on the pages, very similar to those visual images that Bortoft was talking about earlier. What a mess. No pattern at all. You keep looking at it, reading it over, feeling into it. What a mess. No pattern at all. Why the hell did I write all this stuff? But you feel something in there, no matter how diffused or unclear it is, so you keep looking it over. Then suddenly one day, as if a light were switched on, the pattern reveals itself. All the invisibles that flowed into the work suddenly coalesce into a pattern that has meaning. Suddenly, you see what you were doing, where your feeling sense was taking you, what the dreamer inside you was putting into the work. Suddenly, you have a gestalt of the book, of its underlying meanings and thematic interrelationships. And you realize in that moment of perceptual breakthrough that the whole you now perceive is not remotely the book your conscious mind had in mind when you began. The thing has now taken on a life of its own; it has found its own form. And this perceptual understanding you now have can only be found by writing the book. You literally have *written* yourself to the truth of it.

So, there, pulsating in your mind, is the whole complexly interacting, living story that makes up your book. And from that core perception you look upon the geography of the text now lying like a living map in your mind. It literally is a whole world come into being. You can now see how each part of the book is an expression of the underlying pattern. Every idea or concept within the book is an integral, living element of the nonfictional story you have written. Now you can begin to make that pattern clearer and more succinct. You can now begin to concentrate the invisibles you have gathered with your analogical harvesting, to condense them.

At this point, you focus your synaesthetic perception and analogical thinking on the writing again, but with a different goal. You begin removing excess words and thoughts from the pattern, just as a sculptor removes excess stone. You begin to work the lines themselves to enhance that pattern, so that the pattern you now see in the book comes more fully into being. Each section of the book is reworked so that it flows more easily and fully as an expression of that pattern. Form and essence, on this level, begin to echo each other.

You can now see, as well, the thematic threads that have emerged in the book and which are a part of that pattern. During this condensing process you work to develop them, as well. You also begin to condense and develop the various subconcepts and ideas as they emerge and flow through this chapter and that. They are part of that thematic pattern. Symbols make sense now within the whole of the book and you work to condense and develop *them*.

You have the whole picture now, a gestalt from which to work. You have written yourself to where you were going and can now refine all those cautious steps you took as you laid down one concept under another in order to get across the slippery slope. You condense all those elements you now see just as you did your descriptive writing. You condense them into luminous threads that run throughout the book, unseen for the most part, hidden underneath the *now* of the text.

Analogical thinking is one of the great joys of this craft. It is one of the oldest forms of depth perception that human beings have, one of the oldest ways that we have used as a species to understand ourselves and the world around us. We find truth in this kind of perceiving, the eternal verities that Faulkner spoke of, deep aspects of reality that, when articulated, wind their way down inside us and set up a reverberational response from the truth receiver that lives there. We literally think our way to the truths that reside, and can only be found, in the imaginal and mythic worlds, truths that underpin our daily world and that lead to a moral life, a whole life. As Stephen King once said, "Moral fiction is the truth inside the lie. And if you lie in your fiction, you are immoral and have no business writing at all."[17] No matter the form of our writing, we have to find, through our analogical thinking, the truth inside the lie, and if we don't we have no business writing at all.

We find in this kind of thinking a way to *understand* the life we live embedded within. And the more we engage in analogical thinking, the more we educate this capacity in ourselves, the more we give it experience, the more we find in it. Ultimately, it takes you, as it has always taken writers, deep into dreaming, so deep that you find "the secret room where dreams prowl."

CHAPTER FOURTEEN

The Dreamer and the "Secret Room where Dreams Prowl"

It was winter; a strange, violet light was in the sky—a color typical of clear prairie evenings when the air is freezing. Something about the light, and the quiet library, and my being away from home—many influences at once—made me sit and dream in a special way. I began to write. What came to me was a poem, with phrases that caught the time, my feelings. I was as if in a shell that glowed. All the big, dim reading room became more itself and had more meaning because of what I was writing. The alcove at the east end where the literature-browsing books were (a favorite place of mine) was darker and more velvety. My steps, walking back to the boarding house to work, were ritual steps, feet placed carefully on the storybook world.

William Stafford

It is rather our interior self I'm concerned with, and therefore with the language which springs out of the most retiring and inmost parts of us.

William Gass

> *I am learning to see. I don't know why it is, but everything penetrates more deeply into me and does not stop at the place where until now it always used to finish. I have an inner self of which I was ignorant. Everything goes thither now. What happens there I do not know.*
>
> Rainer Maria Rilke

In the forecourt of the Temple of Apollo at Delphi, carved in stone, is perhaps the most famous of all admonitions: *gnothi seauton*—know thyself.

All people must come to know themselves to some extent. But writers, more than most, must. They must learn themselves in ways that many people are never, by circumstances, forced to do—if they wish to truly become writers, that is, someone who is more than a typist of words. They must become, as Wallace Stegner insisted, "exemplars of the examined life."

We have to learn how to remove, as much as possible, unconscious psychologicalisms from our writing (something I will talk more about later). If we are to be good at our craft, we also have to learn how to put ourselves inside the people and things we write about. And most importantly, we have to learn how to get our conscious selves out of the way so that the dreamer inside us can write.

We have to come to know ourselves.

This calls for a great deal of flexibility of self, flexibility of perspective, flexibility of reality orientation. We must have flexibility in how we see and experience the world around us. We must learn, as good actors also must, to shift from perceptual frame to perceptual frame. We have to learn how to take on the underlying assumptions and beliefs of differing matrices of perception (whether those are cultural, professional, psychological, individual, or nonhuman). And we must do so truly; we must take on each perceptual frame as if it were our own.

One way good fiction writers speak of this is to say that they must care for each character they are writing, no matter what kind of character it is. In order for the character to come alive they must be able to see the world from that character's point of view and present them in the book from that point of view—without prejudice. All people, no matter how evil their behavior, believe they are justified in it in some fashion. To be inside each character and write from that character's point of view allows complexity into the writing.

As nonfiction writers, we face the same task. We may have a default set of beliefs that underlies our behaviors and the way we approach life, but we have to be able to step away from those beliefs and see from the other's point of view if our writing is to be true. To do this we have to come to terms with the *other* in ourselves. It is the only way we can deeply understand the *other* out there, and see the world from that other's point of view. The "other" in ourselves consists of the parts of us that we repress in the unconscious and that we then project onto the other out there. Resolving this is the only way we can write people who are real—there are then no cardboard characters, no two-dimensional people in our work.

This is one of the dynamics that puts so much psychological pressure on artists, especially on actors and writers. Most of us have prohibitions on what we believe it is legitimate to feel or think or do. And those prohibitions interfere, often strongly, with our ability to move into different reality frames. So, this work demands personal exploration. It demands that we come to know ourselves. The more we do, the better able we are to be in service to our craft. The more able we are, as Ralph Waldo Emerson described it, to "become a transparent eyeball," to allow what we are seeing and feeling to flow into us living and intact, and then onto the page, without our unconscious beliefs or biases shaping what we are seeing and feeling. The better we can do this, the better our crafting becomes.

Emerson was not the only one to speak of this; his student Thoreau also insisted on its importance when he said: *So much of man as there is in your mind, there will be in your eye,* and Goethe, too, when *he* said: *How difficult it is not to put the sign in place of the thing; how difficult to keep the being always livingly before one and not to slay it with the word.*

Writing that comes from such clarity is the only way our readers can see and experience the imaginal world and what we have found there. The more distortion we keep out of our lens, the more clearly our readers will experience what we have experienced and have captured in language.

Such clarity demands a great deal of self-knowledge. We have to know ourselves well enough that we can get out of the way of the work. If we don't know ourselves we won't be able to determine just how much is in our eye and how much is not. We may *feel* that something is off in the writing, but it will be difficult to figure out just what that offness is. It is, in fact, the sense that something is off in the writing that leads many writers to self-examine. We struggle to learn what is wrong and in so doing we come to know ourselves. The art itself demands it.

But for the writer, most fundamental of all is coming to a relationship with the dreamer, for without the dreamer there is no writing, at least that has merit. And one of the most important things of all, if nonfiction is to become an intentional art just as fiction has, is allowing the dreamer to write what is being written. The statistical mentality must stand aside so that something more than linear thinking enters the work. All fiction writers struggle with the dynamics of this; some nonfiction writers do as well. It truly is one of the most important elements of the art.

In my experience, there are few parts of the self that keep more secret than the dreamer. All of us have a great many parts of the self that live in what Freud called the unconscious. Jung wrote in some detail about this, insisting that the unconscious is a multiple personality, that, in fact, all human beings are multiple personalities. (What we call multiple personality disorder merely being an aberration of a general condition.) The late actress Brittany Murphy spoke of this when she said, "There are probably 800 people living inside of here, so they all pop out in different ways. When I act, those parts use my tears and snot and sweat and bruises, just in different contexts."[1] This is true for everyone of us. During our daily lives, as all of us eventually learn, many of these parts come forward from time to time while, at the same time, our conscious selves step into the background.

All of us know that the part of ourselves that talks to our spouse is not the same part that talks to the policeman who pulls us over for a ticket or the part that delivers a lecture at a university. All of us have experienced those odd embarrassing moments when, in a social situation, some other part of us takes over our mouth and says a lot of things we would rather it not say and then steps again into the background, leaving us standing there, mouth gaping, trying to socially recover. Or the times when we go home to visit relatives and suddenly find ourselves, not the grown-ups we are in our daily lives, but once again the surly teenager or the highly emotional four-year-old. (No one knows how to push our buttons better than the ones who taught them to us.) Or the times when we become incredibly angry and some other part of ourselves comes out and loudly delivers all the irritations and frustrations that we've saved up, seemingly since birth. Then later, when the anger has passed, we find that some things should never be said, for they can never be unsaid. And, of course, all of us know that the part we secretly took to dinner with us, the one that spilled the red wine on the lace tablecloth and felt gleeful about it, is not the same part that accepted the dutiful, and boring, invitation. Difficulty in managing movement from one part of ourselves to another is one of the most common problems all human beings face.

Over time, one way or another, all of us begin to know ourselves. We learn, the hard way, that any part of the self that we repress will become hostile to us. Certainly, it contaminates what we write. So, we begin to do interior work, to make relationship with our unconscious selves, begin to understand their purpose and nature enough that we can start to live as our own best friend. And this, if developed as a way of life, can be taken to incredible depths.

For example, in many respects, the autonomic functions of the body can each be understood to be controlled by a specific part of the unconscious. Indian fakirs have shown that, by establishing a relationship with those parts, they can bring such unconscious autonomic functions under conscious control. Those unconscious parts become the allies of the conscious self and often will, if asked to do so, alter their behavior at the request of the conscious self. But they won't do so in any manner that undermines their primary function, that is, while fakirs can control heart function to an extreme degree—such as lowering heart rate and respiration to nearly undetectable levels or initiating intentional fibrillation—they cannot force it to stop permanently. The only reason that such unconscious parts of the self will agree to alter function at all is if the conscious self understands that. There are certain lines that cannot be crossed without the unconscious becoming unresponsive. Respect for the intelligence and function of the part of the unconscious that is being accessed is essential. The unconscious understands mutually respectful bargaining; it simply won't respond to attempts at control (i.e., demands) by the conscious mind except by becoming silent and invisible once more.

Within the psychological body, the dreamer is as deep in the unconscious as the part that controls heart function. You might say that this part is a part of the autonomic psychological system rather than the physical. Unlike the surly teenager within us, which we can more easily access and affect, the dreamer is very deep in the self. It functions day in and day out without any input or direction from us; it rarely lets us know of its existence. We do know we dream but few of us understand why or what is involved. Most people never have cause to go that deep into the self. But writers do and must.

Those who become writers learn by a slow step-by-step process to become deep and intimate friends with the part of their self that dreams. They learn how to make that slight interior shift that puts the conscious mind on stand-by so that the dreamer inside comes forward and begins to dream words onto the page. They form a cocreative partnership. The dreamer writes, the conscious mind edits . . . but always checking out those edits with the dreamer and as well with the truth receiver. Both have to sign off on the edits before the edits can be accepted as legitimate. The establishment of this relationship takes years; the more honorable it is, the better the creation, the better the writing. You must, over time, become *trustworthy* to your self. You can't, as with the part that controls heart function, cross certain lines. The dreamer responds to violations of its essential integrity or of the relationship between the two of you with silence, better known as writer's block.

To work deeply with the dreamer, you have to establish trustworthiness and like any new relationship that is going to be deeply intimate, it takes time. You have to show, over and over again, that the conscious mind does not harbor any arrogance toward the unconscious. This relationship has to be an equal and mutually respecting partnership. Your conscious mind has to learn its limits and freely recognize that the statistical mentality is not the part that creates the writing. It is merely the part that shapes. Both are essential, both crucially important. But the dreamer's contribution has to be cherished and honored. It has to be understood as primary; *the* most important to the writing process. The conscious mind is secondary.

Most writers do learn how to make relationship with the dreamer, one way or another. Most know how tenuous that relationship can be, how very shy that part is, how easily given to offense, how reluctant to come forward. I think this is why so many writers are so reluctant to speak of their creative process in any detail. The dreamer is exceptionally uncomfortable being exposed to public view. There are very few people *out there* who are likely to treat it with the respect and kindness that you must. Once exposed it can be hurt, once hurt it retreats. And it takes a long time to convince it to come out again. It has to be protected from hostile mental forces.

Stegner comments . . .

> *No writer I ever knew wants to examine too closely what goes on when he is writing well. . . . I have seen a pair of distinguished psychologists meet only stony suspicion and refusal when they asked members of my advanced fiction seminar to volunteer as hypnotic subjects. The idea was to sneak up on their creativity when it wasn't looking. Those young writers did not want their creativity sneaked up on. They felt it to be not only intensely personal, but fragile. Instead of exposing or analyzing it, they surrounded it with a camouflage of routine and casualness. They kept it in its hideout, where it was safe; only at their will, not at that of some investigator, did they turn it loose to make its raids on human experience.*[2]

It takes a long time before we learn how to "perform the holy and sacred act of breaking bread with ourselves" with our inner dreamer. And once we have learned how to, nothing can be allowed to injure it or the sacred relationship we have managed to forge.

To write you must learn how to intentionally dream, learn how to let that part of you flow its dreaming onto the page. But, if you are just starting out, be very careful of speaking of that part of yourself to others. This is *your* secret self and it keeps itself secret for a reason. Your relationship with the dreamer inside you should be held in a special place inside. The same kind of place that only our lovers and our children know. That relationship is built step by step, year after year, as all deep relationships are.

WRITING AS INTENTIONAL DREAMING

Every human being on the planet who is alive or has ever lived has the capacity to enter a similar kind of dreaming state to the one that occurs during writing and does so every day, hundreds of times. Daydreaming is a form of it (all writers are very active daydreamers, often since early life). Mentally working out the solution to a problem, where you are lost in the problem itself, is a form of it. Imaginatively creating anything engages the faculty of dreaming in this way. And everyone who drives a car knows that state of mind. We start for a familiar destination and suddenly arrive, the hour absorbed into the place the dreamer lives.

The dreaming state that occurs in writing, from one perspective, is similar to (though it is not) hypnotic trance. Like such trance states, it can vary from very mild to very deep. And all a hypnotic trance is, is a state where the conscious mind merges into the background of the self and another part, normally unconscious, comes forward. If the conscious mind goes very far into the background, so far it no longer is aware of what's going on around it, no longer aware of what the part that has come forward is doing, it is deep trance. If it is aware of what is happening, it is a lighter trance. The writing trance moves between both of these poles. Sometimes we just dip down into it, letting our feet go slightly below the surface of the water, other times we immerse ourselves completely. At those times it is not uncommon to write for four or five hours and for the conscious mind to be unaware of the passage of time. You reach some sort of ending place, stretch, and find that shadows have lengthened, the whole day is gone.

Daydreaming is a shallow form of the dreaming that occurs at night and while the daydreaming state is useful, the powerful mythic elements that move writing into great art come from the deeper dreaming self that is more active at night. It is that deeper dreaming self that must be accessed in writing.

The best results occur if you are willing to understand the dreamer as a specific personality in its own right, with its own motivations, needs, and desires—if you understand that it is in charge, not you. It is a delicate love affair and no desired lover will respond with more caution, as you hold out your hand, than the dreamer.

The techniques that I have outlined so far in this book—beginning with a focus on feeling, then blending it into a unique form of synaesthetic perception as you write, then becoming so immersed in your perception and the writing you are creating out of it that you enter analogical thinking—will, in and of themselves, put you into the state of mind where the dreamer becomes active in the writing. As you go deeper into analogical thinking, as all sense of self fades, you are, automatically, in the dreaming state that writers need to be in to write.

In contrast to that approach I'll briefly share some of Dorothea

Brande's methods for accessing the dreamer. You will see, that even though our approaches are different, they bear a great many similarities.

Dorothea Brande's approach (outlined in her book *Becoming a Writer)* is very clever. She suggests that you keep a journal next to your bed and the first thing every morning, before you completely awaken, you write while still in the state of mind that exists between dreaming and waking. What she is suggesting is giving the dreamer permission to express itself through language while it is still close to the surface. In essence, this begins a collaborative relationship between the dreamer and the conscious mind where the conscious mind intentionally gets out of the way and allows the dreamer to express itself at a regular time every day.

She emphasizes that nothing should be read before doing this and that no critical thinking should occur during it. She clearly understands that one of the greatest problems facing successful alliance with the dreamer is the grammarian, the language perfectionist, who hides out in the conscious mind.

Grammar is the enemy of the dreamer, so is negative editing and self-censoring. I will talk more about these later but it is crucial when doing this sort of exercise that you not have *any* critical judgments about what the dreamer writes. So . . . wake up, take the journal, and write whatever that part of you wants to write. Don't read anything you have written previously either, just let that part of you write whatever it wants to at the appointed time.

The point of this is to begin the partnership that must exist between your conscious mind and the dreamer. To allow the dreamer to get used to being out in the open and writing. That part needs to learn that it is okay to emerge and write and that you won't do anything to harm or denigrate it.

Another way of putting all this is that Brande recognized that the writing trance is very similar to the state that all of us experience every morning when we are in between waking and sleeping. So, by doing this kind of exercise regularly, you habituate yourself to staying in that state of mind for longer and longer periods and to writing while in it.

What you are doing is encouraging a specific part of you to write and to do so when it is most close to the surface. Because you treat it with respect, it learns to express itself without fear. Once the process is comfortably established, it is time to take the next step that Brande outlines, that is, to write at some later time during the day, after the day has already started, perhaps at ten o'clock or noon or four p.m. What you do is to mention to that part that tomorrow at the specific time you have decided upon, the two of you will sit down and you will let that part write whatever it wants to write. Brande makes a crucial point about this exercise. You have, in essence, given your word to yourself. She calls it "a debt of honor." The debt must be paid at the appointed time. You must keep your word to yourself.

If you keep your appointment, the dreamer will eagerly show up whenever it is that the two of you set a time for writing. And because you have habituated that state of mind, you will drop into it immediately as you begin to write. She suggests altering times as the process continues so that you, in essence, learn to allow that state of mind to occur at any time, making it possible for the dreamer to write.

What you are doing is allowing the dreamer to work in partnership with you, allowing it to express itself, letting it speak more and more, letting it dream out loud on paper. Eventually, as you make friends, as that part comes to trust you, it will gladly begin to participate in the creating that writing is. It will look forward to writing, to dreaming out loud. Dreaming is, after all, what it does best.

As you develop a trusting relationship with the dreamer, it is essential that you be incredibly careful to do nothing to damage that trust. All of us do, of course, sooner or later. And from this we learn just how to be honorable with this part of ourselves. Here are some of the most common transgressions that occur.

1. Speaking of a work in progress, except in the most general terms. This is often a recipe for the writing drying up completely. You can implore all day long once that happens, but the dreamer (as with most parts of the unconscious) never responds well to threats or pressure. Bargaining, yes. Force, never. It is very hard, often impossible, to convince the dreamer to continue writing once what it is writing has been talked about wrongly, or, sometimes, at all. Part of the reason this dries up the writing is that the dreamer makes no distinction between telling a story or writing one down. If you tell it, the dreamer's job is done. Still, I think another, and perhaps more important reason, is the conscious mind taking credit for

something it is not actually doing while getting social plaudits for doing so. Guaranteed to offend anyone.

2. Failing to keep agreements with the dreamer. A deadly sin. This is especially important when it comes to writing. If you have agreed to write on a certain day at a certain time, you must in fact write on that day and at that time. The dreamer hates to show up for work when you are someplace else (like anyone). Brande has some succinct comments on this:

   Now this is very important, and can hardly be emphasized too strongly: you have decided to write at four o'clock, and at four o'clock write you must! No excuses can be given. *If at four o'clock you find yourself deep in conversation, you must excuse yourself and keep your engagement. Your agreement is a debt of honor, and must be scrupulously discharged; you have given yourself your word and there is no retracting it. If you must climb out over the heads of your friends at that hour, then be ruthless.*[3]

3. Exposing the dreamer, unprotected, to external forces. The dreamer has very thin skin and takes offensive behavior very personally. So, don't allow the dreamer to be exposed to those who live in a mechanical frame of mind. Never allow such people to give you feedback on your work. Nothing kills the complexity of life more than reductionism. Nothing insults more than the arrogance of disbelief. For example: some people still have the belief that women are not as intelligent as men. If you are a man, take on that belief and go and talk to a woman and see how well you do. The dreamer should never be exposed directly to outside forces like this under any circumstances, especially not to reviews, people who don't like you, or eviscerating critics, agents, editors, and writing teachers. It will feel abandoned, hung out to dry, and angry that you did not do your job of taking care of it. It will become convinced you are an idiot (which you were). It takes a long time for the dreamer to forgive that kind of idiocy.

4. Insulting the dreamer. Don't. The dreamer is the source of the writing and as such is the most important part of the self when it comes to writing. Arrogance of mind on your part toward the dreamer is a recipe for disaster.

The dreamer is more sensitive than the most sensitive lover will ever be, acutely sensitive to the slightest disrespect, broken agreement, or callous disregard. So, you must understand from the beginning that a great part of the psychological battle that writing is comes from conflicts between the dreamer and the conscious mind. Some of these conflicts are unintentional. They come from limits of perception and constrictions in the conscious mind that do not allow the conscious self to see things that the dreamer is bringing forward in the work. Some of the conflicts occur from bad habits, habits of treating the self poorly, much more poorly than we would treat a stranger. Those behaviors must, of necessity, change. Most writers learn to be kinder to themselves as time goes by, that is, if they wish to continue being writers. Writing is a partnership between the conscious mind and the unconscious. Without the dreamer the conscious mind has no material to edit or publish. You can try to write without the deeper self involved (everyone tries it sooner or later) but nothing written without the dreamer is, in the end, worth much. If the deep self is not involved, the writing is, by definition, superficial. Breaking agreements with the dreamer, treating it shabbily, failing to be your own best friend are things to be avoided at all costs.

Every writer finds their own metaphors to explain their internal complexity, their own metaphors to explain this relationship. Every writer finds their own methods for inducing the state of mind necessary for encouraging the dreamer to write, their own way to make friends with this part of the self, their own way to, in that final moment of trust, let go and let the dreamer write whatever it wants to write.

Some kind of exercise—and all writers find their own sooner or later—that takes you into that dreaming state and lets the dreamer write is essential. Once you can do this as habit you will, sooner or later, fully enter the secret room where dreams prowl.

THE SECRET ROOM WHERE DREAMS PROWL

As I've said, the processes I have outlined so far will take you into the dreaming state that is essential to writing. And it will take you into a deepening relationship with the dreamer inside you. But to get to the secret room where dreams prowl it is necessary to take all this a bit further. There is a place, a state of mind, an experience, that is just beyond analogical thinking. You can only get there through analogical thinking but the place itself is as different from analogical thinking as night from day. You find that place during those incredibly magical moments when the dreamer takes over completely.

Normally, in writing, both the conscious mind and the dreamer take turns. Usually people start out in the conscious mind. In the initial stages of a work writers throw snow at the wall to get everything moving, to build up the inertia to change state of mind, to get something on paper to work with.

Once you get something down on paper that pulsates, it does indeed give you a fix on the state of mind you need. You enter a state of synaesthetic perception that naturally moves into analogical thinking as you begin to think through that perceptual sensing. And as you immerse yourself in analogical thought, you begin to dream. The longer you do it, the more fully the dream deepens. You submerge.

You build up some momentum as you read, then, when you hit the undeveloped or unwritten places in the book, that momentum carries you on. You begin to go deeper into analogical thinking as you think through more and more of the material, trying to refine it, to get on paper what you are feeling your way toward. And the more occupied your conscious mind is with what you are doing, the more the dreamer becomes involved in the writing. Again, it inserts much of its material sideways, when you are busy *over there* with your analogical thinking.

It is rare, however, that the process continues uninterrupted. John Dunning had that happen once, with his novel *Deadline,* where he sat down at the typewriter and six weeks later the book was done. For most of us that's as rare as finding a winning, million-dollar lottery ticket on the sidewalk. Normally, we write for a while, then we lose the thread. Something feels off in the writing. We stop and begin to work it over in our minds and through our imaginative perceptions. The conscious mind, the truth receiver, and the dreamer engage in a dialogue, back and forth, back and forth—trying this in our sensorial imagination, then that—*feeling* how each possibility feels within the text, seeing how each imagined scene looks, and feels, in the work. We keep at it until the thread is found again. When the dream is running well, it often happens that six or eight hours of writing at a stretch occurs without once waking from the dream. Sometimes you can get a week or more. It is exactly like driving a car and becoming aware of yourself only when you have arrived at the destination. It just flows, butter comes out of your pen. The condensation of perception into exactly the right words (however diluted they are) just occurs, of itself.

The great Irish sculptor Michael Quane, though talking about drawing, describes such moments of artistic creation, when everything seems to click:

> *The conscious awareness of the connections between eye, hand and brain diminish with the shrugging off of wariness and hesitation, a stage is reached when it appears that it is enough to will the drawing: all the reciprocating stimuli between brain—hand—eye—brain no longer need to be translated, and trust in the creative mind is achieved. At this point, instinct and impulse cut a swathe through schooled thought and heretofore unimagined possibilities are there for the taking.*[4]

What a nice line: instinct and impulse cut a swathe through schooled thought. He perfectly captures what the experience is like . . .

> *trust in the creative mind is achieved . . . instinct and impulse cut a swathe through schooled thought . . . heretofore unimagined possibilities are there for the taking.*

Or, as Schiller once put it:

> *The intellect has withdrawn its watchers from the gates, and the ideas rush in pell-mell, and only then does [the creative mind] review and inspect the multitude.*[5]

"Has withdrawn its watchers from the gates," oh, how I love that line.

Every book has long periods when the dream is working well, when writing just flows out of such a state of heightened balance. The book literally seems to write itself. And every book has times when the dream isn't working well, when you have to struggle for the dream to emerge into the world, when every fucking word is hand chiseled out of the mountainside, one by one by one.

Part of the reason trouble can arise in the dreaming is because you are asking the dreamer to put the dream in a particular form. When we decide to write a poem, a story, a mystery, or a nonfictional exploration of how to make furniture, that decision, whatever it is, sets parameters around what is being created. We may not know where the book will go once we begin to write but the form in which we are working puts restrictions on what emerges from our dreaming, and the dreamer inside us knows it. So, the dreaming flows through the size and shape of opening that our parameters create. It takes awhile for the dreamer to accustom itself to a dreaming restricted by form (if it ever completely does).

Just as the type of work we are creating sets parameters around what is being created, by the same token, our psychological structure, the deep-seated beliefs we have, the unconscious habits of mind, biases, and perspectives—to put it most simply, how we think of the universe and ourselves—also sets parameters around what is being created. The degree of openness of the door through which the dreaming comes (and the shape of its opening) is determined as well by our psychological structure. These psychological parameters often do interfere with what the dreamer is dreaming because the dreamer doesn't suffer the same limitations as our psychological selves.

Another part of the conflict is perhaps less deep. The dreamer may insist on taking the book to a place that our conscious minds resist. So, instead of writing, we spend time resisting where the dream is taking us. ("No, no, I don't want to write about that, it's too revealing" or "I don't want to kill off that character.") At other times we might be insisting that the book go someplace predetermined by our conscious minds. ("Yes, we *are* going to include the necktie and it *will* be green.") The dreamer resists and we get nowhere.

So, we end up in the fierce psychological struggle that writing is; over time we learn, more gracefully, to step out of the way. We learn through an often painful trial-and-error process to simply follow the threads we sense wherever they are going because every time we don't the writing doesn't work. It dries up. Even if we have no idea where the writing is going, there is always that moment, sometimes after months of struggle, when the pattern that is inside the material suddenly coalesces into understanding. And then we know what "the basement" was doing while we were up here complaining about it. Every time, sooner or later, there is that sudden flash of seeing, of understanding. We see then how remarkable the process is, how what is coming into the world possesses a kind of magic that we, by ourselves, could never have found on our own. So, over time, we learn to trust the process, trust our analogical thinking. (Even if every time, in the midst of it, we are sure that *this* time it's never going to work out.) Most people have to learn experientially that the conscious mind is not the part that writes. They learn, the hard way, that writing happens "in the zone" even if they never define that zone more clearly. And for most of us it takes awhile.

We also have to learn the parameters of the process. We have to learn how to drop into the dream state, how to solve the kinds of problems that generally occur in doing so, and then how to deal with those unique problems that are attendant to the writing process itself. Over time we get better at it and we can drop more easily into the state of mind necessary for the dreaming to take place. We can write without disturbing that state of mind. And we can do so for longer periods of time. We habituate ourselves to this mode of thought, to this way of working and seeing. Eventually, we build up enough trust to allow the dreamer more and more freedom of involvement. We learn to trust the dreamer, the dreamer learns to trust us. Most writers know of this, though they usually speak of it as learning to "trust where the book wants to go."

There are, however, these truly magical moments that occur sooner or later. They usually happen after you have learned the initial stages of the writing process well enough to have habituated them. You are writing one day, firmly in the zone, plugging away and suddenly, like a light switch flipping, you are just in a very different state of being. Suddenly, there is a full-dimensional, sensorial experiencing of a living reality the dreamer has brought alive out of the depths of itself. You find yourself in the midst of a living scene, literally do experience it as a living process just as real and three-dimensional as the world you live in during your daily life. As Gardner said, it is real and this is *literally* not metaphorically true.

This sudden, and magical, experience is difficult to initiate on command, though there are a couple of things that can help generate it. It is completely dependent on immersing the self in analogical thinking. So the first thing that will help you generate it is being able to remain in that state as a habit of mind.

Getting to that experience is much like learning to ride a bicycle.

Things are a bit wobbly in the beginning. You fall often. But there is a state of balance that eventually occurs and once you are in it, you can do a lot more than you could before. You begin to use that state of balance as an expressive form itself.

From your experience of riding a bicycle you perhaps have a sense of what that is like, the invisible state of balance where everything has come into a harmony of function. It's just the same with analogical thinking. You get to that point of balance, you spend more and more time in it and, slowly, you begin to extend more and more trust to the dreamer, to the part of you that takes over when you are in the zone. Usually the writer doesn't realize this is what is happening; they just think they are getting the "hang" of it. (And they are.) They are trusting this way of thinking and perceiving more fully, more completely. They are trusting their balance, themselves, and the skill they have developed. More importantly, they are in service to it; they trust it to lead them wherever it needs to go.

Eventually the trust is deep enough so that, finally, you really do step out of the way and let the dreamer fully dream in front of you without your involvement. In a sense, you go unconscious, just as you do when you take a long drive home and have no memory of all the twists and turns that got you there. But there is a difference. There is that same experience of some other part of the self taking over but when it happens with writing, it would be more accurate to describe it as sitting in the car and suddenly experiencing the whole reality of a trip, the people, everything, without even starting the car. When, during the writing, the dreamer begins to dream deeply, when you finally let go of the reins of control, the dream that unfolds is different from the dreams that arise during analogical thinking. It unfolds as a living experience, occurring without your involvement. Michael Quane has a great description of what this kind of shift is like:

> *It is the automatic condensation of parcels of thought, like the condensating ooze of water droplets from a window pane. It involves a mighty phase change, like gas to liquid. It is a conversion of untetherable thought into footprint evidence of its being.*[6]

Something flows out of the imaginal realm, into and through the dreamer, and emerges, seemingly of its own accord, as a living scene that is as real as any you have ever had. The writer, watching, works to capture it in language as clearly as possible but stands during the whole process as mute, awed, witness to the phenomenon. There is a phase change, a conversion of the dreaming, untetherable thought, into form, footprint evidence of its being. But it occurs without that slow, working, feeling-your-way emergence that is the hallmark of analogical thinking; it is instead a shift from one state fully to another. It just happens, all of a sudden.

Once you have experienced this, the state will begin to occur more frequently, seemingly of its own accord, its duration from a few minutes to perhaps a half hour or so, perhaps, in time, even longer. And your conscious mind, observing it, as Stephen King has often commented, will be as surprised at the story that unfolds (whether nonfictional or fictional) as any reader you ever have will be.

If you are writing fiction, this moment of breakthrough is like suddenly stepping into a living scene that is being generated someplace else. It is a sudden transition. In one moment you are in one state of mind, then immediately, with no discernible movement, you are in another, one that is being generated by some other hand. You are writing analogically, sensing into what you are writing, feeling your way, when suddenly . . .

> *There is a woman sitting on a park bench. She is crying. Her clothes are tattered. She is wearing wool gloves with the finger ends worn through. There is a fluffy wool scarf around her neck. It's purple. The park the woman is sitting in is a winter park. The grass is brown and bare, the trees leafless, the sky faded, a cold blue. By her feet is a brown paper bag, the top rolled over. It is worn looking as if it has been unrolled and rolled again many times. As you watch, a small blue ball, about the size of a tennis ball, rolls to her feet from somewhere to your right, and bumps against one of her shoes. She stops crying and looks up, confused. Her wire rim glasses are fogged. She sniffles and looks around. A small boy runs over, hesitates, then, indicating the ball, slowly walks to her, stoops, and picks it up. He notices as he does so that one leg of her sweat pants is wet with something dark. His eyes round, he steps back, afraid it's blood. At his staring, the woman cries out, picks up the bag, and limps away. Casting quick, nervous, glances around her she turns the corner of the park, and is gone.*

When this happens to you as a writer, you are *in* the scene but not *of* the scene. Yet it's as real as any situation you have ever encountered in your daily world. The colors are as vivid, the sounds as distinct. You can *feel* the breeze; it literally is real. The people move, the scene shifts, things happen. As Gardner says, you wonder what will happen next and then you see what happens next. You observe and if you are a writer you work to write down what you see, hear, and experience as the world you suddenly stepped into unfolds.

While your seeing and perceiving during analogical thinking can approach this kind of clarity, this sudden movement into the imaginal possesses significant differences. You can get a sense of the difference if you think of a photograph of someone taken by a master photographer (or even a very good film of someone), a photograph that seems to come alive as you look at it. Then imagine the actual person standing next to the photograph (or film as it's playing). There is just this kind of living distinction in what is being experienced. And, too, what you are now seeing truly *is* alive. It's not under your control. You are immersed in the scene, can even interact with it in an odd, strange manner (mostly as passive observer), but it's outside your control. Where it's going, you don't know. There's an intelligent direction to it, literally as if you are observing a play directed by someone else. You can't see who is directing it, you can only see the play itself as it unfolds.

Even these descriptions do not do justice to what that incredibly magical moment is like. Gass is right when he says that when we read a writer who has written from this place *in accepting his words we are accepting a vision.*[7] This phenomenon is a specific form of visionary experience, unique to artists.

If you are writing nonfiction, describing an actual scene in which people once interacted, this same sort of living moment can suddenly emerge. It is just as vivid, just as living, just as real. You suddenly know what it was like to be those people, for that conversation to occur. It literally does come alive.

If instead, you are writing about how to build a house or about plant interactions in ecosystems or the dynamics of plumbing, every aspect of the material suddenly comes alive and there is an interactive flow that occurs between all the elements you are perceiving. The plumbing scene you are writing about suddenly unfolds, literally in front of you. The degree of your perception of hidden correspondences and relationships is suddenly enhanced. Exponentially. You literally are in a living scene and the things themselves reveal their natures and their relationships to you. Understandings, insights, other elements of what you are studying, not remotely in your awareness, suddenly emerge, as living entities, into the scene—just as unexpected people emerge in fictional scenes. The book begins to take on its own life, begins to take itself along certain paths that can only be found if you follow where it leads. You, caught up in the wonder of it, write everything down as carefully as you can. Then later, you work to bring that scene alive even more fully, work to deepen it, tease out its implications, help the book to go where it needs to go to be itself.

Writing, as an art form, comes out of these three distinct states of mind: 1) the conscious mind (who later edits what has been written and who actively works to facilitate and support the process of dreaming); 2) the dreaming state that emerges out of feeling the world, synaesthetic perception, and analogical thinking; and 3) this full-breakthrough state.

Most writers spend the majority of their time in the dreaming/analogical thinking state, not the full-breakthrough state; I am not sure how long it is possible to be *in* that breakthrough state, certainly it is not common to be able to stay in it long enough to write a whole book. (There are always exceptions but most of us don't like those people.)

Those full-breakthrough moments seem to be times when the mythic flows directly into the book through the metaphor of the story the book is telling—irrespective of whether it is fictional or nonfictional. These seem designed to shape the book, to take it in certain directions that can only be found through just these moments of mythic intrusion.

Some people seem to have a natural affinity for this full-breakthrough state; they become writers in order to use the thing they are already doing. Perhaps they are natural geniuses at this as Mozart was with music. Stephen King, from comments of his that I've read, seems to have a natural genius for it. I think it is part of the power of his work; you can almost feel this kind of mythic shift resonating throughout his books' images and their language. Most of us, however, learn it more slowly, more similarly to the way I've described it. *Anybody* can do it, it's just that in most of us the capacity is undeveloped. The only way I know to get to the place where you break through into it is to practice the process (or some version of it) that I have outlined here.

These moments of complete breakthrough are, in essence, an experience of living metaphor. The same kind of dreaming that we do at night is in play, full blown. But it is emerging through a *story form* that the conscious mind has predetermined, fiction of some sort, nonfiction of some sort. The imaginal flows into this world through that particular shape. And that shape is a metaphor through which the imaginal, and subsequently the mythic, expresses itself. That is why fiction and nonfiction are, at core, in essence, the same. It's just that the form is slightly different and that difference in form places certain constraints on what you do when you write. It places constraints on how the imaginal presents itself. Whether those constraints are absolute limits or whether the two forms can legitimately blend into one form, actualize the archetype that is underneath all writing irrespective of the form chosen, is something that writers have been exploring a long time.

It beats the hell out of card games.

My experience of this full-breakthrough state, and perhaps it *is* because I am focused primarily on nonfiction, is that these moments occur regularly but not continually. They are more like points of orientation; they keep me on course to the heart of the book. In between those points I write through my analogical thinking and that analogical processing ultimately connects all those points together into one seamless whole. Once that is done, however, the livingness in the book is a great deal more vivid than if those breakthrough moments don't occur. Analogical thinking seems to spread that livingness throughout the book as the points are connected together.

Neverthheless, it should not in any way be inferred from what I am saying that I think analogical thinking is less important than these full-breakthrough states. Most of the writing in any book comes out of analogical thinking; you literally cannot write a book without it. Those breakthrough states, while wonderful and important in their own right, really are like the dreams we dream at night. There's a great deal more in them than we can ever understand, for the whole imaginal realm has come flowing into us and expressed itself through the living dream we just experienced. Unlocking those meanings, or at least as much as we can, is part of what we do later when we work them through with our analogical thinking, as we *compose* the book. Our analogical thinking teases out the implications layered into the breakthrough moments and those implications then flow through the spaces between such points-of-orientation moments.

When we analogically think through those breakthrough moments, we enter into a dialogue with the imaginal, a conversation.

There are, of course, a great many moments in the writing of the book where we don't go this deep, where that full-breakthrough state does not occur. Yet material from the imaginal and mythic realms still leaks into the work sideways. These, more continual, moments lead to the pattern that is hidden in the work, to certain flashes of brilliance in the text, to observations, hidden relationships and correspondences that themselves possess luminescence, and intimations of duende. All of these you later develop through your synaesthetic perceiving as you read what you have written, and then you think them through with your analogical thought.

Most of the writing trance is conducted in just this state of mind and during it, the substance of the mythic world flows into the book in just this sideways fashion. You are thinking with an older part of the self, one that understands that consciousness is not only in here but also out there. You sense from this place the movements of great things.

But from time to time, those great things catch us up in their grasp and take us trembling and awed to the shores of another land. Suddenly, for no apparent reason, the full dreaming state clicks into place. You have moved then into direct, conscious contact with the imaginal world. In that state the mythic flows full force into the work as a living metaphor. But in those moments the writer isn't thinking about the mythic, he's not detached in any way; he's not thinking at all. There is no noticing of anything other than what is being perceived. The writer is caught up in the wonder of the event, seeing and hearing the story for the first time (whether nonfictional or fictional) just as the reader will be in some future time. When you awaken from this state, step once again into your conscious state of mind, there are things on the paper that really have come from someplace else. And they have come directly, while you were watching, rather than sideways as they do during deep analogical thinking.

If you keep practicing the writing process, one day, perhaps when you least expect it, everything will click and there you will be in that moment of balanced, full-dreaming perception. Suddenly, everything you might have heard about that moment will make sense. Suddenly, everything you have sensed about the writers you admire will make sense. Something from some other world really has flowed through them into the work; they really are a bridge between two worlds; their writing really a bridge into something just as real as *this* world seems to be in our daily lives.

SOME SUGGESTIONS

In addition to habituating analogical thinking, there are two other things I can suggest that can help the emergence of the full-breakthrough state. The first is that sometime, when you are deeply engaged in your writing, when you are analogically thinking through your perceiving, while you are in that dreaming state, let that dreaming part of you write whatever it wants to write whether it seems related to your book or not. In that moment of acquiescence you extend trust to this part of yourself. You let it begin to speak in its own voice, however it wants to speak. You give up control and that is of the essence—these full-breakthrough states cannot happen unless you do give up control.

You have practiced all the necessary elements of writing, just as you once practiced all the necessary elements of driving a car. As those elements of driving were internalized as habit, you allowed your unconscious mind to drive the car more and more often. You didn't have to consciously think about the process anymore. This is much like that. Eventually, the unconscious will take over more and more often. But I think there is a further, crucial element to this that is not present while driving a car and it's letting go of control. In this sense it's more similar to landing a plane on a moving aircraft carrier and allowing yourself to completely depend on the flag signals given you by the man on deck. Letting go of control and truly trusting the dreamer to write whatever it wants to is essential.

That trust, again, is highly dependent on the expansion of your sense of reality. It is dependent on your ability to allow the dreamer's world to *be* the world. It is dependent on your not restricting the mythic to the narrow world you have been taught is all that constitutes reality in this place. For as Gass says, "Unless these separate aspects of ourselves and our language speak to one another, respond to one another, there will be no match of the 'thing' to the Form it is said to resemble, no string will stretch from significance to object."[8]

Secondly, I suggest that when you are deep in analogical thinking you allow your experience to extend in a particular direction. And that is the place where analogical thinking becomes a living conversation with the invisibles you have been touching through your perceiving. You will discover, if you do, that you have stepped through a particular doorway and are now in what the Persian storytellers called: "in a certain land, in a certain kingdom." It is a land, a kingdom, to be found on no maps but one that has nevertheless been important to storytellers for centuries. It is sometimes called the imaginal world.

The Persian mystics that Henry Corbin studied said that there was a world Aristotle didn't know of, one where the mythic and the mundane interpenetrated each other. They called it the imaginal world, or as Corbin put it: *the Mundus Imaginalis*. It is the place the human sometimes finds when using the exact sensorial imagination to read the text of the world. There the human can directly interact with the mythic world and the mythic with the human. The imaginal world is the place where the two meet. And storytellers have been weaving what they find there into language ever since storytellers have been.

We use our descriptions of "the visual world," William Gass says, "to remind us about what we saw on our journey to the invisible one."[9] We work as writers to arrive "at those combinations of words which lie nearest the signs made in the soul by the Forms."[10] For, as he says, "These original words come from, and have their home in, the realm of the Forms, for they were sounded in sight of them, as though by a trumpet."[11] That realm of the Forms, as Plato named it (though other Greeks might have called it the realm of the Archi), is the mythic world.

Archi means "the first." They are the primary or first things from which all phemonena come. *Archetype,* the more familiar term, combines *archi* with *type*—meaning "impression," from the Greek "to beat or strike," "to mold." Archetype is the first expression of the archi in form. It means "to prefigure or foreshadow." The archetypes, which reside in the imaginal world, prefigure the forms they become in our world. As those archetypes express themselves, they change. They are modified by where and how they appear.

Every form we see in this world is a modified expression of the archetype that underlies it. The essential identity we recognize as *plant,* for instance, exists as a unique archi in the mythic world. The *archetype* of plant, however, is to be found in the imaginal world. And when that archetype expresses itself into our world, the archetype alters itself to fit the demands of whichever field it grows in. From such alterations, all plant forms come. Luther Burbank, in observing this, said then that "heredity is nothing more than stored environment." Every plant we see is the archetype whose present form has been altered by stored environment. The form a plant takes comes from the demands that environment has made on it and those demands are encoded within its seed as heredity. Goethe's understanding of plant forms came from this same recognition as well.

There is only one plant form, Goethe said, and it's the archetype, or as he called it, the *Urpflanze,* which resides in the imaginal world. All plant forms that we see come from it, expressed in the endless variety that occurs when something extrudes itself from that world into this one. To see this "is a growing aware," as he put it, "of the Form with which again and again nature plays, and, in playing, brings forth manifold life."[12] Or, as Henri Bortoft describes it, "The archetypal plant as an omnipotential form is clearly a different dimension of the plant than what appears in the space time dimension as many plants."[13] When the archetype of plant manifests in this world, he says, "It is inherently dynamical and indefinitely flexible."[14]

The archetype, then, is the first or original pattern or model from which all other forms of it come. Goethe applied this perspective to his writing as well. Not only did he view words as having an archetypal form but also story and myth. For him story and myth existed long before human beings entered the world. This is what the Persian storytellers were talking about when they said, "At one time there was a story and there was no one to tell it," or "At one time there was a story but there was no one to hear it but God."[15] When the archetype of any myth or story then, extrudes itself into this world, the forms they can take, as Bortoft says, are "inherently dynamical and indefinitely flexible." They are as varied as the field in which they take root.

When we write, the themes, stories, and archetypes that express themselves through us alter their form to fit the conditions of our psychological fields just the same way plants do in physical fields. The dreams that flow through us and the mythic elements they contain alter themselves in unique ways as they flow into and through us. That is why the stories that all new writers tell, if the writing is genuine, offer up unique insights, unique treatment of myth, symbol, theme, that can be found no other way. It is the shape of our own field, and how archetypes alter their forms within it, that makes our work unique.

This is what Michael Wood was reaching toward when he said . . .

> *It's not just that all interpretations of a myth are instances of the myth . . . it's that all instances of the myth are interpretations of it, as if they were played from a musical score that everyone knows but no one possesses.*[16]

We have entered, when we enter the imaginal world, the place where the score itself is to be found. As it flows through us we play that music, as all who have found this place before us have done. But as it flows through us, it changes its form to fit the particular shape of our field. The words that come to us in the imaginal world really are sounded, as Gass said, in sight of the Forms. And when we write those words they are filled with substances that come out of the mythic. And whatever those substances are they touch others, as you yourself were once touched by the work of the writers who went this way before you.

The conversation that occurs, that allows you direct access to the imaginal realm, always happens in the same way. You are floating on your raft on the ocean of meaning surrounding you, feeling into the depths with your analogical sensing, fishing, intently attentive to any touches on your line, when suddenly you notice, coming toward you on the surface of the sea, certain Presences. Your analogical thinking has extended itself in a new direction, suddenly the imaginal realm is no longer expressing itself through the metaphor of your book but is conversing with you directly. Suddenly you see the world as it appears through the dreamer's eyes. Suddenly you are in *its* world.

CHAPTER FIFTEEN

The Imaginal Realm

The associative paths are not private to the poet, but are somehow inherent in the universe. An ancient work of art such as The Odyssey *has at its center a long floating leap, around which the poem's images gather themselves like steel shavings around a magnet.*

ROBERT BLY

To anyone who thinks about it carefully, this must at first seem a rather strange statement: "The process by which he works eventually leads him to his goal"—as if the process had some kind of magic in it, some daemonic will of its own. Indeed, some writers—not the least of them Homer—have taken that point of view, speaking without apology of Muses as, in some sense, actual beings, and of "epic song" and "memory" . . . as forces greater than and separate from the poet. We often hear even modern writers speak of their work as somehow outside their control, informed by a spirit that, when they read their writing later, they cannot identify as having come from themselves. I imagine every good writer has had this experience.

JOHN GARDNER

In the magical universe there are no coincidences and there are no accidents.

WILLIAM BURROUGHS

Robert Bly discusses the marvelous Russian tale, "The Maiden King" (or "The Maiden Tsar" in Russian), in his book of the same name. But he comments that, importantly . . .

> *the storyteller does not say exactly where the story takes place: it is occurring "in a certain land, in a certain kingdom." That seems right, because the narrative is happening, one could say, simultaneously in the other world and in this one. A storyteller might say, "Our earth has four continents, and we are going now to the fifth," or "In our planet there are seven oceans; we are going now to the eighth."*[1]

And when storytellers say such a thing, some deep part of us knows that the land we are traveling to is not in this world but in the invisible one. Those words awaken the dreamer inside us. They serve notice that we are going to be traveling into the imaginal world, a place where time is not linear, where everything is more than it seems.

So, when, in the foreword to *Night Shift,* Stephen King says . . .

> *Where I am, it's still dark and raining. We've got a fine night for it. There's something I want to show you, something I want you to touch. It's in a room not far from here—in fact, it's as close as the next page. Shall we go?*[2]

. . . he initiates the same shift. There's a part of us that knows that other world, a part of us that lives partially within it. And there are opening movements in all story forms that serve notice to the dreamer inside us that we are leaving this world now and traveling to another.

> *I remember the day a name changed my life.*

In that moment, the dreamer and the truth receiver inside us begin to reach out toward substances that can only be found in the kind of stories that come directly out of the imaginal. The dreamer inside us begins to reach for the mythic.

Now, in *The Maiden King,* as Bly says, by the time the story begins, the usual kinds of things that happen in these kinds of stories have already happened. Ivan—the boy who is at the heart of the story—has a mother who has died (as mothers in fairy tales often do) and after a while, the father hires a tutor to watch over the boy while the father is working. Of course, we know from the moment we hear that, that odd things, troubles perhaps, are going to come from it. And indeed, one day, they do.

The tutor has taken Ivan fishing on a small raft out at sea . . .

> *The father apparently has wisely asked the tutor to teach the boy how to fish. We each need to know how to "fish." Psychologically, fishing amounts to an inquisitiveness about the "treasures of the deep." We float in broad daylight, on our well-constructed, rationally engineered raft or boat, looking down into the cloudy waters—inhabited by God knows what—the same waters each dreamer fishes in at night. Teaching people how to fish is a just aim in education. We are fishing right now.*
>
> *Fishing is a kind of daydreaming in daylight, a longing for what is below. There are many mysteries down there in those waters over which these two dwarfed, half-abandoned people drift. I suppose we could say that as we brood over the story, we are fishing in that eighth ocean mentioned earlier. . . . Novelists are fisherpeople; so are poets and psychologists. . . . Painters are always going on fishing expeditions. Chagall was amazed at what he saw in the waters beneath his little Russian village, and he spent his life bringing those violinists and horses and brides up to the surface.*
>
> *Sometimes what we discover when fishing is a Presence. An event like that is about to happen to Ivan in our story. The boy and the tutor are looking down into the sea, one might say, for the Presence that swims about in the murky world below the surface of things; and all at once the Presence arrives on the surface of the ocean, coming in from the horizon, seemingly belonging to the sea itself.*[3]

The breakthrough state that happens every so often when you are immersed in analogical thinking, is just like that. You are fishing, concentrating on the depths, feeling for touches on your line, and all at once you find yourself someplace else, inside a living scene that you are watching unfold in front of you. But that breakthrough moment can occur differently. Sometimes you will find yourself in a place where you are not experiencing the imaginal world through the metaphor of your story form, but instead find yourself experiencing it directly. It happens like this . . . rather than focusing your analogical thinking on the depths, feeling for touches on your line, for some reason (no one knows why) one day you look up and out at the world around you *through* your analogical perceiving. And sometimes, if you are deep enough in the dreaming, of a sudden everything clicks—that phase change occurs, but it does so in a special way—and you find yourself *in* the imaginal world, surrounded by Presences who are no longer in the deeps but who are now on the surface of the ocean, coming toward you from the horizon.

The imaginal world is the place we find when we, having followed our golden threads, unsuspectingly step *through* what Blake called Heaven's gate built in Jerusalem's wall. As Henry Corbin says, "One sets out; at a given moment, there is a break with the geographical coordinates that can be located on our maps. But the 'traveler' is not conscious of the precise moment; he does not realize it," does not notice it happening, he just suddenly finds himself arrived.[4]

That describes it perfectly. While you are following a golden thread through your synaesthetic perceiving, as you concentrate more and more fully on the descriptive process, an inertia builds up, and then, when your focus is someplace else entirely, you suddenly end up taking a long floating leap and land someplace completely different, in the imaginal world itself, in the place from which all golden threads come and in which all duende has its roots. And the shock of landing in this new terrain causes us to look up and see the world around us using a very different kind of cognition.

Analogical thinking is now turned as a general mode of perception onto the world itself. Rather than working with specifics, headed toward a goal, you just perceive everything around you through that state. Generally, you are so deep in the experience of dreaming that you don't notice this is what has happened. You just, all of a sudden, break through into an entirely different state of mind. Caught up in the momentum of your writing you reach a chasm and not even knowing it is there you take a long floating leap and land in some new territory. And when you look up from that shock of landing you notice that everything is alive, everything is aware, and everything is interacting with everything else. In the imaginal world, as Rilke said, there is no place that is not looking at you.

Literally, not metaphorically, in that territory *everything* is alive and aware and interacting. Everything has personality, depth, three-dimensionality. The feeling dimension of things is exquisitely perceivable, the whole world throbs, pulsates, with it. The mythic is encountered now, not as some abstract concept in scholarly books, but as a living, breathing reality. Archetype, theme, story, even the symbolic layer that runs through all things, are alive as people are alive. Each expression of them that you encounter possesses its own unique personality just as every person, while recognizable in general as a person, has a unique personality. Each archetype, theme, instance of symbol, like each person, is a unique variation on a core identity. And they are interactive as people are interactive. You don't control them, don't even engage in abstract analysis of what they are. You experience them directly as living, breathing entities. They possess movement, intention, direction.

There is a feeling, strongly present, that you have entered a world a great deal older than the human, a world out of which the human was expressed long ago. And as you travel through this realm you become aware of the movements of great things throughout it and from it into your experience. The imaginal world sends you living experiential realities, concrete universals. They begin to flow into your work of their own accord. (And, as Wallace Stegner observed, the writer and his words then become a lens through which the reader sees, and experiences, those realities.) And you, the writer, never will know the full meaning of those things that have, through this meeting, entered your work. You can *feel* the reality of them, sense their importance, even understand some of their unique aspects, but they come from someplace else, someplace older, more ancient, and a great deal deeper than the human. They are forever beyond a complete understanding. You enter this place and by its very nature you can only be a student, a partaker, a sharer in the mystery of being. You understand in this place what Frank Herbert meant when he said that *The mystery of life isn't a problem to solve but a reality to experience.*

And that reality is a conversation as much as anything else. As Robert Frost said, *These are not monologues but my part in a conversation.*[5] Everything you encounter now is a direct, living expression (in the imaginal realm) of the mythic. And you find yourself, naturally, in an interactive communication with it. Sometimes that conversation will just, seemingly magically, shape itself into written form while you are immersed in the living, pulsating imaginal world. Theodore Roethke described such an experience this way . . .

> *Suddenly, in the early evening, the poem "The Dance" started, and finished itself in a very short time—say thirty minutes it was all done. I felt, I knew, I had hit it. I walked around and I wept; and I knelt down—I always do after I've written what I know is a good piece. But at the same time I had, as God is my witness, the actual sense of a Presence—as if Yeats himself were in that room. The house was charged with a psychic presence: the very walls seemed to shimmer. I wept for joy.*[6]

What a wonderful description of how it feels. The room you are writing in, the world itself, becomes charged with a psychic presence, with Presences, the very walls shimmer with them. During such moments, you understand in your experience the state of being that Euripides and Aeschylus engaged as part of their craft. You understand, in your experience, the world they entered and from which they gathered their perceptual descriptions.

And what is communicated to you, to any writer who enters this realm, *always* has a great deal to do with what you are writing, the particular story you are telling at the moment you enter the imaginal. What is communicated is a *commentary* on that story from the depths of the mythic world. You have suddenly entered a place where the mythic begins directly shaping what you are writing. And when you let that commentary flow into the book, that is when *poesis* occurs—the Making that can only occur when the imaginal has been directly accessed. It is at that moment that what you are writing begins to *become* myth itself.

Samuel Delany was describing aspects of this experience in the following portion of his Author's Journal, in Venice, in October 1965, which he included as epigrammatic material in his novel *The Einstein Intersection*. (TEI is short for that title, Lobey is the protagonist.)

> *Each night for a week I have lingered on the wild flags of the waterfront, palaces crowding to the left, brittle lights crackling over the*

harbor in the warm autumn. TEI goes strangely. Tonight when I turned back into the great trapezoid of the Piazza, fog hid the tops of the red flagpoles. I sat on the base of one nearest the tower and made notes on Lobey's hungers. Later I left the decaying gold and indigo of the Basilica and wandered through the back alleys of the city till well after midnight. Once I stopped on a bridge to watch the small canal drift through the close walls beneath the nightlamps and clotheslines. At a sudden shrieking I whirled: half a dozen wailing cats hurled themselves about my feet and fled after a brown rat. Chills snarled the nerves along my vertebrae. I looked back at the water: six flowers—roses—floated from beneath the bridge, crawling over the oil. I watched them till a motorboat puttering on some larger waterway nearby sent water slapping the foundations. I made my way over the small bridges to the Grand Canal and caught the Vaporetto back to Ferovia. It turned windy as we floated beneath the black wood arch of the Ponti Academia; I was trying to assimilate the flowers, the vicious animals, with Lobey's adventure—each applies, but as yet I don't quite know how. Orion straddled the water. Lights from the shore shook in the canal as we passed beneath the dripping stones of the Rialto.[7]

Immersed in analogical thinking, the boundaries between the imaginal and your daily reality suddenly thin, turn to smoke, fade away. You take a step you didn't even realize was there. The outer world and the inner join together, the mythic begins to flow in. John Dunning speaks of it this way (Rigby is a character in his book):

At the end of my universe is a door, which opens into Rigby's universe. Either side must seem endless to a wayward traveler, who can only guess which is the spin-off of the other.[8]

At such a moment, the mythic begins to flow through you and into the book that you are writing, infusing it with its fragrances. The book suddenly becomes an extension of the mythic world, becomes the mythic itself held for a moment in time in this form that is coming into being. We have immersed ourselves in the waters of what Stephen King has called *that myth pool in which we all must bathe.* And when we write our books those mythic waters flow into our work, into our words. Something more than the merely human is involved.

A doorway has opened and the whole aware universe has come flooding in. You find yourself no longer isolated in your own House.

Francis Spufford captures some of this experience, this sudden phase change in perception, from a reader's point of view, when, in his book *The Child That Books Built* (London: Faber, 2002), he says . . .

> *I learned to read around my sixth birthday. I was making a dinosaur in school from crepe bandage and toilet rolls when I started to feel as if an invisible pump was inflating my head from the inside. My face became a cluster of bumps on a taut sphere, my feet receded and turned into dangling limpnesses too far away to control. The teacher carried me home on her shoulders. I gripped the dinosaur in one hand. It was still wet with green and purple poster paint. After that things turned delirious. I had mumps. . . . When I caught the mumps I couldn't read; when I went back to school again, I could. The first page of* The Hobbit *was a thicket of symbols, to be decoded one at a time and joined hesitantly together. . . . By the time I reached* The Hobbit*'s last page, though, writing had softened, and lost the outlines of the printed alphabet, and become a transparent liquid, first viscous and sluggish, like a jelly of meaning, then ever thinner and more mobile, flowing faster and faster until it reached me at the speed of thinking and I could not entirely distinguish the suggestions it was making from my own thoughts. I had undergone the acceleration into the written word that you also experience as a change in the medium. In fact, writing had ceased to be a thing—an object in the world—and* become *a medium, a substance you look through.*[9]

During movement into the imaginal, you experience a change in medium that is equivalent. The world that you are looking at is no longer a world of form but has instead become a living story filled with the mythic. At first, as in Francis Spufford's experience, what you are seeing is just a thicket of forms, symbols in Spufford's sense of the term, slowly decoded, one at a time. But as you move more deeply into analogical thinking, those textual forms soften, become a transparent liquid, first viscous and sluggish, like a jelly of meaning, then ever thinner and more mobile, flowing faster and faster until, suddenly, you shift, and they are alive as you are alive, their interactive, communicatory expressions flowing toward you at the speed of thinking, until you cannot entirely distinguish the communications they are making from your own thoughts, so quickly do they move inside and become integrated by you.

In that moment the dreamer, that deep part of the unconscious, becomes conscious. You literally look out at the world through the dreamer's eyes. Or, perhaps it is more accurate to say that the dreamer awakens fully and looks at its world through your eyes. And you, standing to the side, look along with it. You see in the imaginal realm what the dreamer always sees, whether you are aware of its perceptions or not. It is this imaginal world that flows into you when you dream at night but in this moment of heightened perception you are literally seeing the world that lies inside and behind your dreams. This is the place that Rilke often wrote of, and Baudelaire, and Goethe, and Corbin. In this place you are the *observed,* not just the observer.

Once we enter this place, we begin to think not just analogically, but mythically. We immerse ourselves in the myth pool that Stephen King speaks of, the dark waters of duende cover us, black sounds reverberate, and imagination itself becomes a form of perception, of cognition, of understanding.

Once in this state, the statistical mentality is no longer active. As Corbin describes it, the *agnostic* impulse—the disbelief in invisibles—that has been inculcated since birth in the Western mind shuts off. You are not just analogically thinking in that moment but literally experiencing the mythic dimensions of the universe as a living, interactive reality. You are aware of the Presences that inhabit that mythic landscape, become aware of the Forms themselves as they express themselves in the imaginal. And they, of their own accord, begin to tell you how to shape your book. They do this, not in words, but through an apprehension of meaning that can only occur through your analogical perceiving. As Corbin puts it, Imaginative consciousness has been activated. Meaning begins to flow into you directly, a *communication* occurs. The thought of the Presences—*their* thought—begins to shape the forms inside your book. Delany comments further . . .

This morning I took refuge from the thin rain in a teahouse with the dock workers. Yellow clouds moiled outside above the Bosphorus. Found one man who spoke French, two others who spoke Greek. We talked of voyages and warmed our fingers on glasses of tea. Between the four of us we had girdled the globe. The radio over the stove alternated repetitive Turkish modulations with Aznavour and the Beatles. Lobey starts the last leg of his journey. I cannot follow him here. When the rain stopped, I walked through the waterfront fish market where the silver fish had their gills pulled out and looped over their jaws so that each head was crowned with a bloody flower. A street of wooden houses wound up the hill into the city. A fire had recently raged here. Few houses had actually burned down, but high slabs of glittering carbon leaned over the cobbles where the children played with an orange peel in the mud. I watched some others chase a red headed boy. His face was wet; he tripped in the mud, then fled before me. The heels had been trod down on his shoes. Perhaps on rewriting I shall change Kid Death's hair from black to red.[10]

When we shift into this last and most complete state of dreaming, we fully enter a distinct and real place, a world that somewhere deep inside us, we recognize. It is a place to which some part of us belongs, for we, ourselves, come from an archetype that has expressed itself in multiple forms over long evolutionary time, forms shaped by the fields in which they have grown. When we reenter the imaginal world, we touch that archetype once again, begin to interact with other archetypes, begin to remember that place from which we once came and which still resides deep inside our species memories.

Corbin asserts that "In offering the two Latin words *mundus imaginalis* I intend to treat a precise order of reality corresponding to a precise mode of perception."[11] That is, when analogical thinking reaches a certain depth and is then directed in a certain direction a unique and precise mode of perception is initiated of its own accord. At that moment a precise order of reality is perceivable in which everything you meet has an intelligent individuality. As Corbin says, "'The pronoun best used when describing the specifics of this dimension is not 'what' but 'who.'"[12]

In this heightened state of perception you directly perceive, through both your feeling and visual sensing, the living mythic world that underlies the world of form. You have extended sense perception from nonphysical touching, from feeling, deep into the world itself, into the mythic repository that the Earth is. And it is a living experience. That mythic world is as alive now as it was when Homer was alive. And when you are in that state of perception certain things, of their own accord, present themselves to your gaze. There is some living thread that connects them all to the myth your book is becoming. And you know it. You know it at a level too deep for words. Rilke poignantly captures this shifted and distinctly different perceiving in his book *The Notebooks of Malte Laurids Brigge . . .*

> *Have I said it before? I am learning to see. Yes, I am beginning. It still goes badly. But I intend to make the most of my time.*
>
> *To think for instance, that I have never been aware before how many faces there are. There are quantities of human beings, but there are many more faces, for each person has several. There are people who wear the same face for years; naturally it wears out, it gets dirty, it splits at the folds, it stretches, like gloves one has worn on a journey. These are thrifty, simple people; they do not change their face, they never even have it cleaned. It is good enough, they say, and who can prove them the contrary? The question of course arises, since they have several faces, what do they do with the others? They store them up. Their children will wear them. But sometimes, too, it happens that their dogs go out with them on. And why not? A face is a face.*
>
> *Other people put their faces on, one after the other, with uncanny rapidity and wear them out. At first it seems to them they are provided for always; but they scarcely reach forty—and they have come to the last. This naturally has something tragic. They are not accustomed to taking care of faces, their last is worn through in a week, has holes, and in many places is thin as paper; and then little by little the under layer, the no-face, comes through, and they go about with that.*
>
> *But the woman; she had completely collapsed into herself, forward into her hands. It was at the corner of rue Notre-Dame-des-Champs. I began to walk softly as soon as I saw her. When poor people are reflecting they should not be disturbed. Perhaps their idea will yet occur to them.*

> *The street was too empty; its emptiness was bored; it caught my step from under my feet and clattered about with it hither and yon, as with a wooden clog. The woman startled and pulled away too quickly out of herself, too violently, so that her face remained in her two hands. I could see it lying in them, its hollow form. It cost me indescribable effort to stay with those hands and not to look at what had torn itself out of them. I shuddered to see a face from the inside, but still I was much more afraid of the naked flayed head without a face.*[13]

In the imaginal world there is always a sense of awe, that unique emotion composed equally of fear and joyful wonder. There is always some deep darkness, the dark water that Lorca spoke of, a water that gathers its darkness from the mere fact of its depth. And there is always what Lorca called black sounds, sounds whose darkness comes from their depths as well. Without this, as Lorca says, there can be no duende.

> *These "black sounds" are the mystery, the roots fastened in the mire that we all know and all ignore, the fertile silt that gives us the very substance of art.*[14]

And "behind those black sounds," he says, "tenderly and intimately, live zephyrs, ants, volcanoes, and the huge night straining its waist against the Milky Way."[15]

When we enter the imaginal world, begin interacting with the mythic directly, we feel Lorca's dark water upon us, hear those black sounds. We feel them flow through us, into us, and into our work. We feel the living thread of connection between the imaginal realm and the writing. The images inside the writing and the imaginal beings we encounter connect and some kind of powerful life force flows from them into the images we are writing. And those images come alive, not only through the activation of the feeling sense, they come alive in a mythic sense. Something from another world is alive inside them now.

This is the place that people sense writers have access to. It is why, even in the midst of our culture's abandonment of the imaginal, writers are still revered. And our job as writers is to enter the imaginal, to immerse ourselves in dark, mythic waters, and then to let those waters flow through us onto the page. This is the ancient work that we have taken on, to travel to the imaginal realm and write accounts of what we find there. In that imaginal world the dreamer inside us steps forward and the conscious mind stands aside and lets the dreamer look through our eyes. We look along with it and begin then to move into and through a forest of living symbols, into a context of interactive texts. We begin to understand, in our experience, what Gass was talking about . . .

> *The dark horse is stabled in the child. So . . . the author who is satisfied to* see *his words, as though at a distance like sheep on a hillside, and not as concepts coasting like clouds across his consciousness; such a writer will never enter, touch, or move the soul; never fill us with the feeling that he's seen the Forms, whether or not there are any; never give us that ride up the hill of Heaven as Plato has, or the sense that in accepting his words we are accepting a vision.*[16]

The fear that writers have as they face the page comes not only from the inevitable and necessary unconcealment of the deep self. There is also a fear of what the journey itself will entail. If you truly are committed, once you sit down in front of the blank page you initiate a process that will unmake you. There is not a writer alive that has not found that when they write their entire personality moves through a process of destructuring and then a later restructuring. We enter mythic realms. Something from out there flows into and through us and it has impacts on us when it does. It alters the nature of our psychological structure. It alters how we see ourselves and how we see the world in which we live. And it allows the *out there* to come *in here*. We, for a time, allow something more ancient than the human to take up residence inside us.

We let the mythic flow into us and it shapes us as much as it shapes the writing the dreamer is doing. We are *dreaming*. And the part of us that dreams is a great deal deeper in the structure of the self than the conscious mind. It is at the root of us, the core, and perhaps it is even deeper than that. Because all things dream it may be that the dreamer transcends the human entirely, that it underlies our species form itself. It may be that, as many have said, we are only part of the dreaming of the world. If so, dreaming underlies us and is more fundamental to us than our psychological selves. When the mythic flows into us, the power of it flows not only through the core of us but perhaps through our species form itself. However deep in us it begins, it percolates upward impacting everything that is layered on top of it. And this *disturbs* things. It affects the balance of our interior world. We begin to *change.* We bring *up into consciousness connections that have been forgotten, perhaps for centuries.*

The great dreams that become written works, such as Tolkien's *Lord of the Rings* (as Peter Beagle once observed), already exist whole and complete in that imaginal realm; writers such as Tolkien struggle in their work to write down something that already has a real existence in that other place. That is what all of us do. The books we write are living things; they have their habitation in the imaginal world. They have a living shape that we must find. To do so, we must follow them home to where they live, personally locate their habitation in the imaginal realm. It is the only way the shape that they must take in our world can be brought into being.

We *know* because we have felt it that our book has its real life, its living origin, in that other world—our writing can only bring forth a shadow of it. And we try, as best we can, within the limits of our skill, talent, and practice to make the book that takes root in our field as alive and real as the true one, so that together they achieve a unity of form, until the one we have written shimmers with the mythic substance of the true book we have at last experienced. Every golden thread, every shivering moment of duende that we capture in our writing comes from that true book that lives in the imaginal world.

When we, through our exquisitely trained and educated facility to *feel,* bring the mythic, living, and true book into form, we engage in *poesis,* the Making. The ancient Greeks meant by *poesis* the writerly shaping of a unique, living text that has its real existence in the imaginal world. It is then that a singular piece of art emerges that has within its depths aisthesis, a conversation with the imaginal, filled with ensouled exchange. It contains a true aesthetic dimension. We immerse ourselves in our craft, working to shape what we are perceiving into a form. Eventually, one day we understand that we are not only the shaper, but the shaped.

CHAPTER SIXTEEN

Poesis

The written word comes forward as the completion of a process, not as the process itself. It quietly omits the context of composition, of discovery. It admits no doubts, no alterations, no unmeant obscurities. A field of rejected alternatives lies invisibly around the chosen word or phrase like dead around the boy who still holds the standard, but we don't realize a battle has taken place; that blood has been shed, ideas denied, feelings changed, accidents allowed to stand; no, the completed sentence stretches itself out in the sun with ease and assurance: its figure is full, even fulsome; it already has a tan. And when many completed sentences lie together to form a treatise or a novel whose composition took many years, and went on in spite of illness, through love affairs, bankruptcy, and divorce, they*—these sentences—will still pretend that the same author authored all of them.*

William Gass

There was a vague assumption that the stories had just come. All I did was write them down. It was weird. I sweated blood over the damn things. Seventeen years later my novel A Disaffection *was shortlisted for prizes and a member of an adjudicating panel asked if I ever revised "or did it just come out?" It jist comes oot, ah says, it's the natchril rithm o the working klass, ah jist opens ma mooth and oot it comes.*

James Kelman

> *Mark Twain, saddled with a cast of characters selected by Henry James, would be quick to maneuver them all into wells.*
>
> John Gardner

Some of the things I have shared about the writing process—synaesthetic perceiving, analogical thinking, dreaming, the breakthrough state—may make it seem that writing is easy if only you can learn to habituate these skills. It isn't. The doing of it must still occur, the shaping must still take place. You must still get all the raw pieces on the pages, then transform them into something whole and complete, a book through which a living thread flows from beginning to end, a book in which the imaginal lives and expresses itself.

The book must become whole, something throughout which you feel an imaginal unity and in which, to the best of your ability, is condensed the diluted luminescence that runs throughout the book, condensed into the flash of a single sentence. Over and over again. The book must still be *composed.*

First you have to get it in raw form, then you must shape it into a coherent, layered, luminous, and living work.

We have something that drives us to do this. Some reason that we decided to be writers to begin with. Some reason we end up writing this book and not that. There is some soul destiny in us being writers and in every book we write. For every book we write is an exploratory journey into the real, into the invisibles that lie behind and inside the world of form, into the imaginal. We actively explore that world through our analogical thinking. And every journey into the real teaches us something about the world in which we live, something about ourselves that we can learn no other way. *Something* drives us on and we are so bullheaded we refuse to quit. We insist on making the journey, a journey that many begin but few finish. There are a great many gifted writers, more gifted than any you have read, who began this process and then decided it was too much trouble, too painful. So, they did something else with their lives, something easier. But those of us who are willing to become desert taking on human form, faces a craggy expression of stone and sand and sun, of silent places and wilderness, of the battering that all writers suffer if they don't quit, we remain bullheaded, we insist on The Making, on poesis.

So we weave the imaginal into our work in all the ways and through all the forms that we know: our sense of feeling, the golden threads we encounter, moments of duende, the sudden unfolding of scene, and those moments of breakthrough into the imaginal itself. And we open ourselves to the process so that the imaginal can weave itself into the work in its sideways ways when we are not looking. Throughout all this, some part of us deep inside constantly feels into the writing to determine its rightness, feels into the book as a whole to determine *its* rightness; we continually seek the form it must become to be itself, and we keep at it until it does.

To do this, as your skill develops, you literally have to read and feel *every* line and *every* word in a work. You have to take it *all* in. When you finally get to the point of tiny refinements, when you are at the point of working for perfection, you have to be *inside* every word, feeling how it feels as you write it and as you read it. You can't let your mind skip over any of the words you have written, each one has to be *inhabited* by you as you read it back to yourself. That is why the writing is so often slow and difficult—you drop down inside this word, feel how it feels, adjust it if necessary. Then do the same thing with the next one, and the next one, and the next one. Eventually you look at the whole sentence; you read it back to yourself and feel how it feels as a whole. Then adjust it if necessary. Then the paragraph, one slow feeling step at a time. Then you look at the patterns in the book, the flow of subconcepts and symbols, of theme, and do the same thing with them. This is what it means to *compose* in language.

The meanings that flow through a book are composed just as a symphony is composed. The meanings hidden behind words and the musical meanings hidden behind notes are equivalents. The words, in their composed form, are a score for meaning, just as a musical score is a score for meaning—the emotional meanings that are underneath and within particular kinds of sound. To write nonfiction as art you must move from writing that is a discourse generated by the statistical mentality to the composing of meaning through the delicate interweaving of your synaesthetic perceptions of the world and the complex living meanings that words are the containers for.

So, we work at our craft, work to shape the imaginal that is flowing into us into a coherent form, work to make it art. And as we do, one day, during our shaping, we suddenly find that we are not only the shaper but the shaped. This writing we do, it's not a one-sided process. Theodore Sturgeon comments on that this way . . .

> *The shaping of a bonsai is therefore always a compromise and always a cooperation. A man cannot create bonsai, nor can a tree; it takes both, and they must understand each other. It takes a long time to do that. One memorizes one's bonsai, every twig, the angle of every crevice and needle, and, lying awake at night or in a pause a thousand miles away, one recalls this or that line or mass, one makes one's plans. With wire and water and light, with tilting and with planting of water-robbing weeds or heavy root-shading ground cover, one explains to the tree what one wants, and if the explanation is well enough made, and there is great enough understanding, the tree will respond and obey—almost. Always there will be its own self-respecting, highly individual variation:* Very well I shall do what you want, but I will do it *my* way. *And for these variations, the tree is always willing to present a clear and logical explanation, and more often than not (almost smiling) it will make clear to the man that he could have avoided it if his understanding had been better. It is the slowest sculpture in the world, and there is, at times, doubt as to which is being sculpted, man or tree.*[1]

With everything an artisan attempts to shape the process is the same, whether a living tree or a piece of wood or these things we hold in our hands that we call books. The books we write are like bonsai, they are living beings, and they respond to our shaping just as bonsai do.

We sit down to write and find our book insisting back. We push here, try tying it there, try to force it away from the sun or toward the light so that we can achieve a certain outcome. The book resists, insisting on its own direction. We fight it and suddenly find ourselves in the fierce psychological battle that writing is. We hit the wall. The writing life suddenly becomes very difficult. Days of struggle ensue. We keep insisting, hammering at it over and over again. And slowly, usually with much resistance, we begin to hear what the living book is telling us. We begin to let go of our certainties. Begin to listen more carefully. And suddenly, letting go of our human exceptionalism, we truly begin to hear what we are being told. We engage in a living conversation—we no longer insist on only our own voice being heard. In consequence we are taken places we never would have found on our own.

We find where we are going by going there one slow step at a time. And many of our steps are those that the book itself insists must be taken.

The words we write come from some place in the depths of us, from some region of being that we can only catch glimpses of from time to time. Those that read our words, and make them their own, find through those words passage into those same depths . . . in themselves. Those passages follow them home and they, in turn, give rise to other lines, sentences, feelings and thoughts of significance, which are then written or spoken and which then lodge within still others. We become part of a conversation that knows no geographical or temporal boundaries, the meanings passing from one of us to another in a great relay race of soul. All writers of the past were part of that relay race (they still are). We become a part of it in our lifetimes and so will others who come, sometimes long years, after us. The book as myth comes into being as we work. And we serve that process to the extent of our capacity to do so. The myth that our book is, if we have done our work well, will continue to speak to those who encounter it, no matter the geography or time in which they live.

Writing that is merely a human being forcing words into a certain shape without regard for their feelings on the matter is not, and never can be, art. You begin to understand, as the process of creation goes on, that what you are doing is a co-creative act between yourself and something that is outside of you. You learn how to sing a song that is always sung between the writer and the living meanings that infuse this world, between the writer and the archetypes that live in the imaginal world, and the Forms that are, ultimately, behind that world. You engage in a harmony where the voice of the human and the other-than-human join together, and where something more than either comes into being.

You must, in a very real sense, steal this art. You must make it your own. You must take it inside you, eat it as you would a food, and let it inform your muscle and sinew as it becomes part of you.

If you read a poem you love out loud a hundred times, becoming subsumed into its rhythms and meanings, after a time, the poem becomes *yours* no matter who wrote it or when. You understand the meaning of it as if it were your own breath, your own flesh and blood. It flows through you and the unique life that is yours shapes it as it emerges from you into the world.

You must make this art your own and then shape it for *your* ends in order to fulfill the soul destiny that awaits you, the destiny that has driven you to write from the moment of your birth.

All writers, then, must learn to play, for it is in playing that such shaping occurs. (And it is in playing that our joy in the word emerges as a unique form of vitality in the work.) Writers play with lengthening the sentence or shortening it to find out what effect that will have. They use long words and short, to see what effect it will have. Someone tells them that real writing does not use clichés and so they write an entire short story using only clichés . . . to see if it can be done. Those same forensic speakers say that readers cannot understand big words so they write a whole book, a complex multisyllabic composition, and find there actually are readers for it. They press the form, always, to see what it can do. But under all that playing is the drive to bring a particular kind of meaning into the world. This playing with form is only a part of the refinement of the craft, the equivalent of playing scales on a guitar or piano. There comes a day when the fingers are limber, the scales integrated at the deepest level of being, the capacity to dream at will is ingrained, and then the whole focus of being, mind, will, and soul turns to the work and what they have made theirs, what they have stolen because they knew on some deep, primal level it was *theirs* already. They take it and turn it into a communication that must be and truly does belong in the world. And one day, soon after, they will suddenly catch a glimpse of themselves in a mirror or the plateglass window of a storefront and realize that they are no longer that young man or woman who set out so long ago to be a writer, too. They have learned to shape and they, often without their knowing, have also been shaped. They have become something much more than they were.

You will not be the same at the end of this journey as you were when you began. I wonder sometimes if that is not the hidden wisdom in the word *poesis*. The ancient Greeks called certain people poets because they shaped the imaginal into form, made poetry of it. But I think those ancient Greeks understood as well that in the process, poesis was also practiced upon the poet by the mythic during their sojourns in the imaginal realm, that the human engaged in poesis becomes, as a result, a unique kind of condensed meaning themself. In some way a part of that imaginal world, and the mythic the human meets there, now lives inside them. And by using the word *poet* those ancient Greeks were recognizing that the writer is shaped as much as they shape. They are someone who has been shaped by the movements of the gods, they have become, through the shedding of their skin, poetry themselves.

On Technique
The First Draft, Revision, Clarity, and Refinement

Once more, an urgent truth lies in a text. But no one has told us that it is there, much less that finding it is of paramount importance. Morever, even if we have somehow turned to the correct page and are looking right at the message, there is no certainty that we will recognize it as a cipher, for it is written in language that, on the surface, looks exactly like everything else in the text. The only signal of a challenge, the only factor distinguishing it from the thousand readers who have examined the passage before us and found nothing, is a vague sense of disquiet: a sense either that there is something curiously "wrong" with the text or that there is something strangely wonderful about it. The only way to reduce this subtle code is by looking at language with new eyes, by radically reinterpreting what seem to be common and obvious verbal structures. And such a reinterpretation is impossible unless we are able, at least temporarily, to transcend our personal assumptions about language itself.

Robert Grudin

Just as the swimmer does not have a succession of handholds hidden in the water, but instead simply sweeps that yielding medium and finds it hurrying him along, so the writer passes his attention through what is at hand, and is propelled by a medium too thin and all-pervasive for the perceptions of nonbelievers who try to stay on the bank and fathom his accomplishment.

William Stafford

[To a critical reader]: "Where were you when the page was blank?"

John Dunning

CHAPTER SEVENTEEN

The First Draft and the Beginnings of Revision

[Perfectionism] is the main obstacle between you and a shitty first draft. . . . [It] will ruin your writing, blocking inventiveness and playfulness and life force. . . . Perfectionism means that you try desperately not to leave so much mess to clean up. But clutter and mess show us that life is being lived. Clutter is wonderfully fertile ground.

ANNE LAMOTT

I worked out a plan, did my best with it, revised it, and finally discarded it. I worked out another, and then others after that, and by muddling along, sometimes reclaiming an element or two from a scrapped approach, I finally came up with something that would do. . . . Writing . . . is like heading out over the open sea in a small boat. If you have a plan and a course laid out, that's helpful. If you drift off course, checking the stars can help you find a new course. . . . [But] sooner or later confusion will **make** *you check the stars.*

JOHN GARDNER

The craftsman works, looking and looking again, from one revelation to another—often by way of mistakes, listening to the material, coming upon unexpected signals.

JAMES KRENOV

> *Many random movements are more apt than a few to contain the right movement . . . from quantity, quality.*
>
> Robert Frost

Sooner or later it will be time to begin writing your book. Like every author you will eventually have to sit down and face the blank page. Most of us face that page similarly: We build up a powerful reservoir of emotion, in whatever way we've found works for us, then we sit down and begin to throw snowballs at the wall to see what sticks. Some of those snowballs do stick—some shatter in a flurry of powder, most of which falls to the ground, some miss the wall entirely. That's how all first drafts start.

These snowballs? They are created out of the core of us, the deepest parts of who we are. They are filled with the energy of our passions and beliefs and the meanings we hold deepest in our secret selves. We are, in this initial creating, getting some of those deep meanings onto the page so we will have something to work with, some place of beginning. We use the built-up energy to get us over the resting state we're in, to get the ball rolling—and, of course, to create enough energy to get us through our fear.

In that tiny, shivering moment of beginning, when I sit down and begin to type the first trembling words of a new book, every time, I, like most writers, am afraid. For when we pull those meanings up from inside ourselves, we reveal who we are. Writing (all art) *reveals* in a way that nothing else you do ever will. And some deep part in every writer and hope-to-be writer knows it. Every time we write, some new part of our self is exposed. We take the deepest parts of ourselves, our hopes and our dreams, our loves and our hates, everything that makes us who we are, the fabric of our lives, our *individuality,* and we put it into the work. We weave it into the writing and stand revealed inside those words. For the work to be good, we *must* be revealed in this way. Of all that we have to offer, the only thing unique about us is who we genuinely are—in the depths of us. To the parts of ourselves who wish to remain hidden nothing is more terrifying than such undefendedness, such unconcealment, such revelation. And, too, there is the fear that comes from opening ourselves to the mythic, to the moment when we begin to let what is *out there* move *in here.* For that act of intentional dreaming changes us; we leave the known boundaries of our cultural and psychological world. We allow our psychological boundaries to go fluid. We turn our back to land and enter deep waters—and we never know what we'll find when we do. It is a certainty, however, that we will not be the same person coming out that we were going in.

There is not a one of us who writes that does not understand the fear that comes from these things. You can get away from it by writing superficial or overly mental crap. (But the work will show it.) You can get used to the writing process, come to love what writing is, and so have some other experience to balance out the fear. You can gain so much recognition and money that your success acts as a counterweight. But every true writer that sits down in front of the blank page trembles at what they are about to do. As Barry Lopez once put it, *If you are not afraid when you write then you are doing something wrong.* It is this fear that indicates that, on the contrary, you are doing something right.

So, we build up a huge reservoir of energy from someplace inside us and make some snowballs and throw them at the page.

> *Just get it down on paper, no matter what it is just get it down. It's the initial writing that's the hard part. Polishing, honing, shaping—that's the easy part; it comes later. So just get it down any old way, any old way at all.*

Like any kind of work, once you get through that initial barrier, once you overcome your resting state, you'll begin to get into the flow of the thing, to forget yourself and your concerns. You'll enter the dream and the dreaming will flow through your fingers and onto the page. You'll lose yourself in the art.

That's one of the things so many writers love about the craft. They love that loss of self, they love that act of creation, and they love the unexpected discoveries (about the self, about the world, about the book) that emerge when analogical thinking and dreaming takes over. But getting into that state is often the hard thing, harder still for the new writer who is just beginning. For the new writer does not yet know he can write, does not yet know he can sell what he has written to a publisher. He works in a void of unknowing, driven only by an insistent urge he cannot deny, that he has tried to deny and has failed in denying. Later, the writer knows he can do it, or at least that he did it once. But there is never any surety that the result will be of value or that he can do it again. That's one of the things that makes the profession excruciating. The writer follows a golden thread and pours his life force, deep beliefs, energy, and time into describing what the thread reveals. He reveals the landscape of his heart's response to the thread he is following. But he never knows where it will go or if, in the end, what he writes will be any good. There is only the desire, rising unstoppably from deep in the self, to follow that touch of the real.

It takes a long time before trust in that touch is, or can be, complete.

So, in the beginning, for nearly all of us, the initial engagement, the work of the first draft, is a hard one. Some writers outline extensively (I don't) and that outline process *is* their first draft. Others outline mildly, just to create the illusion of a form to follow (my preference). Others dispense with any sort of outline at all (John Dunning). They just begin to write and let whatever form emerges emerge. They find the form that somehow appears, magically, out of the writing itself, line by line, page by page, bird by bird.

No matter how you do it, whether your first draft is an outline or you dispense with an outline entirely, the first draft is messy. Every writer finds where they are going by going there, by writing the book (or, as in John Irving's case, by writing the outline). In consequence, the first run through of the material is rough. It's messy, chaotic. *Shitty,* as Anne Lamott says.

It's crucial in this first run at the material to trust the process, to allow what emerges in the initial writing to be rough, messy, chaotic. A perfectionist approach to the first draft creates sterile work. There's no room then for life to get inside what you are doing, no room for the unexpected to manifest itself, no way for the writing to become a living, moving thing.

For many who fail to write, they fail because they try to make the initial draft look like a finished, final draft. They can't figure out why what they've written doesn't look like the books they've read. Writing doesn't work that way; it never has. If you just let it come out of you without censoring it, get that material, whatever form it takes, onto the page, things will show up in the work you could never have planned for or found otherwise. The dreamer inside us has to write how *it* wants to write, not how our minds want it to write. The dreamer has to be allowed to play and talk how it wants to talk. Too much control will kill the process of dreaming. It *must* be messy in the beginning.

So, let's play with it a bit and see how the process looks in some sort of practical terms . . .

CHOOSING WHAT TO WRITE ABOUT

If you are always feeling keenly, there will never be a shortage of ideas for you to choose from; if you pay close attention to what moves you and what angers you, there are always more ideas than time. I (and all writers) always have a lot of ideas and feelings floating around, bothering me, insisting they become a book, or an article, or a story, or a poem. The question, always, is which topic to choose. What do I want to spend years working on, day after day after day? Because writing is so hard, I need something that won't bore me to death halfway through. The ideas that keep coming back to me, that I continue to find interesting over a year or two (or ten), are the ones I ultimately choose. And I usually have three or four (or more) of them percolating in the back of my mind at any one time. If I can't decide, all things being equal, I will sometimes send out query letters to a few acquisition editors asking if they have an interest in any of them. If someone is interested in a particular book idea, that's the one I'll choose to write. At other times one idea just seems more insistent, more interesting, more luminous and that's where I begin.

Though I have already read and thought deeply about potential book ideas before I finally settle on one, when I'm ready to commit I begin to pursue the idea with a different kind of focus. I start some of the heavy lifting; I begin a detailed and focused exploration of what's already been written and published in the field. While this is an integral element of any nonfiction book proposal and will have to be done eventually, doing it now serves two purposes: 1) It's a necessary step in finding a publisher to publish the book. 2) It acts to clarify my thinking.

Amazon.com is a tremendously useful resource for this. In ancient times I used to go to very large bookstores (or a great library if I were close enough) and look over what they had on the shelves, then peruse the books-in-print list. The larger the bookstore (or library) the better sense I would gain of the field, what had already been written on the topic, which publishers had published those books, and just how my own approach differed—how mine might contribute something new.

Now I don't have to travel so far, one of the largest bookstores in the world is as close as the Internet computer in my library.

Occasionally this initial research will put me off the idea for one reason or another and so I go on to the next one. Once I am firmly committed to the book, however, I will usually buy many if not all of the books that exist on the topic (or any I don't already have). Then I read them and mark any passages in the text (with my own strange form of note taking) that I think useful so I can reference them when I begin writing.

This deep read helps with the later proposal development, it allows me to see the strengths and weaknesses of the current books, and it irritates me (thus providing more motive force). There's always something important none of the published authors covered, or covered poorly. My reading of other writers' works also gives me something to bounce off of. It helps clarify my thinking and, in consequence, my work becomes more focused and comprehensive. It orients me in space and time in relation to the thing I am writing about.

All of this is part of gathering a lot of energy from someplace inside me so I can begin to make snowballs to throw at the page.

BEGINNING A FIRST DRAFT

In the previous chapters, from a number of orientations, I've given you experience with how the human capacity for feeling works in writing. I've also encouraged you to examine what you deeply love and hate and the heroes and books that have moved you so you can write about the things that reflect your most basic and strongest feelings. So, let's say you've done all that and have decided to write a book on building a sustainable, energy-efficient house that will create the tiniest ecological footprint possible. Let's say you decide to focus on adobe houses rather than any of the other possible choices (cob, straw bale, or rammed earth, for instance) because there's something in adobe houses that moves you more than the others.

I assume at this point that you've had some experience with adobe one way or another, that you have some amount of knowledge of it. (This isn't necessary, your book could be about your gaining that experience, a kind of how-to blended with memoir and travel book. But for now, I assume you already have some exposure to adobe house building.)

So, two things emerge from this that are central to the book: the feeling that an adobe house gives you and your desire to do something about the ecological state of the world (which is itself powered by your hatred/anger/irritation at the stupidity and foolishness of what currently passes for good house building and sustainable architecture). Love and Hate. This is the at the core of your motivation for writing the book. It's the *why*. When the book gets hard, and it will, coming back to the *why* will help you orient yourself. It will help you remember why you began this imprudent thing to begin with.

You can approach the building of adobe houses from a vast number of starting places, points of view, and voices. I often think about how I want to approach a book for months or years (while writing others) before I decide on just which approach I want to use. I try on this approach, then that one, experiencing how each one feels to the part of me that wants to write the book, that has feelings about the topic, that dreams as it writes. I usually come up with some rough approach to the topic that feels better than the others and that's where I begin. The first thing I then do is to create a provisional title for the book (which always changes as the book evolves and begins to become itself). The provisional title is intended to hold the essence of my reasons for writing the book. It's meant to hold the *why*. Simply rereading the title, then, helps ground me in what I'm doing during these first stages of creating.

Once I have a provisional title, I create a very rough table of contents. I don't like detailed outlining but I do like a very, very loose outline to give me a general sense of where to begin and where I am going. The initial table of contents does that for me and gives me a grouping of topics I feel are integral to the essence and core of the book.

So, for a book on building adobe houses, I might start with this title:

Soil and Soul: The Craft and Art of the Adobe House

As soon as I have a title, I begin a process of free association. I just list whatever phrases seem to me to be central to the book. This is the material that becomes the provisional table of contents.

For a book on adobe houses those initial free-association phrases might look something like this . . .

> *history, material, making adobe bricks, sustainable housing, building permits, wood, wiring, plumbing, site planning, the soul of adobe, energy efficiency, photo spreads of adobe houses, costs of adobe, plastering adobe, natural and historical plasters, different plaster looks, styles of adobe houses, roofing adobe, adobe woodworking: post, beam, and accent wood approaches, flooring,* and so on.

The more time I spend on this the more my mind begins to drop down inside the subject. The deeper I go into it, the more the material comes alive and the more exciting the individual topics become. I will usually spend a week or so on this, revising the title as well while I do so. The topic list often suggests a deepening of the title, revealing things that were not apparent before I began.

I want to make clear here I'm not going for any kind of perfection during the process, just a working title and group of topics that make a rough, working table of contents. I will only find the final form of the book by writing it.

So, now I have a grouping of topics and I turn them into a table of contents.

Table of Contents

Introduction

Chapter One. Sustainability and the Crisis of the Human Ecological Footprint

Chapter Two. The Need for Ecological and Sustainable Housing

Chapter Three. What is Adobe and Why Build with It?

Chapter Four. Building with Dirt, Mankind's Oldest Building Material

Chapter Five. Adobe Houses through Time and from Around the World

What I have now is a really rough outline. Again, the final chapters will bear little relation to this although all of these topics (and a great many more) will become chapters one way or another as the book is written. This just gives me a place to start.

By the time I've finished the rough table of contents I'm beginning to have a sense of the feel of the book, its emotional tone, the poetry of it. To make the point more strongly: the feeling that initially drew you to adobe houses is a golden thread. You are following not so much tiny impulses through the meadow of language here but rather a feeling impulse through the meadow of the meanings in your life. And that feeling impulse has a particular flavor or mood or emotional tone to it. It's the thing that pulls you into the world of adobe houses and it does so because there is something in adobe houses that has deep meaning to you. Though you may not know clearly or completely what that is, there's an important meaning in the living symbol that adobe houses are that touches on the deep meanings in you and your life. There is a resonance there; it's important to trust it.

You are, in a sense, exploring the nature of identity through following your feeling sense into the meaning-world that is adobe houses. You have looked broadly at all the topics in the universe you can write about and this one has captured your attention. It has done so for a reason. (It's often only in the writing of the book that subtle elements of that reason can be perceived.) It's crucial to remember this, for the book should reflect out of itself, in every word you write, to the utmost skill of which you are capable, the exact feeling or emotional tone you associate with adobe houses. (If it does, simply by reading the book, people will have an experience of the invisibles inside adobe houses even if they can't say what those invisibles are.)

Once you enter the world of adobe houses, you will find that there are other, more specific, feeling impulses, other, more specific, golden threads inside that world. You will recognize them as you have recognized all the golden threads in your life: they feel a particular way. Something about them will feel slightly out of the ordinary to your feeling sense. So, when you're ready to begin writing the book, look at the table of contents again. There will be one chapter that will capture your attention more than the others. It will feel more exciting somehow, more luminous, and that's where to begin your writing.

It really doesn't matter where you begin (in the sense of which chapter is most essential to the book's integrity), you just have to begin rightly. Every part of the book will lead to every other part—eventually. All of them inevitably lead to the core of the thing you are writing about. To begin rightly, however, is important. It means beginning where the feeling is strongest, where some luminous thing has reached out and touched you. You begin with trusting what your feelings are telling you.

Robert Bly explores the importance of this when he comments:

> *[Stafford's] life—so different in that way from most of ours—began with a right decision. Many began their lives with what was for them a wrong decision. These decisions return one way or another every day. Stafford—distinctively among contemporary poets—faces decisions about aggression in every poem. All those slyly named "decisions" he talks of when he follows the golden thread to the center of the poem amount to refusals to adopt instinctive pressures. . . . He doesn't want to be led by habit. He wants to make up his own mind.*[1]

And Stafford did so by following his feeling sense. And, always, it led him deep into the heart of what he was writing about. He didn't allow cultural or social pressures to force him along any particular line of thinking. He followed his feeling sense and trusted it. He began rightly. So, trust the instinct you have for what feels right to you. Your feeling for the right will lead you into the heart of your own writing, your individuality will be expressed out of it, and you will, inevitably, find the heart of your book. So, the place to begin the journey is with the part of the book that calls you most strongly.

In this initial, rough table of contents on adobe house building, the part that draws me most is the chapter on natural plastering. On another day it might be another chapter, it doesn't matter. All that matters is that today, right now, this chapter is the most interesting, the most fun. So, that is where I begin. I take all my knowledge of plastering, all I have read about it, and all the *feeling* sense I have about it and I make some snowballs and throw them at the page.

Here is what my first run at the chapter looks like (they always look like this):

> Traditional adobe plasters may be lime-based or clay-based and both are still used almost everywhere on earth except the U.S. In contrast to the cement plasters used in this country natural plasters are not nearly as ecologically damaging. Lime plaster, for instance, makes a strong and durable plaster that naturally inhibits mold, mildew, and many insects. It breathes, is durable, porous, and evaporates moisture. It is much more workable than cement plasters so that troweling is much easier. But beyond this it has centuries of tradition behind it and in those centuries of tradition a great many things have been discovered about how to affect the nature and feeling of lime when used as a natural plaster.
>
> The first, or base, coat of lime plaster is stabilized by the use of natural fibers, plant or animal. Grasses or animal hair, for example, act much like metal rebar does in cement foundations. They provide a longitudinal band tying the material together, allowing it to flex with shifts in humidity and earth stress, and helping prevent severe cracking in the coat. Later, once this coat

has dried and set firmly, topping coats can be applied. Lime can take on a great many properties when other materials are added to the topping coats. Linseed oil increases durability, tallow imparts plasticity, skim milk decreases permeability. The most interesting to me are the many plant additives that human beings, working over long time, discovered to affect both the behavior and beauty of natural plasters.

Prickly pear is one of the primary plants that is used wherever it grows. For a big job, a 55 gallon drum or barrel is filled with rough cut prickly pear cactus, covered with water, and allowed to stand for a week minimum. Then the lime plaster is made, using the prickly pear liquid. Prickly pear is highly mucilaginous. As one text on its use notes: "It helps the lime set, increases adhesion, improves workability, and makes the plaster more water repellent" (*The Straw Bale House Book,* p. 208). An interior wall, finished with a prickly pear lime plaster possesses a slight sheen, much like a semi-gloss paint. The wall is actually a great deal more water repellent than a regular lime plaster and can easily be washed without damage. Some 14 different plants have been or are used throughout the world to impart particular properties to the plasters they are mixed with. All of them are also primary foods (like prickly pear) or medicines (like ocotillo) in the cultures that use them. Prickly pear in particular has been found to be able to reverse type 2 diabetes when taken as a regular part of the diet.

As Anne Lamott says in her book on writing—*Bird by Bird*—a first draft is supposed to be shitty. This one certainly is. It's dull, plodding, boring. The sentences thud down like heavy dumplings on an upset stomach. I pass the test for a first draft (and you will too).

It's very important to not worry about it. Shitty first drafts can be fixed later; that's the easy part. Now, you are doing the hard part, getting it all down on paper. So, just take all the feeling you have and write. Write and write and write until you are all written out. Eventually, often around page 60 or so, you will begin to wonder what the hell you are doing. As John Dunning once put it: "About then I begin to ask myself,

'Just who the hell are these people, anyway?'" This is the moment where the work (and some deep part of you) is beginning to demand more depth of insight, where implications in what you have written begin to insist they be teased out. Here the demand to go below the surface begins to emerge.

You've got enough at this point for the writing to turn into a conversation, into a conscious collaboration between you and your dreamer. So, you begin to refine a bit, begin to get a sense of where you are going.

This is not, by any means, anything like the final editing process that begins after you have a completed first draft. It's an intermediary step that, at the urging of your deep self, begins to lead to other golden threads you didn't suspect existed when you began.

I would normally write a lot more in that natural plaster chapter before playing with it but let's look at it anyway so you can get a sense of what I mean.

The writing is pretty dreadful (the book you are now reading looked much like it once upon a time) and it resembles a lot of published nonfiction, doesn't it? Nevertheless, I'm not worried about that now. I'm just trying to get as much on paper as I can so I have something to work with that can become art. I'm at the point in the book of "who the hell are these people anyway?"

Again, the concepts in a nonfiction book are a living reality for me. They are to nonfiction what characters are to fiction. At his point in time, I begin the work to find out who the hell they are as living beings.

Some of the concepts I've introduced need to be fleshed out. I need to develop their personalities, allow them to become truly alive on the page rather than remain expressions of the statistical mentality. But that's easy once I have something on paper to guide me. Once I have a piece like this (though it's usually much longer as I have said), I can go back to it and readily see where its needs expansion and development.

So, let's go through the material with just that eye and note in the text where expansion is going to be necessary:

> Traditional adobe plasters may be lime-based or clay-based and both are still used almost everywhere on earth except the U.S. **(need more here on what lime and clay plasters are, how they**

are made, and how used in traditional cultures around the planet) In contrast to the cement plasters used in this country natural plasters are not nearly as ecologically damaging. **(need detail on cement, how we got to cement over lime, why people would ever stop using lime, and the ecological impacts of both types)** Lime plaster, for instance, makes a strong and durable plaster that naturally inhibits mold, mildew, and many insects. It breathes, is durable, porous, and evaporates moisture. It is much more workable than cement plasters so that troweling is much easier. **(Query: why does it do these things?)** But beyond this it has centuries of tradition behind it and in those centuries of tradition a great many things have been discovered about how to affect the nature and feeling of lime when used as a natural plaster.

The first, or base, coat of lime plaster is stabilized by the use of natural fibers, plant or animal. Grasses or animal hair, for example, act much like metal rebar does in cement foundations. They provide a longitudinal band tying the material together, allowing it to flex with shifts in humidity and earth stress, and helping prevent severe cracking in the coat. Later, once this coat has dried and set firmly, topping coats can be applied. **(Define topping coats, purpose of base coat, etc)** Lime can take on a great many properties when other materials are added to the topping coats. Linseed oil increases durability, tallow imparts plasticity, skim milk increases impermeability. **(Develop how different topping coats are better in one room than another depending on the purpose of the room. Eventually need to go into history and how to make each of these and just what happens in the process of making them)** The most interesting to me are the many plant additives that human beings, working over long time, discovered to affect both the behavior and beauty of natural plasters.

Prickly pear is one of the primary plants that is used wherever it grows. For a big job, a 55 gallon drum or barrel is filled with rough cut prickly pear cactus, covered with water, and allowed to stand for a week minimum. Then the lime plaster is made, using the prickly pear liquid. Prickly pear is highly mucilagi-

> nous. **(Define)** As one text on its use notes: "It helps the lime set, increases adhesion, improves workability, and makes the plaster more water repellent" (The Straw Bale House Book, p. 208). An interior wall, finished with a prickly pear lime plaster possesses a slight sheen, much like a semi-gloss paint. The wall is actually a great deal more water repellent than a regular lime plaster and can easily be washed without damage. Some 14 different plants have been or are used throughout the wall to impart particular properties to the plasters they are mixed with. All of them are also primary foods (like prickly pear) or medicines (like ocotillo) in the cultures that use them. Prickly pear in particular has been found to be able to reverse type 2 diabetes when taken as a regular part of the diet.

It's always true that some of the most important concepts in the book show up in a very superficial way in the first run at the material. Many times they tend to show up, as Gardner put it, as a pulsation on an otherwise dead planet. This last paragraph on plants in plasters has that pulsation for me. It reveals a whole world in the book that I didn't suspect was going to be there when I started. The dreamer brought something luminous out of the material that I hadn't planned on; it bypassed my conscious mind entirely. As a result the book has just taken on a new dimension, a kind of livingness has emerged. It's this livingness I experience as a pulsation.

Gardner talks about such an emergence like this . . .

> *In fleshing out his characters, the writer does not ordinarily think out every implication of every image he introduces at the time he introduces it. He writes by feel, intuitively, imagining the scene vividly and copying down its most significant details, keeping the fictional dream alive, sometimes writing in a thoughtless white heat of "inspiration," drawing on his unconscious, trusting his instincts.*[2]

Somehow, in the white heat of writing, when I wasn't paying attention, some living thing entered the writing. Because I trusted my instinct, my *feeling* sense, I began with natural plasters and, of its own accord, that living thing emerged. It always works like this. We stagger from one revelation to the next, never knowing when or how they'll show up. I notice, too, as I read the material, there's another area of pulsation for me: the brief discussion on straw acting like rebar. Both these sections have unexpected juice, but the strongest for me right now is the section on plants and that's where I'm going to begin. (That rebar piece will lie in my mind, gestating. When I am done with the plant section there's a good chance some very interesting material will emerge from the dreamer about longitudinal bands and the flexing of plaster.) The other areas that I noted need expansion and development I ignore for now. They don't have much juice and writing about them is the equivalent, for me, of washing the kitchen floor—a chore to be done, no fun. So I skip them—for now.

I'm still following my feeling sense, following tiny impulses through the meadow of meaning. This is the key to the emergence of the book in the form it needs to take to become itself.

This unexpected emergence of plants in natural plasters does something interesting for me; it connects plaster to the livingness of the Earth, to a renewable resource, to some indefinable energy that belongs to living plants. As with generations of people before me, something has pulled me into the wildness of the world. I find there a much older world, one filled with living beings that have been here far longer than human beings. I begin to look at plants with new eyes. I accidently wander into wilderness and suddenly find myself gathering herbs that benefit and change my life.

Plants that are used in natural plastering are woven deeply into the fabric of the indigenous cultures that use them. They are used for building materials, food, medicine, clothing, and tools—often as intelligent companions in life. So, even though I started with how to build an adobe house and then focused in on one small aspect of that—plastering—suddenly I find myself encountering plants and the relationship of those plants to culture over generations upon generations of time. Not only do I have a new chapter, I have a new thread to follow, one that takes me deeply inside the human relationship with Earth and plants and sustainable, renewable habitation.

And a sudden thought occurs to me as I look at the range of uses of prickly pear: "Can it be that how we relate to such a simple thing as prickly pear has ramifications not only to sustainable housing but also to health care, food production, and our culture's sustainable habitation of Earth?" Some slight duende feeling begins to emerge here, so I look a little deeper at it.

It turns out that when indigenous cultures move away from traditional foods such as prickly pear, they begin to develop diabetes in large numbers and a return to a traditional diet corrects the problem. So, when we turn away from plants like prickly pear as integral to the building of our homes, do our buildings become sick? Do our buildings begin to make us sick? Is our relationship to prickly pear really a metaphor for the sickness of our culture in its relation to the natural world? Is this a living example of the impact on us of living our lives through the statistical mentality versus following the road of feeling? When we cut ourselves off from the plant world do we cut ourselves off from the ground of being that gives us life? Do we, literally, lose our roots?

So, just by beginning where the feeling was strongest I suddenly find myself in very different territory, a territory that touches on what matters most deeply to me, and perhaps, to the core of the difficulties of our time. And perhaps I have found some essential truth about the nature of housing, of human relationship to housing, and the housing problems affecting us as a species. And this place I have found has duende in it. As I work with the material I feel that thrill of feeling that goes with duende, feel that long, floating leap and the landing in some other territory of spirit. I know that I will eventually develop and enhance it in the text until I've got it condensed into a living poesis that lies there, shimmering, on the page.

The writing begins to come alive now, to take on some luminous nature. I travel into the plastering of a house and find myself deep inside a continent and our human relationship with that continent. It's in just this way that the dreamer expresses a living symbol into the writing, in just this way that the dreamer activates the symbolic layer that is woven into all things into the writing.

But it was only when I finished that white heat of writing and stepped back, letting my conscious mind come to the fore, that I could see what had emerged. And once I see it, I begin to play with its ramifications, to tease out its implications, to follow where it leads. I re-engage the material and begin to develop it. I take that one pulsating area of the writing and, for now, let go of all the rest. That pulsating area becomes the focus of the writing.

I begin writing outward from it and work to make more and more of the material surrounding it pulsate as well. I begin expanding from that center but I don't worry about where it's going. I don't try to control what's emerging; I just follow the thread wherever it takes me. Prickly pear, and the feeling that emerged with it, becomes the focus. I drop down inside the meanings and begin to think analogically. I let the dreamer write. As I do, more things will emerge that were not remotely in my conscious mind when I began. I go from one tiny revelation to the next.

It's in just this way that the dreamer takes a writer deep into the imaginal and mythic landscapes that generate all books. It's not something that can be planned or that the conscious mind can do. It just happens. I wrote this material on adobe houses exactly as I would have if I were writing such a book; I did not expect in any way that prickly pear would become a focus for me. It just happened. Later, when I stopped and began looking over the rough material with my conscious mind, I felt something more in the section on the use of plants in natural plaster than I did in the rest of the text. It stood out to my senses when I touched it. My conscious mind noticed so I began to follow the thread.

I know now that I have at least one more chapter: The Use of Plants in Natural Plasters. But I suspect there's going to be more than one. As I follow this new thread, it will open up more material, in ways I cannot know until I begin to write. I just follow the feeling. Later, once the rough draft is completed, when you begin to look at the manuscript through your analogical thinking, the underlying patterns that are in there, that your conscious mind hasn't noticed, will emerge to your sight. The whole pattern of the book, the interlocking golden threads and various duendes, will be seen. You can consciously begin then to develop them as a coherent pattern that flows below the surface of the text. The book that can only be found by writing it will have come into existence.

It's in exactly this way that a whole manuscript is written. Day after day after day. And the more days that pass, the more fully you will enter into the process, following the threads that emerge and demand your attention. As time goes by, you will enter the mythic landscape more and more completely. Time will cease to have much meaning, this world will begin to take on more the quality of a dream, and the world inside the book will become more and more real. It will *be* the real world, this other the dream. And from time to time you will pop through into that full-dreaming state where you are *inside* the dream, watching it unfold, from time to time break through into the imaginal world itself where the mythic extrudes itself into the work directly.

You live now inside the world of the book, writing, struggling, working to find your way through the meadow of language by following your feeling sense, one slow step after another. You peel the layers of the book away like an onion, one layer at a time, and as Carl Sandburg once remarked about life, "sometimes you weep."

CHAPTER EIGHTEEN

Problems and Further Revisioning

Everyone I know flails around, kvetching and growing despondent, on the way to finding a plot and structure that work. You are welcome to join the club.

Anne Lamott

How did the writing go? It was a five dollar day with a thousand dollars worth of bills to be paid.

John Dunning

Superlative writing is love lavished on the word.

William Gass

My description of creating a first draft makes it seem as if it might be an easy thing to do, but of course "stuff happens." You can't control where the golden threads you're following will lead you. Sometimes they lead to uncomfortable places, sometimes to truths the conscious mind has no desire to see. So, your conscious mind refuses to see them, the dreamer insists, and you hit the wall. It's then you encounter the fierce psychological struggle that writing is.

At those times, you can feel something wrong in the text but you can't seem to figure out what it is. You back up to a pulsating section and take a run at the material again. Wham! Wall again. Hysteria. Depression. Another run. Wham! Depression. Hopelessness. And again, another run.

Day after day after day. Always searching for what's wrong, trying to lay down those words underneath each other so you can make it across the slippery slope. But failing, again and again and again.

Every writer has to struggle like this when the material just won't work. Inevitably, every time, I find the fault is mine. The dreamer (or the material, or both) is telling me something but, for whatever reason, I can't, I won't, hear it.

Theodore Sturgeon, again, described this kind of experience in his story "Slow Sculpture." In it a man works to get the tree he is growing to grow in the way he sees in his mind and . . .

> *if the explanation is well enough made, and there is great enough understanding, the tree will respond and obey—almost. Always there will be its own self-respecting, highly individual variation:* Very well I shall do what you want, but I will do it *my* way. *And for these variations, the tree is always willing to present a clear and logical explanation, and more often than not (almost smiling) it will make clear to the man that he could have avoided it if his understanding had been better.*
>
> *It is the slowest sculpture in the world, and there is, at times, doubt as to which is being sculpted, man or tree.*[1]

There is always doubt about what is being written, ourselves or the books we write. It's a collaborative process; *both* of us are being written. The book will never be what you originally imagined it to be when you began nor will you ever again be the person you were before you allowed the mythic to flow into you and become the book you did write.

To write what must be written every writer has to learn to hear what the book (and the dreamer) is telling them. The book you are bringing into the world is a living thing, just as a bonsai is. Remember what Gardner said, the writing comes alive and this is *literally* not metaphorically true. You are shaping a living thing and it, and the dreamer, will insist that the book find the shape it must have to be itself. The dreamer will insist that the archetypes that are flowing through it, into you, and onto the page, find the shapes they must have to grow in the reality of *your* field. It's always a struggle to be able to hear what we're being told and more, to acquiesce to it.

The conscious mind has to become highly adaptable to do so. In every book I've written this has forced encounters with my own psychological limitations, my preferences for how reality must be, my unwillingness to hear things I don't want to hear.

Writing forces a maturation in any who follow the craft—though some writers are seemingly able to leave that maturation in the writing room when they emerge from it. You have to become more than you are to follow where the dreamer leads.

For myself, if I keep working with the material, looking deep inside me, hitting the wall and backing off, then taking time to think and feel more deeply into what's happening, there always comes a day when suddenly the material makes sense. The reason I was stuck is suddenly clear to me, what needs to happen obvious. I can never seem to remember, at that point, why it was so difficult for me to figure it out.

I always hit this kind of wall three or four times in a book. Generating the initial energy to begin writing, those messy first snowballs, and this hitting of the wall . . . they are the hardest parts of writing for many of us. Here's Geoff Dyer writing about his experience of it:

> *I thought that the fun part of writing would be the "creative" bit, making stuff up and inventing things. The older I've got, the less fun this has become. I dread it. The part I enjoy is the re-writing. Increasingly, I enjoy the dullest, most clerical stages of the process. Having said that, there always comes a point, after I've amassed enough material and can start knocking it into shape, when I begin looking forward to working on something. Basically, it gets easier and easier each day until the last five or six months are a real pleasure. . . . I always hope I can carry over that momentum from the end of one book to the beginning of another but, unfortunately, it's strictly non-transferable.*[2]

And Hari Kunzru talking about what it's like for him:

> *I get great pleasure from writing, but not always, or even usually. Writing a novel is largely an exercise in psychological discipline—trying to balance your project on your chin while negotiating a*

> *minefield of depression and freak out. Beginning is daunting, being in the middle makes you feel like Sisyphus. . . . Along the way, there are the pitfalls of self-disgust, boredom, disorientation and a lingering sense of inadequacy, occasionally alternating with episodes of hysterical self-congratulation as you fleetingly believe you've nailed that particular sentence and are surely destined to join the ranks of the immortals, only to be confronted the next day with an appalling farrago of clichés that no sane human could read without vomiting. But when you're in the zone, spinning words like plates, there's a deep sense of satisfaction and, yes, enjoyment.*[3]

It is work, this laying down of words one underneath the other to make a passage across a slick mountainside. Persevering, continuing to go at it again and again, coming back to those essential feelings that led you here, to your reasons for writing the book lead, always, to finding a way through the book. There will come a time, always, when from someplace deep inside you, the answer to the problem confronting you will float up into your conscious mind. At that moment you and the book come together as one thing, both changed, both finding the conversation that must be found for the book to become itself.

Depression is the way darkness is made visible to us.

Sometimes, it takes me a long time to find my way, to understand what the problem is, so, sometimes, I wash the kitchen floor. Literally. I take a break and work with my body and hands doing something completely unrelated to writing. By taking myself out of the world of the book and focusing totally on something else, especially if it involves physical labor, I give my unconscious some time and space to work on the problem without my interference. It's often during these kinds of breaks that the answer will just pop up one day, clear and whole in my mind.

At other times, I go over sections that are finished but not yet polished, engaging in the revision process I will have to do later anyway. This is something I really enjoy. It's a process that's a lot of fun for me. So, it gets me out of the depression that hitting the wall creates and lets me play, lets me work with words for the pure joy of it.

Sometimes I wash the kitchen floor metaphorically. I do the bibliography. I format or tidy up the pages. And if none of that works, I finally bite the bullet and go back to places in the book that need more development and begin to flesh them out. I'm never very excited about it; it's just a chop-water-carry-wood sort of thing. But what's interesting is that every time, after I get over my avoidance, when I begin to get into those sections of the book, to drop down below the surface of the thing, it, too, starts to come alive. I begin to find golden threads I never suspected.

For example, with this material on plastering adobe houses, I go back to lime and clay plasters and begin to flesh out that part of it. I start reading about lime-based plasters and move deep inside them, working to understand them from the inside. Then I move to clay-based plasters and do the same thing. Both of them connect me more deeply to Earth again. Lime-based plasters have, for thousands of years, been made, without high technology, from limestone. Clay-based plasters have always been made from clay soils. So, I begin to look more deeply at the nature of rock and soil. I begin to see our human relationship to these things over long historical time. Then I look at the movement to cement plasters and the industrial production behind them. I see the intensely negative environmental impacts of concrete. I begin to look at why we, as a culture, made the move away from more natural, less manufacturing-intensive plasters. And I begin to see some of the ecological problems that have come from that choice.

I learn how small groups of people, using local materials, have historically engaged in a particular kind of relationship with the ground around them, and from it, raised up a house. I see how they made the soil into adobe bricks, then into plasters for those bricks. (They are, in a sense, living inside the Earth when they are done, surrounded by its soil.) I find there is a sense of artisanship about this kind of work that's missing when cement plasters are involved. I begin to discover unexpected aesthetic dimensions in the older plasters.

It turns out that clay soils have many different properties. For instance, different clays naturally possess different colors—in fact, there's a tremendous range of colors, from white to black and everything in between. So instead of paint, the clay itself is used to color the interior of the house. Abandoning paint means the house is less toxic for the people who live there; it also means that the house materials are less toxic to the environment. I also find that clay is not damaging to the skin when it's used as a plaster; it doesn't burn as lime and cement plasters do. In fact, clay is very good for the skin. I discover that the people who use natural clay plasters experience a natural enthusiasm for the work, that the making of mud pies brings up a childlike joy in the person, a kind of joy often lost in those who merely work for a living. I find that when people plaster together, using clay, there is a deep community joy in it, a childlikeness that enters the group, which in some indefinable way brings them closer together. It stimulates community bonding that other plaster forms do not. And in some indefinable way, all that joy and childlikeness and community bonding gets into that house. When the house is done its secret kinesis will be composed, in part, of all those feelings and sharings and bondings. The house comes into this world already a home and the people who live there are surrounded every day of their lives by those invisible things. That home really does become then, in many ways, a kind of medicine for the people who live in it. And I feel in all this the emergence of duende again, something I will, again, intentionally develop more fully as the book goes on.

So, this area that originally felt boring to me has opened up and revealed some of its secrets. I find there's a lot more to it than I suspected. New golden threads have emerged. Something of a gentle, simple humanity, encouraged by a gentle, simple building material, has been revealed.

Then one day, I raise my head out of the manuscript and find I suddenly understand that other place where I was stuck. I can go back to it now and write what needs to be written for that part of the book to become itself.

NEW MUSCLES

Using the capacity for nonphysical touch is wearing, especially in the beginning years. It takes a certain focus of mind, focus of will, focus of *feeling*. It uses muscles that get tired, just as during the building of a house your physical muscles tire. The more you do it, of course, the more your muscles develop and the longer you can do it without tiring. But doing it six to ten hours a day, seven days a week is tiring for anyone, no matter how muscular they are. Eventually that part of me needs a break. One day I wake up and part of me just cringes at the thought of doing it anymore. So, I take a break. I might take a few days off. Other times I take a break in the style of writing I am doing.

By the time I become that tired I usually have large chunks of rough manuscript available to play with. And that is what I begin to do. I begin to use the techniques I discuss in the next chapters to refine and polish the work. This uses different muscles and gives those others a chance to rest. When the rough draft is finally done, I might have polished some of those early chapters forty or fifty times. I tend, when I do this, to go back and polish the chapters that give me the most pleasure. (Chapter One in this book, although it was the fourth chapter I wrote, is the one I initially went back to most often.)

This serves a number of purposes besides allowing that other part of me to rest: it accomplishes some of the revising and polishing the book will eventually need anyway. So the time is spent usefully (from a finished manuscript point of view). It also rekindles my excitement in the book. By continually working with only the roughest areas of the manuscript I begin to forget what a polished piece of writing is like. Moving to a more finished section of the book in this way reminds me; it keeps up my spirits.

This kind of rewriting uses a different part of the self; it gives the deeper parts of me space and time to think about the book. All the meanings I am working with in the material, many of which I have not noticed consciously, are impacting my deep self and that part of me is working with them constantly. When I stop awhile and begin to revise, it allows those deeper parts to rest and think without having to produce anything. They have time to mull things over.

And from time to time, as I write in this different way, I burst through into one of those full-breakthrough states and I write what comes to me then. These breakthroughs serve as points of orientation throughout the book that I then connect together through my analogical thinking. Eventually I will break through into the living reality of the book itself and experience its true form in the imaginal world. When this happens I get a gestalt of it and that's when I begin to weave that gestalt through the fabric of the book.

This is how I do it every time, bird by bird, line by line, page by page, chapter by chapter, section by section. And finally, one day, the rough manuscript is done.

The dreaming is mostly finished now (but not completely). It is now that the revision and editing process begins in earnest. There are a number of techniques you can use to revise the work, to make it more elegant, to strengthen and develop the themes the dreaming part of you put into the work. This is when the book is *composed,* turned into art. And, of course, there will be problems in the text that need to be corrected. My first run at the revision process is designed to catch those problems and to correct them. I do this by focusing eros energy on the text.

EROS

This simply means that you begin, in a particular way, to reread the manuscript *through* your capacity for nonphysical touch. At this point the reading is concerned not so much with feeling your way through the text, one tiny revelation to the next (that should already have been done as you created the initial draft), but reading through the text from a love of the meanings inside the words themselves, from a love of the continually emerging flow of feeling tones that weaves through the material. It's this eros working of the draft that's at the heart of what Gardner meant when he said . . .

> *What the honest writer does, when he's finished a rough draft, is to go over it and over it, time after time, refusing to let anything stay if it looks awkward, phony, or forced.*[4]

Awkward, phony, forced . . . those terms refer to a passage in the text where, during an eros run, the author *feels* something amiss. Even though Gardner uses the word *looks,* what he really means is how the passage feels to the feeling self as it is read.

As you begin this kind of a read the mind stands slightly back, the feeling sense slightly forward. You move into a mild trance where you are simply reading for feel. The author, as reader, is moving into the dreaming state that all writing evokes but with the conscious mind highly attentive to effect. So, if, during such a read you are awakened from the dream, brought out of the trance state, the conscious mind immediately attends to the place in the manuscript that caused the waking.

You feel the incongruency, you wake, then the mind begins to look the material over to try and determine just what's wrong and what needs to happen to make it right. You begin to fiddle with it.

In this part of the editing process the relationship of every line, of every chapter and section to every other, is felt, worked over, held as a living gestalt inside the self. What you are working to do is to get eros energy inside every word. Bly has a nice metaphor for this . . .

> *A shoemaker in the Middle Ages could be in business for years and remain in Eros consciousness, because he knew everyone who bought shoes from him, and he worked on a shoe long enough that love-energy could flow into it.*[5]

You have already done the hard part—making something out of nothing; the concepts and overall form are already laid down on the pages. Many portions of the text are alive but the whole isn't as fully alive as it needs to be, isn't yet one coherent whole. So, during an eros run you focus on the feel of the love energy that flows through the text and you concentrate it, condense it. (Condensing naturally occurs in an eros run. You cut extraneous words. The umms and ahhs, the throat clearing.) In the process of feeling into and loving each section, every word in the text, what you have made will become fully inhabited. From directed eros energy a soul force begins to move inside every part of the manuscript, a dark well of psychic energy begins to flow into every word.

With this kind of focused caring, the thing, be it word or shoe, becomes something crafted with care rather than carelessness. There should be no word in the text you have written that you do not love, nothing you have written that you have not been alive inside of. Brenda Ueland comments that, "A great musician once told me that one should never play a single note without hearing it, feeling that it is true, thinking it beautiful."[6] The same is true of every word you write.

During this stage of the revisioning, I work to face each word in the text (including "and") as I would a human being, attentive and aware, present and caring and genuine. Each word should be as alive to me as if it were a person on the other side of a deeply meaningful conversation. So, I read the entire manuscript now by keeping my alive, aware intention on each and every word as I read it. If I tend to go slightly to sleep in a section as I read, there is something wrong. And every time I drift off, I intentionally emerge from the dream and let my conscious mind work on the passage until it works, until I can remain in the dream as I read it.

At this point, the conscious mind and the deep self work in concert. I nod off, I awaken, then focus consciously. I revise the line, ask how it feels, note the feeling response, compare it to the rest of the material to see if it's congruent with what I am going for, then read it again to see if I stay in the dream. If I do, I go on, if not, I revise again, and so on and on and on.

Your feelings must flow into the fingers with which you touch the words and you must caress them as you would the body of a lover and at a deeper level your love must caress the meanings that reside within and under the words. The words are merely the living membranes within which the real meanings reside. Your heart must beat within the pulsation of the word so that when a reader reads your words, your heart becomes their heart, the sound of your voice their voice. Its meanings will circulate then, as William Gass says, "as one blood between us."[7]

During this part of the read, larger issues like clichéd thought (examined more deeply in the next chapter) and hidden baggage (the chapter after that) are also found.

Clichéd thought can be felt by a certain dullness of mind and a particular feeling that accompanies that dullness. The material just isn't alive but it isn't alive in a particular way. There is a particular kind of feeling that accompanies clichéd thought that, after you have encountered it a few hundred times, you will recognize whenever you feel it. That dead space in the text emerges because the material isn't real—you weren't in-the-moment living it as you wrote it—it's only a repetition of something you heard someplace and, without thinking, accepted as true. So, it can't be vital or vivid to the feeling sense. If it does possess any energy it will be drama-triangleish, not real.

Hidden baggage, if it's unconscious baggage, will appear as a similar dullness but it won't have the "parental" edge that clichéd thought has, the "you can only be moral (or intelligent or good or . . .) if you believe this" edge, the "*everybody* knows this is so" edge.

Embarrassed baggage comes across as a passage with some sort of "don't examine this" kind of feeling. It's the kind of feeling that accompanies lying to oneself or family secrets that must not be examined too closely. It will vary in degree depending on what is being hidden. The more powerful the secret, the more intense the feeling as the passage is read. The prickling of the thumbs is stronger.

Ego baggage comes across, most often, as an arrogance, that is, as you read that section and take on its meanings and mindset, you begin to feel a bit arrogant toward the world or the people around you. When you look through the cognitive spectacles that the meanings in the words become as you immerse yourself in them, whatever you are looking at will tend to lose some degree of essential dignity. You will be distanced from the world; there will be a feeling or sense of detached exceptionalism.

These kinds of things point up larger problems in the text (or in the writer) and generally take a lot of thinking through, a lot of work, to correct.

Another significant problem occurs when implications in some part of the text have not been clearly thought through. There is a particular kind of mind wandering that occurs when reading that sort of material. The words seem to make sense but when you read the passage it's very hard to hold awareness on the page. Often I find I'm missing a crucial segue or have not thought out and developed my premise enough. *Anytime* your mind wanders as you move through the text it's a sign that something is wrong in the material. (You may be overtired, so rest and read it again the next day. If your mind still wanders whenever you read it; it's the text.) It's usually this kind of unclear implication that I first read for during my early eros runs. The only way to solve this kind of unclear writing is to read, very carefully and immediately, every line of text in that section. As you do, tease out the things that need to be said that you have not said. Look for important segues that you have skipped. At the very moment when your mind begins to wander, feel for what needs to be said to keep the mind focused on the text.

At these points of mind wandering I often find I have included too much material—authorial bloat has taken over. Eventually I get mad and just want to cut, so I do. Cutting a lot of the material thins the text enough that the mind moves through it more easily. The segues that are needed then become more apparent.

In essence, hidden baggage, clichéd thinking, and unclear implications cause dissociation. You stop feeling with your feeling sense, lose your connection with the meanings in the text, and get caught up in something else, usually some sort of mentation or psychological circus. (If you find yourself getting into an argument with the part of you that says something is wrong in a passage, that's a form of defensiveness. Generally, there's something under it you don't want to see.) So, as you read through the text, you should be able to stay in your feeling state, in the dream, and have nothing awaken you from it. If something does, you have to work that section until you figure out what's wrong and correct it.

Clichéd thinking and hidden baggage are two of the most difficult problems in a manuscript; they are especially common in nonfiction. They kill livingness in a book; they destroy the art of the craft. So, let's look at them more deeply.

CHAPTER NINETEEN

Clichéd Thinking and Killing the Genuine

Mountains of unspeakable books . . . have been dumped on long-suffering humanity in recent years because mediocre critics have wrongly claimed for them astute perceptions on the problems of, for instance, blacks and women. One might suppose such a vogue would at least help true art on the same subjects; but not so. A really good book or painting concerning blacks or women is as hard to sell now as it ever was. True art is too complex to reflect the party line. Art that tries hard to tell the truth unretouched is difficult and often offensive. It tears down our heroes and heart-warming convictions, violates canons of politeness and humane compromise.

JOHN GARDNER

Art—the arts generally—are always unpredictable, maverick, and tend to be, at their best, uncomfortable. Literature, in particular, has always inspired the House committees, the Zhdanovs, the fits of moralizing, but, at worst, persecution. It troubles me that political correctness does not seem to know what its exemplars and predecessors are; it troubles me more that it may know and does not care . . . The trouble is that, with all popular movements, the lunatic fringe so quickly ceases to be a fringe; the tail begins to wag the dog. For every woman or man who is quietly

> *and sensibly using the idea to examine our assumptions, there are 20 rabble-rousers whose real motive is desire for power over others, no less rabble-rousers because they see themselves as anti-racists or feminists or whatever.*
>
> Doris Lessing

> *Prefab conversation frees the mind, yet rarely does the mind have a mind left after these interconnected clichés have conquered it.*
>
> William Gass

It's common in writing classes, articles, and books to talk about avoiding clichés, so much so that the discussions themselves are clichéd. Perhaps a different approach is in order? As with most things writing, cliché advice focuses on form rather than essence. So . . .

In essence, clichés, like *avoid clichés* or *snow-capped peaks,* fall into one of two categories: advice or information-about-life (*show don't tell, a chain is only as strong as its weakest link*) or descriptive phrase (*bottomless depths, skanky ho*). Such clichés are to be avoided (they say) because, when used, the writing becomes lifeless and the readers bored as all get out—they zone out, catch some z's, nod off, abandon ship, fall asleep at the switch, and at the end of the day find that nothing alive or worthwhile has been said. It's as plain as the nose on your face that such writing is about as effective as a lead balloon, as welcome to editors as a skunk at a lawn party, as useful as tits on a bull. Ashes to ashes, dust to dust.

But, if you remain alive inside your writing, if you inhabit the word, if you are present with what you are saying, if every word you write is bathed in dark water, if you truly engage in communication rather than technique, if you *feel* every word so that it comes alive, sings, reverberates, hums, and touches the reader with intimate caress, you will find that there aren't many clichés in your writing. Clichés normally occur *only* if you let your attention wander, if you take the easy way out, if you don't really feel what you are saying. Nevertheless, clichés can be used to good effect in many situations. They are often integral to art. You just have to use them with awareness. What matters most is if the writing is alive or not, not whether a cliché has been used.

Clichéd thinking, however, is something else again. It's deadly to art, deadly to writing of any kind. It can be used intentionally as an expression of art but almost never is. Regrettably, it is a great deal more common in nonfiction (and fiction) than clichéd phrases. Clichéd thinking is rarely discussed in writing schools, editors almost never spot it, and a lot of books that should more properly be understood to be false art are published and thought to be "just wonderful!"

Clichéd thinking is when an unexamined, umbrella concept or idea, popularly thought to be true in some largish section of a culture (and thus repeated endlessly), is rolled into a written work. It's a form of the advice or information-about-life cliché expanded to, sometimes, book length proportions. It's an everybody-knows-this-is-true, an "of course," discourse. And it usually has a "parental" edge to it, a hidden assertion within the material that one *must* believe it in order to be a reputable member, in good standing, of some particular group (good people, intelligent people, sensible people, moral people, real Americans [or whichever country you wish], white people, black people, women, men, capitalists, socialists, and so on).

Statements such as "Modern medicine has given Americans better, healthier, and longer lives than any humans anywhere have ever experienced before" or "It is through science and science alone that the environmental and social problems that face us can be solved" are representative of the kind of pervasive clichéd thinking that are endemic in the United States (and its writers).

Clichéd thinking is harder to avoid than clichés, for to avoid it, writers must engage in some depth of self-examination. They must examine their beliefs and the ideas they are propagating and determine just why they have them and why they are including them in what they are writing. They must also deeply examine the clichéd thought itself to see if, in fact, it's as true as it seems. Because there is always some truth in clichéd thinking, it's easy for writers to avoid this kind of self-examination, but such examination is necessary all the same. The question must always be asked: Is the belief as true as people make it out to be? Upon examination, it often turns out it is not. For example: A number of studies have found that modern medicine is actually less a factor in American's longer lives than better sanitation and more efficient agriculture and food distribution. As well, there are cultures that use very different approaches to health care and experience longer life spans and greater quality of life than people in the United States do or ever have.

As with the use of clichés, clichéd thinking comes in part out of laziness. The necessity to confront the difficult subtleties of the universe is abandoned in favor of a simpler picture, one that demands no depth of thought or reasoning. The small kernel of truth in clichéd thinking is then applied as a blanket belief to the exterior world, so that the full range of human experience or the subtle complexities of the universe around us do not have to be examined. It is often a kind of either/or thinking dressed up as depth analysis.

Sometimes, clichéd thinking is the result of various kinds of social pressures rather than laziness. Sometimes the pressures are monetary (e.g., the pharmaceutical industry and its lobbyists), sometimes they are social (e.g., range of acceptable sexual expression in a culture), sometimes they are professional (e.g., expectations of other journalists and scientists about what you can and cannot say in print). Sometimes they are all three.

Most clichéd thinking is accepted as true because to not do so puts a person at odds with a group to which they belong. (And we have a basic need to belong; it's deep in our unconscious, a primary driving force.) If clichéd thinking is avoided, the writing that is then created often conflicts with the writer's community and generally leads to problems, including censure, angry letters, and condemnation. As John Gardner noted, *True art is too complex to reflect the party line. Art that tries hard to tell the truth unretouched is difficult and often offensive. It tears down our heroes and heart-warming convictions, violates canons of politeness and humane compromise.*

There is great energy underneath clichéd thinking. Always. Some knowledge or truth is being repressed when clichéd thinking is used. Always.

When the cliché is removed, when a writer begins to really look at what is being described, some powerful living thing enters the writing that was not present before. Much clichéd thinking in the arts exists for only one reason, to repress some truth that is too unsettling to be aired in polite company. When that truth is liberated, there is often tremendous energy in it and the work begins to genuinely approach art.

So, let's play with it a little so you can get an experience of what I'm talking about. Please pay close attention to your internal feelings and experiences as this process unfolds. These are a key to the amount of repressed energy that goes along with clichéd thinking.

Ready? Okay then, here we go . . . **Prostitutes.**

When you read the word *prostitutes* what happens inside you?

Are there images that come? What do you see?

Just be with it a minute and let all the associations you have with that word emerge. What *are* prostitutes? And what feelings, thoughts, and images do you have about them?

I have led this exercise many times with many kinds of people. Usually the associations people have with the word *prostitutes* emerge very quickly, in just milliseconds of time. And though responses can fall along the whole range of the possible they are often very similar.

If you allow the first image that occurs when you think of prostitutes to appear in your mind it is most likely, though by no means certain, to be an image of prostitutes on a poorly lit, city street. They are probably wearing the incredibly tacky clothes that only prostitutes on such dimly lit streets seem able to find. If you allow the image to remain in your mind, there may be the image of cars going by and the occasional reflection of storefront neon lights on black pavement. Then sound may come—of the cars that are passing and the prostitutes calling out to the drivers. There may be images of sex in a car, or in a shabby hotel room. And lurking in the background, there may be the image of a pimp—some man who controls the prostitute.

Rather bleak really.

This is an example of clichéd thinking, an everybody-knows-it's-so kind of image. (The only common alternative to this image, and one that emerges much less often in the exercise, is a high-class hooker in a very fancy hotel or brothel.) So, let's take it a bit further and see this clichéd thinking about prostitutes used in one of its various forms in a nonfictional work. The following piece (in *McMafia,* Knopf, 2008) is by Misha Glenny, someone's whose work I normally admire greatly (*The Fall of Yugoslavia* is a masterpiece).

By any standards, though, this place is the pits. The buildings and streets are in disrepair, brightened up only by the odd, flickering neon sign of a heart or a naked woman pointing to a hovel behind the shop fronts. The brothels themselves are the bottom of this mucky heap. I can barely describe the pathetic aging women listlessly chain-smoking in rooms seven feet by three, ready to service any passerby for ten bucks (yes, ten bucks).

It is impossible to ascertain which of these women are compelled by traffickers and which by economic circumstance, as everybody in the trade, including the women, is wary of careless talk. It may be that high-class call girls enjoy the economic freedom their work affords them. But my short tour around Tel Aviv's brothels made it clear that for most women in the industry, the happy hooker is a preposterous myth. Similarly it brought home how relentless the male sex drive is. Streams of men of different race, age, and class trotted in and out of the brothels as I was visiting them. The Jews are both secular and Orthodox; there are Palestinians from inside Israel and from the West Bank; there are a large number of Americans, West Europeans, and Japanese. Their faces indicate that they have overcome any qualms they may once have felt about their purchase of these services. I wonder if they were told the real stories behind the women they are abusing—women like Ludmila—how many would think again.

Instead of getting the holiday experience of a lifetime, Ludmila was kept locked in an apartment from six-thirty in the morning. At five-thirty in the afternoon, she was driven to a brothel above a pizza parlor on Bugashov Street, where she was forced to work for twelve hours in the high-volume second shift. "I worked seven days a week and had to service up to twenty clients per session," she explained. That is a euphemism. Ludmila was raped twenty times a night.[1]

This picture is very common, isn't it? And it tends to match and reinforce the images you may have had when I first mentioned the word *prostitutes.* But now, let's begin to get out of the cliché a little. The following appeared in *Harpers Magazine* in August of 2007. It is abridged and condensed (a *Harper*'s habit when compiling their Readings section) from chapter 1 ("High Priestesses, Low Victims") of the book *A Woman Whose Calling is Men.*

In America, no matter how vigorously we women break ties with patriarchal dominion, and no matter how thoroughly we subdue the religions from which the patriarchy stabs, and no matter how many millennia have passed since the founding of our woe, our sense of loss subtly lingers within us. It's a quiet but potent malignancy, the awareness of a shadowy brink, a nebulous rooting in sad dislocation. Our moody hormonal design is held responsible, but there's more to it than that. No matter how little of our herstory *we know, most of us women sense, deep down, that somewhere, somehow, we got royally fucked over.*

Women take it out on one another. And women ferociously take it out on men. And whores get the worst of it, from everyone. When contemporary women become manfully successful, as CEOs, surgeons, or airline pilots, everyone but the Taliban is likely to cheer them on. But when they professionally take off their clothes, reveal their clitorises and vulvas, and enable orgasms for money, there's a universal gasp of consternation.

Clearly, there are two kinds of prostitutes. There are whores who take great pride in their work, and there are whores who despise themselves for it. Whenever I consider that disparity, I find myself picturing all whores as one woman. She's naked, waist-deep in a warm pond. All around her is a lush, lovely June. Gushes of color spread over the greenery in wildflower-burgeoning meadows. Big summertime branches are billowing. Her face and torso are absorbing fresh air and sun, and her hands are free to splash herself whenever she needs to be cooled. The rest of her, however, trapped in the murky pond-bottom muck, knows no such pleasure.

That picture makes me face facts: there are whores who have a bad time. Those of us happily sunning ourselves must acknowledge that no whore will truly be emancipated until all whores are. Until the end of the disparity, whores will lack the unity needed to converge in large numbers and proudly "come out" wherever we are, which is everywhere. Sex work is not the sleazy arena where victim-

identified women feel shame. Sex work is the showground, radiating with power, where insightful whore-feminists rebelliously disrobe.

Feminists are insurgents who fight sick male power, but when were they last taken seriously? Now they're just part of the problem. No group understands that more than whores. Whores will be part of the movement toward a truly egalitarian, sincerely pluralistic, far less judgmental American spirit. As whores begin to reclaim their role as the primordial priestesses and the culture begins to perceive it, their advancement will be one of a host of indications of feminine principles pervading the world and feminine principles healing Mother Earth. A prostitute is a comfort station, she's a relief, an oasis on men's battlefields—and a true whore knows to be proud of it.[2]

The author, the pseudonymous Aphrodite Phoenix, is unashamed of human sexuality—neither your nor my inherent sexuality, not the act of sex, not the selling of sex (for her, there is no "ick" factor). "We overtly acknowledge the sanctity of our genitals," she says, "and we don't just bless them as life-giving. We also bless them as pleasure-giving and lucratively so."[3]

For Phoenix, openly acknowledged sexuality *and* the profession of prostitution are essential to feminism, essential as well to the ecological restoration of our world. Sex must be *integrated* into Western cultures as an active and accepted part of what it means to be human, for its repression is inherently connected to the ecological and cultural problems we face. In consequence, she says . . .

We don't just gather in vulva-shaped caves and consecrate our feminine parts; we don't just hold hands and chant earthy phrases and proclaim that our menstrual blood isn't dirty. Such ceremonies are basic. Any mainstream feminist can attend them, with minimal disruption to her patriarch-molded life.

We, the true whores, go much further. We cross the line. We break the rules. We take back the temples. . . . We offer our bodies to the Goddess-hungry world.

And everyone is scandalized. Even our most feminist peers are appalled . . . [but] our sexual insurgence is hardly degradation. It's a gorgeous reawakening, a deep-down liberation, the retrieval of our ancient, erotic sanctity.[4]

This begins to reveal a more complex perspective doesn't it? The author of this book, one of the more powerful writings I have read by a first-time writer, is not a high-priced call girl by the way, just a mother in suburbia putting her children through school and paying the bills (much more effectively, she says, than working at McDonalds).

So, now, let's extend the picture a bit more and look at part of an article by Belinda Brooks-Gordon in the London newspaper the *Guardian.*

In her speech to the Labour conference this September, the home secretary Jacqui Smith made clear her intention to criminalize clients of "trafficked" sex workers and stated that, from October, she will begin work to outlaw paying for sex with those who are "forced into prostitution at another's will, or controlled for another's gain."

Stirring stuff, yet Smith seems coy about giving the actual figures for trafficked workers. The official figures for the police operation Pentameter 1 showed, that despite 55 forces hunting for them, only 88 women were trafficked. Since it is accepted on all sides of the debate that 80,000 work in the sex industry, then the number of those trafficked amounts to 0.11% of those in sex work. According to a recent parliamentary answer, Pentameter 2 improved on that performance with the recovery of 167 victims of trafficking—but that still represents only 0.21% of sex workers.

In other words, the impression Smith gives that the sex industry is rife with trafficking is highly misleading.[5]

The images that people have of prostitutes, as I mentioned, are often clichéd. They almost never include the awareness that these women are mothers and sisters and girlfriends, students and artists. They do not include the awareness that they mow their lawns, take their children to soccer practice, cook food, dance for fun, write books, are politically active, are rarely addicted to drugs, or are deeply thoughtful about the human condition. That is, that they are human beings—normal, average people—just like you and me. And those clichéd images almost never include a baseline assumption that they have the capacity to reason as well as you do, to examine the choices before them and to consciously decide that prostitution is what they really want to do. Most likely, almost certainly, they are viewed as women without choice. As victims. However, according to the Prostitutes Education Network (www.bayswan.org), percentagewise few of them see themselves as victims, and many of them are becoming powerfully active in the political realm . . .

> *It is difficult to estimate the number of persons who currently work, or have ever worked as prostitutes for many reasons including the various definitions of prostitution. National arrest figures range over 100,000. The National Task Force on Prostitution suggests that over one million people have worked as prostitutes in the United States, or about 1% of American women . . .*
>
> *The ratio of on-street prostitution to off-street (sauna, massage parlor, in call-outcall, escort) varies in cities depending on local law, policy and custom . . . street prostitution accounts for between 10 to 20% of the prostitution in larger cities such as Los Angeles, San Francisco and New York [meaning that 80–90% of those engaged in selling sex are not on the street and do not fit the picture the media commonly portrays in their stories] . . .*
>
> *Some researchers suggest that prostitutes, in general, suffer from 'negative identities' or lack of self-esteem. A 1986 study by Diane Prince, however, found call girls and brothel workers had higher self esteem than before they became prostitutes. 97% of call girls liked themselves more 'than they did before.'*[6]

So, a still more complex picture begins to emerge. It is not either/or. Prostitution is not either "the happy hooker" or "the victimized, forced-to-have-sex, economically disadvantaged (possibly trafficked) woman" but rather a much more complex phenomenon that exists across a much broader range. It begins to appear that prostitutes are just people with the full range of work and life experiences that all people possess. If we look deeper the picture becomes even more complex.

Here's some material from Laura María Agustín's powerful *Sex at the Margins: Migration, Labour Markets and the Rescue Industry* (Zed Books, 2007):

> *[Most women choose to work in the sex industry; they are not forced into it and] working conditions vary enormously: giving a blowjob inside a car, or in an alley in the rain, is not the same as doing it as part of a shift inside a comfortable club. People also perceive jobs in different ways: some find working in a brothel less alienating and isolating (than working from home or being a live-in domestic); others prefer working from the street because they feel more independent. Every job is easy for some people and impossibly difficult for others. Many work only part-time or occasionally. As in every sector [of the economic world], workers feel confident and in command of their work when they have more experience. Generalisations about 'sex work' and 'prostitution' can only mislead. . . .*
>
> *Many critics who consider exploitation and violence to be inherent in the sale of sex point to the figure of the 'pimp', traditionally a man who closely controls the movements of street workers, taking their money and threatening them physically in exchange for protection services. Although the classic figure does exist in some times and places, he is unknown to most workers. . . .*
>
> *[And] not only women sell sex. Activists who condemn 'prostitution' as patriarchal violence focus on women (and children) and usually imply that men who sell sex are intrinsically different and few in number. Certainly, the stereotypes concern women, and women are those overtly stigmatized and targeted for rescue. However, male workers abound; researchers and outreach workers estimate they exceed women in some places and times; and men have been called more stigmatized because their presence is not even acknowledged. Those seeking women in 'prostitute' uniform in the streets walk straight past men without seeing them. Transsexual, transgender, transvestite and intergender people are also abundant in the industry, the most well-known being those labeled men at birth and who are changing to, or express, a more feminised state. . . . In the sex industry, gender issues are extremely complex and subtle.*[7]

Agustín next describes the effects of a talk she is asked to give on trafficking and her decades of research to an association established for helping abused women. The association is hosting a seminar on sexual violence.

> *Soon after I begin, I see tension, shock, anxiety and displeasure on the faces in the audience, but it is too late to do anything but go on. At the end, I am asked questions in an acid tone prefaced with references to my supposed opinions: 'these delightful sex clubs you are so fond of', 'those respectful gentlemen you call clients', 'such a wonderful job, prostitution'. My responses all begin the same way: 'I didn't say that, I said one can make a lot of money in the clubs' or 'I didn't say that, I said that the numbers of men who buy sex mean they can't all be perverts' or 'I didn't say that, I said some people prefer selling sex to other available jobs.' . . .*
>
> *Why do they hear things I haven't said? They seem offended that I don't talk about what the media say every day, even though the organisers particularly told me they wanted new information. But here and now, they only want to know why I don't mention slavery, mafias, child abuse, psychological damage and violence. In fact, I have mentioned them, but I don't condemn anyone, and they seem dissatisfied at the lack of outraged indignation. Even when I do talk about clients, the audience feel I haven't, because they want to hear me say terrible things about men. . . .*
>
> *[Later, I tell one of the women that she doesn't have to agree with me, she can tell me what she really thinks.] Sputtering and red-faced, she declares that 'prostitution' is always, in all situations, abuse and violence. It is imperialism, invasion of women's bodies. It is the antithesis of love. . . . The men are cruel, egotistical perverts who should be put in prison. No woman ever, ever wants to sell sex, she is only forced to, and if she says differently then she is lying or doesn't understand her own situation.*
>
> *Later I learn that these feminists have never studied 'prostitution'. No wonder we have a problem. . . . The woman whose blood boiled specialises in changing sexist language, believing that the words we use are overarchingly important to gender equity. She hates my*

> *way of talking and wants me and everyone to change our language, to instead speak in terms of sexual exploitation and abuse, making it impossible to consent to sell sex and making buyers criminals. . . . If 'prostitution' can be universally redefined as sexual exploitation, regardless of whether people say they choose to sell sex or not, then all those who purchase sexual services become, by definition, exploiters. For those who believe men are inherently and biologically aggressive and predatory, this traditional battle of the sexes feels real.*[8]

Agustín brings an elegant nuance to the field. Her writing is clear, powerful, and articulate. It remains rooted in the moment, a succinct articulation of what *is* rather than a lazy repetition of clichéd thinking. So, if I wanted to avoid the use of cliché when writing about a severe thunderstorm, if I focused on what *is*, I might write something like this . . .

> *The rain is relentless; my whole world has contracted to this tiny moment in time. There is me and the storm and between us only this insubstantial metal roof writhing like a living thing, arguing with its fastenings, attempting to fly, a metal magic carpet wanting to escape on the wind. And those screws I had, so sure of myself, put in one-by-one? Only those tiny screws are holding that roof in place. With every flutter of the metal, I can hear them screech, hear them slowly letting go. One-by-one-by-one.*
>
> *And every so often the white, actinic glare of a close lightning strike stabs through the windows and paints everything with stark black and white shadowing. Then the massive thunder comes, the house staggers from the blow and the shadows dance on the walls. I cower and stare out the window, my vision restricted to a few inches beyond the glass. The only things that exist in my world now are the rain, the lightning, the thunder, and this insubstantial house surrounding me. I am cut off, our modern world erased. I am at the mercy of the elements, less than a grain of sand before the storm.*

Quite different from "raining cats and dogs," isn't it? Agustín, too, leaves cliché behind and writes of what she has found, not in a *"short tour around Tel Aviv's brothels"* as Glenny did but from years of study in numerous countries throughout the world. She tears the lid off clichéd thinking and some of that powerful repressed energy begins to spill out, to come off the page, to be freed.

Now, let's extend this further and see how the poet Etheridge Knight develops the nuance of sexuality and gender in one of his poems.

Now you take ol Rufus. He beat drums,
was free and funky under the arms,
fucked white girls, jumped off a bridge
(and thought nothing of the sacrilege),
he copped out—and he was over twenty-one.

Take Gerald. Sixteen years hadn't even done
a good job on his voice. He didn't even know
how to talk tough, or how to hide the glow
of life before he was thrown in as "pigmeat"
for the buzzards to eat.

Gerald, who had no memory or hope of copper hot lips—
of firm upthrusting thighs
to reinforce his flow,
let tall walls and buzzards change the course
of his river from south to north.

(No safety in numbers, like back on the block:
two's plenty, three? Definitely not.
Four? "you're all muslims."
Five? "you were planning a race riot."
plus, Gerald could never quite win
with his precise speech and innocent grin
the trust and fist of the young black cats.)

Gerald, sun-kissed ten thousand times on the nose
and cheeks, didn't stand a chance,
didn't even know that the loss of his balls
had been plotted years in advance
by wiser and bigger buzzards than those

who now hover above his tract
and at night light upon his back.[9]

Etheridge Knight wrote that poem, as he did many of them, in prison. This one, as Robert Bly comments, is "about men raping men; it doesn't fall into the cliché that rape is done to subdue women; and he lets go all the talk of rehabilitation, therapy, everything can be corrected."[10]

Knight's poem touches not only on the collateral damage to young men who are sent to prison (something for which we are all responsible) but on the surprising truth that when we take prison rape into account, we must acknowledge the fact that more men than women are raped every year in the United States. (And that touches on the point Agustín raised earlier, doesn't it? Why is it that, when it comes to this aspect of sex, men become invisible? Just what is it that is being repressed? Is it only our ubiquitous sexuality? Or is there something more? Something deeper?)

Part of Etheridge's power is his tremendous respect for his readers. The poem describes something specific but he lets his readers work with the material themselves; he doesn't tell them how to feel, how to think, or how to believe to remain moral (as Glenny does). He captures something in language then lets it go, like opening a cage door and letting a bird take flight. The bird alights someplace inside us and he trusts us to find that place on our own, to make relationship with the bird in our own way. He trusts the truth receiver inside us and he trusts our capacity to move toward truth, to take in this kind of food and become moral in our own way, at our own speed, in our own time.

There are few writers with that degree of trust in their readers or that kind of courage in their work . . . Stafford is another.

Glenny, in contrast, takes the easy way out; he uses a half page to deliver a clichéd concept without doing the hard work to find out how true his thinking is before he applies it as a general condition. He avoids the hard work of dropping down inside himself to find out just what his own biases and assumptions are and how they surreptitiously are entering his writing.

The situation he describes in *McMafia* actually has nothing to do with prostitution but everything to do with trafficking in human beings and the illegality of sex work. (Legalization would alter the entire frame, just as it did with alcohol and *its* prohibition.) He has conflated slavery with prostitution, accepted the effects of prohibition as inherent to the work, and contaminated any possible discussions of sex work with something very much unrelated to it. He has, through literary sleight of mouth, connected our cultural discomfort with our own sexuality (and with the selling of it) to the trafficking of human beings, to sex work itself, and to economic oppression of the weak.[11] He manipulates how we are supposed to feel by (among other things) the use of specific words: *mucky, pathetic, listlessly, serviced, compelled, relentless male sex drive, abusing, raped*. The result is women as victims, men as victimizers, and the natural expression of human sexuality (and sex work) as something violent, depraved, immoral. And the way his writing is structured makes it nearly impossible to take any other position without seeming morally suspect.

Though carefully hidden in his writing, the main issues in his material are slavery, the cultural repression of sex as a natural expression of the human, and the effects of prohibition on sex work, not prostitution—and those issues are where his writing should have remained focused. Men, women, and children are still captured, owned, and sold as slaves throughout the world, an estimated 27 million of all colors, creeds, and nationalities. Most of them are forced to work as farmers, loggers, miners, child soldiers, and garment workers. Prostitution is only one category of many and not, even then, the largest of them. As the head of the Human Trafficking Centre, Grahame Maxwell (also head constable of North Yorkshire, England) has said, "There are more people trafficked for labour exploitation than there are for sexual exploitation. We need to redress the balance here. People just seem to grab figures from the air."[12]

There are reasons why good writers, why any writer, avoids the hard work of surmounting clichéd thinking: laziness, an unwillingness to engage in interior examination and reflection, an attachment to an identity-defining belief, a fear of becoming undefended or naked inside the work, the desire to not offend one's group, and failure to trust the readers' innate intelligence or capacity to determine the truth of a thing for themselves. But in many instances there is a further element, the cheap and tawdry use of an artificial energy source to power the work. It's called the drama triangle and it's perhaps one of the most common ways poor writers inject motive force into a work. It's deadly to art. Gardner talks about it this way . . .

> *If the storyteller tries to make us burst into tears at the misfortunes of some character we hardly know, if the storyteller appeals to stock response (our love of God or country, our pity for the downtrodden, the presumed warm feelings that all people have for children and small animals); if he tries to make us cry by cheap melodrama, telling us the victim that we hardly know is all innocence and goodness and the oppressor all vile black-heartedness; or if he tries to win us over not by the detailed and authenticated virtues of the unfortunates but by rhetorical clichés, by breathless sentences, or by super-dramatic one-sentence paragraphs . . . then the effect is sentimentality and no reader who's experienced the power of real [writing] will be pleased by it.*[13]

THE DRAMA TRIANGLE

Everyone of us knows what the drama triangle is; we see it every day on television or in newspapers. It goes something like this: some innocent person (often a child or female or both) is walking along minding her own business, just enjoying the wonder and joy of being alive, and out of nowhere comes a bad person (usually male, often a member of a minority, usually poor rather than rich but sometimes a corporation run by white males) and causes some terrible damage to the innocent person, which ruins the otherwise wonderful life she would have had. The innocent young girl is the victim, the bad person is the persecutor (or victimizer), and the final member of the triangle? (There are always three.) Well, that's us, reading the account, or perhaps the newswriter, or maybe an organization that calls for something to be done to "protect the innocent." Usually it is all of those together who form the third member of the triad: the rescuer.

The drama triangle is pervasive and it reduces people to cardboard thickness. The innocent person is naively innocent and good. She possesses no other human characteristics, no greater multidimensionality of self. The bad person is not really a person but something not quite human really. Just bad (and if only we can get rid of all the people like that, we will all live happy lives). The rescuer, usually someone who has experienced some kind of victimization herself, responds in outrage, determined that no one will ever experience that kind of abuse again.

Whether it's health care for all, land mines in Africa, attacks on the Gaza strip (or on Israel), prostitution, carjacking, drugs, or guns it doesn't matter. The story's the same, just the names and locations change. The person who's in the victim position represents the innocent child, now horribly damaged, and we who read her story are encouraged to correlate the innocent, once wounded, child in us with the innocent, damaged, child in her.

All of us have had those moments of betrayal and hurt and we are encouraged by the stories we see to project that old hurt onto this new situation. We project our pain onto the bad man in the current circumstance. And our outrage encourages us to move into a kind of lynch mob mentality to rescue all innocents everywhere, to pass laws, to send the perpetrators to jail and throw away the key, to make the world safe forever from this kind of evil. (And this is a major reason why the United States now has one of every thirty-one adults in prison, in jail, on parole, on probation, or under supervision. The most of any country in the world. Though the United States has only 5 percent of the world population, 25 percent of the world's prisoners are in American prisons.)[14]

All of us know the drama triangle. No writer should ever use it. It is not honorable writing, it is not accurate to the world, it reduces complex questions to one-picture answers that are often wrong, reduces the complexity of human beings to single dimensions. It creates the illusion that a previous state of victimization automatically confers superior wisdom and a moral conscience others do not have. It leverages a common belief, that those who have suffered have a greater degree of insight about what should be done to prevent future victimization (or how to appropriately sentence offenders) than others do. They don't, but it breaks powerful taboos in the United States to say so, something that is very hard for people to do. A previous state of victimization does not automatically confer moral authority or greater wisdom on anyone, or, as Barbara Ehrenreich once put it, "a uterus is no substitute for a conscience."

The drama triangle perpetuates vengeance as justice, removes humanity and human dimension from large segments of the population, creates cascades of unintended consequences, gives the illusion of doing something to address problems (while leaving the actual problems unaddressed), and perpetuates myths about reality that injure democracy and future generations. It is lie dressed up as truth. It pulls on people's unresolved feelings about old pain and uses that unresolved rage to power poor writing. It does not trust people to see what is true for themselves, does not trust them to make up their minds for themselves. It is not moral writing.

All of us engage in the drama triangle from time to time, most of us at low levels. It's a way of relieving the energy that builds up inside us from the daily impact of situations over which we have little control, e.g., inequitable taxation or inner-city congestion. All of us have played or will play it at more intense levels sometime in our lives. We feel victimized by something, we get angry, we decide that no one will again experience what we did, and we become proactive. Over time, we find, as people always have, that solutions created out of the drama triangle ultimately cause just as much victimization as they are intended to relieve. We learn there is a law of unintended consequences.[15]

It *is* possible to find, and institute, solutions to social problems without being in the drama triangle (and thus reduce significantly the emergence of unintended consequences) but the first step is to cease using the drama triangle as a lens through which to view life and through which we design solutions to social problems. Something else emerges then, a very different approach to problems, which can only be found through such maturity of character, such refusal to take the easy way out. As Clarissa Pinkola Estes comments . . .

> *There is no ethnic group on the face of this earth that has not been slaughtered; viz Angles, Saxons, Jutes, Britons. When, after a conflict, the best balanced leaders who have a stake in the future of all persons, are bypassed, and instead power is seized by the angriest and most grudge-holding, whose greatest stake is in the past. . . . Without new consciousness, and without strong reconciling actions, thus erupts a horrible recycling of living out the least of what is human in this world.*[16]

Nonfiction, if it is art, should modify prejudice, not carve it in stone as immutable truth. It should humanize, not reduce people to one-dimensional stereotypes. As Gardner once commented, a writer like Glenny is not using his work "as a mode of thought but merely as a means of preaching his peculiar doctrine. The more appealing or widely shared the doctrine, the more immoral the book."[17]

Clichéd thinking is, by nature, superficial thinking. As with a cliché, you can tell its emergence in a work by a certain fatigue of mind that occurs when the material is read or, more analytically, by the presence of one-dimensional blanket concepts or ideas that remain superficial, starkly good and bad people, or by the utilization of the drama triangle. It can only be avoided, as with *raining cats and dogs,* by a truly descriptive focus on the material at hand. And because the presence of clichéd thinking always indicates the presence of unexamined beliefs and repressed energy, it demands interior self-reflection.

If you find that you have clichéd thinking in your work, if you are writing your material around the drama triangle, the only way out is to look at the material itself and follow your discomfort to where it leads—deep inside, to the place you don't want to see, the thing you wish to hide or hide from. Then when you get there, begin to write what is true in all its difficulty. You will find more power in your work, a huge amount of energy will be released, and you will begin to say something that all of us truly need to hear.

The choice is always there: to be true to your calling or to be true to your wish to not see what is inside you. Both have consequences. With one, you extend awareness further than society wants it to go. With the other . . . well, all of us discover that one. In time.

The singer/songwriter Mike Williams puts it like this:

> *After we cease to be children, we seem to stop discovering ourselves for free. The price of self-awareness rises until it reaches a level we are no longer willing to pay except in moments of extreme duress. So we just stay however partially aware we have become, and muddle along.*
>
> *You are the only person who can decide what your price is.*[18]

The price of self-awareness for a writer is often very high indeed.[19]

CHAPTER TWENTY

Hidden Baggage

> *What the honest writer does, when he's finished a rough draft, is to go over it and over it, time after time, refusing to let anything stay if it looks awkward, phony, or forced.*
>
> JOHN GARDNER

> *The tics of mannered writing, on the other hand, are those from which we gather, by the prickling of our thumbs, some ulterior purpose on the writer's part, a purpose perhaps not fully conscious but nevertheless suspect, putting us on our guard. Think of John Dos Passos at his most self-important, or George Bernard Shaw when he pontificates. . . . Mannered writing, then—like sentimentality and frigidity—arises out of flawed character.*
>
> JOHN GARDNER

> *Every word has to earn its way onto the page.*
>
> BEN MIKAELSEN

We all have hidden baggage inside us, unexamined beliefs, attitudes, and orientations of mind we have internalized. It's part of the human predicament. Discovering, understanding, and deciding what to do about that hidden baggage is an inescapable part of our maturing. It is an inescapable necessity, as well, for every writer who wishes to truly practice the craft, for every unexamined belief, attitude, and orientation of mind you have will flow into and through everything you write. Misha Glenny's material in the last chapter is a perfect example of how that looks—and *feels*—in a finished work.

Hidden baggage attaches itself to your writing through unconscious word choice and sentence structure. *Everything* that you have not self-examined will eventually show up in your work through such unconscious choices. As Gardner puts it, "language inevitably carries values with it, and unexamined language carries values one might, if one knew they were there, be ashamed of accidentally promoting."[1] Once "one has made a strong psychological investment in a certain kind of language," he notes, "one has trouble understanding that it distorts reality."[2] To the conscious mind hidden baggage is out of sight, under the water. But like barnacles growing on the hull of a ship, it impedes the smooth flow of writing. It's an unrecognized friction and weight, hovering unseen just below the surface of the material, holding it back, dragging it down.

Hidden baggage in writing is often unintentional on a writer's part. So, it's crucial, over time, to develop the habit of self-reflection to reduce its presence as much as possible. There will always be something missed (writing is a journey, not a destination) but it should not be missed for want of trying.

Here are some examples of three (of the four) primary ways hidden baggage can emerge in a work. They might be called unconscious baggage, embarrassed baggage, and ego baggage. (The fourth we've already talked about. It comes from clichéd thinking. It might be called cliché baggage, or peer-pressure baggage, or even herd-mentality baggage.)

UNCONSCIOUS BAGGAGE

This kind of hidden baggage comes, very simply, from a lack of interior self-reflection (or a lack of maturity with it). It is common among the young or those who have never discovered the existence of their internal world and thus never realized that the shape of that world comes, in part, from beliefs and perspectives absorbed through family, culture, profession, and language. It is common among people who do not engage in interior self-reflection.

You've already read an example of it earlier in this book . . .

Without guidance, adolescents create their own rituals and values with their own dress, symbols, language, beliefs, and blessings. Because they are created by the adolescents themselves, they do not contain good advice.

As Gardner noted, "by the prickling of our thumbs" we can tell something is wrong in there someplace, even if we don't immediately know what it is. Carl Hammerschlag, the author of that passage, might be said to be lacking any understanding of what Adam Phillips has called "the truant mind."[3] That is, every human being must, of necessity, engage in behaviors that push on accepted convention to enable the individual to determine, for themself, what kind of behaviors work and what kind do not. They must become truant from accepted modes of behavior. To learn to not betray the self, for example, one must first betray the self and find out what happens when one does, and how it feels. One must learn experientially to understand *why* betrayal of the self is a bad idea. It's the only way it *can* be learned.

Adults that have not come to terms with their own truant mind cannot easily understand adolescents and the biological and psychological necessity that drives them to certain acts. (They became good grown-ups too early.) Certainly, they cannot trust the inherent intelligence of adolescents or understand that, like all human beings, adolescents can genuinely create (rather than cheaply imitate) and generally do understand the distinction between the genuine and the false. Hammerschlag doesn't seem to understand that adolescents are human beings, just like the rest of us, and possess the same capacities we all possess. He removes perceptual intelligence from one group of human beings simply because of their age. That Mozart (along with numerous painters, mathematicians, and writers in all times and on all continents) created many of his great works when an adolescent has apparently escaped him.

A lot of nonfiction suffers from this kind of unconscious baggage. Let's look at a more subtle form of it. Here is an example from the book *When Languages Die* by K. David Harrison (Oxford University Press, 2007).

Harrison's book is on an important topic: the nature of language, its formation out of unique cultural engagements with reality, and what happens when languages are lost. There are certain terms in French, for example, that are not directly translatable into English; one culture engages an aspect of reality that another does not and captures that experience in its language. You might say that all languages encode the results of a cultural exploration of the nature of reality. Because every culture, like every individual, experiences reality in slightly different ways, how they linguistically encode what they have experienced gives clues to the nature of reality (as a whole) that it is not prudent to lose. As a specific: Hunter/gatherer groups tend to develop an extreme keenness of perception of the natural world and then to create language to reflect what they have perceived. Many such groups possess a greater sophistication of taxonomy than industrial groups (and their scientists). That is, they see minute and often important distinctions in plants—their ecosystem function and relationships—that are routinely missed by members of industrial cultures, no matter how well they are schooled in universities. These distinctions of perception matter a great deal when wide ecosystem problems emerge, as they now have emerged, for the species as a whole. Harrison comments succinctly on this when he notes: "The longer a people have inhabited and made use of an ecological niche and practiced a particular lifeway, the more likely they will have applied their linguistic genius to describing that ecosystem."[4] (Oh, what a beautiful line: *their linguistic genius.*) Ten thousand generations, or more, of exploration dies when a language dies.

Harrison is well meaning and the book contains important explorations and many unique insights on the nature of language in culture, but he is young and his book is filled with baggage he's unaware of. For instance:

> *Scientists try to avoid being sentimental about what they study. But in working with speakers of disappearing languages, it is hard not to take seriously their own feelings of sadness, regret, even anger at the fate of their language. . . . Linguists and anthropologists have set out to see what science may learn from these knowledge systems. . . . While science may serve the needs of the speech community, this is not scientists' primary goal.*[5]

In this section Harrison glosses over an important conflict between certain forms of scientific study and the natural human empathy for the objects of that study. In essence, he is apologizing for having feelings. The third and fourth sentences I quote, reveal the source of his discomfort—

an internalized epistemological error. He uses the word *science* as a proper noun as in: "to see what science may learn." In actuality, in reality, science is not a living being; it can learn nothing. That this is a common error committed by many writers makes it no less egregious. Science is a tool, like a hammer, used, as a hammer is, for a specific purpose. (Science, in fact, is simply a method of inquiry—and not the only one, analogical thinking is another.) Writing that sentence as "to see what hammer may learn" makes just as much sense. It is an epistemological error, a problem in the software, a misidentification of the nature of reality. It causes a logic interrupt, short circuits analysis, and generates problems in behavior, as all epistemological errors do.

By referring to science as a living being with intelligence and the capacity to learn and to act, human responsibility for using the tool that science is and the human capacity for moral action is diminished or eliminated entirely. Science demands a behavior (because that is what science does) and the scientist conforms to that demand (because one must in order to be a scientist). The scientist has no responsibility for the science he then conducts. Responsibility for individual behavior, for the choices an individual makes, is removed from the actor, the scientist, and moved to some nebulous entity, Science. Harrison is in the midst of a personal struggle, between what he believes moral action entails (caring) and what he has been taught (and accepted) as being correct behavior for a scientist (having no feelings about the objects of his study). The result of this internal conflict is a holding back, a circumspection, a timid apology that flows through his text. This reduces its power and impact and he ends up pleading as he makes his case rather than powerfully letting his writing stand for what he truly believes. These hidden beliefs, about what science is and is not and about the proper behavior of a scientist, cling like barnacles below the surface of the material. They interfere with the meaning and content and flow of the work.

This kind of unconscious baggage is common in the young and in new writers; none of us are exempt. The only way to get rid of it is to write it out over and over again and to learn from the ever-recurring sense of something not quite right in what we have written.

All of us know something is wrong when this kind of thing gets into our writing. We feel it, but don't really understand, in the beginning, what *is* wrong. There's a lingering feeling of something amiss, a prickling of the thumbs. It nags, comes boiling up out of the unconscious at 3 a.m., waking us up, demanding a response, until the reasons are understood and corrected. Every genuine writer who has written something like this walks around with a nagging sense of wrongness and can't let it go, no matter how much they try to shrug it off. So, they keep working with it, coming back to it again and again, until, eventually, they figure it out. With deeply held, and cherished, unconscious beliefs, it can sometimes takes years for that nagging feeling to unconceal itself to the internal gaze, to reveal just what the problem is. Nevertheless, over time, we do figure it out. The writing, the craft, and our own sense of self-respect demand it.

EMBARRASSED BAGGAGE

This next example, hidden baggage that comes out of embarrassment, has some similar roots to Harrison's. It's a piece from Gary Paul Nabhan and Stephen Buchmann's book *The Forgotten Pollinators*. Nabhan is a great deal more accomplished a writer than Harrison and I'm a great admirer of his work. This following section, however, is by his cowriter Stephen Buchmann, and Buchmann falters badly in the writing, something Nabhan never should have allowed.

Their book is an important one as well. It's about the crucial function of pollinators to ecological health, the coevolutionary relationships, often millions of years old, that exist between pollinators and their plants, the accelerating die-off of pollinators, and what that means to the ecological integrity of the planet.

Throughout the book, the writers talk in genuinely loving detail about the nature and life of pollinators. They *cherish* them. They clearly understand that all these pollinators are *needed*. And they know as well that pollinators are a great deal more important to the functioning of the earth's ecosystems than human beings. Nevertheless, read how Buchmann describes the capturing and ultimate disposition of some pollinators he is studying in an area of the Sonoran desert near Tucson, Arizona.

> *I took a swing at an extremely fast-flying gray blur of a bee, but missed. It was a male digger bee. It was an old friend to me: a big*

> *gray* Centris pallida *female, a harbinger of spring. In fact, I began studying the mating habits of this species with another friend, entomologist John Alcock, nearly 20 years ago. . . . I then swept up as many kinds as I could capture that day, recording their nectar sources and periods of activity. Back at the Arizona-Sonora Desert Museum at day's end, I dumped my catch onto a piece of notebook paper and sorted the pile of now quiescent bees into groups to show Gary. . . . In all, during just a few morning hours, I had collected solitary and primitively social native bees belonging to 6 families, 20 genera, and perhaps as many as 50 different species. . . . The possibility of nabbing something new to science—by intensively sweeping our nets through the canopies of even the most common tree—was not an unrealistic expectation for the day's bee hunt.*[6]

In this particular passage Buchmann uses language that is exceptionally incongruent to the content and writing in the rest of the book. Worse, he uses sleight-of-mouth technique to hide what he's really saying.

Nabhan and Buchmann's book is concerned with protecting pollinators, some of them considerably rare and endangered. Most of their writing uses language that reflects this. But in this section, hidden baggage, much of it due to embarrassment I suspect, emerges in language that is very different in tone. Here Buchmann "takes a swing" at a pollinator, "swept up" others (a term all too close to cleaning a floor), "dumped" them onto a "piece of notebook paper" (continuing the image of floor cleaning), sorted the "pile" (continuing it yet again) and "nabbed something new to science." Nabbed.

The way the material is written conveys a picture of a happy-go-lucky sort of guy, just hangin', knockin' back some brewskies, playin' a little badminton with the guys, and catchin' some rays . . . and a few interestin' critterz, too. A nice guy really with no shadow side at all. But Buchmann's language conflicts with the rest of the book and even with his statement "an old friend to me."

It is incongruent to take a swipe at an old friend, a swipe that, if successful, will result in its death. And make no mistake about it, all the bees he captured, he killed. But he hides this truth, intentionally, in perhaps the most egregious part of the piece when he talks about the *"now quiescent bees."* That is, the dead bees. That he killed.

This is sleight-of-mouth technique. The phrase *quiescent bees* is structured so the reader's mind will slide over the truth it is meant to conceal—that he killed a lot of pollinators, some of which, no doubt, are endangered. The phrase brings up images of resting, not dying, and his use of it is intentional so we won't emotionally feel the impact of what he's done.

As Harrison did, he then talks about science as if it were an intelligent being, something capable of action, something that, unrelated to the humans involved in it, objectively, and without repercussion, searches out information about the world. Buchmann is merely the servant of the process, with little or no responsibility for his actions. (A more subtle element in this is his mention of the digger bee as "an old friend to me." What is actually true is that he did not know that particular bee, so it was not, could not be, an old friend. The statement is, in fact, a lie. He was talking about the *species,* not the individual bee at all. This type of communication hides a particularly dismissive, fairly patronizing orientation common among scientists who speak of science as a living being. It is bias, hidden in innocuous-sounding words.)

It's clear from the development of the piece that Buchmann knew exactly what he was doing. He knew he killed the bees, he just didn't want to say it. He could feel the incongruency between killing them and the orientation of the rest of the book but did not know what to do about it. He reveals throughout the book that he possesses a high degree of intelligence and self-awareness, but he has not resolved this particular conflict. So, in embarrassment, he hides it. He does so not only through the sleight-of-mouth phrase, *"now quiescent bees,"* but also through the way he developed his persona, his *voice.* And, in actuality, that persona development is only a more sophisticated sleight-of-mouth technique. By pulling the reader into the fact of his goodness, wrapping them up in his brewski persona, he tricks them into missing the reality of his predator nature and the shadow side of his scientific pursuits.

Every writer runs into this kind of problem. It's an internal conflict that arises from unintegrated values—the person who eats meat but won't kill their own food. When unintegrated values emerge in a writer's work, it's readily recognizable. The writer cringes somehow when the topic emerges, hides the truth because of what it says about them. And by the prickling of our thumbs we know something is wrong in the text. What is apparently being said doesn't match what is really being said. One communication on top, another hidden underneath.

Unintegrated values are difficult problems to resolve. The only viable solution, as most of us learn by first trying everything else we can think of, is facing the conflict directly and struggling toward resolution.

Nabhan and Buchmann's book would have been far more useful and much more deeply human if they had, together, openly addressed the conflict. Since all people struggle with unintegrated values, their open engagement would have helped their readers in their own struggles with unintegrated values. It would have helped them be more deeply human, more able to deal with the subtle internal conflicts that face all of us when culture/ecosystem clashes occur.

Nabhan and Buchmann's failure is, however, even more damaging because this particular conflict is central to the topic of their book. It points up a significant problem with the use of science. If simply using the tool impoverishes ecosystem health, what do we, as a species, do about our use of the tool when we use it to study ecosystem function? That question is central to the conflicts that face us as a species and sooner or later it must be addressed. Directly. If Nabhan and Buchmann had addressed it directly, their book would have gone a long way toward a more sustainable solution to the challenges facing pollinators. But they simply refused to follow the implications of what Buchmann was feeling. They conveyed important information but they failed to deal with the personal transformations necessary for that information to be useful in changing societal patterns of behavior. If information, by itself, were enough, everything would already be different. There would be no ecological crisis. We've got information—by the bucketful. What we don't have are the interior shifts necessary to put all that information into practice in the world.

They failed to follow the golden thread—in this case, the feeling they have for pollinators—where it ultimately led. There would have been . . . *implications* if they had, and those implications would impact deeply held beliefs that Buchmann, and Nabhan apparently, have no wish to examine, or take responsibility for.

In essence, Buchmann's hidden baggage remained hidden from a failure of character, a failure of courage, and the book, and all of us, are the poorer for it.

EGO BAGGAGE

This next example is representative of ego baggage intentionally hidden in a work for manipulatory ends. I want to approach this one comparatively so I will start with Norbert Mayer's poem, included earlier in the book. As you read the poem again, notice what happens inside you as its meaning penetrates.

Just now
A rock took fright
When it saw me,
It escaped
By playing dead.

Just sit with it awhile and notice how you feel. Notice that a particular kind of feeling emerges. Notice, as well, whether you like it or not, whether you feel better about yourself and life or worse.

Now, read this next quotation and notice what happens inside you. In particular, notice what happens to the feeling that is still lingering inside you from Mayer's poem.

Really, all you and your pet rock can share is, you both fall at the same speed.[7]

Interesting, isn't it?

I have recited these two pieces many times over the past decade to a great many people. The responses are very consistent.

When I read the first piece, as the meaning of the poem penetrates the room, people laugh in the most delightful way. A spontaneous laughter just bursts out of them and they wriggle around in their seats, excited, happy. They become more childlike. Their breathing deepens, their eye focus softens, their skin tone relaxes, there is often a flush of color to their skin. They are happy and feel a great deal of joy.

The poem reminds people of something a part of them has long known to be true: that the world is alive and aware and watching us, that stones are alive but that you have to look really quick if you want to see them move, that as Baudelaire once observed: *Man walks through forests of physical things that are also spiritual things, that watch him with affectionate looks.*[8] A particular, and important, experience moves inside a person who hears that poem. It can be termed, as Gregory Bateson might have, an epistemology or way of experiencing reality. It includes within it a particular orientation of perception, what Bateson called the sense of aesthetic unity. It extends livingness to what we normally consider to be inanimate matter.

The second piece, by Ken Wilber, carries within it a very different kind of meaning, doesn't it? It contains within it the antithesis of that sense of aesthetic unity, of that particular epistemology, of that way of feeling and seeing the world. But it contains more than that merely, it also contains baggage from the author who penned it, a commentary that goes along with the overt meaning, and that baggage is very much intentional on Wilber's part. Here, look at his sentence again . . .

> *Really, all you and your pet rock can share is, you both fall at the same speed.*

It has been most instructive to see how this second piece affects people when I read it. There may initially be a short, sharp, snort of laughter from one or two people in the audience but nothing like that spontaneous joyful laughter that emerged so immediately upon hearing Mayer's poem. Those who become entangled in the meanings of Wilber's sentence experience a particular kind of dissociation. It distances them from their feeling sense and moves them into a particular kind of mentation. Their sense of the livingness of the world dissipates. Surfaces rather than interiors—and lack of connection to the world around the self—become more prominent. The childlike joy, wonder, and hope that so filled the room dissipates, as if some kind of hole has opened in the floor and all the life is draining out of the room. An odd, uncomfortable, existential emptiness takes its place.

You, most likely, felt it as well when you read Wilber's statement. It's a familiar feeling, isn't it? Almost everyone has felt it sometime in their lives. Many people feel it every day. A lot of people take Prozac in order not to feel it. Ever.

Every time I speak, when the people hear what Wilber has written, the light that shone so briefly in their eyes is extinguished. Their breathing becomes shallow and high in the chest. Their skin dulls. They sit immobile in their seats, apparently afraid of spontaneous gestures. And the sadness in the room is as palpable as the hopelessness that now holds everyone in its arms. It feels of ancient human misery and lost children and the death of growing things and the uselessness of going on.

Now, some people will say, Wilber among them, that that first state of being, the one that came from reading the poem, was a kind of projection onto the world of a childish part of the self, that to mature, all humans must give up such childish thinking and feeling. They will say that believing rocks, plants, or animals have consciousness or awareness—that is, interior depth—is anthropormorphizing, that is, the projecting onto nature of human attributes. They assert that, in fact, nothing is out there but lesser life forms and dead, inanimate matter; that we are the only intelligent form of life on a ball of rock hurtling around the sun. And that science (and by this they mean a mechanicalist view of life that is anthropocentric in its orientation) conveys the only realistic description of the world. And, in a modified form, this is just what Wilber *is* saying in that particular sentence. Let's look at that sentence as it appears within the paragraph from which it comes.

> *Of course, we also share all lower world spaces—the physical (such as gravity), the vegetative (life), the reptilian (hunger). Since we also contain a reptilian stem, we can also share with lizards, but it becomes less fun, doesn't it? Down to pet rocks, with shared mass and gravity. Less depth, less to share. Really, all you and your pet rock can share is, you both fall at the same speed.*

The important thing here is not how reasonable this sounds but how you feel when you interiorize it (for that is the greatest clue to its nature). How dissociated do you become? How in touch with your sensate perceptions do you remain? How *alive* do you feel? Usually, at this point in my comparison of the two statements, I make the observations that those who take that position are guilty of anthropocentric mechanomorphism, the projection of a mechanical nature onto Nature centered around a human exceptionalism; that human beings have a lot more in common with plants (and lizards) than with a car; that there is a pattern that connects everything that has been expressed out of the ecological matrix of this planet; that the connection between things is a great deal more important than the parts; that the first step of intelligent tinkering is to know you don't know what you are doing and especially to realize that you must save all the parts (and this includes older ways of thinking); and that a human being with a life span of eighty years should have one attribute firmly in place before making determinations about a living system as complex and ancient as the 4.5 billion-year-old Earth—humility.

> *Really, all you and your pet rock can share is, you both fall at the same speed.*

A reductionist view of life oriented around a hierarchy of value is deeply embedded within Wilber's sentence. The meaning he put in there is specific and intentional—that is, there is no consciousness or awareness in rocks, there is no possibility of empathy between a rock and a human being, the only thing you can share between yourself and a rock can be explained through a reductionist physics—the rate at which you both will fall. (And even this is inaccurate. Even from that reductionistic perspective, you can also share getting wet together, biodegrading together, being part of the ecosystem of Earth together, being used by the powerful for their own ends together.)

If he was simply arguing for that position and allowing the hearer to determine for herself what her feelings and thoughts on the matter are, it would be fine, however much one might disagree with its accuracy. But the meanings that Wilber poured into this sentence are contaminated, intentionally, by other things.

While the communication appears to be simply a statement of fact, an emotion-free observation, it's not a pure sentence, meaning by this that the overt communication has a number of attachments clinging to it, like leeches to the legs of a man staggering out of a swamp.

The use of the word *pet* as a modifier before *rock* gives the game away. It was an intentional word choice, designed to produce a number of specific effects. The first is a form of the "Have you quit beating your wife?" dilemma. By structuring the sentence around "pet" rocks, he limits the topic and creates a similar dilemma. Most people who experience the livingness of stones and accept that experience as a legitimate perception (for instance, the members of many indigenous cultures), don't think of them in terms of "pet" rocks but as "stone people." Not pets but a wild and specific archetype expressed in multiple forms, of which rocks are only one expression, mountains being another. And this type of relationship crosses cultural lines. The sixteenth-century (North India) ecstatic poet Mirabai touches on this when she says . . .

> *I praise the mountain energy night and day.*
> *I take the path that ecstatic human beings have taken*
> *for centuries.*[9]

Any attempt to respond to Wilber's sentence as it stands forces the responder into the pet rock frame of reference, a place where Wilber can control the content and direction of the conversation.

Secondly, the sentence engages in the denigration of alternate perceptions of the world under the guise of conversational humor. It's a clever, but unfortunately not uncommon, form of name-calling. That is, if you believe you can share anything with rocks (specifically: your "pet" rock), you are foolish and certainly very, very naive about the true nature of reality. Wilber, by contrast, is not any of those things and he not so subtly sniggers at anyone who believes otherwise ("it becomes less fun, doesn't it?").

Wilber's sentence holds within it a very specific denigration of a certain perception of reality, a perception common to children and many ancient and indigenous cultures, under the guise of an objective-observer communication. (This is a common form of what Annie Le Brun calls the assault on the imaginal realm.) Robert Bly describes that sort of transaction like this:

> *The boy and his father—the love unit I think has been most damaged by the Industrial Revolution—are traveling together. The*

boy sees in the groves "the invisible king" and then his daughters, but the adult father does not. The father in a rationalist's way dismisses the boy's questions.

"Calm down, my boy, no need for all this—
It's dry oak leaves making noise in the wind."

"I see the spot very clearly, my boy—
an old gray willow, that's all there is."

We sense how many European and American fathers have done that to their sons; the poem says that the rationalist viewpoint simply opens the boy further to the dark side of consciousness, and the poem ends with the boy dead in his father's arms.[10]

Wilber is in fact, doing exactly this but he does it sideways, through subtle name calling, use of a logical fallacy, and using "science" and "rationality" (or his versions of them) as the arbiters of what reality is and is not. Many people who read his sentence know something is wrong with it simply from the feeling response it engenders; the feeling response is often a strong one as well because of the subtle insults layered into the material. It takes awhile to understand the sophistication of Wilber's constructions. He is very good at it.

And the issue this ego baggage is covering? It's an important one. It touches deeply on matters of import to us and our time: Is the earth (and its parts) alive or not? If it is, how should human beings interact with it? (Does a hierarchy of value based on how much an organism thinks really work? Is it even true to reality?) Further, will this one alteration in epistemological orientation make a difference in the degree of environmental damage the earth is currently experiencing? That is, how much environmental devastation is the result of an improper paradigm? Of an improper approach on the part of human beings toward their planet? Have scientists been guilty of a serious epistemological error the past two centuries? Is reductionism an improper approach to studying the world? What are the alternatives?

And do they work better? Can blending a sense of the aesthetic unity of the world (and the empathy that goes along with that) with what we now call science produce more sustainable results for the human species?

There is increasing evidence in many scientific disciplines that Earth should be thought of as alive and treated as such. There is increasing evidence that human beings are only specific examples of a general condition ubiquitous within the Gaian system that we know as this planet—that intelligence and awareness is an inherent condition in all self-organized systems and their parts. There is increasing evidence that the apparently firm line between the living and the nonliving may be an illusion. There is increasing evidence that reductionist approaches are not suited to solving the problems before us primarily because they cannot perceive the invisibles and the interconnectivity that lie at the heart of living systems. However, by using this particular technique, Wilber moves the discussion away from the real issue into areas he can control and to the personalities of those who hold opposing views. In essence, he cheats, forcing the reader to his point of view through manipulation. He abandons an open and direct discussion of the issue.

Instead of releasing what he is saying, as Etheridge did, like a bird taking flight that will find its own place inside us, instead of allowing his argument to stand on its own merits, to be judged by the intelligent examination of his readers, Wilber manipulates the reader into a limited orientation, inserts a personal commentary about people who hold different points of view, through the use of a denigrating technique, however subtle it is, designed to exert emotional control over the discussion. He shows contempt for his readers.

Underlying Wilber's communication is an overriding desire to create an ultimate and final description of reality. Something foundational. It allows of no alternatives; soft complexities have no place within it. Because it is evangelical and absolute in nature (a common attribute of ego baggage) it cannot accept that those who disagree with it possess intelligence or the capacity to reason.

The great English philosopher Mary Midgley comments that . . .

> *world pictures like this are not primarily science. The science that is supposed to justify them is really a small part of their content. They*

> *are actually metaphysical sketches, ambitious maps of how all reality is supposed to work, guiding visions, systems of direction for the rest of our ideas.*[11]

Arguments such as Wilber's (and Dawkins's and . . .) are a form of intellectual imperialism representing a conceptual monoculture as Midgley accurately describes it. Such imperialists have set out to conquer the superstitious natives inhabiting the dark continent, the place where the general populace lives. Midgley makes the point that arguments such as Wilber's rest in a belief in human beings as "an isolated will, guided by an intelligence, arbitrarily connected to a rather unsatisfactory array of feelings, and lodged by chance, in an equally unsatisfactory human body."[12]

"The really strange and disturbing thing about" it, she continues, "is the alienation of the human operator from the system he works on. He appears outside the system. He is an autonomous critic, independent of the forces that shape everything around him."[13] He has no relation to the world from which he has been expressed, no feeling connection to the other life forms on the planet. Such systems of thought are not science, she notes, not reason, but behavioral examples of an unexamined, "exuberant power fantasy."

Of all forms of ego baggage this one is perhaps the most dangerous to real writing, to the craft, to the ability to dream.

Ultimately, ego baggage in writing is a form of violence against the reader; it's immoral writing. Regrettably, it is not all that unusual, especially in nonfiction.

Writing that has baggage attached suffers from it, sometimes terribly so. It may be a somewhat minor problem, as in Harrison's work, more serious, as in Buchmann's, or egregious, as in Wilber's. It takes work to get this kind of baggage out of the writing. It takes effort of will and a willingness to engage the interior world. True art occurs more readily when the artist is aware of these kinds of impacts and diligently works to move out of his own, and the work's, way. It occurs when he can shape meaning in as pure a form as possible, craft it expertly in language, so that nothing but the meaning flows into the reader, so that as much of the hidden baggage as possible is removed from the work. To write morally, we must examine ourselves. We must have the courage to engage the shadows within us and make them conscious. As William Gass says:

> *To think for yourself—not narrowly, but rather as a mind—you must be able to talk to yourself: well, openly, and at length. . . . That side of you which speaks must be prepared to say anything so long as it is so. . . . To speak well to oneself . . . we must go down as far as the bucket can be lowered. Every thought must be thought through from its ultimate cost back to its cheap beginnings; every perception, however profound and distant, must be as clear and easy as the moon; every desire must be recognized as a relative and named as fearlessly as Satan named his angels; finally, every feeling must be felt to its bottom where the bucket rests in the silt and water rises like a tower around it.*[14]

CHAPTER TWENTY-ONE

Some Subtle Refinements of the Art

We can feel in this quotation Logan's powerful phrasing—the words leave his hands bent permanently into their phrases and the phrases are curved so as to carry emotion better. He has a great gift for the phrase that carries deep emotion—and carries it somehow invisibly, in ways impossible to pin down. In his work, he shows himself again and again able to create a poem without the hectic surface that so many poets depend on to carry emotion. Instead he moves us simply by moving language. . . . He writes a poetry in which heavy, turgid sensuality, whirling like water in a ditch after a sudden rainstorm, is mingled with luminous spiritual leaping and a desire that everything in the world shall shine from within.

Robert Bly

The sentence, then, if it is to have a soul, rather than merely be a sign of the existence somewhere of one, must be composed by our innermost being, finding in its drive and rhythm, if not in its subject, the verbal equivalent of instinct; in its sound and repetitions, too, its equivalent feeling; and then perceive its thought as Eliot said Donne did, as immediately as the odor of a rose—fully, the way we see ships at anchor rise and fall as though they lay on a breathing chest.

William Gass

> *Circus knife-throwers know that it is indeed possible to be perfect, and one had better be. Perfection means hitting exactly what you are aiming at and not touching by a hair what you are not.*
>
> John Gardner

> *The difference between the right word and almost the right word is the difference between lightning and a lightning bug.*
>
> Mark Twain

As you have seen in this book, there is much more to nonfictional writing than simply getting some words in a row, words that to whatever extent accurately describe what it is you are writing about.

It *is* true, that if you are writing a descriptive phrase, say of driving up to a house on a misty morning, that that descriptive phrase is an instance of what forensic writing freaks call verisimilitude. All that ten-dollar word means is that the writing is an accurate reflection of the true world (*veri* meaning "truth," *similitude* meaning "similar" or "like," i.e., "truth similar" or it's "like true," you know). But a great deal more is going on than that. The house sets mood and tone, it acts as a character in the story, bringing its own personality into the mix. The character of the house may foreshadow something that comes later. It may be the initial emergence of the symbolic layer of an object in the text as a living expression. *Every* line you write has more in it than mere verisimilitude. And the more that is layered into a line, the more real that line becomes, the more real and satisfying the book.

At minimum, besides its surface meaning, a line should possess the proper feel. It should feel alive. It should, at the same time, also possess the proper sound. So, even if a line has been inserted only for descriptive purposes (adding a visual vividness to the book at that moment in time) it should also possess an integral kinesthetic quality *and* a sound quality that is congruent to the rest of the material within which it is embedded. These elements carry deeper meanings hidden in them that affect the reader; they work on very deep levels.

There should always be a complex layering of meanings and purpose in every part of the work. That layering is what the word *composed* means when it is applied to writing. It is this layering of the work that, in many respects, makes it art.

Bly's comment on Logan's writing . . .

> *the words leave his hands bent permanently into their phrases and the phrases are curved so as to carry emotion better. He has a great gift for the phrase that carries deep emotion—and carries it somehow invisibly, in ways impossible to pin down.*[1]

captures what Bly is talking about perfectly; the first line elegantly demonstrates the communication he is making about Logan: *the words leave his hands bent permanently into their phrases and the phrases are curved so as to carry emotion better.* He does, in his description of Logan, what Logan himself does in his poetry. Through this you get not only a description but a feeling experience of what Bly is talking about. This is a beautiful example of written description as art.

Many of the techniques I discuss in this chapter, when applied to the writing that comes from following golden threads, from writing generated out of intentional dreaming, work to create exactly this effect: *words bent permanently into their phrases and the phrases curved to, invisibly, carry emotion better, in ways impossible to pin down*. The result is an important layering of meanings within the lines; it, through an act of *composing,* turns written description into art.

It's during this revisioning that the writer begins to go for perfection, working to turn the shitty first draft into a seamless and layered whole. This is where the clunky sentences are reworked, the excess fat removed, the presence and movement of living symbol, theme, and archetype refined, strengthened, and intentionally woven more subtly into the text.

John Gardner perfectly describes this moment in the writing process . . .

> *But at some point, perhaps when he's finished his first draft, the writer begins to work in another way. He begins to brood over what he's written, reading it over and over, patiently, endlessly, letting his mind wander, sometimes to Picasso or the Great Pyramid, some-*

times to the possible philosophical implications of Menelaos' limp (a detail he introduced by impulse, because it seemed right). Reading in this strange way lines he has known by heart for weeks, he discovers odd tics his unconscious has sent up to him, perhaps curious accidental repetition of imagery: The brooch Helen threw at Menelaos the writer has described, he discovers, with the same phrase he used in describing, much later, the seal on the message for help sent to the Trojans' allies.[2]

As the writing process deepens, as the work reaches the final-draft stage, for most writers the exterior world takes on less and less substance, the world inside the book more and more. Thousands of details are simultaneously held in the mind as living realities. For a time, nearly every line is easily remembered and can be recalled at will. You have broken through to the core of the book and, at this point, the book and every part of it is held as a living gestalt inside the self. It is now that the brooding starts, that the revising process begins in earnest. Now the writer begins to go through what has been written to consciously discover what invisibles the dreamer has put into the writing. (Or, at least as many of them as they can see.) Those things are then mulled over, brooded upon, understood as much as possible at that moment in time. Then the writer begins to consciously work with what they have found: the hidden relationships between every part of the text, between words, sounding patterns, image reverberation, symbol emergence, melody line, syllabication, and so on.

As I mentioned in chapter 18, the first thing I do during revision is to work with eros energy in the text. I begin to read through the book by feeling what I have written to see if what I have written allows me to dream or whether it wakes me from that dreaming. I begin to put eros energy into each word, work to condense the feeling in the work, work to bring it all alive. When that is done, I work with unclear implications and then clichéd thinking and hidden baggage. Once those larger issues are out of the way (or at least as much as I can get them out of the way), my read-through tends to focus on other elements in the work. Tentativeness is perhaps the next thing I check for.

TENTATIVENESS

Often, as writers work their way through the text, feeling their way to where the book needs to go, what they are doing is very much like Gary Snyder's description of his poem "Rip Rap." The writer has been laying down words, one slipped under the end of another, "on the glassy surface of some insight that one couldn't stand on otherwise." This naturally creates a kind of tentativeness in the work just as it does in the steps of someone trying to create a safe passage across a slippery slope on a mountainside.

You lay the words down just so, then you put your weight on them to see if they hold. If they do, you rest in that spot and carefully lay down others in front of you and then test *them* for stability. You make the path by walking it, slowly, carefully, one step at a time. It is only later, when you have arrived at your destination, that you know the path is sound (though of course there were many missteps along the way). Once you have made the path from the beginning of the book to its end, you have to start at the beginning again and work to remove this naturally occurring tentativeness from the text. You will know it when you feel it; tentativeness has its own feel. It usually creates a slight hesitancy in your feeling state as you read. Unless there is something more problematic underneath it (such as self-worth issues) tentative text can usually be altered with fairly minor adjustments of wording.

To check for hesitancy, you begin going over and over the path you have laid down, from beginning to end, until you flow easily from initial word to ending word. As you read through the material again, you no longer have to work carefully with each step you take; the foundation is already there. From slow hesitant steps you move toward a jog, then a run. Now that you trust the ground beneath you, how fast can you go?

The quicker you go, the more you will notice that the material has a somewhat wavelike movement as it slows down and speeds up in the different sections of the text. What you are primarily feeling for is your ease of movement through that text, irrespective of whether the text itself is fast or slow.

Hesitancies in the text, if the ground is solid below them, are usually easy to rework. Just a word here and there makes all the difference and these words and alterations will, unless there is a deeper problem in the text, generally appear clearly in the mind as you need them with only a tiny bit of work necessary to evoke them.

READING FOR FEEL

After reading for hesitancy, I begin to read simply for feel. (In some ways this is just a refined form of an eros read.) At this point in time I want every word to be the right word. I want every word to feel completely congruent to me as I read it. During this kind of read, certain sentences or passages will stand out because they don't quite feel congruent with the surrounding material. It's more a matter of feel now than content in the material. I may have said what I needed to say but now I need to alter it so that it flows seamlessly into the rest of the passages.

Here are a few examples of what I am talking about . . .

Early in chapter 6 "It Burns the Blood Like Powdered Glass" I was working with a particular feeling/image, one that was particularly strong for me. I embedded it within a longer passage containing a series of feeling/images. This is the feeling/image as it was originally written:

> *writing in which you sense the forest wolves standing behind you without having to turn around*

It took about six months for me to get it right. Here it is in final form, embedded within a portion of that longer passage:

> *I believe in writing that burns the blood, in which you feel forest wolves tensing behind you, writing filled with wilderness, writing that forces the margins, writing that challenges, that insists, that bleeds when it's cut . . .*

Now feel the kinesthetics of that passage with the first form of the feeling/image in place . . .

> *I believe in writing that burns the blood, writing in which you sense the forest wolves standing behind you without having to turn around,*

> *writing filled with wilderness, writing that forces the margins, writing that challenges, that insists, that bleeds when it's cut . . .*

It's very different in its impacts, isn't it? It feels funny. There is a sense that something is off, not right. It took some time for me to get it right; I had to keep going back to it and revising it over and over again until the feeling/image flowed smoothly while still conveying the experience I was going for. During those revisions, I was reading for the feel of the flow of the words.

Here's another example . . .

Some of the more important phrases I've used in this book did not actually start out as mine but began their life as another writer's work. For some reason they captured my attention and I began to use them in my teaching, often for many years. As I worked with them over time I found myself distilling them into their essential feeling flow. (This also included sound distillation, which I will discuss in a moment.) I took a concept initially articulated by someone else and made it mine. I only discovered this when I went back to find the citations for the phrases I was using in this book and found, much to my surprise, that they had altered a great deal over the years.

For example, this phrase that I used much earlier in the book . . .

> *The writer piles up meaning behind the word like water behind a dam*

. . . came initially from something Robert Bly wrote. But here is what he actually said when he wrote it . . .

> *The Spanish "surrealist" or "leaping" poet often enters into his poem with a heavy body of feeling piled up behind him, as if behind a dam.*[3]

You can see the origins of my line, can't you? But mine is, in many ways, very different. If you read the two lines, one after another, you can see that Bly's original line feels very different when it is read. It is not as unwieldy as my original wolves line; in fact, it's pretty good. But it hasn't been smoothed down by long use and verbal repetition and the dependent phrase that comes after the comma weakens the power of it. To Bly, that line, while important, was only part of the larger point he was making. It was most likely an observation that emerged in the heat of his writing rather than a magnetic point, as he might put it, around which the writing arranged itself like steel shavings on a sheet of paper. But for me, when I became entangled in its meanings, it became, and remains, a seminal concept. Bly planted a seed within me but the plant it became was shaped by my soil and so became my own. (It works this way, I think, for all writers.)

My long, out loud, working of the line resulted in the meanings I had found in it being distilled to their essence until nothing else remained. You can tell, if you read them back and forth, that my long use of the phrase resulted in a smoother flow of feeling than the original that started me off. The concept underlying the two phrases is similar—though the movement from "feeling" to "meaning" in my version alters it in interesting ways.

I go through just this process with every line in the book and I read the text through for this kind of flow a great many times. The degree to which you can do this depends on the amount of time you have (deadline?), the skill you have developed in using your feeling sense as a perceptual tool, and the degree of skill you have (at this point in time) in being able to craft this kind of flow.

FURTHER REFINEMENTS

After I have read for feeling flow, I begin to look at some of the other elements of the writing. I begin to look at symbol and image, begin to work with foreshadowing and repetition. I begin to look at symmetry and mirroring in language, begin to listen for sound patterning, syllabication, and melody line.

Foreshadowing

The most common example of foreshadowing can be found in the cheap horror flick. Usually, sometime early in the film, the camera will pan around the kitchen and linger just a bit too long on the knife rack. Often, this is repeated a number of times during the initial stages of the film as characters move into and out of the kitchen. And, of course, eventually, later in the film, the camera pans again, lingers on the knife rack a moment, and one of the knives is missing. The big one.

Normally, the viewer, except in very crude films (or unless they have learned to look for it) will not notice these early foreshadowings. These parts of the film merely seem to be an instance of verisimilitude, that is, an innocuous visual of the physical world to make the film or book seem real. But such images build up in the unconscious of the reader and indicate that something of import is going to happen. They are very subtle cues to a meaning that is going to emerge later in the book (or film) and upon which the plot—or idea—line depends.

As a book is being written, foreshadowing images spontaneously emerge out of the dreamer's dreaming. The writer rarely notices it when it happens. He may feel there is something important in a scene that insists on being included but he can't know why until the first draft is complete. It's only later, when the conscious mind is looking things over, that these kinds of events are consciously noticed and developed further.

As an example from this book: the rutted road David Hoffmann and I traveled to visit Dale Pendell, foreshadows the osteopath's crash. The images of us being slammed around inside the car foreshadow the physical reality of the crash, and broken neck, that the osteopath experienced. The reader's unconscious tucks that initial description of the road someplace inside and, when the car crash emerges, a completion or fullness in the story line occurs.

I felt compelled to describe that rutted road in detail but until I later wrote the words the osteopath told me, I didn't know why (and that was a week or two later). Nor did I know why I had felt so compelled to mention, in chapter 1, the long drop down to the bottom on the side of the mountain road I traveled. Many people had gone off that road before the county put up guardrails in the 1980s. But even then, that early in the book's writing, I had very specific images of a car going off that road into that deep, deep ravine and a sense that that image had to be included in the book. (The Dale Pendell story was written into the book months later.) I noticed as I was writing that there was some compulsion on me when I hit those passages but I had no idea why, I simply followed the urging of the dreamer, acquiescing to its demands and doing the best I could in the initial run-through to get the descriptions in place, capturing the feeling that was upon me at that moment. It was only after the rough manuscript was done that I noticed what had been occurring. It was then that I began to work the draft over, bringing that material forward, developing it more clearly and fully, recognizing it as an important thread that ran, however minimally, through the book.

Foreshadowing is a regular component of fiction, it works as well in nonfiction, for foreshadowing is an integral element of dreaming and our search for meaning. To the part of us that searches for greater meaning in the things that happen to us, that knows that there is a great deal more in random events than happenstance, tiny movements, like those contained in foreshadowing, mean much more than they appear to. Although the dynamic has been superficialized in film to a ridiculous degree, foreshadowing is integral to the art of writing, all writing. *Something* occurs and, in a moment of foreshadowing, the deep self feels in it a meaning out of the ordinary. And while our conscious minds don't notice that something extra has been layered into a passage, the deep self does. That invisible thing is held deep in the self as a crucial element of the dream being dreamed.

The dreamer inside us puts it in, the dreamer in the reader extracts it out. *All* readers have the capacity to take in the meaning built up in invisible layers under the surface meanings in a book. Because of the common nature of the dreamers inside us, readers have the capacity to grasp deep meaning in a writing from the subtlest of cues.

Subtle cues build up in works of fiction as in dreams. The name a character possesses, the color of his shirt, the pacing and rhythm of his sentences—all change who and what he is. Simple background information imparted offhand in the story—whether a man's father was "rich, or had owned elephants"—would immediately change the nature of his character. As Gardner notes, "Subtle details change characters' lives in ways too complex for the conscious mind to grasp, though we nevertheless grasp them."[4]

For it is not the conscious mind that grasps these details. It is the unconscious mind, used to working with the nature of meaning, that takes them into itself and understands their import. The dreamer within the reader intuitively understands foreshadowing. When it's present, the work becomes more legitimately dreamlike. It approaches the real more closely and as a result, the reading of the book is more fulfilling, more satisfactory to the reader and the dreamer inside them. The work *feels* right at a level too deep for words to easily explain.

Because the dreamers within human beings are of an identity with each other, the dreamer-in-the-writer and the dreamer-in-the-reader are, in essence, involved in a conversation, a communication. Our conscious minds are, in many ways, only bystanders in the process.

Foreshadowing, again, emerges of its own accord. Introducing it through "mere intellect," even if expertly done, makes the book mechanical, a paint-by-numbers process. The important thing is to understand the nature of foreshadowing and to look for instances where it has spontaneously emerged in the book, *then* to develop it consciously, to hone and shape it with awareness—and as well, respect. The dreamer hates self-important meddling.

Symbol

Symbols, like foreshadowing, emerge and return in different parts of a book of their own accord. They are activated by the use of the feeling sense, for when we touch any part of the world with our nonphysical kinesthetic sensing, part of the meaning flow that is released includes the symbolic layer within that thing. The symbolic is an integral layer of the complexity that makes up everything we encounter. The symbols then flow through the dreamer into the writing; they emerge without the conscious mind's participation.

When beginning this book, I had no idea that water (and its inhabitants) would emerge as a potent symbol. Nevertheless, as the manuscript developed I began to notice that water, the concept of immersion, large inhabitants of bodies of water, and communications from those inhabitants kept showing up in one form or another. They became essential symbols in the work.

When you begin to revise the manuscript for symbol development you can see, as you examine the text, the slow movement of the text toward the emergence of a symbol. It slowly rises into view then moves back under the surface again. Nevertheless, once it becomes a part of the material, it remains a presence from the first page. Just because you first notice it on page 65 doesn't mean it wasn't already there on page 1.

Once you notice this movement, you can begin to work it consciously, to insert or enhance subtle clues in the text indicating that movement more clearly. You can go back to the beginning of the book and start to work with this thread alone. As with everything else, you read the text and feel for the movements of this particular element. You work toward strengthening the line. It takes a light hand—you are subtly enhancing flow and movement here, not creating billboards on a highway. Doing this takes symbol movement and sands the rough edges from it, eases its way, uses it as an integral element in the composition of the book.

I want to emphasize something: What these kinds of symbols mean is irrelevant. Dissecting a book for symbol is about as useful as diagraming a sentence to find its meaning. Forensic approaches are useless to understanding any part of the craft except the least important bits. Symbol emerges *by itself* from the dreaming of the dreamer through the use of the feeling sense. It is a particular layer of the complexity that reality is, which is activated and released through our dreaming and feeling/sensing. The dreamer's movement into the imaginal frees symbols to emerge, seemingly of their own accord, out of whatever is being perceived. The writer opens a channel inside herself and something enters in from someplace else. The dreamer understands the living nature of symbols, knows they are not two-dimensional concepts, and innately knows how to work with them. They are part of its meat and drink. But the symbols themselves reside someplace outside of and beyond the dreamer. They come from deeper layers within the multitudes of phenomena we experience in our lives and they have deep roots in the imaginal realm. They are filled with mythic substance. The opening in the dreamer simply allows their movement from out there to in here and onto the page. A forced symbol is a terrible thing in a book.

Symbols are worked similarly to foreshadowing. After the first draft they are noticed by the conscious mind, their implications teased out and developed. They become part of the composing that then occurs. You, as writer, work with them, but you don't create them and you certainly should not think you understand what they mean better then the dreamer. There is *always* more in them than the conscious mind can find. They are living realities, filled with meaning and feeling. A writer working with them can feel their impacts, feel the livingness of them, but can never tease out of them *all* the meanings they contain. That is why, when a writer allows symbol to emerge of its own accord, he will never see all that is in the book he has written. Each reader will find something new in the symbols that have emerged within a book. A great book can be read every year, for a lifetime, and new insights and truths can still be found in it, most of which the author did not consciously know were there.

It's crucial to trust the symbols that emerge, to strengthen and develop them as part of composition but their essential nature is beyond the writer and must be respected for what they are. They are not owned.

Reverberation or Mirroring of Image

Mirroring, or reverberation, of image is also something that helps deepen the dream and make the reading more powerful. Cheap instances of this occur daily in newspapers (those newspapers that are still in business anyway): "Headless Body Found in Topless Bar" is perhaps the most famous. I first noticed mirroring being used when, as a teenager, I was reading Roger Zelazny's *Damnation Alley,* a science fiction novel loosely based on Hunter Thompson's book about the Hell's Angels.

> *Tanner said, "Hope not," and wolfed down more food. He wondered, though, if they were anything like his old pack, and he hoped not, again, for both their sakes.*[5]

Zelazny's main character Hell Tanner was once the leader of a motorcycle gang, The Angels, before they were killed off in "the big raid." Many times throughout the book Zelazny refers to The Angels (and several other motorcycle gangs) as a "pack." The word "pack" brings up images of animals, especially animals hunting in packs, which itself brings up images of killing and eating. So, when Zelazny uses the word "wolfed" it strengthens those associations and mirrors or reverberates the initial image. Wolfing food means eating it quickly without chewing it much or tasting what is being eaten and this brings up images of wildness, something not civilized, animal-like. It very clearly develops the image of "wolf pack" and the hunting, killing, and eating dynamics that belong to hunting packs.

Images such as these, by their very nature, always have mythic elements within them. Zelazny (and Delaney), almost alone of the New Wave writers of the 1970s, developed a sophisticated writing style that blended image, myth, and dreaming. *Damnation Alley* is set in a time not long after a world war; the environment of Earth has been severely disrupted. So Tanner's wildness, his barbarianism, his uncivilized nature, are essential to the story line of the book but not just for the usual clichéd reasons. The territory the characters in the book have to traverse is filled with the stuff of dreams and myth: giant bats, mile-long snakes, devolved cannibals. And it's Tanner's wildness that allows him to move into that territory successfully. He enters a mythic territory, crossing the United States to bring needed medicine to Boston, and survives only because he is wild, untamed. He can cross into and through the imaginal because he has no civilized belief systems that interfere with his doing so. He innately understands the territory he encounters—which none of the other characters do. So when Zelazny began working with those images—wolfed and pack—images he had already picked up from Hunter Thompson, they deepened. They became a portal into the deep, mythic wildness of Earth. Tanner, to the reader, *feels* a coherent part of that mythic territory.

As with symbol and foreshadowing, most images like this (wolf, pack) emerge on their own as the first draft is written. They are generally a bit rough—the jewel is there but it has not yet been cut and polished. It's only later, when the conscious mind sees the images that they are intentionally developed and shaped. Often, then, the images can be layered in interesting ways, as Zelazny has done.

Verbs (such as wolfed) that are used to describe action can be chosen to subtly enhance, mirror, and develop images already in the reader's mind. They set up a reverberation or echo of images that are already flowing through the book. It is a fairly simple thing to read through the finished manuscript with this eye and look for instances where particular images have emerged and to strengthen them with the use of verbs that reflect, develop, and deepen a particular image.

Images can also move (or mirror or reverberate) from one area of focus to another; this might be called concept mirroring. (This is part of the power of metaphor.) Mike Williams does this in his book on the music business when he writes:

> *Steve and the other members of his semi-communal farm have built their own houses by hand, using scrap lumber and mountain ingenuity. They have built well, and have demonstrated that it is possible for ordinary people to accomplish extraordinary tasks. This was a wonderful place for me to decide to take the scraps of my career and build a future.*[6]

That really is a nice use of image. The initial images, of scrap lumber being used by a mountain community to build nurturing and enduring homes easily moves over to the feeling/experience of a man using the scraps of his career and life to build a future that is enduring and nurturing.

When an image like either of these shows up there is often a resonance to it when the material is reread. It can be seen then that that image has been emerging, on its own, over and over again in the book. Once noticed, it can be strengthened and subtly shaped to even more powerfully affect the reader.

There is not a one of us that has not needed, at one time or another, to take the scraps of our lives and find a way to build something more out of them than we have.

Symmetry of Language

Perhaps the most elegant work done on symmetry of language is that of Richard Bandler and John Grinder in the development of Neurolinguistic Programming (NLP). Their book *Frogs into Princes* (Real People Press, 1979) is a masterpiece on the subject. They give some exceptionally good examples of the impacts and consequences of both symmetry and lack of symmetry in language.

They start with an example of a communication that possesses symmetry. It begins with an imagined communication from a client to psychotherapist Virginia Satir . . .

> *Well, man, Virginia, you know I just ah . . . boy! Things have been, they've been heavy, you know. Just, you know, my wife . . . my wife*

> *was run over by a snail and . . . you know, I've got four kids and two of them are gangsters and I think maybe I did something wrong but I just can't get a grasp on what it was.*[7]

Bandler and Grinder then give a response Virginia Satir might have used . . .

> *I understand that you feel a certain weight upon you, and these kinds of feelings you have in your body aren't what you want for yourself as a human being. You have different kinds of hopes for this.*[8]

In spite of the snail bit (which I think breaks state too much to be useful), notice how you feel when you finish reading that communication.

Read it again to make your awareness of the feeling more conscious.

Now, read their example of lack of symmetry, which they use as contrast. Pay close attention to how your feeling state changes as this next interaction proceeds . . .

> *Well, you know, things feel real heavy in my life, Dr. Bandler. You know, it's just like I can't handle it you know . . .*
>
> *I can see that Mr. Grinder.*
>
> *I feel like I did something wrong with my children and I don't know what it is. And I thought maybe you could help me grasp it, you know?*
>
> *Sure. I see what it is you're talking about. Let's focus in on one particular dimension. Try to give me* your *particular perspective. Tell me how it is that you see your situation right now.*
>
> *Well, you know, I just . . . I'm . . . I just feel like I can't get a grasp on reality.*
>
> *I can see that. What's important to me—colorful as your description is—what's important to me is that we see eye to eye about where it is down the road that we shall travel together.*
>
> *I'm trying to tell you that my life has got a lot of rough edges, you know. And I'm trying to find a way . . .*
>
> *It looks all broken up from . . . from your description, at any rate. The colors aren't all that nice.*[9]

The feeling after this second interaction is very different, isn't it? The therapeutic responses feel rather cold and uncaring, don't they? It feels that way because there is very little empathetic rapport; the responder is not engaged in symmetry of language but rather is engaged in its antithesis.

In the first example, symmetry occurs because Virginia Satir uses the same sensory language as the client in her response. The communication from the client uses kinesthetic language: "heavy," "run over," "grasp." Satir's response matches that: "weight," "feelings," "body."

In the second example the initial communication occurs in that same kinesthetic language but the response uses visual terminology: "see," "focus," "looks," "color," "eye to eye."

Languaging that starts out in one sensory modality and has a response to it in another creates an interrupt in communication. It's like static; it interrupts the flow of meaning through language. In writing it awakens the reader from the dream.

Unless you are intentionally doing so for some reason the book itself demands, you should never juxtapose different sensory frames in this kind of way. Linguistic response should always occur in the same sensory modality unless there is a specific and well-thought-out reason for not doing so. This kind of symmetry in language is something that needs to be examined in any finished work after the first draft is done.

I read the final draft forty or fifty times, each time reading it with a different ear. One of those reads, repeated multiple times in order to make sure nothing is missed, is simply for language symmetry. If I do find places where there is lack of symmetry (and I always do) I revise that section to be more symmetrical while still working to keep the original intent. So, at minimum such a section retains its original communicative purpose but it also carries other meanings within it, one of which is this kind of symmetry. Symmetry allows the words to become more invisible so that nothing remains but the meaning itself. It contributes, as well, to the musical nature of the language. It's like a background of violins in a story. Lack of symmetry is having a horn blare out in the midst of those background violins. It awakens the reader. It interrupts the musical flow of the language.

Also: Written passages are often more vivid if you include more than one sensory modality, e.g., seeing, feeling, and hearing. So, when you are describing a scene or a person you can include two or three sensory takes on that scene or person. It increases vividness, the lucidity of the image in the mind's eye. Just be careful of crossed modalities.

Sound and Sound Patterning

Each part of the text will, as the book develops, find its own natural rhythm, its own beat, its own melody. A book, in essence, has its own song. As William Gass says . . .

> *Language without rhythm, without physicality, without the undertow of that sea which once covered everything and from which the land first arose like a cautious toe . . . can never be artistically complete.*[10]

While these essentials emerge spontaneously out of the dream the dreamer dreams, they will be unpolished in the rough manuscript just as the other elements I've been discussing are. Sooner or later, as the editing proceeds, it will be time to work on the rhythmic patterning, beat, and melody embedded within the text. And so the manuscript gets read again, this time paying attention only to those things—essentially the sound patterning that is within the book. Sentences are then revised to confirm and strengthen that already-present patterning. It should also act to reflect the meanings embedded within the text.

As an example of this kind of reflection, shortened sentences and shorter words cause a faster movement through the text. Longer words and sentences slow the movement down and allow the reader to sink into the piece in a more reflective frame of mind. The following sentence demonstrates this perfectly:

> *Walnut Tree Farm was a settlement in three senses: a habitation, an agreement with the land, and a slow subsidence into intimacy with a chosen place.*[11]

The first sense, habitation, is one word and the reader moves through it fairly quickly. The second sense is captured in a longer phrase and the reader moves more slowly. The final sense is captured in a very long phrase indeed, a beautifully articulated phrase. The length of that last phrase, the words used, and the particular beauty of its construction, cause in the reader a slowing down that experientially matches the "slow subsidence" communication itself.

This is just a brief glance at how this can work. So, let's get a bit deeper into it. Let's start with punctuation . . .

Punctuation

A type of backbeat, or drum patterning, is created in a written work through the punctuation that surrounds the words. Short words and short sentences create a faster backbeat, longer ones a slower. As bibliographer D. F. McKenzie says . . .

> *The material forms of books, the non-verbal elements of the typographic notations within them, the very disposition of space itself, have an expressive function.*[12]

Punctuation controls pace of reading and, along with word and sentence length, helps generate the particular beat that is specific to every work. (It is closely related to syllabication, which I talk about in the next section.)

So, during one of my reads, I go through the work again reading *only* for beat and I spend some time specifically working only on that element of the book. You might think of it as listening to a musical composition by solely focusing on the drums. Punctuation serves one primary purpose: to control how fast or slow the meanings that are embedded within the words, sentences, paragraphs, pages, chapters, and sections of a book move. (This is why there are no hard and fast rules to punctuation; focus on rate of penetration or movement of meaning creates its own, inevitable, punctuation. The punctuation should reflect that flow dynamic rather than exist for its own sake.) It can be said that what each style of punctuation does is to allow the reader to rest to differing degrees at different points during their reading of the book. This, in essence, works to move the meanings into the reader at different rates of speed.

To a much lesser degree, punctuation affects meaning, as the famous (and overused) Panda story of eats, shoots, and leaves illustrates. A panda walks into a restaurant. The waiter comes over and the panda orders.

After he eats, the panda stands up and shoots the waiter, then he goes outside. The customers run after him asking, "Why did you do that?" "Because that is what I do," the panda replies and hands them a dictionary. They open it to:

> *Panda, a bear indigenous to China. Eats shoots and leaves.*

Nevertheless, punctuation is generally more important for controlling meaning flow than meaning itself.

The writer should be working with the punctuation to control the rate of meaning penetration into the reader by creating different degrees of rest. The reader is then not bombarded with incoming meanings with no rest and no time to savor the meanings they are receiving. In this, as in many aspects of writing, the writer's intuition is paramount. You do it by feel, by your own sense of a need to rest or need to move rapidly through the text. You are working here by feel to intentionally shape rate of meaning flow.

The brilliant Hungarian writer Peter Nadas comments on the importance of following your own intuitive sense of punctuation rather than rules handed down from some forensic authority.

> *I felt I was putting punctuation marks here or there because that's how others were doing it, without comprehending their relation to me: so my marks had only a global meaning but no personal value. And the more faithfully I served this consensually accepted global sense, the more I distanced myself from my personal requirements.*[13]

It's crucial to follow your own feeling sense of how punctuation should occur. This leads naturally into a feeling for the secondary function of punctuation, its beat patterns. By using this secondary aspect intentionally, you create a rhythmic patterning to the work that impacts at the deep level of the self where music itself impacts its listeners.

This beat dynamic should be used to facilitate the communications embedded within the text. If, for example, you are writing about the physiological and mental impacts of amphetamines, a very fast beat would enhance the meanings in the text. (Minimizing the feeling element of the writing and emphasizing the mental, visual elements from time to time would enhance it as well.) The reader would, simply by reading the material, have an experience of an amphetamine state of mind. (Dale Pendell's book *Pharmako/dynamis* is a perfect example of this type of amphetamine topic/underlying beat/minimized-feeling interplay.)

The beat pattern in a text should, for the most part, be enjoyable, unless you have a specific reason for its being otherwise. Amphetamine use often causes a dissociation in the people who take it for any length of time. By occasionally inserting a discordant beat toward the later stages of an amphetamine description (and eventually making it a primary beat pattern), the reader would not only have an experience of the fast, mental pacing that is the hallmark of amphetamines but also the initial and, if you wish to take it that far, later stages of dissociation—and paranoia—that accompanies long term overuse. (Philip Dick was exceptionally good at this.)

Beat patterns can be intentionally altered to create a great many effects. The beat, if it mimics the beat of a resting heart, will have one impact. If it mimics the beat of a racing pulse, another. You can increase the rate of beat from a resting heart to a racing pulse (as they often do in the background of scary movies) and the reader will follow along into that state of being. This will enhance the feeling impacts of what you are writing about at a level too deep for conscious recognition. Many thrillers use exactly this style of writing to enhance tension in a story line, to stimulate—by playing on the reader's tendency to pace rhythmic patterns—feelings of fear. These feelings then are generated not only by the tension in the storyline but by how the beat pattern is developed. Form echoing meaning.

Punctuation beat can be a great deal more complex than that, it doesn't have to remain that simplistic. There can be layered beat patterns; there can be interwoven patterns from several different sound sources (which is where syllabication comes into play). It takes practice but the beat patterns created by punctuation can become a conversation, a communication to the deep self in the reader, in and of themselves, a conversation that flows deeply in the text, much deeper than the conscious mind can hear. And that beat patterning, like symbols, tends to emerge naturally from the dreamer and be found, when reading for revision, already within the text.

These unique patterns that naturally develop in your writing are intimately interwoven into your individuality, your original voice and style.

Your writing will, if you follow your feeling sense, emerge as a form of song, *your* song, what is sometimes referred to as the writer's voice. But you don't have to seek for it, it emerges naturally out of you, following your feeling sense into and through the writing, and the readers will feel it as well. As Willa Cather once commented:

> *[Every story] must leave in the mind of the sensitive reader an intangible residuum of pleasure, a cadence, a quality of voice that is exclusively the writer's own, individual, unique. A quality that one can remember without the volume at hand, can experience over and over again in the mind but can never absolutely define.*[14]

Your job is simply to shape and refine it, to learn over time to hear and understand it, and eventually to create through it just as you do through the words.

So, when you read back through the text, pay attention to that pattern of sound in the back of your mind: ba dah, ba dah, ba dah, do wah, ba dah. Pay attention to how it changes and alters itself as it the text flows from one section to the next. Pay attention to whether or not it has an elegance of development, if it flows from one rhythmic patterning to another with ease. If it is discordant, should it be? Does that discordance match what is happening in the text? Pay attention to whether the beat pattern matches what is being talked about in the text (generally it does somewhat, that is part of why it has emerged in the way it has in that section). Pay attention to how it makes you feel when you hear it, to see if that feeling matches the feeling in the text you have written. Again, it usually will be somewhat, or very, similar. Writers intuitively alter punctuation patterns to match what they are writing about in every section of the book. When you pay attention to the sound patterning in a book you are generally just working to enhance that pattern, to act to compose it rather than let it remain in its unfinished form.

Syllabication

The number of syllables a word has also creates a beat pattern because there is a patterning to the way the words are sounded out and where emphasis falls. (As Jerome McGann says, "The means by which literary works secure their effects are never purely linguistic.")[15] You can easily hear this patterning in such words as *quantity* and *ratiocination*.

There is a close relationship, as I've said, between the beat pattern of punctuation and that of syllabication. Emphasis or accent is placed on a certain syllable of a word and that controls how the word is said, somewhat similarly to the way a comma controls reading speed in a sentence, there's a slight pause just after it occurs. Punctuation just controls the flow of meaning into the reader in a slightly more emphasized form than word syllables do.

One of my reads through the text is concerned solely with the beat pattern in word syllables. (And I might read for this ten or fifteen times until I'm satisfied with it.) The words chosen in each sentence and paragraph should fit together to enhance the beat line encoded in their syllabic nature.

The punctuation of the sentences should synchronize with and emphasize the syllabication beat. Periods, paragraph indents, sections, and chapters, for example, are points of emphasis where there is a longer rest than a syllable break allows. The end of a chapter often represents the end of particular sound pattern movements; there's a flourish and a final ending beat. Commas, semicolons, parentheses, and dashes are closer in impact to the syllable accent.

You can tell by feel if a word interrupts the beat line that the rest of the words (and punctuation) create. I do several read-throughs focused solely on syllabication beat and once I get that how I like it, I then read for both syllabic beat and punctuation beat to make sure they are working together. Again, syllabic beat tends to emerge of its own accord as the dreamer writes the book. What you are doing here is intentionally refining and deepening that element of the book.

Here, in my poem *A Thought,* is an example of intentional syllabication used for both sounding purposes and creating a specific state of mind.

Thomas Huxley,
Darwin's strongest defender,
observed
that "No rational man,
cognizant of the facts,
believes that the Negro

is the equal
still less the superior,
of the white man."

The assertion
that the degree of rational "thinking"
of any species
is illustrative of its position
on the ladder of evolutionary hierarchy
is only a decision
by an organism
(and specific people)
with a vested interest
in what is being decided.

What does
    a bristlecone pine
        do
    during six thousand years
of life?

What does
    a blue whale
        do
    with the largest brain
on Earth?[16]

I wanted to use larger, multisyllable words to capture the technical intellectualism of many scientists who study the natural world and yet do it in such a way that the words themselves, and the way they are set down, possess a syllabic rhythm and pattern that experientially creates a movement into and through that state of being.

I began with a fairly easy stanza, written in an intellectual tone, that would capture the attention of the reader and work to slightly move them into that intellectual orientation. But the core of that kind of intellectualism possesses a certain rushing element to it that goes hand in hand with

Earth-disconnected mentation. That second stanza is designed to capture that, to create that sense of rushing and to generate an experiential movement into that kind mentation.

So I pulled the reader in with the first stanza and then got them to rushing along mentally with the second. But I didn't want to leave it there, I wanted to experientially move the reader into a different orientation entirely, one that is the antithesis of that intellectual mentation. So, I did two things: I slowed the final stanzas down and I asked questions for which technoscience has no answers. The reader is then moved not only into a slowness of perception but also into a different kind of thinking.

You can feel the different movements the piece contains as you read through it. The ending state, the feeling tone and pace of it, is very different, isn't it? But I particularly like the second stanza as an example of a multisyllabic patterning that in and of itself possesses a congruent sounding and that, at the same time, initiates the kind of state of mind that the stanza is describing.

If you read it aloud and work with it a bit you will find that there is a particular kind of beat to that second stanza that the syllables of the words enhance and strengthen. Notice as well the state of mind you move into as you read it, then, by comparison, note how that state shifts as you read the final two stanzas.

I do want to emphasize that I did not write this poem from an analytical or mental orientation, which my discussion might seem to indicate. I came across that line of Huxley's in something I was reading and it captured my attention. (It irritated the hell out of me.) So, I began to try to tease out the implications I was feeling in it by following the thread where it led, by feeling my way. It was only afterward, when I stepped back, that I saw where I was going with it and then began to work consciously to strengthen those dynamics and movements in the poem.

Word Sound

Word sound is another important element in the sound of your writing. Each word has its own poetic or tonal sound and the words should be positionally related to each other in such a way that the musical tone of each word blends harmoniously with the ones near it (unless, for some reason, you intentionally don't want them to). Word sound then will flow along as you read much like a melody line in music. Daniel Soar reaches toward this truth when he says . . .

> *Sometimes language aspires to perfect contextlessness: never-ending incantation, pure sound. This is something it never can achieve; but it can play with the idea.*[17]

So, on another read through the book I read for sound relationships, or the musical tonality of the words themselves and how that melody line flows through the text.

The sounds of the words (their tonal melodies) can be combined in such a way to make the reading of a sentence a very pleasurable experience. It keeps the reader in the dream because they are hearing, as they read, a kind of lullaby, a crooning of the writer through the words. These sound characteristics can be developed just as any musical composition can be. The song can be slow, gentle, caressing or move into rapid, loud, and demanding rhythms. The words can possess hard, choppy sounds, or soft, flowing sounds and these sounds should match the communications within the text itself. "Caress" has a slower, softer sound, for instance, than the word "touch."

When working with the tonality of words you begin to work with what Robert Frost called the audile imagination—a wonderful phrase . . .

> *You recognize the sentence sound in this: You, you . . . ! It is so strong that if you hear it as I do you have to pronounce the two yous differently. Just so many sentence sounds belong to man as just so many vocal runs belong to one kind of bird. We come into the world with them and create none of them. What we feel as creation is only selection and grouping. We summon them from Heaven knows where under excitement with the audile imagination. And unless we are in an imaginative mood it is no use trying to make them, they will not rise. We can only write the dreary kind of grammatical prose known as professional.*[18]

Frost understood that it was possible to *hear* analogically or, to put it another way, to think through feeling/hearing as well as through the combined feeling/seeing that most writers use. He used not only the phrase *audile imagination* to describe this but also *imagination of the ear*. Both essentially mean the same thing, that is, the perception of the imaginal through the hearing sense, but there is something more grounded to my way of thinking in that second phrase, more easily graspable to the feeling sense.

Writers learn to develop the sound and rhythm of their writings by practice and love of the craft. I love, as many writers do, the sound of a good sentence—just for the sound of it. I have found the best way to improve the sounding of my own work is to read passages aloud and then listen to how they reverberate in the room.

One of the major problems for most writers is that they don't know how to read a line aloud. They tend to hurry through the material, failing to stop and savor each word and phrase and the relationships between them. They forget to live inside the word as they say it. They haven't learned how to let the meaning of the word emerge from the word itself, in its own time, and then float there, shimmering in the room.

Through speaking my writing aloud (in hundreds of workshops, lectures, and readings) I began to overcome this in myself. I began to get a sense of just how words vibrate in relation to each other. I began to learn how their melodic natures interacted. And I began to understand the importance of silences.

Silences are as important in writing as the words themselves. If you learn how to speak the things you have written aloud you will find that there are certain points in the work, especially during moments of duende, where silence becomes a meaning in and of itself. In a sense, silence itself becomes a word.

Silence, you could say has the same relationship to words as 0 has to integers. There are certain things that cannot be done in mathematics without the use of 0; there are certain things that cannot be done in language without silence. And I am not really talking here about the pauses that naturally occur between words because of punctuation, though there is a valid point that can be developed about that. What I am talking about here is when silence itself becomes a living meaning, vibrating in the room. Readers must be drawn into, be allowed to explore the silences that live between the meanings in your words. Without learning to speak aloud what you have written, it's nearly impossible to learn the importance of that kind of silence. (Or develop a sense of timing.) That kind of silence only emerges out of a living interaction that occurs between listener and speaker. Once learned, it can be inserted into the written material intentionally and the work becomes the better for it.

My writing improved considerably after I began learning to speak the material aloud because the audile element of the word and the livingness of silences began to emerge as specific elements in their own right. And this, I found, was an essential, third element that must be combined with both seeing and feeling—though I believe, from my experience, that it is subordinate to these other sensory mediums. If sound comes first for someone, then they are, almost by definition, more inclined to be a musician than a writer. Nevertheless, this sound element is crucial. When it begins to become a living part of the work, the work itself takes on an incredibly vital dimension that truly is essential to the work becoming art.

I think Gass captures this when he says . . .

> *Above all, the written word must be so set down that it rises up immediately in its readers to the level of the ear, and becomes a vital presence in their consciousness. It asks, that is, to be performed; to be returned to the world of orality it came from; it asks to be said, to be sung.*[19]

Gore Vidal was a master of this. Johnathan Raban comments . . .

> *During the 1970s, Vidal's essays increasingly took on the form of dramatic monologues scored for his own voice. . . . Years of writing plays probably helped to equip him with the exceptional ability to replicate the sound of speech on the page, with every pause and change of tone clearly registered in a system of precise punctuation intended as much for the ear as for the eye. He turns his readers into listeners, alert to the sly sotto voce aside, slipped in between parentheses, the sudden rise in pitch, signaled by a satiric question mark, the lethal afterthought, preceded by a long dash, at the end of what had seemed a finished sentence. His best essays are aural performances in which—as in stand-up comedy—the timing is everything.*[20]

If the book you are writing contains highly technical terms, as parts of my book *The Lost Language of Plants* does, sound relationships are still crucial. Many people get so caught up in technical language they forget it has its own beauty of sound, just as all words do. A unique sound patterning, never present to such an extent in nontechnical works, will emerge simply because of the kinds of words used. Technical words have their own sound logic and they can be developed just as words that occur in common usage do. *Mucilaginous,* for example, has a very musical sound to it as do terms like *terpene, alkaloid,* and *tannin.*

Each word that you use in a text, no matter what kind of writing you are doing, must be faced as you would a person with whom you are becoming intimate. Each word must be embraced, it must be *heard,* and an essential part of every word is its musical tonality. Its sound. And the essential musical expression or tonality of a line (and the words inside it) is directly related to the feelings that that line is intended to capture inside itself. Herbert Spencer understood this when he said, "variations of voice are the physiological results of variations in feeling." So, as feeling shifts through the text, the sounding of the material, of necessity, must shift along with it. An essential element of the revising of a text then becomes checking for congruency between shifts in feeling and the sounding of the material. I have found that if I work with a sentence or phrase over time, I naturally begin to find its essential musical expression, its essential tonality. This happens naturally because as I work with the line, I become more immersed in its feeling and that naturally shifts how I speak the line and how I write it. Feeling, speaking, writing of the line all take on a congruency automatically.

Here's another example of my taking something someone else said and making it my own; again it's a phrase originating with Bly . . .

> *A human body just dead looks very like one still alive, yet something invisible has left it. In writing, as in life, it is the invisibles that make all the difference.*

Here is how it appeared originally . . .

> *A human body, just dead, is very like a living body except that it no*

> *longer contains something that was invisible anyway. In a poem, as in a human body, what is invisible makes all the difference.*[21]

There is a distinct difference in the sounding of the two, isn't there? Long verbal use during a decade of teaching this material naturally began to smooth off the rough edges, to distill the sentences down to essence, and to enhance the sounding of the concept. Again, Bly was articulating a concept that occurred to him in the heat of writing (he wrote it in the 1960s). He refined it then to the extent it mattered to him for that piece but it was not, I think, a primary or central concept to what he was writing. It was, in a sense, a one-off observation. (I find that Bly, in his commentaries, tends to throw off these kinds of astonishing concepts by the score, a single one of which, to another writer, would take a major effort to produce.) Nevertheless, the concept, for whatever reason, captured my attention as crucial for me, and I began to use it as a central element of my teaching and writing.

This sound transformation, I think, points up an interesting experience common to writers who perform written works: when you verbally express a piece of writing over time, it begins to become a part of you. You eat it in a way you can't if you merely read it. It's the out-loud repetition of it that begins to make it an essential aspect of who you are. The more you digest it, the more you live its meanings from within itself. The deep meanings inside it, that were only sensed in the beginning, begin to reveal themselves more and more clearly. And, if it is a line like this (rather than a completed poem you are using) it begins to alter itself. It begins to extrude itself through who you are. The concept begins to emerge more and more strongly through the speaking of it, forcing a change in the lines you are speaking until the lines themselves are distilled to the maximum extent they can be. And one of the more important elements of that distilling is the removal of any words that interfere with the melody, the musical sounding, of the line.

You can see the distinctions between how the lines changed over a decade of use from how they were originally written. This is exactly how the book you have written should change as you rework the text. Multiple reads through the text should be for exactly this kind of thing. How much you can alter the material along these lines depends on how long you have to work with it. For most of us—not a very long time. (Most of us, after all, are trying to make a living; most of us write on deadline.) There were ten years of work on just those lines. So, all of us do the best we can with the time we are given. The more you practice the craft, the faster you'll be able to alter lines in just this way. The more you do it, the more it becomes second nature.

Meaning and Symbol Sound

And finally, every meaning that a word contains and the larger meanings that flow through a text have their own musicality, separate from the words themselves. As a gross example, if you pay close attention you can sense that there is a kind of interior sound that goes along with the experience of intimate love and a very different one that goes along with the memory of a hated enemy. You might say that every feeling tone has its own sound (an insight that musicians intuitively understand).

These kinds of sounds are inherent in meanings themselves. Meaning exists outside of and beyond words, we have only created words to hold it, similar to the way a bucket has been created to hold water. I read for the musicality in meaning flow as well. I get to this by *feeling* the flow of meaning as it moves through the text and as I feel this, at the same time, I hear the musical nature of those meanings. (And I should add here that symbols and images have their own musicality as well. So, it is possible to read for the sound flow of symbol and image as well.)

Repetition

I tend to like repetition, not only of sound, but of concept. As Robert Bly says . . .

> When a sound is repeated in a certain way, the sound becomes alive and runs away.[22]

I found through listening to Robert Bly's public performances in the early 1980s that when a poem is read the first time it gets the listener's attention. The truth receiver begins to listen to what is being said. If immediately read again, the poem penetrates much more deeply inside the self. It is *heard* the second time while the first time much of it is missed. This technique is also used by Anthony Hopkins when he acts. He has a tendency in his films to say the same thing in three different ways: "So, you want us to cut him loose, abandon him, let him go?" There is a certain kind of poetry to such repetition and I find it deepens the communication of the material if concepts are repeated in several different ways in succession and then again, in a similar way, later in the book.

Some people find this repetitious; it does take work to avoid it becoming tedious. Nevertheless, I tend to follow my feelings in this, putting in as much as I want as the book is being written and only honing my uses of repetition later. I write the initial concept into the text to capture the reader's attention, then I repeat it in different language for a deeper penetration, then I will often repeat it a third time, which I feel sets it in place. People, I have found, tend to hear material better if it is repeated three times in succession. But each repetition needs rephrasing. And I like each rephrasing to have its own musicality and for every such phrase to musically blend into the phrases around it. I find doing so enhances the penetration of the meaning.

The repetition of a concept in slightly different language, in two or three succeeding paragraphs, does something besides help its penetration into the reader. It is an essential element of working with the sound that is integral to concepts. It's a kind of alliteration.

Every time a concept is repeated in slightly different language, the concept itself is slightly altered. It's the same concept but the angle of view has shifted slightly. Every concept, like every image and symbol, has its own sound. Repetition like this creates an alliteration of concept sound as the material moves through the succeeding paragraphs.

You might say that this kind of sound patterning is a sound inside sound, a sounding that lies below physical sound, something even more invisible than the below-conscious-notice patterning of punctuation, syllabication, word sound, and the musical composition that those together create under the surface of the text. It is an added dimension to sound patterning.

There is a rhythmic patterning to all writing, or there should be. It is integral to the craft itself. The underlying musical and beat patterns in a text have a great deal to do with the depth of the dream that the reader experiences when reading. In a sense, the underlying music lulls them to sleep. It deepens and maintains the dream. A good writer writes in stages (or layers) and one of the later stages of refinement of the work is this working with the rhythmic patterning of a piece. It is laid down layer by layer just like multiple tracks in a recording studio. Each work you create should be like a song, it should have a beat, a melody, a rhythm. And those elements should be intentionally developed just as the other elements of the book are.

Most readers don't notice the rhythmic patterning consciously. If it's finely tuned the piece begins to take on a harmony of expression that makes it a much more elegant work than it would otherwise be. It is this sophisticated layering process, where each level is smoothed, refined, developed on its own, that gives a work depth, and complexity. A particular kind of mastery of the craft flows through it.

So, as you read what you have written during this stage of the editing process, the focus is on the rhythm and beat of the work. Each word is read to hear its pattern of sound, each sentence is read to hear its cumulative pattern of sound, each paragraph, each chapter. And each section of the book that has a discordant rhythm is changed, altered, so that, too, on this level it remains congruent, the pattern consistent. (Unless of course you intentionally want a discordance in that section.)

You will also notice that there will be movements to the work, just as there is in a classical composition of great length. By noticing these movements you can intentionally enhance them, strengthen the way they are already working in the text. You can enhance movement toward crescendo or develop a slow background beat as an intentional act. You can, as I mentioned earlier, weave two beats together so they strengthen each other or act as counterpoint to each other. Part of what this does is keep the attention of the reader on the work. As Bly remarks these "shifts in tone keep our feelings alive as we read."[23] Works *naturally* have this variation in sound patterning. When a work contains a monotonous patterning, continually repeated (as too many nonfiction works do), the reader begins to sleep, but not to dream. The book becomes boring. By intentionally composing through the underlying sound patterning of the book the deep self remains engaged in the work, the whole work alive, changing, altering, moving. All the layered parts should work together as a coherent whole, enhancing each other, supporting each other.

Again, there are specific kinds of communications within the musical patterning of a work just as there are in musical compositions. It may be hard to say just what those communications are but on some deep level all human beings know that music contains meaning. When we hear it we begin moving through particular kinds of emotional experiences, certain kinds of feelings are generated within us, a certain type of feeling sense is activated. Music itself is a language that all writers touch upon when they inhabit the word.

It takes a while to develop competence with these elements of the craft but you should not be put off by that complexity, just pay attention to the rhythmic patterning of the piece you are working on. Find your own rhythms and melodies, the ones that make you happy, that say what you want to say. It doesn't have to be of the complexity of a classical symphony to be either important or valuable. Remember: punk rock occurred because a lot of young musicians were fed up with the stupid complexity of rock and roll, musicians, and music schools after the 1960s. They just wanted to rock and roll.

Joan Jett is a perfect example of someone following her feeling sense and allowing her unique genius to come out of that sensing. From this she created brilliant work out of simple ingredients. She allowed herself to be ignorant (one of the hardest things of all) and to follow the golden thread that was calling her to find out where it was going. She allowed herself to play what was in her to play, abandoned music teachers, and found her own form—with virtually no knowledge of music at all, just the desire to play. Her "fuck you" is, frankly, great art. The music studios rejected her demo tape—so she released it on her own label. If I remember rightly, there were six hits on that one tape. Great music came out of her insistence on following her own intuition, a music that touched many of us.

If you want to take this further, both Bly, in *American Poetry,* and Gardner, in *The Art of Fiction,* discuss some of the more theoretical aspects of sounding. Still, remember: all these techniques are there to serve you, you do not exist to serve them. So . . . don't get caught up in all the bullshit; these are just some thoughts. If they are useful, use them. If not, shitcan them. Start slowly. Play with it. Have fun. Don't forget, a primary reason we come to this work is because reading makes us happy.

In the beginning of this kind of editing just notice rhythmic patterning that has emerged spontaneously in your work and adjust your punctuation to enhance that patterning. Trust your feelings. If you follow the thread that is calling you, you will get wherever it is you are going.

MOVEMENT CYCLES

Most books also possess movement cycles very deep inside the writing. These are generally expressions of natural cyclical patterns that affect all life forms. As with theme, symbol, archetype, and sound patterning, these cyclical patterns emerge within the work of their own accord.

The most common is the birthing cycle; it goes something like this . . .

The baby is in the womb, held in the only world it has known, then contractions begin. The universe begins to compress, begins to force movement into some new state, a state the baby has no experiential knowledge of. There is a forced change of status. But the process is lengthy. There is a pressure to move, but the cervix takes time to dilate. Literally, there is no exit. The universe demands a change from one state to another but there is no way to get there—Sartre's no exit and the origin of despair.

This process continues until finally there is an opening; the cervix dilates enough to allow passage into the birth canal. The baby enters the canal, experiencing tremendous compression as he is forced through that tiny opening. (That squeezing, that compression of the self, turns out to be essential to a healthy adaptation to the new life, the new state of being.) Then there is the emergence on the other side, into loving arms and the new life.

There can be, of course, aberrations or theme variations in this process: long labor with no opening and an eventual caesarean birth, emergence into nonloving arms, twin birth, breech birth, and so on. All are variations on the original dynamic. (All can be written into a work.) But the basic pattern is something that is deep in mammal memory. When we encounter it deep inside a story line, the dreamer in us understands it and the process that is unfolding. It makes the story seem right at the visceral level—for this is perhaps the oldest pattern that we know. It's not surprising, then, that it should emerge as the primary movement cycle in most books; it is, for instance, the commonest cyclical pattern in adventure stories and thrillers.

Other powerful movement cycles are the cycle of the seasons, the movement of the tides, the moon cycles, day and night cycles, and loving sexual intimacy—that is, the intitial meeting, movement into intimate foreplay of varying degrees of intensity, sensitive and communicational intercourse, climax, the slow subsiding into afterglow, then the more conscious interactivity that comes with the decision to be permanently intimate. All of these can (and have) emerged in writing, all can be developed consciously to strengthen their presence in a work. If you look for them during your editing process you can engage in the same kind of slight adjustments of text as you do with sound patterning or image mirroring.

This is the final dynamic I examine. When everything else is done, I look for the overall cyclical patterning so that the tides that move within the writing as the moon passes over can be strengthened and confirmed.

Among nonfiction writers, for example, Raul Hilberg has consciously worked with these kind of movement patterns—in his writings on the holocaust. The chapters in his classic *The Destruction of the European Jews* mirror the thematic movements that Beethoven's developed in his symphonies, which are, themselves, based on deeper patterns in the world.

These kinds of patterns connect the readers to some of the most powerful unconscious patterns that affect their lives. It makes the work more real, more like life itself and something deep in the reader knows it.

LAYOUT AND THE BOOK AS PHYSICAL OBJECT

When a reader picks up your published book, they really do enter a specific and unique world. That world is composed not only of the meaning-filled dreaming in your story but also the physical book itself.

The physical elements of the book, and the way those elements combine, hold within them particular meanings, too, and those meanings also impact the reader—powerfully—at deep and often unconscious levels. As such, the physical book should be produced with those impacts consciously in mind. The book's form should be designed to reflect the meanings within the text.

Regrettably, this is rarely the case. Most publishers are concerned with cost and so produce their books as cheaply as possible.

If at all competent, the publisher will create a cover that is visually compelling in order to entice potential buyers to pick up the book and at least look at it. But primarily, the cover should, in its design, color choices, and content, reflect the deep meanings that reside in the text—not just be visually appealing so someone will buy it. (I have been very lucky with most of my books in this regard, many writers are not.) However, the interior structure of most books is often poor, bad layout on stark white paper with a bland type font.

As a writer you will have no control over most of the book's design. By contract, none over cover, none over title, none over type of paper used, and none over type font. However, you can, by how you develop your manuscript, create a text layout that will accentuate the impacts of your work and that layout will often be allowed to flow through into the actual production. This attention to layout in the manuscript is, in part, what D. F. McKenzie was referring to when he said that *The material forms of books, the non-verbal elements of the typographic notations within them, the very disposition of space itself, have an expressive function.* Some of Raymond Federman's work provides good examples of this. He wrote his books for the eye as well as the ear—as Margalit Fox comments in the *New York Times.* In his first book *Double or Nothing,* she says . . .

> *each page is a carefully arranged, self-contained collage of black text on an open white ground. The net effect—one of fragmentation, displacement and emptiness—suits the subject matter of the book, the loss of the narrator's parents and siblings in the holocaust.*[24]

Simply shifting text can create, and accentuate, different feelings. You can, if you wish, begin to play around with the emotional effects and impacts of layout when you go back through the text during your editing passes. Paragraph and chapter breaks are part of this process but you can also break up the page by the use of indents, quotations, and epigraphs as I have done in this book. This can accentuate not only different feeling experiences within the text but different voice emergence at different places within the story you are telling—as examples, this can affect how the words are sounded within the reader's mind as the author's single-point-of-view voice is telling the story, (*You, you. . . !*) or it can be used to generate multiple-point-of-view communications that play back and forth from different ego states within the author, (*Really?*) or even voice plays between the book's author and the other authors being quoted. You can also use layout to develop pauses, especially duende pauses, as an integral element of your communication.

The layout of my poem about Huxley and Darwin and Blue Whales was designed with this in mind. The line breaks in the final two stanzas were designed to help break up the linear train of thought developed in the first two stanzas and facilitate a movement from linear thinking into a nonlinear moment of duende pause.

Like other aspects of writing, the more you practice it, the better you will become at it.

Often the interior designers at the publisher will support this process—they don't normally get to do much interesting work. If they are good, they will actively work, no matter what the book is, to create an interesting title page and beautiful chapter headings and initial paragraph indents for the chapters. This will greatly enhance the feeling impact of the book. However, if they catch on to what you are intentionally doing, they are wonderful allies and will often work to enhance the layout you have developed for your text.

The kind of type font that the designer decides on can also enhance the effect of the layout. Different fonts have tremendous impacts, enhancing or diminishing either the feeling sense or its dissociation in the reader. There are many powerful unconscious associations that go along with different fonts. A good designer knows it and utilizes that knowledge to enhance the power of the book.

Unfortunately, the paper color and quality is a place where publishers can directly save money—and they often do. A natural or light cream color to the paper enhances the *feeling* aspects of the book. A stark white paper stimulates mental dissociation. A texture to the paper—and the kind of texture can vary considerably depending on intent—will also enhance the feeling aspects of the book. A smooth paper with less tactile sensation will diminish it. Regrettably, because it's cheaper, most publishers go for a stark white paper with no texture.

Once upon a time, knowledge of the unconscious touches of typeface styles, paper texture and color, and layout upon the reader was an integral part of the printer's—and publisher's—art. It is regrettably becoming a lost art. There are a few small presses that regularly incorporate it into their work. A few of the New York presses still do it once in a while (David Godine more than most). Robert Harrison gives a recent example—Douglas Brinkley's *The Wilderness Warrior: Theodore Roosevelt and the Crusade for America* (Harper, 2009):

> *Brinkley's book . . . is laden with many small affectations. Panoramic, sepia-toned photographs of Roosevelt contemplating a shoreline adorn the inside boards; the pages are rough-cut; and an elaborately descriptive table of contents parrots the look and feel of nineteenth-century sportsmanship and adventure books like Roosevelt's own demi-luxe edition of his badlands adventures. . . . [Brinkley's book] belongs to what the poet and literary critic Susan Stewart has called a distressed genre—"distressed" in the sense of furniture beaten and stained to seem time-weathered, or pre-faded blue jeans, or Roosevelt's own custom-made, frilly buckskin hunting outfit. . . . Like such costumes, Brinkley's book comes to us antiqued and pre-worn as it slipstreams behind Roosevelt's own flare for self-mythologization.*[25]

By mimicking the styles of older books and an older time, the book's designers created a specific terrain for the reader to enter when she picks up the book. The visual and kinesthetic impacts help deepen the reader's immersion in the story being told.

This kind of attention to the physical form of the book *is* an essential aspect of the story you are telling. I wish it were better understood—and supported.

One of the best explorations of this neglected part of the publisher's art, by the way, is John Dunning's *The Bookman's Wake.*

SOME FINAL COMMENTS ON TECHNIQUE

While I have made it seem that I take all these elements and work them in some sort of linear order, that's an oversimplification. I do read first with eros energy for feeling flow but I can't completely separate all the other areas of refinement from one another. They are too interwoven. So, when I read for feeling flow there are times when I get caught up in sound patterning because it is the sound patterning itself that is interfering with the feeling of that section. Sometimes, in teasing out implications in a thing, I get caught up in foreshadowing or symbol development or image mirroring because those things are signaling to me a need for a development I have been missing and *that* is why the feeling is off.

Like learning to drive a car, writing begins with the conscious mind involved in a lot of thisses and thats. It takes a lot of practice before the process becomes intuitive, before the behaviors necessary to operate a car drop below conscious level and become automatic, before you can drive by feel alone. If driving remained a conscious act, everyone would drive as inexpertly as we did when we were learning.

The goal with any new skill set like this is to get to the place where it becomes automatic, where you can do it by feel, where you only have to pay attention with your conscious mind if something is going wrong. The behaviors involved in writing are too complex for the statistical mentality to overtly control. Linear thinking processes simply are not complex enough to successfully drive a car or write a book.

Nor is writing a linear process—this is partly why it's so difficult to teach in school settings. Writing is nonlinear. It possesses the same kind of interlooping, interweaving, interconnecting parts and dynamics that all complex systems (such as Earth ecosystems) possess. When you pull on any one section of such systems, the whole system itself is affected. It's simply not possible to dissect such complex systems into their component parts without destroying the most important elements of what you are working with. It is simply not possible to control, or understand, such complexity with the linear mind.

In learning how to write, you are working toward the moment when some deep part of the self finally gains an intuitive grasp of what you are doing, finally understands all the things that are involved. As you keep working with it you begin to "catch on" as Gardner puts it. You catch on not only to the dreaming state necessary for writing but also, at a very deep, intuitive level, to every component of the craft and how those components work with one another. You understand, over time, how they are inextricably interconnected. You begin to get a sense of the whole thing existing in a state of dynamic balance in which any little alteration affects everything else. (This is why a simple name change for a character can alter a whole book.)

It's much like juggling; when you get all the balls up in the air there is that magic balance point that suddenly comes out of nowhere, a moment when something more than the sum of the parts comes into being. You begin to work then with something invisible, yet that invisible thing produces tangible, seeable, results.

Juggling is a simple example of a complex, nonlinear system existing in a state of dynamic equilibrium close to the threshold of self-organization. It's a good metaphor for what happens when a writer finally begins to "catch on."

At first you have juggling balls here, juggler there. A dynamic system separated into its parts, not in dynamic equilibrium. When the juggler picks up the balls and throws them up into the air, for a moment, they are still isolated parts. But then there is that magic moment when the juggler finds the balance point. At that instant he and balls become one unified whole existing in a state of dynamic equilibrium; they have crossed a threshold of self-organization. Juggling occurs.

But once it does, immediately, the juggler begins to slightly move his hands and feet—this way and that way—to maintain the balance point. Tiny perturbations, that is, exceptionally tiny disturbances of the balance point, a slight movement of a ball this way or that, indicate to the juggler just how that perturbation can affect the dynamic equilibrium. So, he moves his body, his feet, his hands to keep the balance point intact. But there is no way for any juggler to think those perturbations through consciously; it takes too long, by the time he does, the balls will have fallen. The conscious mind is too gross a tool, too slow, too focused on parts rather than wholes. So, at a very deep, unconscious level some part of the juggler takes in that perturbation, extracts the meaning within it, and then alters his movements to maintain the balance point. Those perturbations are *communications* but they have to be analyzed extremely quickly and a response initiated in order to not drop the balls. It must be done by *feel,* intuitively, that is by some other part of the self than the part that thinks linearly.

This is a simple example of the behavior of whole systems that chaos theory or nonlinearity attempts to explain. There is an inherent indeterminancy in these kinds of systems. There is no way to predict what perturbations will occur at any moment in time nor is there a way to predict a living system's responses to them. You can start off with two identical-as-possible jugglers at the same spot on a performance floor and you will never be able to predict where they will end up in the room nor the movements they will use to juggle the balls. The most you can say is that they will most likely be in the same room and, if they are good, they will probably manage to keep the balance point intact.

When you begin to "catch on" to writing, this same process occurs. You will, eventually, find your balance point. It has a certain feel to it that you will recognize over time. It's the moment Hari Kunzru described as: *when you're in the zone, spinning words like plates.* In that zone, tiny perturbations of the storyline occur and you intuitively respond without having to think about them. You can't tell where the book is going because you are engaged in a communication rather than a paint-by-numbers process but you aren't thinking about that, you are spinning words like plates. You're involved in the communication occurring between you and the balance point of the book you are writing. You focus on keeping your balance, eventually you are finished writing, and you look around and suddenly notice you have traveled some distance from where you began. You may still be in the same room where you started but where in that room you find yourself has a lot more to do with the communicatory dynamics of keeping balance than it does intent.

This means that as you begin to edit the manuscript by feel, you are working to keep that balance point, that thing that is more than the sum of the parts, intact. And though you can focus on this aspect of the book or that, all the elements that make up the complex living system that a book is are acting on the book simultaneously. It's not possible to completely separate them out and look at them linearly. You learn how to work with all of the parts simultaneously just as a juggler does.

It's only when you run into trouble in one particular area that it's sensible to isolate that thing (punctuation perhaps) and focus on it separately from the whole. After you finish working on it you have to reimmerse yourself in the whole again, sense the balance point, and keep your invisible fingers on it, feeling how it feels, sensing its integrity. When you again sense something off in the text and step back from it you may find the next thing demanding your attention is sound or image mirroring.

Getting too mentally hung up on technique will keep you in a linear mindset. It will kill your capacity to write altogether. The ability to analyze and problem solve technique issues develops naturally as you work at the craft. Simply focusing on the feel of the thing will get you to every one of these techniques eventually and, most likely, to many others—trimming authorial bloat, for instance. If you go by feel, you will eventually learn how to cut everything that does not belong in a work and add everything that does. You cut primarily because you have the gestalt of the whole living book inside you and you begin to just chip away the excess material. It just takes practice. Cutting for cutting sake just substitutes technique for aware perception.

Of course, in this process you will make errors of judgment many times, errors that other writers will see, some of whom will "share" them with you. Sometimes shaming is an element of that "sharing," just as it is in any schoolyard. Nevertheless, finding your own way is essential. If you go by feel you will find your own unique solutions to problems in the text. You will find ways to do the disappearing coin technique, as one young magician did, that were assumed to be impossible. You will come to your craft then without having to impose a universal matrix on your work that has been handed down from on high by forensic grammarians. Abandoning such universal matrices is the way unique art is created, how your own style is found, how your own genius is unleashed.

In the end the final appeal must be made to how the material feels to *you* and to nothing else. Trust yourself. It is your art, your crafting, your journey. Do it the way that seems best to you and trust your feeling sense. It is your only true guide to the art. As John Gardner said . . .

> *Art has no universal rules because each true artist melts down and reforges all past aesthetic law. To learn to write well, one must begin with a clear understanding that for the artist, if not for the critic, aesthetic law is the enemy. . . . [f]or the young writer, as for the great writer he hopes to become, there can be no firm rules, no limits, no restrictions. Whatever works is good. He must develop an eye for what—by his own carefully informed standards—works.*[26]

CHAPTER TWENTY-TWO

Grammar Nazis and Editors-from-Hell

Language pedants hew to an oral tradition of shibboleths that have no basis in logic or style, that have been defied by great writers for centuries, and that have been disavowed by every thoughtful usage manual. Nevertheless, they refuse to go away, perpetuated by the Gotcha! Gang and meekly obeyed by insecure writers.

STEVEN PINKER

The grammarian is often one who can neither cry nor laugh, yet thinks that he can express human emotions.

HENRY DAVID THOREAU

When I write, grammar is my enemy.

WILLIAM STAFFORD

And when I split an infinitive, I mean it to stay split.

RAYMOND CHANDLER

Language is an invention intended to capture something that by nature is ever changing, moving, and flowing. It is designed to capture life—so that it can be held in the mind as memory or communicated to others. As such it has to be as fluid as life itself. It must be as adaptable as water to the landscape over and through which it flows. (There is a reason, as Jay Griffiths observes in her book *Wild,* that when we know a language we are considered to be *fluent* in it.)

The writer, when touched by a golden thread, begins to track it through an invisible landscape, a landscape composed of meanings the guide to which is his feelings. His job is to capture that elusive thing in the flow of words on a page so that when readers encounter it, that elusive thing flows into them. For a moment then, the reader enters inside of the experience the writer described. A writer's first and major allegiance is to the following of that thread and its eventual embodiment in language. Rules of language usage, conventional punctuation, and grammar have a distant, secondary place in the craft. Cut-in-stone rules are the least important element of the craft, a living, breathing conveyance of meaning is what matters.

You may run into problems after you craft your work; you may run into Grammar Nazis and Editors-from-Hell. This chapter is designed to help you with some of the common forensic depredations you will encounter.

Editing must, to be of any use, focus first on the effect of the sentence. The work must first be synthetically read. The analytical meaning of it is secondary. The question is: Does this sentence create the desired effect? Did it capture the living essence within it? Does the reader feel it? And if not, why not? Whether the sentence "makes sense" in the normal usage of that phrase, is irrelevant.

Gertrude Stein's *It looked like a garden, but he had hurt himself by accident* is a perfect example of what I am talking about. It doesn't "make sense" by the "normal" rules of writing, but the impact on the self, its effect, is brilliant. It illustrates perfectly that writing is a communication, not a technique. Synthetical reading then, as William Gass describes it, is very different than analytical reading. Analytical reading dissects the sentences and looks at their form. Synthetical reading, in Gass's words, "integrates every element and *responds*."[1] The good editor must be able to read synthetically first, analytically second in order to fulfill her main function, that of making sure the writing does what the writer intended.

Regrettably, most people, and this includes most editors, are taught, early on, that rules of grammar are *the* important things. As a result, many writers (and editors) end up as stiff and wooden in their skill as the rules themselves. Being able to utilize the rules of grammar, sentence construction, and so on, may produce writing that is technically correct but if writing is composed from this orientation there will be no life in it, no luminous quality, no greatness of spirit. It will feel, and be, mechanical.

Language and rules of grammar, again, are meant to serve us. We are not meant to serve them. Both, it is important to keep in mind, are only human-created conventions, they are not inevitable laws of Nature. The imposition of inflexible rules can kill the ability to say what is necessary to be said and so the rules must serve the writer, not the other way around. When writing rules interfere with capturing the living, always-changing, ever-moving luminous thread that is being followed, when they interfere with the conveyance of meaning, with what must be said, then the rules of grammar must be abandoned. Humans created them, any human can break them. With impunity. Ultimately, there are no inviolable rules of grammar. (That's right, none.) For every grammatical rule that someone insists is unbreakable, there will be a writer that breaks it in a way that makes its breaking art.

The most common response to that statement by the way, by many writing teachers and editors, is, regrettably, that the rules must be understood before a writer can break them. Poppycock. (Dandelionscrotum?) By approaching the craft without a lot of preexisting limitations cluttering up the mind a great many ways to do things can be discovered that would not have been discovered otherwise. Such statements show one thing only, a lack of trust in the essential integrity of the young writer. Writers are obsessive, driven people. They explore their craft no less ardently than an adventurer seeking the source of the Nile. Their allegiance is to saying what they feel forced to say by the daimon inside them that drives them to write. *They* know better than anyone if they have fallen short and that feeling of incompleteness will never let them rest. They will chew on that feeling of incompleteness endlessly—until they figure out what is wrong. Ultimately, they will attain a great deal of perfection in the craft because of it. The grammatical conventions they then adopt will be based on a much deeper core of the craft than top-down-imposed analytical rules. They will come out of an understanding of essence and that essence will determine form, as it should. As young writers explore essence, their form will become more sophisticated. Automatically. Young writers must be trusted to find their own forms of usage. *That* is what William Stafford was so earnestly trying to communicate through his particular teaching approach.

So, let's look at some of the common editorial inflexibilities that a burgeoning writer might encounter. This list will by no means be exhaustive; I just mention the most common ones I have experienced.

SPLIT INFINITIVES

I have always loved that Chandler quote at the beginning of this chapter—his note to an overactive editor: *And when I split an infinitive, I mean it to stay split.* I have sent it to a couple of editors on necessary occasions, none of them apparently understood the sophisticated humor in it, that Chandler was using a split infinitive to make his point.

The most recent foolishness surrounding a split infinitive occurred during the inauguration of Barack Obama as President of the United States. The Chief Justice, John Roberts, refused to say the oath of office as it is written (and must be said for it to be legally binding) because it contains a split infinitive. The result was that Obama appeared to stumble when saying the oath and Roberts had to repeat it, correctly, the next day for it to legally take effect. What a great example of the foolishness of blindly following grammatical rules.

The no split infinitive "rule" came out of what Steven Pinker calls "a thick-witted analogy to Latin, in which it is impossible to split an infinitive because it consists of a single word."[2] This thick wittedness eventually made its way into a great many books on proper grammatical structure, including *The Texas Law Review Manual on Style,* where it then began to spread everywhere like some sort of virus, eventually reaching the highest court of the United States. The reality is that the split infinitive rule is considered to be the invention of self-appointed grammarians with no legitimate basis in usage, i.e., it doesn't matter and never did.

SENTENCE FRAGMENTS

Sentence fragments can be, and often are, an exceptionally sophisticated technique for creating emphasis, developing mood, and establishing voice. They are also a legitimate side effect of the use of punctuation for sound patterning. Unfortunately, most editors hate them, I think primarily because they don't understand them. Most likely they were taught in school that fragments were bad things. The question, however, is not whether a sentence is a fragment, but whether or not the fragment works. If it works it is considered to be a *stylistic fragment* (yeah, it's an industry term) and, as such, a legitimate, and intentional, technique of the craft.

A stylistic sentence fragment causes a certain kind of emphasis to be placed on a section of the text that would not occur otherwise. It creates that emphasis by the powerful reading pause a period generates; comma pauses are much weaker. That emphasis alters the way the meaning of the fragment penetrates the reader. It literally alters a reader's perception of the material.

> *Just as Gerry was about to give up, he saw that bright, green hat bobbing along in the crowd. Finally.*

Now, let's shift it around and see how it works.

> *Just as Gerry was about to give up, he finally spotted that bright, green hat bobbing along in the crowd.*

The impact of the piece is very different isn't it? The emphasis moves when the word *finally* is used as a fragment. But the meaning held in the sentence is quite different as well, a different emotional state is expressed just by altering that one thing. A different voice emerges.

The main error that new writers make when they use sentence fragments is that they end up, unintentionally, with a disconnected phrase or clause. Usually this is a disconnected prepositional phrase or dependent clause. Every so often there might be a disconnected verbal phrase, though I think it much less common.

Dependent clauses, as sentence fragments, usually start with what are called subjunctive coordinators: *as, because, if, that, though, when, since,* and so on.

Because he lost his book.
When you get home.
After the party.

Disconnected prepositional phrases start with a preposition such as: *by, for, from, into, with,* and so on.

Into the wind.
With my sister.
From the side of the car that had been hit.

Nevertheless, any of these can work as intentional stylistic fragments:

He got out of the car and took a piss. Into the wind.

The reader (and writer) don't really need to know why this works. They can tell it works because it is inherently satisfying when it is read (the only real criteria for whether something is a stylistic fragment or an unworkable sentence fragment). It *feels* right. This next one, on the other hand, does not:

Then I attended the University of Colorado. A university that was a bad experience.

You can tell there is something wrong with it because there is something unsatisfying about it. It *feels* funny.

Stylistic fragments that are used to create intentional impacts on the reader just feel right. *Like this.*

When those two sentences are read, the reader stops completely after the word *right* and that forces an emphasis on the next sentence: *Like this.* And then the reader stops again. By juxtaposing a short, sentence fragment with a longer sentence a much greater emphasis falls on the second, shorter sentence. As well, that second stop is longer, deeper, and more powerful than the first. The reader enters a moment of silence where the power of that second, fragmented sentence almost reverberates in its intensity. It concentrates the attention on that moment with a particular kind of insistence, emphasizing the importance of the communication. It gives a kind of commentary about the sentence that immediately preceded it. And it expands awareness in particular directions, sometimes uniquely so . . .

He got out of the car and took a piss. Into the wind.

The initial sentence creates a particular image in the reader's mind. The fragment that follows it gives a wry commentary about the person in that image. It also develops character. Very succinctly. A hard-to-pin-down, but very clear experience of that person's character emerges from the use of the sentence fragment. The fragment also works to establish a certain kind of voice in the text. If that sentence were written differently, eliminating the fragment, something entirely different happens . . .

He got out of the car and took a piss into the wind.

This creates a very different kind of meaning even though the words are identical. In the first example, a sense of the character's stupidity comes across. In the second the action becomes a determined act, an "I don't care" behavioral statement. And just as in the Robert Frost example of *You, you* . . . ! how the words are pronounced is very different because of the structure of the sentence. There is a wry irony that emerges in the first, fragmented sentence, which the second sentence does not, and cannot, possess.

Stylistic fragments are also an integral element of the sound patterning that occurs in any writing and can be used to give a kind of short, punchy, and powerful rhythm to certain sections of the work. This, in part, develops mood.

So. You, too, are a liar. Capital L. Small i. Small a. Small r. Period.

Or

Don't. Fucking. Move.

I like sentence fragments. A lot. I think they can be used to create a great many sophisticated effects when writing. This next example, used earlier in the book, creates another type of impact, slightly different than those discussed so far.

> *Most likely you are remembering how it feels to share closeness with a dog, even with a particular kind of dog. A nice dog. A friendly dog.*

The reader reads the first sentence and moves into a specific state of mind and then stops at the period. Then, just slightly, the gestalt is expanded: A nice dog. And then expanded again: A friendly dog. It just eases the readers into a slightly expanded perception. They move from a generalization into a specific and when they get to that specific, they linger a minute. There is a certain savoring of the reality that underlies the words and that is enhanced by the second fragment. And after that one, the reader just stops a minute and that reality reverberates a bit. I like the effect—especially in contrast to the rest of the paragraph—and I like the sound patterning, the melody, and the alliteration of the line.

Sentence fragments are an essential part of the craft. They possess a long history of use by writers. They exist for a reason. They should be left alone by all editors . . . unless, for some reason, they do not work. That is the only criteria upon which they should be judged. If you do run into an editor who hates fragments, any fragments, and seems to have no idea of the concept of *stylistic fragments,* you might find this section of use. Maybe. If you're lucky.

CONJUNCTIONS AND CONNECTIVES

A coordinate conjunction is a word such as: *and, but,* or *or;* a subordinate conjunction, again, is a word such as: *as, because, if, that,* or *though.* Both are used as connectives, for words or descriptive phrases (i.e., dependent clauses) that expand on the meanings in a sentence. Editors are often highly particular about how these are used, in general, in my opinion, too much so.

A lot of editors and writing teachers don't like dropping final connectives, as in:

> *I have spent the last two decades working among herbalists, plant people, vegetalistas.*

Most want to alter the sentence to read:

> *I have spent the last two decades working among herbalists, plant people, and vegetalistas.*

Again, the only legitimate reason to argue with leaving out the coordinate conjunction (i.e., the connective *and*) is whether or not the intended effect doesn't work. In this sentence, my intention is to have the sentence read with a certain emphasis on the final word and also to create a certain sound patterning when it is read. And, in fact, leaving it out does create exactly the effect I wish.

A final connective in a string of nouns weakens the emphasis on the final word in the sentence. Without the connective, herbalists, plant people, vegetalistas are all read with equal weight, perhaps there is even a slightly stronger emphasis on the last word. When the connective is used, the sound patterning trails off and the final word is much weaker. The mind begins to wander a bit in the second example, in the first it does not.

Such usage is perfectly acceptable; there are no legitimate rules against it, just convention.

Editors and writing teachers also tend to have a great deal of trouble with the use of both coordinate and subordinate conjunctions to begin a sentence. There is even a clichéd phrase about it: NIC—"no initial coordinators."

Connectives such as *however* and *but* are some of the simplest ways to connect a sentence to a preceding idea, thought, commentary, or discourse. A rule, the justification for which can be found no place in the English language, against the use of Initial coordinators has been taught to children throughout their schooling. Don't use *but,* or *and,* or *so* to start a sentence. There is no reason for this and very few comprehensive texts on the English language exist that actually insist it should be followed. It is perpetuated by undereducated (or is it overeducated?) writing teachers, many with MFAs, or English teachers in the public school system; most of us learned it as children and now follow it as if our little bottoms will be spanked if we don't. Anyone who relies on members of either of those groups for the final word on proper writing is NEVER going to be good at the craft, nor to understand, and be able to use, the inherent flexibility of the English language. *But* and *and* are, within the English language, like all of the other coordinators, perfectly acceptable words with which to begin sentences.

SINGULAR THEY

This is probably one of the most difficult grammatical problems facing contemporary writers. It is a prime example of the natural and important shifting of language in response to cultural change being resisted by rule-foolish grammarians, most of whom don't understand the nature and history of the English language.

So . . . I want to emphasize: the use of the singular they is, and has always been, proper English usage. (By the phrase "singular *they*" I mean the use of the terms *their* and *them* as well.) I will go into some depth as to why in a moment, I just want to note here that the rule prohibiting it came into vogue in the nineteenth century from the activities of social reformers who were intent on reforming how the lower classes spoke. I do not mean by this that only the uneducated used the singular *they*—Jane Austen used it extensively—but rather that a certain segment of the population decided on the rule and made it their goal to eradicate the use of the universal they among the "lower orders." It was, and still is, part of the mandatory schooling movement.

I have particular problems with restrictions on the use of the singular *they* because of what it does to writing as an art form. I hate the prissy restrictions on its use and the forced adoption of techniques that can, and often do, ruin good writing.

Formerly, for about a century, the pronouns *he, his,* and *him* were used by most (not all) writers as universal pronouns, covering both genders. The feminist movement of the late twentieth century highlighted, correctly, the problems attendant with universal masculine pronouns. A great deal of social pressure was created and, as a result, people felt they were engaging in sexist languaging if they continued to use *he* as a universal pronoun. The discomfort became culture wide over a fairly short period of time and the culture as a whole began to reject the use of gender specific language, specifically the words *him, he,* and *his* as universal pronouns. That created a problem—there was no legitimate, culturally accepted, substitute that could fulfill the needs for universal pronouns in either writing or speaking.

Most editors suggest the use of alternating *he* and *she* throughout the text, or the combined phrases *he and she* or *his and her,* sometimes *he/she,* or sometimes even the deplorable *s/he*. None of these really work. By their use, all a writer is doing is signaling he's sensitive about the issue—it's poor writing and all good writers know it. If a writer is clever, he can usually get away with alternating *he* and *she* throughout the text—if they don't occur in too close proximity. My experience, however, is that these alternatives to the universal pronoun *he* are just too clumsy. They ruin careful composition. They awaken the reader from the dream and they interfere significantly with the sound patterns in the text. As a writer, I feel they need to be rejected for those reasons alone.

The general populace, however, understands that these clumsy alternatives will not work; they have already abandoned them. What has happened is what always happens when language begins to change; people as a group begin to find a solution that truly does work. It is here that the conflict arises.

The culture is choosing the gender-neutral pronoun *they* as the word of choice. Grammar Nazis everywhere are outraged and are doing their best to make them stop. (It's a terrible thing when the lower orders make up their own minds. They just don't know what's good for them.) Unfortunately, writers suffer the impacts of this most directly. It's upon them that the editors work out their frustration; appeals to logic and good sense generally fall on deaf ears.

Still, let's look at what really is true, within the English language, about the use of the singular *they*.

Just to warm things up a bit, both *The Oxford English Dictionary* and *The Cambridge Grammar of the English Language* support the use of the singular *they,* as does *The Cambridge Guide to English Usage*

(2004). "Gender/universal *their* provides a gender-free pronoun," it says, "avoiding the exclusive *his* and clumsy *his/her*." It further comments:

> It avoids gratuitous sexism and gives the statement broadest reference. . . . *They, them, their* are now freely used in agreement with singular indefinite pronouns and determiners, those with universal implications such as any(one), every(one), no(one), as well as each and some(one), whose reference is often more individual. . . . For those listening or reading, it has become unremarkable—an element of common usage.[3]

The Chicago Manual of Style (at least my 1993 version), as usual, avoids making any definitive, or deeply thought out, statements on the issue. Its writers just comment that a lot of people think differently. (Wow! Thanks.)

In truth, the *only* time that the singular they cannot legitimately be used is if the sentence in question is directly referring to a specific individual, e.g., Tom. "Hey, there's Tom. Geesus! Look at their hat." That kind of construction doesn't work and any reader or listener can tell so immediately. It feels, and sounds, wrong.

However, this sentence: *The reader will very rarely mistake the proper use of this word for they are very capable of understanding what you are doing and why* is, in fact, correctly constructed. You can tell because, for some reason, it feels and sounds right. The reason that it feels right is that "they" is not, in fact, a plural pronoun in the common meaning of that term, nor is "the reader" singular.

The semantician Henry Churchyard makes the point that nearly all semanticians are now making about the singular *they*. The term can legitimately be used "with a morphologically and syntactically singular antecedent when what it refers to is semantically collective and/or generic and/or indefinite and/or unknown."[4]

That is, if a sentence contains a word such as *reader,* as my example above does, what that word refers to is a semantically collective term. A reader, reading that passage, knows that I am referring to all readers, *not* some specific, individual reader. While the word *reader* appears to be singular, semantically it is plural. Because the sentence does not refer to a specific person (Tom) the use of the singular *they* is not only acceptable but proper English usage.

Singular *they* is, in fact, a "semantically bound variable, rather than a simple referential pronoun," as an entry at Wikipedia puts it.[5] It is a distributive construction that applies across a range, that is "all entities in a group" and that *includes* a single member of that group. Distributive expressions such as *they* are neither singular or plural, they are indeterminate. The insistence by editors that *they* should never be used with what they are calling a singular antecedent is, in fact, wrong. While *they* can be held to be a plural pronoun under certain circumstances, in most it is instead a distributive expression.

That editors do not understand this shows a lack on their parts of knowledge of English usage, grammar, and history. While the universal *he* did enjoy about a century of primary use, the use of the singular *they* has been in common use since the thirteenth century, a much longer duration. For much of that time, it was *the* term of choice for a universal pronoun. (Interestingly enough, some writers in the eighteenth and nineteenth centuries refused to ever use the universal *he,* believing it too sexist. They were shouted down by the mandatory school reformers.) The controversy over singular *they* is exactly the same as that over split infinitives. The problem is human created, not inherent in usage.

If you are interested in studying this further, Steven Pinker's *The Language Instinct,* and the Internet sites Wikipedia, Mark Liberman's Language Log, and Henry Churchyard's anti-pedantic site are good places to start.

Eventually, singular *they* will win out simply because it sounds best to the ear, it works better than any of the alternatives when writing, and it is preferred by the general populace who can tell, intuitively, that there is nothing wrong with it. It is proper English and it solves the cultural problem facing us quite nicely.

Eventually editors will roll over on the issue—perhaps in their graves, as it might take another generation for them to come to their senses.

SOME FINAL ADVICE

If you are lucky, you will not run into a Grammar Nazi or Editor-from-Hell early in your career. They can put a writer off writing and I sometimes wonder if that is not their objective—jealous they are not the writer perhaps. Even writers such as John Gardner ran into them.

> *The editor of one of my novels . . . insisted on changing my punctuation, forcing it to conform to some rule he learned at Yale and denying absolutely that punctuation can be an art. One of the characters in the novel was unable to remember people's names and used any name that came into his head. The editor fixed all this. When I howled, he said nothing, and he refused to change anything back.*[6]

So did John Steinbeck. He includes a marvelous description of his experiences in one of the letters he wrote to his publisher Pascal Covici (which appears as the final passage in *Journal of a Novel*). Here's a sample . . .

> *Sales Department*
> The book's too long . . . [People] won't buy it.
>
> *Writer*
> My last book was short. You said then that people won't buy a short book.
>
> *Proofreader*
> The chronology is full of holes. The grammar has no relation to English . . .
>
> *Editor*
> No Irishman ever talked like that.
>
> *Writer*
> My grandfather did.

Editor
Who'll believe it? . . . Let's see if we can't fix it up. It won't be too much work. You want it to be good, don't you? For instance, the ending. The reader won't understand it.

Writer
Do you?

Editor
Yes, but the reader won't.[7]

Everybody goes through this. Nobody likes it much. It's exasperating.

The best thing you can do to prevent trouble is to try and get into your contract a provision that the publisher cannot make major alterations of the text without your permission. This is usually defined as anything that will substantially change the meaning of what you wrote. Luckily, I had this in my contract for *The Lost Language of Plants*. Specifically:

> *Once the work is accepted by the publisher for publication, no material change may be made without the Author's approval, except that the Publisher shall have the right to copyedit the Work in accordance with its standard style of punctuation, spelling, capitalization, and usage.*

"Accepted for publication" generally means once they have paid the rest of the advance that is due *upon receipt of an acceptable manuscript*. Basically, once they give you the rest of the advance, they cannot make any material changes.

I knew I was in trouble when, during a lunch with the project editor, she told me she had read some of my other books and I was lucky—I was finally going to get to work with a good editor. After her subsequent ravaging of the manuscript, I had to write a 30,000 word defense of the manuscript showing that the massive alterations she wanted would substantially change the meaning of the work, that is, that they would be material changes. I prevailed but it took a lot of time and aggravation to do so. The book went on to win numerous awards and, most gratifying, the primary areas that readers have told me they liked over the years are the ones she wanted to cut or substantially alter.

If you do have to defend your work, some of the material in this section may be of use. I hope it is. Editors will usually show some semblance of reason if you can give them a clearly articulated explanation, backed up by a history of use by other authors and semanticians, for what you have done. Usually. Contractual wording such as *the right to copyedit the Work in accordance with its standard style of punctuation, spelling, capitalization, and usage* can be problematical if the editor does not understand the usage of punctuation as part of sound patterning or the importance, and legitimacy, of the singular they.

The other thing you can do to help protect the language usage you have decided on is to remember that edits fall into four categories: good edits because you missed something, irrelevant edits, partly relevant edits, and very relevant edits.

I stroke editors extensively for the good edits, after all those edits save me from looking foolish in public. I freely give them all the irrelevant ones with a lot of nice comments when I do so (even if my preference is for how I wrote it). I take all the relevant edits, the ones that really matter in the text, in trade for doing that, often apologizing for my intransigence as I do so. And I give up about half of the partly relevant ones, keeping the ones that matter the most to me.

This works better after you have run around the house screaming at how stupid the editor is and have gotten it out of your system.

Remember, language is there to serve you in the working of your craft. It is not there to be served. To be a writer, you cannot abjectly bow to forensic thinking. You have to come to own your way of languaging, and understand why you do so, so you can fight for it. Otherwise forensic speakers will steal the work from you, make it speak with their voice, not yours. They will tame you, all in the name of good grammar. James Kelman makes the point thusly . . .

> *[Tillie Olsen's] work offered a different way of seeing for myself, finding ways to hijack third-person narrative from the voice of imperial authority. Prose fiction was exciting at this level.*

> *Somebody was punching fuck out of ye but ye went away and attended the cuts, and came back with Daddy's axe. Tillie's work was a weapon. The true function of grammar. Make yer point. Writers need to learn these lessons. If you do not then you will not tell the story. You might tell other stories but not the one you could be telling. These bastards think they own the language. They already own the courts. They own everything. They want to block your stories, and they will, if you let them. So go and do your work properly. Ye will need every weapon.*[8]

So . . . when you experience these things, keep your weapons sharp and, if all else fails, keep in mind something John Dunning told me long ago: *illigitimi non carborundum.* (Don't let the bastards grind you down.)

CHAPTER TWENTY-THREE

Some Final Words on the Writing Life

Real secrets have been forgotten, real clues are being missed, a wholeness of vision that was once adequate has been lost.

John Gardner

We need only a modicum of awareness to assess the extent to which this gradual victory of exterior language over the inner life corresponds to a reality that crushes anything that does not serve its own expansion. This invasion of the inner world by an outside force intrinsically opposed to it has taken on catastrophic proportions. Why should we not see this as the equivalent of an oil spill? . . . A kind of rational violence now threatens all sensorial expression.

Annie Le Brun

The wordsmiths who serve our imagination are always devoted to communication. Clarity is always their method. Universality is their aim. The wordsmiths who serve established power, on the other hand, are always devoted to obscurity. They castrate public imagination by subjecting language to a complexity which renders it private. Elitism is always their aim. The undoubted sign of a society well

> *under control or in decline is that language has ceased to be a means of communication and has become instead a shield for those who master it.*
>
> John Ralston Saul

> *The first act of disobedience is contemplation.*
>
> Sign carried by French protestor, 2009

We writers, those of us who are more than typists of words, are all of us working class no matter how much some of us like to pretend otherwise. We plumb the imaginal, and through it the mythic. We channel the flow of dark waters from that world into this. There is not a one of us who does not have grease on his hands, not a one who does not deal with the dark fertilizer that comes from our own wastes, the waste of our cultures, from our old lives and the skins we have shed, from the inherent tragedy of human limitations and limited sight. How few of us really belong at a party for the literati. Or should. We be working people, not dilettantes. We be writers.

Every book we write, through some different slant or approach, is another journey into the imaginal. Each one a part of our search for truths that are woven deep within the fabric of the world. They are our reports and in them you can read of our travels to the imaginal. Some will always be better than others. Alexandre Dumas authored more than three hundred plays, novels, travel books, and memoirs. But he is popularly remembered only for two: *The Count of Monte Cristo* and *The Three Musketeers*. All of us only practice this craft, following our feelings here, then there. As we learn, we try this, then that. If we are lucky, if all the cosmic tumblers for some reason known only to the gods suddenly click into place one day, if we are able to bring that living book out of the imaginal into this world without distorting the shape it must take in our field to be itself, we may be able to write something that will last and be remembered. Immortality is part of what we seek but, really . . . it's the least of it.

What we do we do as a way of life and we do it because we must. We have been called to become part of a conversation, a great relay race of soul, that has been going on for as long as there have been storytellers.

It has been calling us from the moment we were born. Somehow, even in the first moments of life, we sensed some part of that conversation, sensed the meanings with which it is concerned. And some deep part of us knew we must be a part of it, too. Every fiber of our being, then and now, demands it.

Everything I have spoken of in this book is about becoming an active participant in that conversation. It is about *becoming a writer, too.* When we learn the elements of the craft that allow us to write truly and dream deeply, when we begin to find our balance point, start accessing the imaginal as a habit of mind, then we do in fact join that conversation. We become part of a conversation with the mythic and with all the storytellers who have encountered it and with all the readers who care about it, a conversation that has existed since human beings have been. We become members of a nation that is and has always been unbounded by time or geography.

We are not, however, the only ones who work in the imaginal realm; all real artists do, no matter their medium. Scientists used to, though they tended to be called natural philosophers then; the last generation of them were born before WWII and included James Lovelock, and Barbara McClintock, Jane Goodall and Louis Leakey. That is why Goethe could be both a poet and a botanist and do both with genius. Why Leonardo Da Vinci could be an inventor, a sculptor, painter, and architect. Why so many could do so much in so many fields. All of us have genius inside us and it is analogical thinking that unlocks its potential, analogical thinking that unlocks those secrets from the world and raises them up inside us to conscious awareness. Analogical thinking can be applied to anything and everything with which a human comes into contact. And behind every form we explore through that thinking—plants or words, music or painting, woodworking or healing—we will always find the imaginal world. Analogical thinking is a way of knowing, of understanding, that is far older than what we now call science. And a writer's work is to travel into that imaginal realm and bring back what he finds there and encapsulate it in living language for others to experience. Our writings are lenses that focus the vision of our readers—not that of exterior sight but of insight. When someone reads our work, if we have done our job well, they see the worlds, touch the understandings, we have found. It is only through our human exploration of the imaginal that certain aspects of this world in which we have been born *can* be found; without finding them we can neither inhabit our planet or ourselves sustainably. The capacity for art exists within us for a reason.

That is why the continuing assaults on the imaginal realm possess so much danger, why the reduction of science to some form of mechanicalism, devoid of the imaginal, is so fraught with peril, why the domestication of poets and writers, of all artists, is damaging our culture as much as oil spills damage our land (and now our seas). Perhaps at no time in the history of writing have so many written so much while so few fulfill the ecological function of the writer.

Annie Le Brun, in her powerful book *The Reality Overload: The Assault on the Imaginal Realm* (Inner Traditions, 2008), remarks that we must wonder, "if there is a relationship among the crisis in poetry, the collapse of certain ecological niches, the rise of religious fundamentalism, and soil desertification."[1] She locates the blame for much of the ecological devastation we struggle with *inside* us, not so much in our behaviors as in the historical moment when we, as cultures, abandoned the imaginal, the dreamer, and the mythic for "practicality" and the literal. She condemns what she calls "the devaluation of the dream" and the dreamer inside us, commenting . . .

> *No doubt, when we contemplate all the calamities that the twentieth century so generously supplied, stumbling upon a particular tragedy such as this disappearance of the dream would, by comparison, appear far smaller in scale—if it was not a disaster that could create many far greater ones. Indeed, this calamity is an amputation that strips us of everything we might have used to blindly rediscover the world from the most remote reaches of our solitude. Evidence for this resides in the fact that at the onset of the present era, no one has expressed anxiety at the disappearance of the "definitive dreamer" who we may not yet have ceased to be. It even seems that in this disappearance some find a cause for rejoicing, for perhaps some have been working—consciously or otherwise—to bring about this catastrophe.*[2]

We have, in our Western cultures, become literalists, lost the understanding of the importance of dreaming. And there are many among us who do indeed rejoice in that loss. But there are still mavericks among us, people who insist on extending awareness further than society wants it to go, people who explore the imaginal and bring to us ways of seeing and living that we need to survive as whole peoples. One such is Bill Mollison, the father of permaculture.

> *[My father] never tired of stories, and many of his stories were dreams of what was possible. . . . I know that I got caught up in his dreams; I continue the dreams of a dreamer. And in the end, every one of us is alone, except for those who dream our dreams. . . . At all times, I have felt myself outside, an outsider. If I see people rushing somewhere, I turn at right angles to their path. I know that everybody is usually wrong, or usually the victim of mass persuasion, conformity, infectious plague. So lemmings press into the river, mammoths stampede over cliffs, locusts drop into the ocean, bodies of all sorts pile up in death. I think that anyone who daydreams is an outsider; they are imagining worlds different from those about them; they are nowhere real. . . . When we design, we are always building for future floods, future fires, future droughts. And planting a tree a few cm. tall that will be future forest giants, throw future shadows. Future populations will need future soils and forest resources, shelter, security. So somebody needs to range ahead in time, scout out the next century. We are not day-dreaming; we are time scouts, finding places now for what will be needed then. All this must be imagined or pictured, not on a screen, but in our mind. We must watch distant horizons and adjust our courses in terms of distant signals, hints carried on the winds. . . . For a social animal, foreseeing future peoples, it is normal to daydream; why else would a bee gather honey, and seal it in a wax cell? And if we succeed, then a sustainable system is self-governing, so when they say, "What are you doing?" we can truthfully say, "Nothing." . . . Everything I do now is in a real sense, experimental; it is done to see if it will work well, or not at all. . . . In the long term, we need to devise sustainable living systems, therefore we need models [not only from cultures that have shown their capacity for sustainability but those that arise out of our dreamers].*[3]

But how hard it is now for our Western cultures to love the dreamers among us. How many future dreamers are now medicated when they show impatience with sitting in those graveyards of the imagination we call schools? How many future dreamers are derailed from their journey, forced away from the road of feeling into a dissociation of self through a constant immersion in mechanical thinking? How many future dreamers' capacity for writing is destroyed through the pressure of forensic grammarians, those terminally humorless people who force the free-wandering traveler in dreams into a straight ditch of safely channeled words? Why is it that there are no courses, no schools, in this country that teach children how to dream—as a way of life? How is it that there is no program of instruction that allows people to major in the imaginal? That teaches them *how* to engage it? How is it that we have forgotten that the United States itself came out of dreaming? That it, itself, came from imagination. "There exists in most men," Charles-Augustin Sainte-Beuve observed, "a poet who died young, whom the man survived." Has that become true of our cultures, and of ourselves, as well?

So, I would ask a question: *What happens when you break off a part of Nature?*

This question, rarely asked, is one of the most important questions of our time. It is at the center of the problems we now face as a species. It is also crucial to the kind of writing we do.

If you think about it carefully, the answer is obvious: *Any piece of Nature, broken off, immediately begins to degrade.* Everything here in this place is meant to be biodegradable (including ourselves).

The consequences of this truth are pervasive.

All parts of our technological civilization are things broken off from Nature. We go into Nature and cut trees to make houses. Soon we find that our houses need endless upkeep. The shingles wear out, the paint peels, the wood rots. Nature works to biodegrade what has been broken off from it and we spend a great deal of time and money and energy trying to prevent it from doing so. It's a battle we can never win. Nature is, and has always been, a self-replicating and self-maintaining system. It is exceptionally ancient, complex, and sophisticated compared to us or our technology. Nature possesses highly complex mechanisms designed to facilitate that biodegrading process for biodegradability is one of the primary things upon which all life in this place depends.

All pieces that are broken off from Nature degrade, are subsumed back into the ecological matrix of the planet, and are then used in the growth of new life. This is the main reason why infrastructure always breaks down and must be replaced. If civilization is kept below a certain level of development, there is enough ecological interest produced from the foundational ecological capital so those things that do biodegrade can be replaced without damaging ecological integrity.

One question leads to another: *"What happens when a culture is broken off from Nature?"*

It's obvious, isn't it? It begins to biodegrade as well. And its behaviors express that degrading process.

Ecologically? It begins to utilize ecological capital. It burns the house to keep warm in the winter.

Socially? Read the newspapers. Watch the television.

Artistically? That is, *"What kind of literature does a culture that is broken off from Nature produce?"*

Whatever that emptiness is, we know it when we encounter it. It's common in the flat poetry of the universities, the dead-end literary forms of Bellow, Updike, and Roth (that they possessed a mastery of their form is irrelevant); it fills the hundreds of thousands of nonfictional works that are published every year, works that, for the most part, are nothing more than exercises in dissociated mentation. It produces literary forms that orient themselves solely around the human and, especially, its aberrations.

You find those dead forms prolifically circulating in the writing schools, in every school that pretends to teach children "literature." The living beauty of language is ignored and the children sit immobile in classrooms dissecting the dead husks of words gathered from forensic expeditions into the morgues most literary works are. There is so much dust in those rooms it's astonishing that anyone there can catch a breath, can breathe at all, still live.

It doesn't matter what that type of writing (or teaching) is called; it matters how it feels. And within it we feel the devaluation of the world and of some essential aspect of ourselves. "True art is moral," Gardner insists. "It seeks to improve life, not debase it. It seeks to hold off, at least for a while, the twilight of the gods and us."[4] And art that is broken off from Nature, automatically, debases life; it *is* the twilight of the gods and us. We killed the livingness of Nature—now we find Nature may return the favor.

As Gregory Bateseon once remarked, the choice to view the world as a collection of nonliving parts with whom no one can legitimately have empathy, parts that can be disassembled and studied at leisure, is an epistemological error. It is inextricably interwoven with what he calls the loss of our sense of aesthetic unity. Geoffrey Hartman speaks of this phenomenon as well; he uses the powerful term "aestheticide" to describe our cultural loss of the aesthetic sense.

Literature not born in sight of the Forms is deeply flawed, and innately so. It is not literature but rather a forensic study of the falling apart that occurs once human beings and cultures are broken off of Nature. It is dead-end literature because it studies something broken off from Nature, something dying, something dead.

Writers in our time are caught up in a great conflict between two competing worldviews. It is in many ways the great problem our species now faces: whether the world is alive, filled with intelligence and soul, or whether it is just a ball of resources hurtling around the sun, there for our use in any way we see fit. Writers are at the core of this conflict, for no writer can create genuine work if they accept the reductionist orientation. The degree to which a writer can enter the mythic, the expansiveness of the dream they create, is completely dependent on the paradigm in which he or she lives. As Gardner remarks . . .

> *For the writer who views his characters as helpless biological organisms, mere units in a mindless social structure, or cogs in a mechanistic universe, whatever values those characters may hold must necessarily be illusions.*[5]

And so the characters, and the story, lose the interest of the reader. There is no reason to care for them, no reason for us to enter the dream.

That reductionistic view is becoming more pervasive every day. The Western cultures, as now constructed, cannot abide the imaginal or its dreamers. As Annie Le Brun comments, "We cannot miss a demented desire for control that aims at a limitless expansion of the rational field."[6] The intent is, she says, to "cause us to unlearn our ability to discern by taking away our ability to feel."[7] And that depends on getting people to not only distrust their feeling sense but to abandon and distrust the place from which feelings arise, the body.

Lorraine Daston comments . . .

> *Embodiment embraces subjectivity and, by implication, life; disembodiment deals death to the self in order to attain objectivity. . . . Whether certain features of the individual self—sensory acuity, say, a probing theoretical imagination, or laser-like powers of concentration—might be a help rather than a hindrance in figuring out how the world works, or whether objectivity might possibly conflict with other epistemological ideals (truth, precision, explanatory scope) are not questions that exercise [a rationalist's interest].*[8]

The loss of our feeling sense results in a desertification of our interior landscapes. Those Presences, golden threads, moments of duende, and deep meanings that are a part of the imaginal, *are* the sources of the fecundity of our interior landscapes. True literacy is not the ability to read the printed word but the ability to read the text of the world around us. And it is completely and utterly dependent on our capacity to feel.

The flatness of most nonfiction comes from removing feeling from the work in an attempt to make it seem "objective" or "adult" or "even-handed and not shrill." As a result, it has no vitality. It has abandoned feeling for a form of dissociated mentation. There is no response of the heart to what is presented to the senses. Its very form *is* aestheticide. That loss of the feeling sense and the resultant loss of access to the imaginal is what John Ralston Saul is exploring when he speaks (in his book *Voltaire's Bastards*) about the dictatorship of reason in the West.

> *The more these conflicts are examined, the clearer it becomes that certain of our most important instincts—the democratic, the practical, the imaginative—are profound enemies of the dominant rational approach.*[9]

And that dominant approach, as Mary Midgley comments, often "seizes on a particular pattern of thought as the only one that can properly be called rational and extends it to quite unsuitable topics. This intellectual imperialism," she continues . . .

> *constantly favours the form over the substance of what is being said, the method over the aim of an activity, and precision of detail over completeness of cover. That formal bias is not in fact at all particularly rational, though it is often thought of as being so.*[10]

If we are to write nonfiction as art, dissociated mentation, and our ingrained agnostic reflex, have to be abandoned for something else, something that has its roots hooked in the real universe, not the virtual one we have been taught about in schools.

The greatest act of subversion an artist can now commit is to reclaim the capacity to feel, to restore the aesthetic sense, to regain a sense of aesthetic unity—and then to speak and write truthfully in their own voice of what is found when they do. And . . . they must do so unashamedly, unapologetically. Insistently.

When we reclaim our capacity to feel, we travel deep inside our sensate perceptions and, ultimately, find ourselves once again inside the meanings that underlie this world. We once again find the imaginal. We can reclaim it then—if we wish—and incorporate it once more as a crucial expression of a whole human life, as an integral element of our human cultures.

If we reclaim our capacity to feel, if we then reach out with the nonphysical part of ourselves and touch things outside us (as human beings have always done), we will eventually find that we are touched in turn. In that moment, we discover that there is a lot more to this life than a dead, to-be-dissected universe and the human concerns (and aberrations) in which we have been immersed. We move into experiences of aisthesis, into contact with the mythic realms that infuse all great writing. We enter the world of the dreamer, and the dreamer, by its very nature, knows nothing of reductionism; it resists from its core the assault on the imaginal and the dictatorship of reason.

We understand then, as we create from this place, as we liberate the dreamer within us, why the old gods have been banished from the world and who it is that benefits. We suddenly discover why it is we have been trained to believe that there is no consciousness in the world, in the things outside us. We discover why we have been trained to not extend awareness further than society wants it to go.

Fuck you then, becomes operational—behaviorally, linguistically—as it must for all artists. The courtly, dissipated language that the courtiers of power have forced upon us, you must understand, is designed to undermine the feeling sense. If ye can't say fuck, then ye are fucked as James Kelman might put it.[11]

It is our job to reclaim our feeling sense, reclaim the imaginal, to counter the assault on the imaginal realm, on our dreamers, and on the dreamer within us. It is only those who have reclaimed the feeling sense and touch the imaginal who can reliably be trusted to speak truth to power. And it is always the powerful that seek to assault the imaginal for the imaginal is always outside and beyond their control. So, too, are the dreamers. Only if those who engage the imaginal are controlled will cultures as a whole accept the surface of things for the depths, accept the literal for the metaphorical, accept the virtual for the real.

Those who have access to the imaginal will always see through the surface to what is underneath for they *feel* what is underneath all surfaces. Automatically. They will never settle for the virtual. Thus, they are, by definition, dangerous.

With this book, then, I invite you to become *dangerous*. For it is only in the restoration of the imaginal to our range of personal experience, to our culture, and the restoration of the dreamers to their place in all cultures, that real solutions to the problems that face the human species in our time can be generated. It is the only way that sustainable habitation of our world can occur. It is the only way we can become truly human. That is why I said in the beginning of this book:

> *This book has not been written for the literati, the illiterati (critics), or the alliterati (graduates of MFA programs). It is for all the children who stayed up late, covers over their heads, flashlight on, reading when they were supposed to be sleeping. It is for every child who read a great line, and when the meaning of it penetrated them, felt the hairs rise on their arms. It is for every child who has felt touched by the greatness of this craft and then, when they were, heard someplace deep inside a tiny voice speaking, saying something*

like, "I wish I could write like that, I wish I could write something that would make other people feel like I just felt. I want to do that too." You can and what is more, you must.

You must because the world, in this time, needs what you can bring. We *need* Gunslingers of the Imaginal. Silent men and women who spend years in small rooms capturing invisibles in language. Men and women who ride into town on horses birthed from mythic wombs and who then shake the foundations of established power. Men and women who carry the oldest weapons known, the true and the real, shimmering and powerful, inside the words they write. Nothing frightens the powerful more. We need the dreamers, all of them. For only the dreamers can understand that . . .

The word is drawn out of stillness
like the sword out of a stone.

Only they can understand what that sword is—and what it can do. Only they can see that when those words are drawn out of stillness and woven into this page, there is a wake, rippling through dark waters, trailing behind them, leading all the way back into the imaginal. Inside it is a power older than the first storyteller. Inside it is the restoration of our world. Can you sense it?

So, reach out and touch it and tell me . . .

How does it feel?

Epilogue

I found the Earth poets clustered together on the wooden porch of the store. They were laughing at something one of them had said. The joke still hung in the air like drifting dust from a passing wind. I cleared my throat. They stopped talking and turned to look at me.

"Can we help you?" one of them said.

I suddenly felt shy, gawky and coltish, and my foot scuffed at the dust beneath my feet.

"Well . . . what is it?" he insisted.

I took a deep breath and told them I wanted to be a poet too. Like them. The two who were leaning their chair backs against the wooden front of the store laughed. The skinny one, the one with his feet propped up on the porch railing, looked like he'd tasted something bitter. His narrow mouth curved down, he hawked and spat. A small shock of dust puffed as it landed in the dirt near my feet. The oldest one, the one nearest the steps, gave me a peculiar look and I saw a shadow pass behind his eyes—gun-metal cloud dampening the face of the moon.

He glanced at his friends and a secret look passed between them; an emotion I could not identify skittered across their faces. The bitter one shook his head like "it's your funeral." The laughing ones shrugged. The old poet turned back to me and raised his arm, pointed. I could see the veins twisting along the back of his hand, skin brown from the sun, fingers wrinkled and worn. There was a nicotine stain between the first two joints of the finger.

"You see that hill up there?" he asked.

I took my eyes from his hand and looked. A hardwood forest, autumn leaves a fractured rainbow, swelled out from the meadow and surged up the hill, covering the sharp ridge above. I nodded.

"Well, go on up there and get some water and bring it back. I'm a bit thirsty."

I looked at the hill, then at him. Looked around for a bucket.

"No," he said and something in his tone caught my attention. "To be a poet you have to go into wilderness and bring back water for the thirsty in buckets made of words." There was an odd cadence to his voice. He looked at me keenly and, of a sudden, his blue eyes were translucent, the bunching eyebrows an archway over some kind of door. Just as I felt myself falling he blinked, and the door closed. His glance held me a moment longer, then he turned back to his friends. I watched him lift his nose and turn his head a bit to the side like a hound to the hunt, as if he were searching out the scent of that laughter that had hung in the air.

I paused, hesitant, then turned and began walking toward the hill. I stopped once and looked back but they paid me no mind. My shoes scuffed through fallen leaves, red, gold, and brown furrows trailing me. A slight wind sprang up, a hint of winter in its fingers. Just as I started into the forest I heard one of the others say, "Mind you now, don't go and spill any." A couple of them laughed and I heard chairs scraping the wooden floor of the porch. Then trees older than poets and maybe even language closed around me. I stopped and took a deep breath. Then . . . I began to listen for the sound of water.

By the way—
This book you just read?
It's a how-to book.

THE APPENDICES

On the Business of Writing

As for the advance of $500. I leave that up to you—since we did hold up the manuscript all this time. If you can see to giving us some of the advance back, that would be fine.

PUBLISHER OF CROSSING PRESS 12/21/93

WHEN RETURNING A MANUSCRIPT

CONTRACTED FOR, WRITTEN AND ACCEPTED,

THEN, A YEAR LATER, ABANDONED

Look as much as you want, you will never find the word "integrity" in a book contract.

JOHN DUNNING

A verbal contract isn't worth the paper its written on.

SAMUEL GOLDWYN

APPENDIX A

The People in Publishing and the Business End of the Profession

In many respects, authors are the least important member of the publishing team.

MARCELLA LANDRESS, ACQUISITION EDITOR, SIMON AND SCHUSTER'S FIRESIDE BOOKS, AT A WRITING WORKSHOP IN WHITEFISH, MONTANA, 2001

Do you mean to tell me that you are going to base our relationship on a signed piece of paper?

PUBLISHER OF ONE OF MY EARLY BOOKS WHEN CONFRONTED BY A FAILURE TO KEEP CONTRACTUAL AGREEMENTS

There has always been a tension between publishers and writers. We are dependent on each other but neither one of us generally likes the fact. If publishers could find a way to publish without having to deal with authors, most probably they would. And, in fact, some deal only with long-dead writers so that they can avoid the problem of authors entirely. As well, some writers would prefer it if they could avoid publishers completely. Some publish their own material for just that reason. It's an uneasy alliance we have.

I have worked with New York publishers and small and medium-size independents on eleven books. I have published my work through my own imprint three times. I know all three worlds. Of the seven outside book publishers I have worked with Storey Books was the best followed closely by Inner Traditions. Penguin Putnam, a New York publisher, was by far the worst.

Every writer's experience is different. New York publishers are great for some writers but never will be for others. Some writers blossom at small presses, others just don't. All publishers are good for some writers but terrible for others; everyone finds their place in the publishing world experientially. Nevertheless, all writers, unless they win the writing lottery, will generally be treated abysmally by a publisher sooner or later. "Welcome," as John Dunning told me long ago, "to the trenches."

The first thing you need to realize is that if you decide to be a writer, to take on this work as your calling, then, among all the other things writing is, it is also a business. It is crucial that you treat it as such in some fundamental respects. It is a matter of respecting yourself, your craft, your calling, and making sure that you do everything you can to minimize financial conflicts between yourself and your publisher. Those kinds of conflicts eat up time and energy and hope and belief and interfere with the capacity to create, to write, and to enjoy the craft.

It's important then that you learn to read and understand your contracts fully. If you don't understand the contract you are being asked to sign, then don't sign it until you do. (Even if you have an agent. Agents possess the same limitations everyone else does; you should still be able to understand what they are asking you to sign.) Publishers, when they offer you a contract, are usually comfortable with several weeks or a month before they receive the signed copies back in the mail. So, take your time, spend it wisely, and study the contract until you understand what it is you are signing. There are many resources to help you, among the best and easiest is the Authors Guild. They will review your contract for you for free. They are especially good at catching nasty, little, crooked-as-a-bent-screw contracts, which, regrettably, do exist.

It's important, as well, to understand the realities of the profession. That is, understanding what a contract means in the real world (rather than just the legal world), understanding the money dynamics, the sales realities, and, also, just who and what these people are that you're working with.

THE PUBLISHERS

There were over 400,000 books published or distributed in the United States in 2007. Of those about 300,000 were published in the United States. In 2003 (the last year for which I can find figures), the larger houses, that is, the New York publishers, only published about 23,000 books. University Presses published about 12,000. The rest were published by the small and medium-size presses.

The six largest publishers in the world (aka The Six Sisters) are Bertelsmann, CBS Corporation, Hachette, News Corp, Pearson, and Verlagsgruppe. There are six large New York publishers, 300–400 medium-size publishers scattered throughout the country, and about 86,000 small presses (which includes self-publishers). The six large New York publishers are: Random House, Penguin Putnam, HarperCollins, Holtzbrinck, Time Warner, and Simon and Schuster. Four of those are foreign owned, that is, by one of the Six Sisters. Those New York publishers take in about half the U.S. publishing revenues each year. The rest go to the small presses and medium-sized publishers.

Sales figures for a "successful" fiction book is about 5,000 copies, nonfiction 7,500. A large publisher needs to sell about 10,000 copies of a book to break even, a medium-size press about 5,000, for the small presses, it depends on their size and structure. (For my own publishing company, the break even point is about 1,000 copies.) Of the 1.2 million books tracked in 2004 by Nielsen Bookscan, only 25,000 of them sold more than 5,000 copies; the vast majority sold fewer than 100 copies. The *average* sales figure for a published book that year was 500 copies.[1]

The New York Presses

The big New York publishers are owned by large corporations. These corporations, it is crucial to understand, care nothing about writing, the craft, the art, or its impact on human culture, Earth, and future generations. They would be just as happy selling laxatives or diapers (both if they could find a way to do so—actually that is kind of what many large corporate presses do do). The corporate New York publishers (there are still a couple of independents) care almost solely about the money and will act in all ways to maximize it. (While smaller presses care about the money as well, they are generally owned by someone who likes publishing, not a corporation that thinks the scatalogical bottom line is all important. For small presses, things other than money enter the mix.)

New York presses no longer like mid-list authors, that is, authors whose books sell less than 20–30,000 copies or so the first year. And they generally won't keep a book in print if it is selling less than 2,000 copies a year thereafter. Very few books do this, even very good ones.

In the middle of the last century, when the New York publishing houses were owned by individuals who cared about the craft, editors would sometimes spend many years developing a writer they thought had talent. Robert Ludlum's first book, for example, took two and one-half years of editing and rewriting before it was considered good enough to print. The editor at that house saw something in Ludlum's first rough manuscript that led him to believe the time was worth it. And it was; Ludlum's books went on to sell hundreds of millions of copies and earn a great deal of money. But this sort of intensive development is so exceptionally rare now that you should discount it ever happening for you.

It's more accurate now to regard the current New York publishers as packagers, not publishers. A packager is a specific industry term. It means someone who sees a need for a book in a certain niche and who then finds a writer to write it for them. They then pitch the whole thing to a publisher, often before the work is written. The writer is often considered as an employee in such an instance, the whole thing a work for hire. Packagers have always been interested in selling a specific product; they are not interested in helping writers develop their craft.

Publishers in New York want a book they can put into publication with as little work as possible. So, they look for books that fill some niche they perceive needs filling; books that need no work, no editing. This saves them a great deal of time and money. They don't care about the product, only the financial returns. In order to minimize costs and maximize those returns, as the big corporations bought up the prestigious New York houses, they generally fired all the good editors with large salaries and replaced them with new MFA graduates in their twenties and thirties. These replacements will work at a much lower salary but they also know a lot less about writing and the craft, very little about writers, and almost nothing about the livingness of language. In general, they are poor editors and their job is not to help refine the work, or help a writer develop, but only to get the book out the door as quickly as they can with as little cost to the publisher as possible. The New York houses do keep a few really good editors to work with their high-end literary writers (the prestige end of the business) not out of good will but out of PR value. Basically, New York publishers are into assembly line production. They want the product out the door as fast as possible with as little involvement in it as they can get away with. They no longer, for the most part, care about what is in the book, they just want the writers producing product that is going out the door and money coming back in.

Most writers want to publish in New York for a lot of reasons, perhaps mostly because they still have a sense of the old world that New York publishing once was. Regrettably that world is dead and gone. (I don't think we are the better for it.) That old publishing world is in the foreign country of the past where people acted and spoke differently than we do now.

There are some other reasons writers want to publish in New York.

They think the money will be better (the advances will be), that there will be a more powerful PR push on the book (there won't be), that there will be more prestige (only in your mind), and that the editing and published product will be better (they won't be—often they will be worse). They think they will be joining the company of all the writers they have loved and whose work has meant so much to them (not usually). It takes a long time for the reality of what New York publishing is *now* to really sink in, for the illusions to fade. But your illusions will fade if you publish there (unless you win the writing lottery, in which case you will have a great time). New York publishers are generally the worst kind of publisher you can work with. Remember: They are *corporations,* big corporations. Unless you are a high-end writer whose books make them a lot of money, a prestige writer who has won a major award (the Pulitzer), or are lucky enough to end up at one of the very few independent New York presses that still exist (David Godine) your experience is more likely to be that of a cow going through a rendering plant than the picture your imagination paints.

New York presses tend toward conservatism as all large corporations do. They tend to dumb down the material they publish. (They think more people will buy it—and they do. For a while.) They tend to go for conservative writers that say acceptable things, that have degrees, that fit into the status quo. They generally do not publish cutting-edge material that will upset people (unless it's half the country against the other half). They are prone to killing books that conservative groups boycott (sometimes that liberal groups boycott). So, working there, if you are doing anything leading edge, especially if it includes the word *fuck,* is likely to be problematic. There is, as well, little consistency in staff.

Editors tend to leave the New York houses through mergers, downsizing, cost cutting and emotional attrition in high numbers. If you do work with a New York house you will likely not experience editor continuity—sometimes even through a single book. Too, a downsizing economy can result in the conglomerate canceling contracts wholesale (a regular occurrence), putting moratoriums on buying new books, or shortchanging your marketing campaign (such as it might have been anyway). New York houses suffer from all the problems huge corporations suffer from, just more so. Most writers at a New York house are just a tiny cog in a very large machine and are treated as such.

If you do decide to go into New York (almost everyone does sooner or later) just be prepared for these kinds of things and watch your wallet.

The Small Presses (i.e., The Independent Presses)

A larger small press (the medium-size) will publish about as many books a year as Random House did in the 1950s. Like those old New York publishers, they tend to be a lot more responsive to their writers. They are also small enough that they can respond to emerging trends as they are happening—and they are often more on the cutting edge in what they publish. The small independent presses are most often the ones that develop new fields, new niches, new writers. Once these fields and writers are established, New York tends to skim off the cream with higher advances (but the material tends to become more stale after they do so—such publishers are just too conservative by nature). Undeterred, the smaller presses just keep on doing what they have been doing. And while the New York publishers are averse to risk taking, smaller presses excel at it. In general, small presses are much better able to respond to downturns in the economy. Unlike the New York houses, which, as this book was being written, were bleeding red ink in buckets, many small presses experienced their best year ever.

In many respects the smaller presses carry on the true essence of publishing. The small presses are the ones that take chances on unknown writers, that take chances on new areas of writing, that tend to uphold freedom of speech. (However, this doesn't mean they are any more trustworthy in terms of contracts.) They don't generally spend much time developing new talent, though, their one diversion from the presses of old. But then, almost no one does any more. And, the small presses primarily focus on nonfiction; fiction is still, mostly, in the hands of the big presses (though this is slowly beginning to change).

At a small or medium-size press a good first year's sales on a book is 5,000–7,000 copies, then 2,000–3,000 the second year, and about 1,000 thereafter for a few years before the book begins to taper off. However, contrary to popular misconception, books published by small presses often sell in the hundreds of thousands of copies. (If you read anything by Jason Epstein—former managing editor of Random House—on the current state of publishing, you will never know it nor that *all* small publishers extensively support their backlist, something the New York houses rarely do.) What's more, most of the better sellers at the independent presses are how-to or self-help books.

Here are some sales figures (as of 2010) from Chelsea Green Publishing:

The Straw Bale House, 130,000 copies
The Four Season Harvest, 120,000 copies
The Man Who Planted Trees, 202,000 copies
Don't Think of an Elephant, 277,000 copies

Here are some from Inner Traditions:

The Heart of Yoga, 130,000 copies
The Acid-Alkaline Diet, 110,000 copies
Vibrational Medicine, 200,000 copies
The Reflexology Manual, 102,000 copies

And some from Storey Books:

Build Your Own Low-Cost Log Home, 220,000 copies
The Backyard Bird Lovers Guide, 111,000 copies
The Classic Zucchini Cookbook, 500,000 copies
The Soapmaker's Companion, 113,000 copies
Feng Shui, Dos and Taboos, 338,000 copies

If you publish with a small press, which I think is the best approach for new writers, you will often have a much better experience than with a New York press and your books will be supported as backlist forever. (Storey Books' first publication, *The "Have-More" Plan*—521,000 copies sold so far—was first published in 1943. And perhaps the first American bestseller, Thomas Paine's *Common Sense,* published in 1776 by a small press, sold 500,000 copies its first year and is still in print today.) It is also not uncommon for publishers like Storey to actively repackage their older books if sales on the title slow. I have seen them turn slow sellers into very good sellers again through this approach; they are always working to get renewed life out of their backlist.

And now, just a short comment on Amazon.com sales figures. Here is a chart to help you figure it out:

Sales Rank	Books Sold Per Week
75–100	250–275
100–200	225–249
200–300	150–224
450–750	75–100
750–3,000	49–75
3,000–9,000	15–20[2]

University Presses

I haven't worked with a university press, so much of what I say here is from conversations with writers who have and from reading industry reports.

University presses were, at one time, publishers of books that had scholarly merit but would often sell only a few hundred copies. They were looked at as publishers of exploratory academic and scientific works, and occasionally works that were more popular in orientation but somewhat unusual, not considered fare for a commercial press. The were not expected to make a profit; they supported new research and new avenues of study—that was felt to be a valuable end for the culture in and of itself. All that changed with the conservative financial approaches lauded as essential business practice after Reagan's election in 1980. Most of the university presses were expected to become profit-making enterprises (as most universities were as well); most of them have failed to do so. Though some university presses have in the past published books that sold hundreds of thousands of copies (e.g., University of New Mexico Press's *The Education of Little Tree*), most of them have never been viewed as a source of the bestseller. It has never been their function.

Because of this shift in orientation this is perhaps the worst time to work with a university press—though some exceptions, such as Oxford, remain good choices. Unfortunately, and quite unethically, some of the university presses, many with notable names, have resorted to requiring authors whose books they accept for publication to pay the costs associated with doing so.

Bad publisher. Bad.

Vanity Presses

These presses normally have the author pay the cost of production while the press handles publication of the book and, sometimes, distribution. They then share, to various extents, the revenue from sales. Occasionally one of these publishers does produce a best seller (*The Celestine Prophecies*) but it is rare and usually happens because of the author's drive and marketing and a great deal of luck. I am not a fan of these publishers. I would not recommend them if you want to do this work as a profession.

On-Demand Publishers

Because it saves publishers a lot of money on storage and up-front printing costs, there is a strong drive among publishers to go to on-demand publishing. This means every book is only printed if someone orders it, one at a time. There are some publishers that are solely on-demand publishers. The technology, in my opinion, is not yet up to it but these kinds of publishers are making inroads and I suspect they will take more and more of the market as the technology improves. I haven't been impressed, so far, by their quality or sales figures. At this point, they seem to inhabit a niche somewhere between vanity presses and the very small publishers. I can't yet recommend them if you want to do this as a profession.

Self-Publishing

I have published three of my own books under a corporate imprint that I partly manage. It has worked very well for me but it usually does not for most people. If you are going to self-publish you should join the Independent Book Publishers Association (ibpa-online.com). They are one of the best sources of support for finding printers, editors, and so on. You should have a number of printers give you a bid on your project and send you samples of their work before you hire them. There are a great many printers that charge the self-publisher exorbitant prices for simple print jobs. The average cost for 6,000 copies of a 200-page book should be about $1.00 per book—black-and-white interior, 4-color cover, not including shipping. For 3,000 copies it should be about $1.50 or so per book. It should not be $5.00–$10.00 per book.

The best success will be had if you have a well-developed platform, a well-developed speaking circuit, and some wider recognition in the world for what you do and who you are. All these should occur before you even consider self-publishing. Finding a distributor is *the* difficult problem for most self-publishers. You have the books but how do you get them into the stores? Most distributors don't want to work with those who self-publish; the numbers of books that sell are just too small for them to make money on it.

I do know a number of people who have self-published and who have several thousand books still moldering in their garage simply because they didn't have an established base and enough experience before they went forward. Susun Weed is a notable exception. She began her own press, Ash Tree Publishing, when no one would publish her first book *Healing Wise.* Her four self-authored titles have sold over three-quarters of a million copies and she now has a number of other authors in print whose work seems to be selling decently as well. The original, *Healing Wise,* has sold more than 100,000 copies. It is still selling strong.

She commented once that self-publishing is like giving birth but instead of push push push and the baby coming out, the baby comes out and you push push push. And she has and does. So will you have to do if you self-publish. It *can* be lucrative—if you approach it professionally. If you use a distributor, on a $20 book you should net about $6.00 per book after distribution, printing, and shipping costs. The bookstore usually buys them for half cover price; they make $10 on a $20 book. If a publisher publishes you, you will make about $1.00 per book sold—see "The Money."

THE MONEY

The money for most writers is poor when compared with most trades. There are, in fact, a great many better ways to make minimum wage—that is, if you are working solely for the money. You should understand going into this that, on average, writers make about $1 per book sold (in 2010 dollars). While this varies a bit from book to book, it is a good rule-of-thumb figure to keep in mind.

In general, an author will receive a percentage of half the cover price. Usually this is stated in the contract as a percentage of net receipts. It used to be that authors could count on the net being, except with special sales, half the cover price. Now, that is not always the case. Many publishers now sell their books for 60 and even 70 percent off cover price. Some publishers will pay the author a percentage of the full retail price of the book (usually around 5 percent). This is the better way to go but most small presses won't do it.

What percentage you receive depends on how you negotiate the contract. Most publishers will offer you as little as possible and will have a limit on how high they will go. It is not uncommon to be offered 6 to 8 percent of net sales in a contract. Most publishers will usually agree to 10 percent if you ask for it—though many times not if it is your first book. They will almost always agree to a graduated scale based on sales, that is, 10 percent for the first 10,000 sold, 12.5 percent for the next 10,000, and 15 percent thereafter. They know that most books never sell more than

10,000 copies so they feel pretty comfortable agreeing to this. So, if the cover price of your book is $13.00 (as some of mine are) and you get 10 percent of half the cover price (assuming they are only doing 50 percent discounts), then you get 65 cents for every book sold. It takes a long time, and a great many books sold, to make any money from this. Most books, thankfully, sell in the $20 range. That produces about $1 per book in royalties (again, in 2010 dollars).

Here is how that works out in the real world: If you are getting $1 per book in royalties and the average book sells 5,000 copies the first year, then you will make $5,000 from the first year's royalties. The second year, if your book is a good seller, you will make $2,500, the third year $1,000, and so on. Most books have a very limited life. (And though small presses do support their backlist, many of those titles sell less than 100 copies a year.)

Nevertheless it is possible to make a very comfortable living as a writer. There are three elements to doing so: 1) Write books that are deeply moving to you, that you care about deeply and that you fill with the luminous, the imaginal (this will tend to build up a readership for what you write that is a great deal more loyal than if you simply write something for the sake of writing something and getting published); 2) Write a book a year for ten years (this will result in accumulated royalties that, together, do help to make a living income); 3) Go on the road and promote your books—and by this I DO NOT MEAN bookstore signings. I mean lecturing and teaching workshops as widely as possible and not dry ones either, your public speaking must, of necessity, become performance art. (This is also a part of what is known among publishers as the author platform. They prefer these days for you to have a platform, that is, a ready-made audience for your books.)

Once you have a published book, it is much easier to get lecture dates at conferences and to teach workshops, and it is easier to fill those lectures and workshops. The books help fill the workshops, the workshops help sell the books, a nice self-reinforcing cycle. Going on the road to lecture and teach (colleges are usually miserable for this, by the way) spreads knowledge of you, your work, and your books, pays you for doing so, and allows you to sell your books at those events for the full cover price.

Generally, publishers will allow you to buy your books from them (no, you don't get them free) at half of the cover price. So, on a $20 book you will make $10 for every one you sell, plus, if you have been clear in your contract, another $1 in royalties for each one you buy from them. (Unfortunately, some publishers, New York presses in particular, do not pay an author royalties on books they themselves purchase for resale and some publishers prohibit authors from reselling their books under any circumstances. Fools come in many shapes and sizes but some publishers and most hedge fund operators express the archetype succinctly.)

Some of your books, in spite of your best efforts, will not do well. Many of them, however, will. The result is accumulated royalty payments that can, together, make up a living wage. If you can do a book a year for ten years, the chances are that you will be getting royalties on eight of them by the end of that time—if you do the kind of writing I advocate in this book. At minimum, by the end of that time, you should be making $12,000–$15,000 per year on royalties and $12,000–$30,000 on workshops and lectures. *At minimum.* Many mid-list writers (and I mean *many*) make $50,000 per year or more from their writing and workshops, and that is often enough to live on and live well. But it is not just money, it is some of the best money you will ever make. It comes to you from your being yourself and doing something you love; it *feels* different from money earned any other way.

Roy Blount Jr., the president of the Authors Guild as I write this book, is wonderfully succinct about this . . .

> *Look. It was imprudent of us, in the first place, to become authors. We could have become something regular, but we managed not to. We were lucky, but we were also determined. There was something stuck in our craw (from the Indo-European root* gwrogh-, *windpipe), and we resolved to make a living using that snag (from the Old Icelandic* snaga, *a kind of axe) as an instrument of expression. Thank heaven we didn't realize how unlikely were the prospects of our pulling this off. . . . Money gained by writing books or articles is no more equivalent to money gained by drawing a paycheck (not that there is anything wrong, necessarily, with that money) than fish*

caught with a homemade harpoon in desert island surf is like fish you get in the store.[3]

Too, this kind of money comes out of a life that is based in a kind of freedom that is hard to find anymore. And that makes the money even more fulfilling to receive.

You can make a good living at this profession; don't let anyone tell you differently. And one of the most wonderful things is, once a book has paid off its advance, you get checks (sometimes almost monthly) while lying around the house thinking interesting thoughts about what you can write next—year after year after year.

Advances

Many new writers have heard of the huge advances that some writers receive and the expectation all new writers have is that they will receive them as well. Generally, most writers don't and never will. While the larger presses will often give advances to new writers in the $10,000 to $30,000 range, the smaller presses tend to keep advances in the range of $500 to $5,000. Occasionally they may run in the $7,000 to $10,000 range but that is somewhat uncommon and is usually given to experienced writers with a strong platform and a number of books under their belts. (All this is in 2010 dollars by the way. If you are reading this in the future, long after this book was published, this may be, and probably is, wildly inaccurate.) The newer a writer you are, the less your advance will generally be. (And yeah, I know that so-and-so got $100,000 for her first book and that the bidding war took the second one up to $5,000,000, but that's not *normal.* It's Abby Normal.)

Normally, advances are split into two or three segments. Half or one-third on signing of contract, the second half or next one-third on receipt of acceptable manuscript, the final one-third on publication or after editing has been completed.

I don't like the one-third approach. Publishers generally pursue it to keep initial costs down (or to ensure that the writer responds to edits in a timely fashion) in spite of the fact that the authors are the cheapest part of their costs. I repeat: *The author is the cheapest part of most publishers' costs.*

Printing, storage, salaries, and overhead are all often much more. Printing costs on a trade paperback in 2010, for example, should run about $1 per book for a good-quality print run that does not include color photographs in the interior. And as for translations: It is not uncommon for a German writer to get a $1,000 advance for an American translation of his book and the translator to get $7,000 for the translation. Again, the author is the cheapest part of most publishers' costs.

Advances are not real money, by the way, they are just a noninterest loan against royalties. (And, by the way, if a publisher accepts a book that you have written under contract then, for some reason, decides not to publish it, the money is yours to keep. Unless your contract contains nefarious elements, you are then free to sell that book anyplace else you like and get paid for it again.) Since advances are noninterest loans against royalties, they have to be paid back from sales. As such, many books never pay off their advances. After fourteen books, I now prefer little or no advance. Since the advance is paid off by deducting it from royalties, it can take a year or more to pay it off. If I do not take an advance, I begin receiving payments almost immediately and I can count on that income flow as I plan my year.

Money, it is important to understand, is a shapeshifter (as most of us learn sooner or later). It turns into tires or clothing or house repairs. Large chunks rarely become savings and neither do most advances.

In general, royalty payments come twice a year, usually around March and September, though which months a publisher uses for their accounting differs from publisher to publisher. Some writers get checks nearly every month.

While some writers do manage to write something that results in a bidding war among the New York publishers, most receive very moderate advances. In 1991 John Dunning received $8,000 for *Booked to Die,* his breakthrough book. (And that was after five books and seventeen years of work—plus a ten-year dry spell.) Sales were vigorous enough that his advances were in the half-million dollar range three or four books later. As he said, "Twenty years of work and now I'm an overnight success." This is the norm, not the exception.

In spite of this, it is possible to make a good and happy living as a writer.

ROYALTY STATEMENTS AND CONTRACTS

Statements from many presses are often late, and many times incomplete. This is usually a small publisher's worst failing. Most publishers tend to look at contractual terms that bind their behavior as guidelines rather than legal agreements—though they often look at the author's contractual agreements as legally binding obligations. They can be rather loose in their performance but be upset if you are loose in yours.

If you order books from them, they will make you pay interest on monies due if you run past thirty or sixty days net. If they fail to pay foreign rights monies due you for a few years or so, they will be offended if you ask them for interest on it (not a bad contract point to keep in mind by the way). You should understand this double standard up front.

You should also understand just what it is you have done when you sign a book contract. Most writers don't.

What you have done when you write a book is to create a work in which you own the intellectual property rights. When you sign a contract you *lease* those rights to the publisher for certain considerations, some financial, some behavioral. At root, they give you money, you lease them the work. Technically, you don't sell them the book. This is something to always, *always* keep in mind. The work is *yours* not theirs. They must abide by the contract they signed with you in order to be able to keep publishing the work. Most authors do not realize this and few of those who do are willing to hold publishers accountable for violations of contract.

If a publisher does violate the terms of contract, that is considered breach of contract. They have failed to conform to a behavior to which they are legally bound. That they then send you your statement or royalties (after you complain) does not mean the breach is made whole. You can overlook it, but a breach is a breach and it means that you can take steps to invalidate the contract and take back the use rights to your book if you wish to. Because of the aggravation, time, and cost involved (and the problem of finding another publisher), it's rarely worthwhile doing so unless the publisher is financially crumbling or innately crooked. Most publishers, like most businesses, are just sloppy at business. Just because they are a publisher doesn't mean they know what they're doing.

In general, publishers will pay you as late as they can under contract, well, actually, for some of them, as late as they can get away with. The good ones will just be as late as they can legally be under contract. The very good ones will pay you as soon as they can do so under contract; these are as rare as unclaimed diamonds on a sidewalk. Like everyone else, publishers like to keep their money as long as possible so they accrue as much benefit from it as they can. In some instances this means keeping it as long as possible to get as much interest from it as possible. In other instances, they keep it because they don't have enough to pay everyone and they only pay monies due in accordance to the level of irritant the author (or creditor) becomes. In some instances, they don't have the money and never will and will put you off as long as you are willing to be put off. I have experienced all three of these. The bigger small presses generally tend to have the money and to pay it on time under contract, so, generally, do the New York houses. Storey Books and Inner Traditions are very good about it. It is usually the really small presses that are a problem.

Again, publishers are often very poor at keeping agreements while they will expect you to keep yours. They will be put out if you do not. *To be fair, many writers do not approach the craft as a profession.* They are late with manuscripts and their editing responses, do not understand the financial realities of the profession, and are generally unprofessional in their transactions. You should look at it as a business and become as professional as you would like your publishers to be.

Sooner or later, once you begin meeting other writers, you will start to hear publisher horror stories. With smaller presses it often has to do with hiding money due creditors, including the authors. They are also often exceptionally poor record keepers when it comes to foreign-rights payments.

Unless you are extremely lucky you will experience troubles of your own. It is important that you stay on top of the publishers with whom you have contracts, that you know when every royalty statement is due and make sure it comes on time. If it does not you should contact the publisher and ask when it will be there; you should ride herd on them until it arrives. (The squeaky wheel really does get the grease.) It is important that you go over every part of the statement when you receive it until you clearly understand it and know whether or not you are being paid what you are supposed to be paid.

I also suggest you run in-depth Internet searches on your books on a regular basis, every four months or so. You will get a good sense of the market penetration of your books and which groups of people are finding them interesting and, if your experience is anything like mine, you will find all your foreign-rights titles—some of whom you were never told of nor paid for. Regrettably, this is one area that many publishers regularly fail to be responsible. Running this kind of check is one way to keep tabs on contract performance.

It's a good idea to have the name and number of a competent intellectual-rights attorney from the beginning of your career (authors organizations can help you with finding one—so can googling). You should use them if the publisher acts outside contractual agreements and is not willing to correct in response to your concerns. Failure to act with alacrity can result in your never getting paid.

Here are some good horror stories.

- A medium-size small press goes bankrupt due to a lawsuit. They then take the assets of the corporation (the printed books and contracts) and run them through three dummy corporations in order to make tracking what they have done difficult. The only person who got paid was the author who hired an attorney three weeks after the statement was late. In all other cases the publisher was able to keep the rights to the books and keep on publishing them without ever having to pay creditors, including the authors.
- A university press accepts a book for publication but tells the author that they have no money for publishing it . . . unless she wants to do the fund-raising for publishing it herself. So she does. She raises over $30,000. The publisher then prints only 1,000 copies of the book, using the rest of the money to make up shortfalls in their budget. The book sells out very quickly and scores of events the author scheduled to promote the book have to be cancelled because there are no books to sell. When she inquires about reprinting the book, the press tells her she must raise an additional $10,000.

- A small California press is in financial trouble and they convince their main author, a very nice, very nonconfrontational Buddhist, to raise money for them so his next book can get published (and the one after that as well). He does so. The press is very nice and easy to get along with but the author never does receive the royalties due for his three award-winning books. When he finally decides to force the issue, ten years later, the press tells him that while they like him very much, his failure to exercise his rights over the past ten years means he did not want them and that they have reverted to the publisher who is now under no obligation to pay him. Ever. (A position that is legally incorrect by the way. Bad publisher. Bad.)
- A publisher has a contract with an author that contains a provision (now common in most contracts) that all books that they sell at 50 percent or less off the cover price will pay 10 percent royalty to the author. Books sold at greater than 50 percent off cover will pay only 7 percent. Upon inquiry, the publisher tells the author that very, very few of their books sell for more than 50 percent off cover price. Usually such exceptional discounts are special sales of one sort or another. It turns out, after the contract is signed, the book published, and royalty statements begin arriving, that 98 percent of their sales are for 55 percent off cover price. This saves them 30 cents per book in payments to the author. Permanently. There is no remedy as the contract, as with all contracts, specifies that no verbal agreements are binding in any way, only written addendums.

These kinds of problems are legion and are only minor examples. My favorite is Judith Appelbaum and her book *How to Get Happily Published*. She had to sue to get a proper accounting and payment for substantial subsidiary rights royalties. (I have always hoped they would change the title of the book.)

A good publisher is worth its weight in gold. You will find which ones are good after a while but . . . get a hard hat and welcome to the trenches.

ABOUT EDITORS: WHAT THEY ARE AND WHAT THEY ARE NOT

There are a number of different kinds of editors. The size of the publisher you are working with will determine if all of these positions are filled by different people or if one person does several of them. What follows is the general organizational structure for a largish small press; I will look at how it is different for New York publishers afterward.

The Acquisition Editor

In general, the first editor you have any contact with is what is called the acquisition editor. This is the person who receives all the crap that gets sent to the publisher in the form of proposals, letters, pleas, whole manuscripts, e-mails, attachments to e-mails (with photos), boxes of shells, sand, beads, feathers, sections from the Bible, and letters about what will happen to the editor (usually a disease or financial disaster of some kind) if he or she does not accept the to-be book.

If you intend on sending a proposal to a small press, look them up online and get the name of the acquisition editor so that you can send it to that person directly.

At Inner Traditions, the publisher of this book, the acquisition editor is Jon Graham. (He would appreciate no more rocks or crystals and, please, no more magic sand mixed in with the manuscripts.) He receives about 10,000 submissions per year; Inner Traditions publishes about 60 books per year. So he has to review about 30 proposals a day, 7 days a week, to stay on top of it. Sometimes he has an assistant. Sometimes not. (They tend to burn out while he, for some reason, does not.)

It's important to understand the realities of the acquisition editor's job, to visualize the tiny rooms they sit in, the stacks of papers on every flat surface, and the hundreds of internal and external e-mails, letters, and phone calls awaiting them daily. I will talk about them a bit more in the proposal section, nevertheless, this is the first editor you will encounter when you begin writing, and as with all editors, it is important to understand their world in order to interact with them most effectively. They are the most underappreciated editors at any publishing house.

The Managing Editor

The next editor you will encounter is the managing editor. The managing editor is responsible for maintaining the overall publishing picture. They are basically organizational administrators who run the day-to-day operations of the press. They will interact with you to a certain extent once your book is accepted and a contract initiated but their main job is running the day-to-day editorial operations of the publishing house and handling any problems that arise. This includes conflicts between you and the house or you and the editor that edits your book. Normally they possess exceptionally good people skills and can be very helpful if you are having conflicts. They rarely edit books, though occasionally they do one or two just to keep their hand in.

The Book or Project Editor

Once your manuscript is finished and accepted you will be assigned a book or project editor to work with during the editing process. More accurately, this editor is the substantive editor. She is usually a she and she will work with the manuscript you send her in great depth. There is no one with whom you will be more manuscript-intimate than this person. They are the only person at the publishing house who will read your work with any depth or detail, or perhaps read it at all. A good one will get inside your skin and see the world from your point of view. That is, in fact, their primary function. Their job is to understand the material you have written from *your own point of view* and to determine if your material does actually capture what you are trying to say, then, to switch into the reader's point of view and see if it really does convey what you mean it to convey. They should be able to observe their reading reactions to the manuscript to determine if your writing is creating the response in the reader that you intended. Their job is to then help your work become the best it can be for that book and for this moment in time in your writing life. They should have a depth knowledge of the craft and of technique. They should be able to discourse intelligently with you about both. If you are a very new writer with few writing skills, they should be able to communicate with you in such a way as to help you improve your work while at the same time not crushing your spirit.

Not all of them can do all these things.

If you have left something out of the book that should be in it or if you have included material that should not be, it is their job to recognize it and to let you know about it. Normally, substantive editing will result in them asking for more of this and less of that. They should have good reasons why they are asking for those things and should be able to tell you why if you ask.

Not all of them can do this either.

While their job is to be your advocate they must, at the same time, represent the needs and desires of the publisher. This puts them into a very delicate position. *You must remember that in almost all instances their primary allegiance will be to the publisher for that is who pays them.* It takes a lot for an editor to be willing to take a stand that endangers that paycheck. If there is a conflict you will generally lose.

Many substantive editors at small presses now work on a contract basis (some, like those at Inner Traditions, are, fortunately, still on salary). This saves the publisher a lot of money but it does have an impact on the editors. They don't have a lot of job security nor do they have a reliable paycheck. This does affect their behavior and unless they are being paid by the hour (many work per page) they will want to get though the editing job as fast as they can. The faster they work, the more money they make.

Unfortunately, the skill level in editors has gone down substantially the past thirty years; about 30 percent of the time (if my experience is anything to go by) you will get one who does not understand to any depth what she is doing. If you are just starting out, you won't notice, as they will probably be better than you are. Later on, it will slowly begin to dawn on you that something is amiss. If you are writing as craft, as art, you will find that fewer of them understand what it is you are doing, especially with nonfiction. This will force you to be exceptionally clear about what you are doing so that you can explain it if problems arise. (Irritating.)

Most editors, however, love the craft and take their job seriously. They will normally do their best to be your advocate and to help you be the best you can be. They generally work very hard to support the vision the author has about the book.

The Copyeditor

The next editor of note is the copyeditor. They are normally freelancers, hired on a contract basis. This is the person who reads the manuscript to check for errors in text, to make sure it is formatted properly, and that there are no glaring grammatical errors. Almost none of them will limit themselves to this job description. All of them spill over, irritatingly, into substantive editing of one sort or another. Usually, their worst fault is trying to substitute their grammatical preferences for yours. Very few of them understand writing; they are *grammarians* and *spell-checkers* by nature, not writers. They often base some degree of personal self-worth on their knowledge of grammar and feel that grammar rules are laws of nature. They can be, if allowed free rein, exceptionally destructive to a manuscript.

When you begin life as a writer many of these people will know a great deal more than you do and their feedback and comments can be very helpful. Eventually, if you are truly driven in the craft, your skill will surpass theirs. That is when the trouble begins—for help with this, see the chapter "Grammar Nazis and Editors-from-Hell."

OTHERS PLAYERS OF NOTE

There are a number of other people you will encounter to one extent or another, all of whom will have an impact on your career: the publisher, the head of marketing, and the agent.

The Publisher

The publishers of most small presses (especially the medium-size) are, very much like the publishers of the New York houses in the early- to mid-twentieth century, people who love the work. They like being publishers and they like the independence of running their own companies. Some of them, not all, are very good at their work. If you visit the publishing house, something I suggest you do (it is the best way to get a sense of the place and whether or not you will like it at that house), you will usually get to meet the publisher and shake fingertips. They do like to meet their authors but they won't remember you later because you are just one of hundreds. Most of them are very nice and exceptionally well groomed. They often use aftershave.

Head of Marketing

The head of marketing is the person who creates the sales strategies for the publishing house and makes sure they are implemented. They will rarely, if ever, read your book. Some publishing houses, unfortunately, come up with title, cover, and marketing campaign for your book without anyone but the editor ever having read the thing—sometimes before reading, sometimes before the book is even written.

And make sure you understand: by contract you will have no control over the titles of your books or their covers. (My suggested titles have been used only twice in fourteen books. My preferred title for this book was and is *Inhabiting the Word*.) Most small presses, however, will work with you to make sure that whatever title they use will at least be tolerable to you—they complain about it but they will do it. (The New York houses don't care and, unless you're famous or the book likely to sell millions, won't allow you much input of any meaningful sort.)

The head of marketing will decide on title (often along with the publisher and managing editor) and market insertion and sales strategy. Often they will have significant input on cover. If the house you are with is a good one like Inner Traditions or Storey Books, they will already understand the niches they publish to exceptionally well and will know how to market to them effectively. Many small publishers, unfortunately, like the New York houses, have very little idea of how to market books. With the small presses it is more a matter of common human limitations and an inability to reason. With the New York houses it is more the arrogance of a large corporation. Badly aimed .22 versus a shotgun approach; neither one is very accurate. So, if unlucky, you will find yourself irritated by the lack of marketing skill or by the strangeness of it. And, by the way, the large box bookstores that the marketers insist on trying to get your books into? They are the worst place for your books to end up; their return rates are monstrous.

It is buzz, word of mouth, and a timely entry into the right niche that sells books. An excellent marketing team can help but they are very rare to find. (And yeah, I do realize that a tiny fragment of the authorial world wins the writing lottery: A first book is published and it takes off and the author makes millions forever after; this is very uncommon and many of those who have this experience have a great first book and never have a great second one. Here's what reality is: For every lottery winner there are a million people who just buy tickets.)

Your increasing exposure through workshops, lectures, and powerful writing is what will be most effective in increasing your visibility and sales. At a certain point, everything just takes on a life of its own from the momentum you have built up. The publisher, if good, can get your book into the markets that it belongs in initially, but the book will have to find its own legs to sell well. Often this is more a matter of luck than anything else. Usually it comes out of just plain hard work over a long period of time.

Triage

If your proposal is accepted by the acquisition editor, it will then be sent to the managing editor with a recommendation to buy. Copies of the proposal will be made and the publisher, managing editor, and head of marketing will review the material and decide, as a group, whether to publish it or not. The acquisition editor may or may not have some voice in the decision.

The head of marketing can usually kill any project he thinks will not sell. The publisher can usually overrule everyone and publish what he wants or kill any project he does not like, after all, it's his or her company. Generally, it remains a group decision.

The Agent

Most writers want an agent. You won't believe me, but most don't need one. You especially do not need one if you are selling nonfiction, even if you plan on selling nonfiction to New York houses. (For fiction, agents are *almost* always still necessary. Almost—but in an eighty-year career Andre Norton never had one. Ever. And . . . this is beginning to change, more small presses are publishing fiction every year.) To understand agents, you need to, very frankly, look at the money involved.

Most agents now get 15 percent of any monies you make from your books (they used to get 10 percent). This means that if they get a $10,000 advance for you, they get $1,500. If they are a New York agent that is not enough to pay their lunch tab for a month, much less their rent, phone, computer costs, overhead, secretary, and assistant. You should figure a New York agent needs $100,000 per year just to cover expenses (rents are often $5,000 per month for an office there, sometimes a great deal more). They've got to sell a lot of books to make that money, $1,500 is nothing to them.

If you become popular, if your books really begin to sell, if film rights are in the offing, you need an agent. The more money that is involved, the more an agent can make from you and the more time he or she can spend on your career. For new writers, just starting out in nonfiction, agents are, truly, a waste of time and money.

The majority of professional writers are not agented and they do just fine. You just have to read the contracts carefully, make sure you understand what you have read, and be able to negotiate the contract to a mutually agreeable form. (The Authors Guild, again, is a great help for this.)

VARIATIONS ON A THEME: THE NEW YORK HOUSES

If you are publishing with a New York press the organizational chart will be a bit different (unless it is one of the very rare independents that still exist). The person who is equivalent to the publisher will be the Editor in Chief. This is usually someone who oversees a division or several divisions of the publishing conglomerate. They are sort of a combination of small-press publisher and managing editor. If the Editor in Chief manages many divisions they will generally work more like the publisher of a small press and there will be a senior editor who manages the division you are being published by, who is, in essence, the managing editor of that division.

The book editors at the New York houses tend to be on salary rather than contract (though not always). They often act as acquisition editors as well. However, if you send a proposal to a New York publisher without an individual editor's name on the envelope, it will go to a slush pile reader. *Don't ever do this* if you want to be successful. New York houses almost never buy from the slush pile. If you are sending to a New York house, look online and find out which person at that house handles the kind of book you are writing and send your proposal to them. Unless you count the slush pile reader, there is generally no separate acquisition editor at a New York house.

The head (or heads) of marketing at a New York house will usually be one or two sales staff of varying degrees of seniority who are supposed to focus on marketing for that particular division. They dress in salesmen suits and know as much about the field as Wall Street bankers knew about CDOs. They spend very little time on any one book; they focus on moving units of *x* in order to build up their scatological bottom line. A book is generally just a unit of income to them. It has no transcendent value at all. It is they who usually title your book (along with a lot of other books) in one, hour-long meeting with your editor and the Editor in Chief.

If you do sell something to a New York house, the Editor in Chief, the senior editor, and/or your book editor will all enjoy meeting you, just as those at the small presses do. The lunch is fancier, the carpets thicker, the hush deeper, the suits more expensive. That's all. They won't necessarily know what they are doing any better than someone at a small press; often they will know less.

APPENDIX B

The Art of the Book Proposal

(Training in the Big Lie)

Although [editors are] skittish and sometimes blind to real talent, they are often ambitious idealists; they would like nothing better than to discover and publish a great book—or even a moderately good one. This means they can be worked.

John Gardner

The book proposal is a form of the short story and should be written like one—as entertainingly as possible.

Stephen Harrod Buhner

If you only learn one thing about book proposals, learn this: they are a specific genre of *fiction*. If you can understand that, you are over the greatest hurdle that faces you. It took me years to figure that out and none of the books on writing proposals mentioned it—I'm not sure the books' authors understood it.

The book proposal is a form of short story and should be written like one—as entertainingly as possible. The book proposal is always and every time: a lie, a fabrication, a fiction, a fantasy, made up, not true, never to be true, and not related to the book you will write except in the most tenuous of ways. Get this into your head, make peace with it, and free yourself from the restrictive notion that a proposal should have some relation to the real world. It doesn't and shouldn't.

The book you write and turn in to your publisher will be very different than the book the proposal describes. This is because good writers never know (and can't know) where their books will go nor what they will be until they write them. The book you do write will sort of be along the same general lines as your proposal, but it will not be what the proposal described. If you can make your peace with this, and feel unashamed of lying, you can write a great and powerful book proposal every time. And you can do so very quickly. They need take no longer than a few weeks.

The second thing to understand is that acquisition editors, in whatever form, *want* to buy books. That is their job. You just have to give them a reason to buy yours. If you let yourself see the proposal as fiction, it will free you up to write entertainingly and well. It will free you up to focus on what's important: giving them a reason to buy your book.

When acquisition editors read a well-written proposal, they get a sense of how that writer writes. This will affect them just as much as the topic of the book itself, perhaps more. It makes them want to buy the book for you have done one thing that most proposals never do. You have entertained the acquisition editor. That, in and of itself, will endear you to that editor. They will want to buy what you have proposed.

Like most forms of short fiction, the proposal should hook the reader as completely and as quickly as possible so they'll keep reading to the end. See it as a story form and begin to develop your skill with it.

THINGS YOU REALLY DO NEED TO DO FIRST

I shouldn't need to say this but regrettably I do. **Do some research on the publishers you intend to send proposals to.** Acquisition editors receive a lot (*as in: A HUGE NUMBER*) of proposals that have nothing to do with the kind of books their house publishes. This irritates them. (And you don't ever, ever want to irritate the acquisition editor.) If it is a gardening publisher, don't send them something that is outside that category. You can often push the edge a bit, just not very much. (You might be able to send a gardening publisher something on how wild plants and garden plants interact in ecosystems, for example, but you generally can tell from the publisher's list if you can actually get away with it.) A publisher that publishes books on politics does not respond well to books about who built the ancient pyramids. So . . . after you have done your Amazon.com research and come up with all the books that have some bearing on the one you are going to write, pay attention to who published them. Make a list of those publishers, then, go to each of their websites (if they don't have one, you probably should not be publishing with them—especially if this is your first or a very early book). Look carefully at the kinds of books they publish and make sure that yours is within their range. Also—read their submission requirements and, as closely as you can, adhere to what they want to see in one. Also—find out the name of their submissions editor (this may or may not be the same person as the acquisition editor. At a small press, it usually is). It's much better to send your proposal to a specific name than merely to the press itself.

This initial research will save you and those editors and publishers a lot of time and trouble. It will show, as well, that you are professional in your approach and that you actually have done the initial research that all writers should do before they send in a proposal. And . . . if you want the proposal back, send a stamped, self-addressed envelope for their use. I often don't want the proposal back and in those cases I invite editors to throw it away ("If my proposal isn't what you are looking for, just throw it away—and thanks, in advance, for taking the time to read it.") However, *always* include a letter-size SASE for them to send either a rejection or acceptance letter to you even if you don't include a 9 x 12 envelope for the return of the proposal.

DEVELOPING THE PROPOSAL

Primarily, proposals should accomplish the following things: 1) Very loosely identify the focus of the book; 2) Excite the publisher enough to want to offer you a contract; 3) Offer a platform for your credentials; 4) Showcase your writing skills.

They should contain the following sections:

1. Cover letter
2. Proposal cover page
3. Overview of the book
4. About the Author
5. Style
6. Format
7. Competing Works
8. Markets
9. Time Frame
10. Table of Contents
11. Content of Chapters
12. Sample Material from the Book

Everything in the proposal except the cover letter should be double-spaced type. This is necessary for both manuscripts and proposals as it allows the editors to make notations in the script, between the lines of type. After awhile, they just get used to reading double-spaced writing—single-spaced type looks funny to them. Like most people, they dislike change.

The Cover Letter

Acquisition editors receive thousands of proposals a year. They don't have time to read them in depth—unless something catches their attention. So, you have to hook them and hook them quickly.

The cover letter is a form of politeness that feels necessary to me and most writers, though many acquisition editors don't care about them. In consequence, they tend to skim cover letters very quickly. A good cover letter is easy to read, almost as a gestalt. It doesn't waste the editor's time. It is short and to the point and it gives the editor just enough of a taste of the book and your credentials to take you seriously. And . . . to make them curious.

The cover letter for the proposal should be short, one paragraph, or, at most, two. It should be succinct and have a hook, something like this perhaps . . . (opposite top)

Or (opposite bottom)

Hi,

I am enclosing a proposal for my book *Soil and Soul: The Craft and Art of the Adobe House.* I believe it will fit in well with your books on sustainable home building and I think you'll like it. (If you don't I have enclosed an SASE for your use.)

I am the author of 12 books of nonfiction and one of poetry (11 of them still in print) which have been nominated for 11 awards and won 8. My books have been translated into 12 languages including Russian, Korean, and Chinese. I travel and teach extensively each year throughout North America and the UK and I think I could give the book a good deal of public exposure.

If you have any questions, please don't hesitate to call.

All the best,

Stephen Buhner

Hi,

I am enclosing a proposal for my book *Soil and Soul: The Craft and Art of the Adobe House* for you to look over. I believe it will fit in well with your books on sustainable home building and I believe you will like it. (If you don't I have enclosed an SASE for your use.)

While this is my first book I have been a columnist for the regional *New Voices Magazine* for the past 8 years and have worked extensively for the past 15 years with the health of desert river ecosystems and the history and building of sustainable habitation in the Southwest. This book is an outgrowth of those experiences.

If you have any questions, please don't hesitate to call.

All the best,

Maria Epstein

Proposal Cover Page

This is just a form of title page:

> **SOIL AND SOUL**
>
> **The Craft and Art of the Adobe House**
>
> By Stephen Harrod Buhner
>
> A Book Proposal
>
> Copyright 2010 Stephen Harrod Buhner
>
> All Rights Reserved

Overview of the Book

This is the most important part of the proposal. It's best if one page in length, two at most. If this is your first book it should be one—very succinct—page. The overview should be written somewhat like a short story; it should pack a punch, be entertaining, and give a sense of the content and feel of the book.

On the opposite page is the overview I submitted for the book you are reading now (then titled *Inhabiting the Word*).

You can tell from reading this that while it does bear some relation to the finished book, there are a great many differences. There is a lot more in the finished book, things I did not know were going to be in there, than there are in this overview. The overview was written several years before the book was finished and I notice my writing style has changed considerably as well.

OVERVIEW

The Importance of *Inhabiting the Word*

Vaclav Havel, the playwright and former president of the Czech Republic, was imprisoned for many years. All of his mail—including the letters he wrote—was read and censored. He said it was good training for a writer. Because he could say nothing, he was forced to learn to say everything in nothing. ("The tragedy of America," he later noted, "is that being able to say everything, all too often you end up saying nothing.")

The art of saying everything in nothing is essential for inhabiting the word. It forces the writer to drop down below the surface of the word, to learn to ensoul it, and imbue it with *meaning*. This involves a transition from merely using technique (the dry, dusty bones of the dead and dissected writings that passes for instruction in most schools) to the communication of meaning through the luminous power of still-living language. The hidden power within language is then shaped into a kind of food that feeds not only the mind but the soul of the readers. This ensouled meaning flows into their deepest selves and powerfully affects their perceptions, of themselves and their world.

This is the art of nonfiction. It is an art that anyone can learn who wishes to do so, for all of us know the touch of *meaning* upon us when we encounter it. All of us can learn to find deeper meanings within ourselves and develop skills to shape them into a living language that touches others. All of us can learn how to inhabit the word. First and foremost, it is this process that this book explores. Only after this most essential aspect of writing is examined does the book move on to the business of writing nonfiction and how to make a living at it.

About the Author

This section should be one page, similar to the overview. It should pack a punch and capture the editor's attention. It should also include more material the editor can skip at this point but can read later if the proposal is of interest. That lengthy, extra material is useful for the decision making that occurs during triage: the meeting between the managing editor, the publisher, and the head of marketing.

Here is what my one-page blurb looked like for the proposal for this book:

> Stephen Harrod Buhner is an Earth poet and the award-winning author of twelve works of nonfiction and one book of poetry. Reviewers have recognized the skill of his writing in many publications, and his works have won, and been nominated for, numerous awards.
>
> His work has appeared or been profiled in publications throughout North America and Europe including *Common Boundary, Apotheosis, Shaman's Drum, The New York Times,* CNN, and *Good Morning America.* Stephen lectures throughout the United States and the UK (from March through October) on herbal medicine, the sacredness of plants, the intelligence of Nature, the states of mind necessary for successful habitation of Earth, and the art of nonfiction. He is a tireless advocate for the reincorporation of the exploratory artist, independent scholar, amateur naturalist, and citizen scientist in American society—especially as a counterweight to the influence of corporate science and technology. Part of this advocacy entails teaching about the power of language to shape behavior and culture. This interest in language has found an outlet in his unique insights on the nature of creative nonfiction and the teaching of writing.
>
> His most recent works are *Healing Lyme: Natural Healing of Lyme Borreliosis and Its Coinfections* and *The Taste of Wild Water: Poems and Stories Found While Walking in Woods.* He lives in Silver City, NM.

This section was followed by a list of awards won, a listing of all my published books (including sales figures), memberships (Mensa, PEN, Authors Guild, and so on), magazines for which I have written or in which I have been profiled, places where I have been invited to teach, comments by contemporaries, some short excerpts from reviews of my writing (not copies of reviews).

This material *does not* look, and should not look, like the normal CV a person might use, which is generally boring and overly serious. It is designed to give me credibility with the publisher and head of marketing so they realize I'm serious about my work, have been at it a long time, and really can produce a book that is salable and competent. To do this well, you have to learn how to step outside of yourself and see yourself as someone else (who likes you) might. It's very important that you do not write it as if you were sending it to some inflexible parent figure whom you are trying to impress. You are simply stating who and what you are and what you do.

I alter what I say and how I say it depending on the publisher I'm approaching and the topic of the book being proposed. If I were proposing a book on adobe houses, I would stress the years I have spent creating ensouled habitation, working with wood, and my understanding of remodeling techniques and design. If I were proposing a book on the traditional uses of herbs among the indigenous cultures of southwestern New Mexico, I would stress my work with herbal medicine, plant ecology, and indigenous cultures.

Basically, you want to make yourself sound like the best thing to come along since the invention of sliced bread. At the same time, you have to be detached from your biographical description, as if you were writing about someone else. This means that your personal-worth issues, which can masquerade as a self-deprecating "I'm-not-worthy" description or as an arrogant "I'm-better-than-all-living-beings" description, have to be uninvolved in this particular piece of writing. This is often hard because most of us have been taught so thoroughly that we must not talk about ourselves in a positive light (too self-aggrandizing) that we have no tools for doing so. Many people simply don't know how to talk about themselves well. If you find this difficult, you might ask a good friend, one who really cares about you, to do this for you. If, once you have read their description of you, you begin feeling really uncomfortable and begin raising all kinds of objections your self-worth issues are probably being activated. These will stand in your way to being a successful writer. So, let your friend write this for you and damn the consequences.

About the Author, Part Two: Platforms

The term *platform* means two things to a publisher: your experience and history in the area the book is about and what kind of public exposure you have or might have. While you can get published if you have no platform, publishers definitely do like it if you have one. I don't often use the term *platform,* it's a publisher's or agent's term and I don't especially like it. But they use it and so it makes sense to understand what they mean by it. Because this is often a relatively undeveloped area for young writers, I suggest you consciously focus on developing a platform as it will help you immensely.

Part of the usefulness of the love/hate list (featured in the first exercise in this book) is that it will point up areas that are deeply meaningful to you. Upon reflection you might just notice that a lot of your life activities have already been occurring in those areas. Rather than saying that you worked as a remodeling carpenter, you can then say you worked with human habitat restoration. That makes a huge difference in what is heard. Rather than saying you worked in a health clinic, you can say you were deeply involved in community health activism for five years, as clinician, educator, and advocate. It makes a difference.

I also suggest that if you are serious about being a writer you begin developing writing credits any way you can. This kind of public writing exposure is very much a part of "platform." Many small or local magazines welcome contributions they do not have to pay for. As a caveat: magazine writing, of any sort, is some of the most irritating writing you will do. The editors, unless you are writing for something like *The New Yorker,* will usually overedit your material—they generally aren't very good at editing so you will be forced to work harder on an article than you do on most of your books. The result will not be better material. Nevertheless, early in the game it is important to get more writing experience. The pieces you get published will give you something to put on your résumé—it does help.

I found that regularly writing on deadline for small magazines was very useful. I think it some of the best training that exists for a writer. You don't have time to overthink what you are writing or to tinker with it forever; you have to produce something by a certain time. You are forced to learn how to work with speed and still do good work. And, you will get a lot of experience in how editors screw up good copy. As Robert Heinlein once put it, "They don't like the smell unless they can pee in it and stir it around with a pencil." It takes awhile to get over the outrage from this kind of nitrogen redistribution. But all writers do have to get over it and this starts the process with material that is not so lasting as a book.

It's also useful if you have some ideas of how you can promote the book. That is, ideas of where you can speak to promote the book, workshops you can give, lectures you can offer. This is often seen as an extension of platform. It is very rare that a book will just take off on its own (though some of them do, especially if they are good, meet a need, and find a good publisher). So, some sort of plan for taking it out into the world through the normal, everyday fabric of your life will help sell the idea to the publisher. By this, I don't mean doing bookstore signings. A few bookstores, such as East/West in Seattle, Washington, *can* be good venues. They often arrange for authors to conduct weekend workshops that are tied in with a Friday afternoon (or mid-week) booksigning. But, most bookstore signings are badly attended, badly conducted, and will not get you the kind of exposure you need to develop sales or your career. (Bookstore *talks* on the other hand can sometimes be very helpful.)

Finding out which bookstores are useful and which ones are not is fraught with peril. Sitting alone at a bookstore table, with piles of your books and one attendee who is in the audience simply due to tired feet, is one of the most miserable experiences on the planet. Editors often don't care so much what kind of platform you have; they're more interested in how it is presented. If you are a housewife with little work experience and less platform, this can still work well for you. If you decide to do a book on restoring adobe homes, the fact that you knew nothing and spent a year immersing yourself in learning how to do it can be a huge point in your favor. It makes the book a combination how-to, memoir, and journey of personal growth. It shows just how a regular person with no experience can do this kind of remodeling and it appeals to a very specific market, one that buys a great many books.

You have to learn how to put what and who you are into terms that make it seem perfect that it is you, and no one else, who is writing the book. *Anything* can be used effectively for this purpose.

An Aside on Websites

I think having a website is a good idea; it contributes significantly to the existence and development of your platform. Publishers now commonly look to see if a potential author has a website—it's easy for them to look yours over if they are thinking about publishing you. You can develop a decently interesting website for a reasonable amount of money and then improve it later if you wish.

Mine (gaianstudies.org) emerged because I was tired of people asking me for an in-depth bio and photograph—usually publishers or event coordinators. It saved me a lot of time—I just sent them to the website and told them to take what they wanted. The site also gave my readers a way to find me and to communicate if they wished, something I have found to be increasingly important as the years go by. I receive about three hundred e-mails a month now (again, in 2010) and though it takes a lot of time to respond to them, I like the contact I have with the community of people who read my work. These e-mails keep me connected to the people who are reading me and give me concrete information about which of my books and what parts of my books people are most moved by. It helps me stay on top of who I am to the people who buy them. My work fulfills a need and it makes sense to be attentive to that need over the course of my career as it develops, matures, and changes—as the times, and all of us, change.

And besides, without the fans, those of us who write (or entertain in any form) would have to go back to work for a living. So, it makes sense to be available to them and to treat them with as much kindness and respect as a person who sits in a little room by himself all day long can.

These kinds of websites are an integral part of a platform for a writer and, I think, will only develop in importance over time.

Style

That is, what kind of voice does your book have: formal, informal, scholarly, technical, or what? I tend to like a conversational, informal style of writing that goes deep into the material. I say this in every proposal and then develop why that will be a good thing for the book I am proposing.

Format

Basically, length and any additional information that seems necessary, such as, the presence of illustrations. For this book I said:

> The book is approximately 95,000 words in length. It will contain numerous sidebars and epigrammatical material. No illustrations are planned at this time.

(As it turned out, for this book sidebars were unnecessary and the book ran about 165,000 words including endnotes and bibliography. Remember . . . a proposal is fiction.)

Competing Works

This is where Amazon.com is indispensable. You can pull up every book that is available (in print or out) that pertains to the material you are working with. I list a number of these, usually around ten or twelve, then discuss why they are not as good as mine will be, what their limits are, and then just why mine is better or unique.

If I am intent on the proposal being accepted someplace, no matter what, I will usually buy these books up front and use them in my proposal development (and later in my writing of the book as resources and irritants). If I have three or four proposals in development and any will do, I will not usually buy the books but will use the Amazon site to develop my content and commentary on them.

The publisher generally likes to see that there are some books published that touch on your topic. Publishers feel that if there are books out there then there is a market for those kinds of books. If there is nothing out there, oddly enough, publishers don't see this as an opportunity. It is rather a confirmation that no one cares about books on that topic, otherwise someone would have already published something on it. Stupid reasoning but unfortunately common.

If there are no books similar to yours in print find some that are somewhat related so you can spin yours as a development of an existing market.

If they know there is a market and that all the books out there are poor, they will get more excited about yours. Remember, publishers *want* to buy new books. You just have to give them a reason to do so. They *know* that this kind of information has little to do with what your book will actually do in the marketplace but they don't pay attention to that knowledge. (It's a living-in-denial sort of thing.) They need a rational excuse to buy your book and if you give it to them, while entertaining them, and showing that you are competent (at least in the proposal), your chances of acceptance are much greater.

The Market

Who is going to buy this book and why? This part of the proposal is entirely fiction but the editor, publisher, and head of marketing always want to see this in the proposal. Some sort of weird author test, I guess.

The truth is that books find their own legs . . . or not. Sometimes the marketing department can, because of established markets, get the book into places no author would be able to (National Forest gift shops, for instance) but usually, books find their own markets and develop their own selling momentum. If they can.

So, make something up and make it sound plausible. For a book on restoring adobe houses I would play up sustainable housing groups, SW home enthusiasts (a huge market, especially if the book contains photos), do-it-yourself homeowners, and solar home groups. Given that I would be developing natural plasters made partially with plants, I would also look at herbalist groups, native plant societies, and those interested in indigenous peoples' foods and building approaches.

Get excited about it and make it sound plausible. It is all fantasy; remember that and have fun making it up.

Time Frame

The book will be finished in twelve months. This is the usual time frame, sometimes a book will take longer, sometimes shorter but most publishers want the book within twelve months of signing the contract. This one, differently, was a twenty-four-month contract.

Authors are notoriously late with manuscripts. If you are a first-time author . . . don't be late with the book. Even if you have to crawl on hands and knees over a field of broken glass.

If you really want to change the world: keep all your agreements and only make agreements you are willing to keep. This is perhaps the easiest thing any human being can do to reduce conflict in the world and change it for the better and the one thing that almost no one will do.

While many publishers may not have integrity, there is no reason for you not to.

Table of Contents

For a book on adobe houses I would use the one we explored in chapter 17 on the first draft of the manuscript. Remember, the table of contents is all fantasy as well. Have fun with it.

Chapter Content

This is just an expanded table of contents. Take each chapter and make up a short paragraph about it that sounds plausible, exciting, and fun. Crib unashamedly from published sources.

Sample Material from the Book

I generally write up something moderately short, well written, and potent (if I write up anything at all). While I try to get the facts right in a general sense (nothing is worse than being caught out by the acquisition editor) I don't flog myself with it. What I want them to have is a sense of the interestingness of the material, my writing style, and how the material might be worked.

This sample material is, in reality, just a short story or two about an apparently nonfictional subject. No one will ever see it (besides three or four people at the publishing house). It is not intended for publication. I plagiarize, use material without attribution, gloss over sections that would demand my doing a lot of research, and make stuff up. I do focus as much as I can on the flow and feeling of the work; I want them to have a sense of how I will work the material, what it will feel like to read it. This material is just part of convincing the publisher to buy the proposal; it has no other function. It is not real, remember that. It is only a story.

THE REALITIES OF THE PROPOSAL

Most writers don't have the time to spend months or years on a proposal. Many proposals do not sell and most writers don't make enough money to waste large amounts of their time on proposals that do not sell. Two weeks to a month are enough for any proposal. As you write the proposal, each section should flow into the next. Each should be enjoyable to read. Each should give the publisher a reason to buy your idea. (No part of it, however, will be as polished and developed as the final material will be; this is practice writing, due to be thrown away.)

Remember, no one will ever see this thing except, perhaps, four people at the publishing house. After they buy the book, they most probably won't look at it again—that is, unless your book on adobe house remodeling turns into a book on soapmaking in which case they will use it to prove that you did not fulfill the terms of contract.

If the final book looks nothing like the proposal, as long as it does in fact cover adobe home remodeling, they won't care.

OTHER FORMS OF THE PROPOSAL

There are a couple of other forms a proposal can take and I often use them as well.

The Proposal Letter

Sometimes this is called an inquiry letter and some publishers prefer it as it cuts down on bulky proposal submissions. Simply, this is a letter, one to two pages, that outlines a book you would like to write. The letter should include one paragraph each about the book, about you, about the market for it, about how it fits in with that publisher and an SASE. It should be as compelling as possible. I have sold a couple of books this way. Often, the acquisition editor will ask for a brief proposal if he likes the inquiry letter so that the buy committee can have something to look over, but, unless you screw that up, the book has already been accepted by the acquisition editor.

The Brief Proposal

Usually this is a truncated form of the full proposal and does not include sample chapters from the book. I will sometimes write up a full proposal leaving off the sample chapters and send it to publishers. If they then request more material, I can write something up in a week or so and send it back to them. This saves me wasting my time writing sample chapters. The other material in the proposal is much easier to develop than the sample chapters. I think this is the most time-efficient proposal of all. I can usually develop this kind of proposal in a week, two at most.

The Completed Manuscript Proposal

Some publishers, if you are a first-time author, want to see the completed manuscript before they will decide on publishing you. This occurred for me and is not all that unusual with a small press. I recommend for most first-time writers that you put together a proposal and begin sending it out and *at the same time* you begin writing the book as well. Every writer needs to complete a book, just to show they can, to themselves if no one else. Writing the whole thing will do three things: 1) Get some of the million words of bullshit that are in every writer out; 2) Give you the experience of finishing a book; and 3) Give you a completed work to use as your proposal.

Then, if you still have not sold it, start another one and begin sending that one out in proposal form as you are working on it. Remember: *There are only a finite number of "no's" in the world.* (And also remember, *Dune,* perhaps the best-selling science fiction novel of all time, was rejected twenty-six times before Chilton, a publisher of car repair manuals, took it on. "I might be making the mistake of my life," one editor wrote in turning it down. [Too complex and involved he thought. Readers just won't buy that kind of thing.] *Yep. You did.*)

SUBMITTING PROPOSALS

Once you have a proposal completed you have a choice, to send it to one publisher or to many. If I have a strong feeling or preference I will usually send it to one publisher at first, saying in the cover letter that this is an exclusive submission because I really want to publish with them. This is an effective approach for a writer with an established career. If this is your first or second book I would recommend sending your proposal to many publishers at once, generally five to ten. Then, every time a rejection comes back, send out a fresh proposal so that you always have the same number circulating.

You have made a decision to be a writer and you must never cease putting pressure on the wall. As I wrote earlier in this book:

> *If you keep the pressure up long enough, eventually the wall will begin to crack. Eventually, always, an opening, will appear. However, you cannot control where or when it occurs. As William Stafford commented, "Dawn comes, and it comes for all, but not on demand."*

So, you keep sending out proposals, writing more, insisting that a crack appear, raging against the lack of response, and writing and sending out still more proposals. Eventually, the world will acquiesce to your insistence. *Always.*

APPENDIX C

Further Reading, Resources, and Recommendations

Most books on writing are dreadful, excruciating demonstrations of the reality that some very good writers can't write about writing and some very poor writers have too inflated a sense of their own understanding of the craft. For the very beginning writer I believe Brenda Ueland's book *If You Want to Write* to be the best followed by Dorothea Brande's *Becoming a Writer*. William Stafford's books are probably the next I would recommend. Stafford was a conscientious objector in World War II, a difficult time to be one, and he carried his belief in nonviolence into his writing and teaching. He felt it wrong to force, either poem or student, into any particular position. He let both of them find their own form. (He was rarely asked back a second time to speak at writing conferences.) He is very easy on the sensitive spirit, perhaps one of the most supportive and intelligent writers on writing I have read.

John Gardner and Robert Bly are more demanding. They are very insistent on elegance and commitment in the craft. Some people don't like their books on writing because they feel judged by an inflexible gaze as they read them.

John Gardner was the first writer who wrote about writing in a way that made sense to me. He opened my eyes to what the craft entailed and what it could become. I had read a lot of books on writing and could not figure out why none of them seemed to make sense. It took me a long time to discover it was because the books were senseless.

Gardner could read twenty-seven ancient and medieval languages by the time he earned his Ph.D. at the age of twenty-five. (Yeah, he really was a genius.) This scholarly bent shaped his opinions on writing as did his work as a professor, sometimes in directions I don't agree with. Nevertheless, anyone who really wants to learn the craft should read him. He and Robert Bly were nearly alone in demanding a return to moral writing and an abandonment of the statistical mentality in the craft. Gardner's condemnation of sloth and lack of morality in the craft, and his naming of names, caused him a lot of problems with the literati. (Gore Vidal once called him the "late apostle to the lowbrows." Oh, my.) Unfortunately, Gardner died in a motorcycle crash in 1982 when he was 49 and all of us lowbrows are the poorer for it.

Robert Bly is, and always has been, a working writer. He did not make his money as a college professor, commenting that he had seen too many of his friends destroyed as writers by doing so. He made his money by public speaking and writing—and he wrote a lot. Two months out of the year, he went on the road doing readings, lectures, and workshops—something that influenced me in my own decisions in that direction. He did not feed at the public trough but let the market decide whether he was offering something useful. His survival depended, unlike most literary writers, on his readers paying him for his work. There is, in consequence, something very grounded and real about his work that many other writers on writing are missing. Bly, too, named names in his condemnation of the lack of soul in American literature and had some of the same troubles that Gardner experienced.

After these writers, I think I have gotten the most from reading the letters of writers to other writers, their editors, and their publishers (Steinbeck and Chandler, for example), and from commentaries by writers about their work, often included as introductions to collections of their short stories (e.g., Roger Zelazny and Alfred Bester). I think Raymond Chandler's essays, especially "The Simple Art of Murder," are essential reading.

I think that both the *New York Review of Books* and the *London Review of Books* are excellent for writers to read. The *New York Review* has gotten better since Bly lambasted them in the 1960s and both journals, while other media cowered, have been some of the few to really do real reporting on the state of the world at the beginning of the millennium. Generally, the writing is topnotch and reading such writing regularly helps with the craft immensely. The *New York Review* tends to be a little too NewYorky at times; the *London Review* occasionally allows ridiculous material into print, usually a review by a writer who doesn't like the writer she is writing about, often for some politically correct reason rather than legitimate critical reasons. (This is not uncommon. See if you can find, anywhere in those publications, a straight, unembarrassed review of Tolkien's *Lord of the Rings,* Kipling's *Kim,* or anything by Buckminster Fuller.) Still, they are both publications of integrity and are generally well written. (I think *Harper's* good as well.)

If you are interested in the conflict between reductionist rationalisms and the imaginal world, which I touch on repeatedly in this book, the best books I have so far read about it are John Ralston Saul's *Voltaire's Bastards: The Dictatorship of Reason in the West* (especially the first third of the book), Annie Le Brun's *The Reality Overload: The Modern World's Assault on the Imaginal Realm,* and Mary Midgley's *The Myths We Live By.* They are hand grenades disguised as books. I also touch on many of these issues in my own *The Lost Language of Plants* (Chelsea Green, 2002).

SUGGESTED BOOKS ON WRITING

Robert Bly, *American Poetry: Wilderness and Domesticity* (New York: Harper and Row, 1990).

———, Introduction to *The Darkness Around Us Is Deep: Selected Poems of William Stafford* (New York: HarperPerennial, 1993).

Dorothea Brande, *Becoming a Writer* (New York: Harcourt, Brace, 1934).

Raymond Chandler, *Later Novels and Other Writings* (New York: The Library of America, 1995). Especially see "The Simple Art of Murder."

John Dunning, Introduction to *The Holland Suggestions,* paperback ed. (New York: Pocket Books, reprint ed. 1997). His first book, plainly, but the introduction is worth its weight in gold.

Robert Faggen, *The Notebooks of Robert Frost* (Cambridge, Mass.: Harvard University Press, 2006).

John Gardner, *The Art of Fiction* (New York: Vintage, 1991).

———, *On Becoming a Novelist* (New York: W. W. Norton, 1999).

———, *On Moral Fiction* (New York: Basic Books, 1978).

William Gass, *Habitations of the Word* (Ithaca, New York: Cornell University Press, 1985). Perhaps the book of his that I like most, see especially chapters 4, 8, 11.

———, *Reading Rilke: Reflections on the Problems on Translation* (New York: Alfred A. Knopf, 1999). Especially the chapter entitled "Lifeleading."

Anne Lamott, *Bird by Bird* (New York: Pantheon, 1994).

Annie Le Brun, *The Reality Overload: The Modern World's Assault on the Imaginal Realm* (Rochester, Vt.: Inner Traditions, 2008).

Rainer Maria Rilke, *Letters to a Young Poet* (New York: Dover, 2002).

John Ralston Saul, *Voltaire's Bastards: The Dictatorship of Reason in the West* (New York: The Free Press, 1992).

David Shields, *Reality Hunger: A Manifesto* (New York: Alfred A. Knopf, 2010).

William Stafford, *Crossing Unmarked Snow: Further Views on the Writer's Vocation* (Ann Arbor: University of Michigan Press, 1998).

———, *Writing the Australian Crawl: Views on the Writer's Vocation* (Ann Arbor: University of Michigan Press, 1978).

———, *You Must Revise Your Life* (Ann Arbor: University of Michigan Press, 1986).

Brenda Ueland, *If You Want to Write: A Book About Art, Independence, and Spirit,* 2nd ed. (St. Paul, Minn.: Graywolf Press, 1987).

WRITERS' ASSOCIATIONS

There are a number of good writers' organizations in the United States. Here are a few of them . . .

The Authors Guild

Writers are eligible for membership in the Authors Guild if they have published three articles or stories in nationally circulated magazines in the past eighteen months, or, if they have published a book with a non-vanity press, or, if they have a book contract with a nonvanity publisher.

The guild offers a contract-review service, for free. If you are a new writer and do receive a book contract, you can join (2010 dues: $90) and they will review the contract for you and offer suggestions for revision. I am not particularly fond of that service as they tend to be, for first-time writers, a great deal too stringent regarding terms and conditions. (It's a political thing, writers vs. publishers.) They are perfect, however, for spotting contracts by disreputable presses that possess, shall we say, sleazy clauses that are unethical and designed to take advantage of first-time authors with little experience. For this reason alone, you should join and submit your early contracts to them. I personally know several authors who were royally screwed by their publishers and would not have been had they used the Guild.

The staff is, generally, very helpful with and responsive to inquiries and I have enjoyed the contact I have had with them. The Guild attorneys tend to be like attorneys everywhere; you can't get a definitive answer on anything, even the weather raining on them as they speak. The Guild is vague on fair use (which I hate), publishes a regular journal that I read cover to cover (and am continually irritated by), and works diligently to protect the rights of writers (which I am very appreciative of). The Guild tends to sue large corporations on the behalf of their members regularly (which I enjoy), maintains a great censorship watch (which I appreciate immensely), and are, generally, sensible about the problems facing writers. They do tend to be a bit too NewYorky for me; writers west of the Mississippi are, shall we say, somewhat less important in the hierarchy of value. Nevertheless, I love being a member and perhaps you will, too.

Here is their contact information:

The Authors Guild
31 East 28th Street
New York, NY 10016
212-563-5904
www.authorsguild.org

PEN

There are two chapters of PEN in the United States, the eastern branch and the western. Their entry requirements for membership are listed below. I belong to the western branch, PEN USA, and enjoy it very much. PEN has fought to protect writers for years, especially those imprisoned by totalitarian regimes because of their work; I admire them immensely. This alone made me very proud to have been invited to join (any writer can apply, you don't have to wait to be invited).

Eastern PEN (which is centered in New York City) tends to be a bit snooty; they seem to think that western PEN (which is centered in Los Angeles) lets in the rabble. (I looked deeply in the mirror this morning. I wonder . . . could they be right?)

Eastern PEN (www.pen.org)
Cost of eastern PEN membership is $100 per year.
Membership requirements (verbatim from their website):

> The standard qualification to become a Member of PEN is publication of two or more books of a literary character or one book of exceptional distinction (i.e., winning a major national prize). Also eligible for membership: editors who have demonstrated commitment to excellence in their profession (usually construed as five year's service in book editing); translators who have published at least two book-length literary translations; playwrights who have had two productions of their work mounted in professional theaters of 250 seats of more; and literary essayists whose publications are extensive even if they have not yet been issued in a book.

Western PEN (www.penusa.org)
Membership requirements (verbatim from their website):

> Full membership in PEN USA is open to professional writers, journalists, editors and translators who have a professionally published body of work.
>
> Anyone interested in becoming a Full member must submit an application in addition to a resume of published work and the Full membership fee of $79. The membership committee meets to determine whether the writer is eligible for Full membership. Applications are accepted throughout the year.

Here is their physical address and contact information:

PEN Center USA
P. O. Box 6037
Beverly Hills, CA 90212
(323) 424-4939

There are other writers organizations but these are the ones I know most intimately and most admire.

A FINAL THANKS

To Jon Graham. For believing and for all the dialog that occurred during the writing of this book; it's a lot better for it. And thanks are due, as well, for that French protestor quote (which is from a photograph he took of the young woman wearing the sign): *The first act of disobedience is contemplation.* If only the outraged everywhere understood it.

FULL DISCLOSURE

I had help with this book. During the writing the following music was instrumental. Michael McGlone's *To Be Down,* especially track 5; Robert McEntee's *The Coin of the Realm,* especially track 7; Eliza Gilkyson's *Paradise Hotel,* especially tracks 6–10; Ellen McIlwaine's *Spontaneous Combustion,* especially tracks 1 and 8; and five albums that approach as closely as any can to perfection: Greg Brown's *Covenant,* Eliza Gilkyson's *Lost and Found,* Christine Kane's *Rain and Mud and Wild and Green,* South by Southwest's *Live on Radio,* and Mike Williams' *The Radio Show.* Thanks to each of them for the golden threads.

If you pay attention to the music inside this book you will see some of those performers inside it, as Bly once said . . .

> *Anyone who knows the work of Guillen, Salinas or Alberti will also see Juan Ramon Jimenez in their poems, seated quietly on the sandy bottom, clearly visible through the sunlit water, like a magic water creature.*[1]

All these albums, except *The Radio Show,* are available through cdbaby.com (a great place to buy music by the way). All the albums are produced by small, i.e., independent, record companies.

If you've never heard Ellen McIlwaine before, she is the best female lead guitar player I know of. If you really want to astonish yourself, listen to some of the material (such as "Losing You") on her first album.

Mike Williams has done four very good albums, three of them in the early '70s on his label B. F. Deal Records. His albums can often be found on eBay—they are only available as LPs; they are worth finding. (C'mon Mike, rerelease them.)

IN MEMORIAM

James Krenov died September 9, 2009, during the last weeks of my finishing this book. He had gone blind in 2002 and spent his last years making wooden woodworking planes by feel alone. His daughter said, as *The New York Times* reported, that when he died he was holding a piece of sandalwood he had shaped and smoothed. He loved the smell, she said, and so he always kept a box of shavings of both it and Lebanon cedar beneath his bed. He loved to savor their fragrance.

Notes

BEFORE BUYING THIS BOOK

1. David Simpson, in "At the Opium Factory," *London Review of Books* 31, no. 20 (October 22, 2009): 23–4, comments on this necessity when he says:

   For some time the Anglophone publishing industry has been keen on fiction of the global south, at least when it takes the form of magical realism, where the paranormal is staged as the ordinary and the imagination is freed from the familiar laws of gravity. Here, in the (to us) remote corners of the undeveloped or developing world, the colours, smells and flavours are more intense, life is more meaningful and death less absolute than in the grey industrial or post-industrial landscapes of the north, the cradle of modernity and modern empires. . . . Franco Moretti has speculated that this novel (Amitav Ghosh's *Sea of Poppies*) and others speak to the world system from the periphery in ways that would be impossible if they were set in Europe or North America: they hold out the possibility of re-enchantment in our disenchanted world.

   Which is why they sell so well in the industrialized north; they meet an essential need not addressed by the dead-end New York literary forms.
2. Raul Hilberg, *Sources of Holocaust Research* (Chicago, Ill.: Ivan Dee, 2001), 204.
3. Ibid., 9.
4. Leah Price, "The Tangible Page," *London Review of Books* 24, no. 21, (October 31, 2002): 38.

CHAPTER THREE. ON THE ART OF NONFICTION

1. Michael Dirda, "Wake Up and Dream," *New York Review of Books* LVII, no. 1 (January 14, 2010): 49.
2. Maya Jaggi, "You Can't Help Being what You Write: An Interview with Tom Stoppard," *Guardian,* 6 September 2008, a quotation from *The Real Inspector Hound,* published by Avalon.
3. James Krenov, *The Fine Art of Cabinetmaking* (New York: Van Nostrand Reinhold, 1977), 47.
4. Cited in: Rachel Donadio, "You're an Author? Me Too!" *New York Times,* 27 April, 2009; also: Terry Nathan, "The Rewards of Reaching Out," in *The Independent,* Manhattan Beach, Calif.: Independent Book Publishers Association (November 2008), 7.
5. Raymond Chandler, "The Simple Art of Murder," in *Later Novels and Other Writings* (New York: The Library of America), 986–87.
6. James Hillman, *The Soul's Code* (New York: Random House, 1996), 3–4.
7. Raymond Chandler, "The Simple Art of Murder," 988.

CHAPTER FOUR. YOU MUST BEGIN WITH SOMETHING DEEPER IN THE SELF

1. Robert Bly, *American Poetry: Wildness and Domesticity* (New York: Harper and Row, 1990), 37.
2. Carl Hammerschlag and Howard Silverman, *Healing Ceremonies* (New York: Perigee, 1997), 44.
3. Robert Bly, *The Winged Life* (San Francisco: Sierra Club Books, 1986), 3–5. Note: I cheated a bit on this one and condensed the material to read as one unified piece. Here's how it would look without that condensation:

   When we fight for the soul and its life, we receive as reward not fame, not wages, not friends but what is already in the soul, a freshness that no one can destroy . . . [This] soul truth, which young people . . . pick up from somewhere . . . sustains them. The soul truth assures the young man or woman that if not rich, he or she is still in touch with truth; that his inheritance comes not from his immediate parents but from his equals thousands of generations ago; that the door to the soul is unlocked; that he does not need to please the doorkeeper, but that the door in front of him is his, intended for him, and the doorkeeper obeys when spoken to.

4. Richard Keeling, *Cry for Luck* (Berkeley: University of California Press, 1992), 41, 47.
5. Henry Beston, *Herbs and the Earth* (New York: David Godine, 1990), 4–5.

CHAPTER FIVE. "THE ROAD OF FEELING"

1. Christopher Benfey, "The Storm Over Robert Frost," *New York Review of Books* LV, no. 19 (December 4, 2009): 50.

CHAPTER SIX. "IT BURNS THE BLOOD LIKE POWDERED GLASS"

1. There has been a considerable amount written on this that is fairly crucial to read given the state of things. A good place to begin is with any of Chris Hedges articles cited in the bibliography.
2. William Stafford, *A Scripture of Leaves* (Elgin, Ill.: Brethren Press, 1989), 7.
3. William Stafford, *Writing the Australian Crawl* (Ann Arbor: University of Michigan Press, 1978), 118–19.
4. Ibid., 78.
5. Federico García Lorca, *In Search of Duende* (New York: New Dimensions, 1998), 51.
6. William Gass, *Reading Rilke: Reflections on the Problems of Translations* (New York: Knopf, 1999), xvi.
7. John Gardner, *The Art of Fiction* (New York: Vintage, 1991), 42.
8. Stephen Harrod Buhner, *The Taste of Wild Water: Poems and Stories Found While Walking in Woods* (Silver City, N.M.: Raven Press, 2009), 5.

CHAPTER SEVEN. THE SKILL OF DUENDE

1. I read this story of this dolphin child years ago though I have told it many times in workshops and lectures. The original can be read here: Lyall Watson, "The Biology of Being: A Natural History of Consciousness" in David Lorimer, ed., *The Spirit of Science* (New York: Continuum International Publishing Group, 1999).
2. Robert Bly, *Hearing Gary Snyder Read,* Unicorn Broadsheet Series 2, no. 3, 1971.
3. Robert Bly, *Leaping Poetry* (Boston: Beacon Press, 1972), 1.
4. Lorca, *In Search of Duende,* ix–x.
5. Ibid., 53.

6. Antonio Machado, *Twenty Proverbs,* Robert Bly and Don Olsen, trans. (Marshall, Minn.: Ox Head Press, 1981), proverb #6.

CHAPTER EIGHT. FOLLOWING GOLDEN THREADS

1. Robert Bly, ed., *The Darkness Around Us Is Deep: Selected Poems of William Stafford* (New York: HarperPerennial, 1993), 135–36.
2. Ibid., viii.
3. Stafford, *Writing the Australian Crawl,* 39.
4. Bly, *American Poetry,* 101–02.
5. William Gass, *Habitations of the Word* (Ithaca, N.Y.: Cornell University Press, 1985), 222.
6. Stafford, *Writing the Australian Crawl,* 18.
7. Gass, *Habitations of the Word,* 249.
8. Bly, ed., *The Darkness Around Us Is Deep,* viii.
9. Ibid., ix.
10. Basho Quotations, accessed online 7/28/09, yenra.com/quotations/basho.html.
11. Robert Bly, *News of the Universe* (San Francisco: Sierra Club Books, 1980), 126.
12. Ibid., 282.
13. Carol Emery Normandi and Laurelee Roark, *It's Not About Food* (New York: Perigee, 1999), 26.
14. Krenov, *The Fine Art of Cabinetmaking,* 34.
15. Robert Bly, ed., *Selected Poems of Lorca and Jiminez* (Boston: Beacon Press, 1973), 63.

CHAPTER NINE. "A CERTAIN ADJUSTMENT OF CONSCIOUSNESS"

1. John Gardner, *On Becoming a Novelist* (New York: Norton, 1999), 119–22.
2. Quoted in Hillman, *The Soul's Code,* xii.
3. Gardner, *The Art of Fiction,* 30–31.
4. Ibid., 36.
5. Brenda Ueland, *If You Want to Write* (St. Paul, Minn.: Graywolf Press, 1987), 57.
6. Christopher Benfey, "The Storm Over Robert Frost," *New York Review of Books* LV, no. 19 (December 4, 2009): 50.
7. Robert Grudin, *The Grace of Great Things* (New York: Ticknor and Fields, 1990), 6, 45.
8. Ueland, *If You Want to Write,* 148–49.

CHAPTER TEN. "THE SECRET KINESIS OF THINGS"

1. Quoted in Bly, ed., *The Darkness Around Us Is Deep,* vii.
2. Ibid., viii.
3. John Dunning, *The Bookman's Wake* (New York: Scribner, 1995), 58.
4. Gardner, *The Art of Fiction,* 37.
5. Grudin, *The Grace of Great Things,* 5–6.
6. Gary Scharnhorst, ed., *Mark Twain: The Complete Interviews* (Tuscaloosa: University of Alabama Press, 2006), 34–35.
7. Hal Foster comments on this same phenomenon when he says:

   "It was left to the Bourgeioisie of the 20th century to incorporate nihilism into is apparatus of domination," [Walter] Benjamin remarked during the depression of the 1930s, with an eye on the embittered realisms and bankrupt surrealisms of the time. To reflect on this nihilism, but also to have updated it and pushed it further, is the ambiguous achievement of the Aarholian line of Koons, Murakami and Hirst.

   Hal Foster, "The Medium is the Market" *London Review of Books* 30, no. 19, (October 9, 2008): 24.

CHAPTER ELEVEN. AISTHESIS

1. Basho Quotations, accessed online 7/28/09, yenra.com/quotations/basho.html. The poem continues:

   Your poetry issues of its own accord when you

   And the object become one—
   when you have plunged deep enough into the object
   to see something like a hidden glimmering there.
   However well phrased your poetry may be,
   if your feeling is not natural—
   if the object and yourself are separate—
   then your poetry is not true poetry
   but merely your subjective counterfeit.

2. Odell Shepard, ed., *The Heart of Thoreau's Journals* (New York: Dover, 1961), 210.
3. Norbert Mayer, "The New Berserkers," in Ralph Metzner, *The Well of Remembrance* (Boston: Shambhala), 1994, 135.

4. Gardner, *On Becoming a Novelist,* 30.
5. Lorca, *In Search of Duende,* 49.
6. Quoted in John Banville, "Emerson: 'A Few Inches from Calamity,'" *New York Review of Books* LVI, no. 19 (December 3, 2009): 33.
7. Rainer Maria Rilke, *Ten Sonnets to Orpheus,* Robert Bly, trans., *Mudra/Zephyr Image Magazine* (1972): sonnet #7.

CHAPTER TWELVE. SYNAESTHETIC WRITING AND THE BEGINNINGS OF ANALOGICAL THOUGHT

1. Wallace Stegner, *One Way to Spell Man* (Garden City, N.Y.: Doubleday, 1982), 44.
2. Mark Twain, Letter to Emeline Beach, 10 Feb 1868, accessed online: twainquotes.com/writing.html, accessed 7/28/09.
3. Gardner, *The Art of Fiction,* 36.
4. Gardner, *On Becoming a Novelist,* 20.
5. Gardner, *The Art of Fiction,* 36.
6. Gass, *Habitations of the Word,* 221.
7. John Lancaster, "Bond in Torment," *London Review of Books* 24, no. 17 (September 5, 2002): 23.
8. Gass, *Habitations of the Word,* 248.
9. Stegner, *One Way to Spell Man,* 13.

CHAPTER THIRTEEN. ANALOGICAL THINKING

1. Stegner, *One Way to Spell Man,* 44.
2. Bly, *News of the Univese,* 212–13.
3. Gass, *Habitations of the Word,* 207.
4. Henri Bortoft, *The Wholeness of Nature: Goethe's Way of Science* (Edinburgh, Scotland: Floris Books, 1996), 51.
5. Ibid., 53–54.
6. Buckminster Fuller discussed this in a number of his books. See, for example, *Synergetics* (New York: Macmillan, 1975), 81–90, especially page 85.
7. Bly, *American Poetry,* 262.
8. Douglas Miller, ed., *Goethe: Scientific Studies, The Collected Works,* vol. 12, (Princeton, N.J.: Princeton University Press, 1995), 39.
9. Gardner, *The Art of Fiction,* 37.
10. Ibid., 36.
11. Ibid., 38.

12. Quoted in Archibald Macleish, "An American Storyteller," *Time Magazine* (July 7, 1999).
13. Bly, *American Poetry,* 274–75.
14. Quoted in Ange Mlinko, "Little Philadelphias," *London Review of Books* 32, no. 6 (March 25, 2010): 26.
15. Quoted in Hazard Adams, *Critical Theory Since Plato* (New York: Harcourt Brace), 1971, 627–29.
16. Quoted in Stegner, *One Way to Spell Man,* 44.
17. Stephen King, *Secret Windows* (New York: Book of the Month Club, 2000), 326.

CHAPTER FOURTEEN. THE DREAMER AND THE "SECRET ROOM WHERE DREAMS PROWL"

1. Ryan Gilbey, "Brittany Murphy Obituary," *Guardian,* 21 December 2009.
2. Stegner, *One Way to Spell Man,* 45.
3. Dorothea Brande, *Becoming a Writer* (New York: Harcourt, Brace, and Company, 1934), 54–55.
4. Michael Quane, "Phase Change," in Jim Savage, ed., *Drawing Texts* (Aghabullogue, Ireland: Occasional Press, 2001), 70.
5. Quoted in John Gardner, *On Moral Fiction* (New York: Basic Books, 1978), 13.
6. Quane, "Phase Change," in *Drawing Texts,* 69.
7. Gass, *Habitations of the Word,* 264.
8. Ibid., 259.
9. Ibid., 255.
10. Ibid., 256.
11. Ibid., 257.
12. Quoted in Bortoft, *The Wholeness of Nature,* 265.
13. Bortoft, *The Wholeness of Nature,* 84.
14. Ibid.
15. Quoted in Robert Bly and Marion Woodman, *The Maiden King* (New York: Henry Holt, 1998), 5.
16. Michael Wood, "Let's Cut to the Wail," *London Review of Books* 31, no. 11 (June 11, 2009): 17.

CHAPTER FIFTEEN. THE IMAGINAL REALM

1. Bly and Woodman, *The Maiden King,* 5.
2. Quoted in Stephen King, *Secret Windows,* xvi.

3. Bly and Woodman, *The Maiden King,* 8–9.
4. Henry Corbin, *Mundus Imaginalis, or the Imaginary and the Imaginal,* online: hermetic.com/bey/mundus_imaginalis.htm, accessed 7/28/09.
5. Robert Faggen, *The Notebooks of Robert Frost* (Cambridge, Mass.: Harvard University Press, 2006), 267.
6. Quoted in Sophy Burnham, *For Writers Only* (New York: Ballantine, 1994), 12.
7. Samuel Delany, *The Einstein Intersection* (New York: Ace, 1967), 12.
8. Dunning, *The Bookman's Wake,* 57.
9. Quoted in Thomas Jones, "Liquid Fiction," *London Review of Books* 24 no. 8, (April 25, 2002): 9. Also: Francis Spufford, *The Child That Books Built* (New York: Picador, 2002), 64–65.
10. Delany, *The Einstein Intersection,* 124.
11. Corbin, *Mundus Imaginalis,* online, accessed 7/28/09.
12. Ptolemy Tompkins, "Recovering a Visionary Geography: Henry Corbin and the Missing Ingredient of our Culture of Images," online: seriousseekers.com/NewsandArticles/article_tompkins_p_recoveringvisionary.htm, accessed 7/28/09.
13. Rainer Maria Rilke, *The Notebooks of Malte Laurids Brigge,* M. D. Herter, trans. (New York: Norton, 1949), 15–16.
14. Lorca, *In Search of Duende,* 49.
15. Ibid., 61.
16. Gass, *Habitations of the Word,* 264.

CHAPTER SIXTEEN. POESIS

1. Theodore Sturgeon, "Slow Sculpture," in *Sturgeon is Alive and Well* (New York: Putnam, 1971), 73.

CHAPTER SEVENTEEN. THE FIRST DRAFT AND THE BEGINNINGS OF REVISION

1. Robert Bly, ed. *The Darkness Around Us Is Deep,* xx.
2. Gardner, *The Art of Fiction,* 68–69.

CHAPTER EIGHTEEN. PROBLEMS AND FURTHER REVISIONING

1. Sturgeon, "Slow Sculpture" in *Sturgeon is Alive and Well,* 73.
2. Quoted in Bly, Anonymous, "Writing for a Living: A Joy or a Chore?" *Guardian,* 3 March 2009.

3. Ibid.
4. Gardner, *The Art of Fiction,* 114.
5. Bly, *American Poetry,* 91.
6. Ueland, *If You Want to Write,* 9.
7. Gass, *Habitations of the Word,* 264.

CHAPTER NINETEEN. CLICHÉD THINKING AND KILLING THE GENUINE

1. Misha Glenny, *McMafia* (New York: Knopf, 2008), 109. Note: Belinda Brooks-Gordon, in her book *The Price of Sex* (Devon, UK: Willan Publishing, 2006), comments people like Glenny "do not seem able to accept that some women choose to sell sex and have trouble supporting those who do, preferring instead to use the violence, in the use of personal testimony, as a tool to pursue the impossible task of abolition at the expense of all in sex work. Personal testimony is typical of revivalist evangelical gathering. Personal testimony turns personal suffering into performance art. It is significant that personal testimony is such an important tool in abolitionist tactics. The parallels with revivalist religion include emotional manipulation and hysteria, as well as the framing of conflicting ideas as a battle between the 'good'—those who accept their moral statements about sex work—and the 'evil'—those who don't" (page 207).
2. *Harpers Magazine* (August 2007): 23–24.
3. Aphrodite Phoenix, *A Woman Whose Calling is Men, Book Two: Her Visions and Advocacies* (Boca Raton, Fla.: Universal Publishers, 2007), 28. This is a remarkable book, probably the best book about sex work by a sex worker in print. And . . . it's a how-to book.
4. Phoenix, *A Woman Whose Calling is Men,* 18.
5. Brooks-Gordon, Belinda, "Playing Politics with Sex Workers," *Guardian,* 16 October 2008. It turns out, however, that even these figures are misleading; many of the "trafficked" women were labeled trafficked through semantics, not reality. Under the law that led to the Pentameter raids, trafficked means any prostitute who was assisted with international travel even if it was intentional and desired on the prostitute's part. Government pronouncements proclaimed that 528 "traffickers" had been arrested. A *Guardian* newspaper in-depth study of the Pentameter raids found that, on the contrary, as the article title states: "Inquiry fails to find a single trafficker who forced anybody into prostitution." The author comments that his research found that government-issued

statements regarding the numbers of trafficked sex workers "were either based on distortions of quoted sources or fabrications without any source at all." Nick Davies, *Guardian,* 20 October 2009.

6. Prostitutes Education Network, Online at bayswan.org/stats.html, accessed 12/28/08.
7. Laura María Agustín, *Sex at the Margins* (London: Zed Books, 2007), 68–69.
8. Agustín, *Sex at the Margins,* 172–74.
9. Etheridge Knight, "For Freckle-Faced Gerald," *The Essential Etheridge Knight* (Pittsburgh, Pa.: University of Pittsburgh Press, 1986), 19.
10. Bly, *American Poetry,* 107.
11. Jenny Diski in her article "Rumour is Utterly Unfounded," *London Review of Books* 31, no. 19 (October 8, 2009), traces this kind of moral crusading back in time, attaching it more to our culturally repressed sexuality, fear of the other, and a desire to sell newspapers than anything else. She notes: "In the 1920s, white slavery was a delicious danger: sinister aristocrats and foreign traders (often Jews or Indians) repeatedly abducted blonde, blue-eyed women, although no evidence of this was ever produced." The current obsession with trafficked sex workers is the same; it's the white slavery scare reworked for a later era.
12. Nick Davies, "Inquiry fails to find single trafficker who forced anybody into prostitution," *Guardian,* 20 October 2009. There is an apparently inexhaustible degree of emotive numbering that occurs in this area. As the television show *Frontline* reported, "When it comes to statistics, trafficking of girls and women is one of several highly emotive issues which seem to overwhelm critical faculties. Numbers seem to take on a life of their own, gaining acceptance through repetition, often with little inquiry into their derivations." [pbs.org/wgbh/pages/frontline/slaves/etc/stats.html, accessed 7/27/09] *Frontline* (and others) indicate that out of the 27 million people worldwide who are considered to exist in a state of forced bondage, that is, slavery, and whom can then be trafficked as chattel possessions, only about 700,000 of them (according to the FBI) are trafficked. But these figures vary widely from year to year among the various groups, from lows of 400,000 to highs of 4,000,000, and these are the same groups talking about the same years. (The UN, in 2001, changed its figures for human trafficking in 2000 from four million to one million.) Part of the trouble is that the definition of trafficking is very fluid and often based on emotive attitudes about sex and sex work, not the reality of whether someone is or is not being trafficked. Trafficking is, in essence, part of the worldwide slave trade, the economic point of which is forced labor, not sex per se. Forced

labor will be used in whatever area in which it will produce economic benefit to the slave owners. Two excellent books on the subject are Benjamin Skinner's *A Crime So Monstrous* (New York: Free Press, 2008) and Kevin Bales's *Disposable People* (Berkeley: University of California Press, 2000).

13. Gardner, *The Art of Fiction,* 116.
14. These figures can be found a number of places including Wikipedia: http://en.wikipedia.org/wiki/Incarceration_in_the_United_States (accessed July 13, 2010).
15. Here are two examples of the Law of Unintended Consequences; they aren't unusual:

    1) Laws creating indefinite detention without trial and without recourse to habeus corpus did not begin with the second Bush administration. They began with laws that incarcerated sexual offenders (who had completed their sentences) for indeterminate periods, up to life, if they were felt—by a single person or committee—to possibly present any future danger to society. A life sentence for something someone *might* do. The rationale was upheld by the Supreme Court and then extended to *accused* terrorists who, even if found innocent of terrorism, can be held for life in maximum security prisons. This rationale will be extended to other *possibly* dangerous people over time for that is the way governments work. Always.
    2) The woman who was one of the primary voices for mandatory airbags in automobiles in the United States reportedly demanded them because her child was killed in an automobile collision and she was convinced that an airbag would have saved her child's life. The auto companies insisted that airbag technology had not been tested enough to determine safety; the public outcry overrode their objections and airbags were mandated by Congress. The first casualties of airbags? Children. They were killed, sometimes decapitated, by deploying airbags.

    The law of unintended consequences always works this way when the drama triangle is used as a lens through which to view the world and solve problems.

16. Clarissa Pinkola Estes, from "Letter to the Prince on the Anniversary of Kristallnacht," accessed on Wikipedia, 9/17/09.
17. Gardner, *On Moral Fiction,* 117.
18. Mike Williams, *The Hop of the Small-Time Toad* (Denver, Colo.: Bread and Butter Press, 1981), 61.

19. I want to emphasize that the purpose of this chapter, which has numerous elements, has *nothing* to do with prostitution. Rather, it is intended to show that such topics, which possess strong but relatively unexamined emotional dynamics, are a great deal more complex than most writings about them reveal. Although many people on both the left and right wish to permanently stop all forms of prostitution—the left because it demeans women and is an expression of the patriarchal domination of women, the right because it is immoral—neither group is willing to genuinely look at what women who work as prostitutes think about it. Once you do, it becomes clear that the issue is far more complex than commonly thought. This complexity runs through nearly every aspect of our lives and cultures. It touches on gender relationships, on politics and power, how individuals feel about their own sexuality and that of others; it touches on social welfare movements and the motives of their proponents, on how religionists feel about sexuality, and a great deal more. Thus, a nonideological, non–group think, exploration of the issue presents an opportunity for a work of great depth and subtlety, that is, for art.

CHAPTER TWENTY. HIDDEN BAGGAGE

1. Gardner, *On Becoming a Novelist,* 15.
2. Ibid., 12.
3. Adam Phillips, "In Praise of Difficult Children," *London Review of Books* 31, no. 3, (February 12, 2009): 16.
4. K. David Harrison, *When Languages Die* (New York: Oxford University Press, 2007), 25.
5. Ibid., 9–10.
6. Stephen Buchmann and Gary Paul Nabhan, *The Forgotten Pollinators* (Washington, D.C.: Island Press, 1996), 86.
7. Ken Wilber, *A Brief History of Everything* (Boston: Shambhala, 1996), 149.
8. Quoted in Bly, *News of the Universe,* 44.
9. From "Why Mira Can't Go Back to Her Old House" in Robert Bly, trans., *Mirabai* (Penland, N.C.: Squid Ink, 1993).
10. Bly, *News of Universe,* 33–34.
11. Mary Midgley, *The Myths We Live By* (London: Routledge, 2004), 119. Note: Lorin Stein in "Huffing Along" *London Review of Books* 24, no. 15 (August 8, 2002): 17–18, explores this same dynamic in evangelical fiction, specifically Stephen Carter's *The Emperor of Ocean Park.* Stein's comments make clear

that, while the overt beliefs of each writer are very different, the motivations of both Ken Wilber and Carter are similar. They write not so much in defense of what they believe but rather use their writing to impose those beliefs on the reader from without. The motivations in both cases are evangelical. (Midgley brilliantly explores the identical nature of evangelical foundationalists and religious evangelicals in her book *Myths We Live By.*) Neither can allow their readers to come to their own decisions regarding either Science or Christianity. Neither has any inherent trust in the individual's capacity to choose—or to reason. If any choice is made that lies outside the author's frame, the choice is wrong and occurs either because of the intellectual limitations of the individual or their succumbing to improper thinking—usually because of some sort of moral weakness—inflicted on them by deluded outside forces.

12. Midgley, *The Myths We Live By,* 91.
13. Ibid., 114.
14. Gass, *Habitations of the Word,* 213.

CHAPTER TWENTY-ONE. SOME SUBTLE REFINEMENTS OF THE ART

1. Bly, *American Poetry,* 209.
2. Gardner, *The Art of Fiction,* 69.
3. Bly, *American Poetry,* 50.
4. Gardner, *The Art of Fiction,* 46.
5. Zelazny, *Damnation Alley,* 102.
6. Williams, *The Hop of the Small-Time Toad,* 64–5.
7. Richard Bandler and John Grinder, *Frogs into Princes* (Moab, Utah: Real People Press, 1979), 10.
8. Ibid., 11.
9. Ibid.
10. Gass, *Habitations of the Word,* 122.
11. Robert Macfarlane, "Force of Nature," *Guardian,* 16 September 2006.
12. Quoted in Leah Price, "The Tangible Page," *London Review of Books* 24, no.21 (October 31, 2002): 36.
13. Deborah Eisenberg, "The Genius of Peter Nadas," *New York Review of Books* 55, no. 12 (July 17, 2008): 50.
14. Quoted in *The Authors Guild Bulletin* (Spring 2008): 21.
15. Quoted in Leah Price, "The Tangible Page," *London Review of Books,* 37.

16. Buhner, *The Taste of Wild Water,* 6–7.
17. Daniel Soar, "It Had Better Be Big," *London Review of Books* 24, no. 15 (August 8, 2002): 19.
18. Quoted in Bly, *American Poetry,* 294.
19. Gass, *Habitations of the Word,* 263.
20. Jonathan Raban, "The Prodigious Pessimist," *New York Review of Books,* LV, no. 20 (December 18, 2008): 66.
21. Bly, *American Poetry,* 32–33.
22. Ibid., 195.
23. Ibid., 209.
24. Margalit Fox, "Raymond Federman, Avant–Garde Novelist and Beckett Scholar, Dies at 81," *New York Times,* 13 October 2009.
25. Robert Harrison, "A Great Conservationist, by Jingo," *New York Review of Books* LVI, no. 17 (November 5, 2009): 44.
26. Gardner, *The Art of Fiction,* 15–16.

CHAPTER TWENTY-TWO. GRAMMAR NAZIS AND EDITORS-FROM-HELL

1. Gass, *Habitations of the Word,* 225.
2. Steven Pinker, "Oaf of Office," *New York Times,* 22 January 2009.
3. *Cambridge Guide to English Usage,* 2004, 538.
4. Henry Churchyard, Online at: crossmyt.com/hc/linghebr/austheir.html, accessed, 3/1/09.
5. Http://wikipedia.org/wiki/Singular_they, accessed 3/1/09.
6. Gardner, *On Becoming a Novelist,* 107.
7. John Steinbeck, Letter to Pascal Covici, 1952, included as the final passage of *Journal of a Novel.* My copy: xerox from John Dunning, np, nd.
8. James Kelman, "Make Yer Point," *Guardian,* 11 August 2007.

CHAPTER TWENTY-THREE. SOME FINAL WORDS ON THE WRITING LIFE

1. Annie Le Brun, *The Reality Overload: The Assault on the Imaginal Realm* (Rochester, Vt.: Inner Traditions), 2008, 3.
2. Ibid., 6.
3. Bill Mollison, *Travels in Dreams* (Tyalgum, NSW, Australia: Tagari Publications, 1996), 10–12.

4. Gardner, *On Moral Fiction,* 5.
5. Gardner, *The Art of Fiction,* 43.
6. Le Brun, *The Reality Overload,* 56.
7. Ibid., 42.
8. Lorraine Daston, "Saintly Resonances," *London Review of Books* 24, no. 21 (October 31, 2002): 16.
9. John Ralston Saul, *Voltaire's Bastards* (New York: Vintage, 1993), 25.
10. Midgley, *The Myths We Live By,* 13.
11. Or as Chris Hedges puts it, "The capacity to exercise moral autonomy, the capacity to refuse to cooperate, offers us the only route left to personal freedom and a life with meaning. . . . Rebellion allows us to be free and independent human beings, but rebellion also chips away, however imperceptibly, at the edifice of the oppressor and sustains the dim flames of hope and love. And in moments of profound human despair these flames are never insignificant. They keep alive the capacity to be human. (Chris Hedges, "Calling All Rebels" online @ CommonDreams.org, accessed 3/8/2010.)

APPENDIX A. THE PEOPLE IN PUBLISHING AND THE BUSINESS END OF THE PROFESSION

1. All figures, except the 400,000 books sold or distributed, which is from Bowker, are from www.parapublishing.com, accessed 9/14/09.
2. From: www.rampant–books.com/mgt_amazon_sales_rank.htm, accessed 1/05/09.
3. Roy Blount Jr. "From the President," *The Authors Guild Bulletin* (Winter 2009): 4.

APPENDIX C. FURTHER READING, RESOURCES, AND RECOMMENDATIONS

1. Bly, *Selected Poems of Lorca and Jimenez,* 4.

Bibliography

Agustín, Laura María. *Sex at the Margins*. London: Zed Books, 1988.

Anonymous. "Writing for a Living: A Joy or a Chore?" *Guardian,* 3 March 2009.

Applebaum, Anne. "Yesterday's Man?" *New York Review of Books* LVII, no. 2 (February 11, 2010): 10–11.

Applebaum, Judith. *How to Get Happily Published,* 4th ed. New York: HarperPerennial, 1982.

The Authors Guild Bulletin (Spring 2008).

Bandler, Richard, and John Grinder. *Frogs into Princes*. Moab, Utah: Real People Press, 1979.

Banville, John. "Emerson: 'A Few Inches from Calamity.'" *New York Review of Books* LVI, no. 19 (December 3, 2009): 33–35.

Basho. Quotations. Online at: yenra.com/quotations/basho.html, accessed 7/28/09.

Benfey, Christopher. "The Storm Over Robert Frost." *New York Review of Books* LV, no. 19 (December 4, 2009).

Bester, Alfred. *Starlight*. Garden City, New York: Doubleday, 1976.

Beston, Henry. *Herbs and the Earth*. New York: David Godine, 1990.

Blount, Roy, Jr. "From the President." *Authors Guild Bulletin* (Winter 2009): 4.

Bly, Robert. *American Poetry: Wilderness and Domesticity*. New York: Harper and Row, 1990.

———. Introduction to: *The Darkness Around Us Is Deep: Selected Poems of William Stafford*. New York: HarperPerennial, 1993.

———. *The Eight Stages of Translation*. St. Paul, Minn.: Ally Press, 1991.

———. *Leaping Poetry: An Idea with Poems and Translations*. Boston: Beacon Press, 1975.

———. *News of the Universe.* San Francisco: Sierra Club Books, 1980.

———. *Pablo Neruda: Twenty Poems.* Madison, Minn.: The Sixties Press, 1967.

———. *Selected Poems of Lorca and Jiminez.* Boston: Beacon Press, 1973.

———. *Times Alone: The Selected Poems of Antonio Machado.* Middletown, Conn.: Wesleyan University Press, 1983.

———. *The Winged Life: The Poetic Voice of Henry David Thoreau.* San Francisco: Sierra Club Books, 1986.

Bly, Robert, and Jane Hirschfield. *Mirabai: Ecstatic Poems.* Boston: Beacon Press, 2004.

Bly, Robert, and Marion Woodman. *The Maiden King.* New York: Henry Holt, 1998.

Bortoft, Henri. *The Wholeness of Nature: Goethe's Way of Science.* Hudson, New York: Lindisfarne Books, 1996.

Bowden, Charles. "The Wisdom of Rats." *Harper's Magazine* (January 2010): 13.

Brande, Dorothea. *Becoming a Writer.* New York: Harcourt, Brace, 1934.

Brooks-Gordon, Belinda. "Playing Politics with Sex Workers." *Guardian,* 16 October 2008.

———. *The Price of Sex: Prostitution, Policy, and Society.* Devon, UK: Willan Publishing, 2006.

Broughton, Irv. *The Writer's Mind,* vols. 1–2. Fayetteville: University of Arkansas Press, 1989, 1990.

Buchmann, Steven, and Gary Paul Nabhan. *The Forgotten Pollinators.* Washington, D.C.: Island Press, 1996.

Buhner, Stephen Harrod. *The Lost Language of Plants.* White River Junction, Vt.: Chelsea Green Publishing, 2002.

———. *The Secret Teachings of Plants.* Rochester, Vt.: Bear & Company, 2004.

Burnham, Sophy. *For Writers Only.* New York: Ballantine, 1994.

Cambridge Guide to English Usage. Cambridge, UK: Cambridge University Press, 2004.

Chandler, Raymond. *Later Novels and Other Writings.* New York: The Library of America, 1995.

Cheney, Theodore Rees. *Writing Creative Nonfiction: Fiction Techniques for Crafting Great Nonfiction.* Ten Speed Press, 2001.

The Chicago Manual of Style, 14th ed. Chicago, Ill.: University of Chicago Press, 1993.

Churchyard, Henry. Online at: crossmyt.com/hc/linghebr/austheir.html, accessed, 3/1/09.

Clouse, Barbara Fine. *265 Troubleshooting Strategies for Writing Nonfiction*. New York: McGraw Hill, 2005.

Corbin, Henry. *Mundus Imaginalis, or the Imaginary and the Imaginal*. Online at: hermetic.com/bey/mundus_imaginalis.htm, accessed 7/28/09.

———. *Swedenborg and Esoteric Islam*. Westchester, Pa.: Swedenborg Foundation, 1995.

Davies, Nick. "Inquiry fails to find single trafficker who forced anybody into prostitution." *Guardian,* 20 October 2009.

Delany, Samuel. *The Einstein Intersection*. New York: Ace, 1967.

Dirda, Michael. "Wake Up and Dream." *New York Review of Books* LVII, no. 1 (January 14, 2010): 49–52.

Diski, Jenny. "Rumour is Utterly Unfounded." *London Review of Books* 31, no. 19, (October 8, 2009).

Dunning, John. *The Bookman's Wake*. New York: Scribner, 1995.

———. Introduction to *The Holland Suggestions*. New York: Pocket Books, 1997.

Eckermann, Johann Peter. *Conversations with Goethe*. New York: Da Capo Press, 1998.

Eisenberg, Deborah. "The Genius of Peter Nadas." *New York Review of Books* 55, no. 12 (July 17, 2008).

Epstein, Jason. *Book Business*. New York: Norton, 2001.

Faggen, Robert. *The Notebooks of Robert Frost*. Cambridge, Mass.: Harvard University Press, 2006.

Felstiner, John. *Can Poetry Save the Earth?* New Haven, Conn.: Yale University Press, 2009.

Forche, Carolyn, and Philip Gerard. *Writing Creative Nonfiction*. Cincinnati, Ohio: Story Press, 2001.

Foster, Hal. "The Medium is the Market." *London Review of Books* 30, no. 19 (October 9, 2008): 23–24.

Fox, Margalit. "Raymond Federman, Avant-Garde Novelist and Beckett Scholar, Dies at 81." *New York Times,* 13 October 2009.

Franklin, John. *Writing for Story*. New York: Plume, 1994.

Gardner, John. *The Art of Fiction*. New York: Vintage, 1991.

———. *On Becoming a Novelist*. New York: W. W. Norton, 1999.

———. *On Moral Fiction*. New York: Basic Books, 1978.

———. *On Writers and Writing*. New York: Addison-Wesley, 1994.

Gass, William. *Fiction and the Figures of Life*. Boston: David Godine, 1989.

———. *Finding a Form*. New York: Knopf, 1996.

———. *Habitations of the Word*. Ithaca, N.Y.: Cornell University Press, 1985.

———. *Reading Rilke: Reflections on the Problems of Translations*. New York: Knopf, 1999.

———. *The World Within the Word*. Boston: David Godine, 1989.

Gilbey, Ryan. "Brittany Murphy Obituary." *Guardian,* 21 December 2009.

Glenny, Misha. *McMafia*. New York: Knopf, 2008.

Goldberg, Natalie. *Writing Down the Bones*. Boston: Shambhala, 1986.

Gordon, Karen Elizabeth. *The New Well-Tempered Sentence*. New York: Ticknor and Fields, 1993.

Griffiths, Jay. *Wild: An Elemental Journey*. New York: Jeremy P. Tarcher, 2006.

Grudin, Robert. *The Grace of Great Things*. New York: Ticknor and Fields, 1990.

Guelberth, Cedar Rose, and Dan Chiras. *The Natural Plaster Book*. Gabriola Island, B.C., Canada: New Society Publishers, 2003.

Gutkind, Lee. *The Art of Creative Nonfiction*. New York: Wiley, 1997.

Hacker, Diana. *A Writer's Reference,* New York: St. Martins Press, 1989.

Hammerschlag, Carl, and Howard Silverman. *Healing Ceremonies*. New York: Perigee, 1997.

Harrison, K. David. *When Languages Die*. New York: Oxford University Press, 2007.

Hartman, Geoffrey. *Scars of the Spirit: The Struggle Against Inauthenticity*. New York: Palgrave Macmillan, 2002.

Hedges, Chris. "Calling All Rebels." Online at: CommonDreams.org, accessed 3/8/2010.

———. "Chris Hedges on Alex S. Jones' 'Losing the News'." Online at: Truthdig.com, accessed 8/14/2009.

———. "The Creed of Objectivity Killed the News." Online at: Truthdig.com, accessed 2/1/2010.

———. "The War on Language." Online at: Truthdig.com, accessed 9/29/2009.

Hefron, Jack. *The Best Writing on Writing*, vol. 2. Cincinnati, Ohio: Story Press, 1995.

Hilberg, Raul. *Sources of Holocaust Research*. Chicago, Ill.: Ivan Dee, 2001.

Hillman, James. *A Blue Fire*. New York: HarperPerennial, 1989.

———. *The Soul's Code*. New York: Random House, 1996.

———. *The Thought of the Heart and the Soul of the World*. Woodstock, Conn.: Spring Publications, 1995.

Jaggi, Maya. "You Can't Help Being What You Write: An Interview with Tom Stoppard." *Guardian,* 6 September 2008.

Jones, Thomas. "Liquid Fiction." *London Review of Books* 24, no. 8 (April 25, 2002).

Keeling, Richard. *Cry for Luck*. Berkeley: University of California Press, 1992.

Kelman, James. "Make Yer Point." *Guardian,* 11 August 2007.

King, Stephen. *Secret Windows*. New York: Book of the Month Club, 2000.

Krenov, James. *The Fine Art of Cabinetmaking*. New York: Van Nostrand Reinhold, 1977.

Kundera, Milan. *The Art of the Novel*. New York: Grove Press, 1988.

Lamott, Anne. *Bird by Bird*. New York: Pantheon, 1994.

Lancaster, John. "Bond in Torment." *London Review of Books* 24, no. 17 (September 5, 2002).

Lappe, Marc. *Of All Things Most Yielding*. San Francisco: Friends of the Earth, 1973.

Le Brun, Annie. *The Reality Overload: The Assault on the Imaginal Realm*. Rochester, Vt.: Inner Traditions, 2008.

Le Guin, Ursula. *Steering the Craft*. Portland, Ore.: Eighth Mountain Press, 1998.

Leopold, Aldo. *A Sand County Almanac*. New York: Ballantine, 1991.

Lessing, Doris. "Questions You Should Never Ask a Writer." *New York Times,* 13 October 2007.

Lorca, Federico Garcia. *In Search of Duende*. New York: New Directions Publishing, 1998.

Macfarlane, Robert. "Force of Nature." *Guardian,* 16 September 2006.

Machado, Antonio. *Twenty Proverbs,* translated by Robert Bly and Don Olsen. Marshall, Minn.: Ox Head Press, 1981, proverb #6.

Macleish, Archibald. "An American Storyteller." *Time Magazine* (July 7, 1999).

Macmillan, Stephanie. "Artists Raise Your Weapons." Online at: CommonDreams .org, accessed 12/10/2009.

MacShane, Frank, ed. *Selected Letters of Raymond Chandler*. New York: Columbia University Press, 1981.

Metzner, Ralph. *The Well of Remembrance*. Boston: Shambhala, 1994.

Midgley, Mary. *The Myths We Live By*. London: Routledge, 2004.

Miller, Douglas, ed. *Goethe: Scientific Studies; The Collected Works*, vol. 12. Princeton, N.J.: Princeton University Press, 1995.

Mlinko, Ange. "Little Philadelphias." *London Review of Books* 32, no. 6 (March 25, 2010): 25–26.

Mollison, Bill. *Travels in Dreams.* Tyalgum, NSW, Australia: Tagari, 1996.

Moyers, Bill. *Fooling with Words.* New York: Morrow, 1999.

Neider, Charles, ed. *The Autobiography of Mark Twain.* New York: Harper and Row, 1959.

Normandi, Carol, and Laurelee Roark. *It's Not About Food.* New York: Perigee, 1999.

Pendell, Dale. *The Gold Dust Wilderness.* np: privately printed, 1971.

———. *Pharmako/Dynamis.* San Francisco: Mercury House, 2002.

———. *Pharmako/Gnosis.* San Francisco: Mercury House, 2005.

———. *Pharmako/Poeia.* San Francisco: Mercury House, 1995.

Phillips, Adam. "In Praise of Difficult Children." *London Review of Books* 31, no. 3 (February 12, 2009), 16.

Phoenix, Aphrodite. *A Woman Whose Calling Is Men*, vols. 1–3. Boca Raton, Fla.: Universal Publishers, 2007.

Pinker, Steven. "Oaf of Office." *New York Times,* 22 January 2009.

Price, Leah. "The Tangible Page." *London Review of Books* 24, no. 21 (October 31, 2002).

Prostitutes Education Network. Online at: www.bayswan.org/stats.html, accessed 12/28/08.

Quane, Michael. "Phase Change" in *Drawing Texts.* Jim Savage, ed. Aghabullogue, Ireland: Occasional Press, 2001.

Raban, Jonathan. "The Prodigious Pessimist." *New York Review of Books* LV, no. 20 (December 18, 2008).

Rilke, Rainer Maria. *Letters to a Young Poet.* New York: Dover, 2002.

———. *The Notebooks of Malte Laurids Brigge.* New York: Norton, 1992.

———. *Ten Sonnets to Orpheus.* Translated by Robert Bly. *Mudra/Zephyr Image Magazine,* 1972, sonnet #7.

Robb, Laura. *Nonfiction Writing from the Inside Out,* 4th ed. Santa Barbara, Calif.: Para Publishing, 2005.

Root, Robert, and Michael Steinberg. *The Fourth Genre.* Boston: Allyn and Bacon, 1999.

Ruas, Charles. *Conversations with American Writers.* New York: Knopf, 1985.

Saul, John Ralston. *Voltaire's Bastards: The Dictatorship of Reason in the West.* New York: Vintage, 1992.

Scharnhorst, Gary, ed. *Mark Twain: The Complete Interviews.* Tuscaloosa: University of Alabama Press, 2006.

Shaw, Eva. *Writing the Nonfiction Book (The Successful Writer's Guide)*. Loveland, Colo.: Loveland Press, 1999.

Shepard, Odell. *The Heart of Thoreau's Journals*. New York: Dover, 1961.

Shields, David. *Reality Hunger: A Manifesto*. New York: Alfred A. Knopf, 2010. (I accessed an unofficial proof published by the author in 2009 while writing this book.)

Siegel, Lee. *Falling Upwards: Essays in Defense of the Imagination*. New York: Basic Books, 2006.

Simpson, David. "At the Opium Factory." *London Review of Books* 31, no. 20 (October 22, 2009): 23–24.

Soar, Daniel. "It Had Better Be Big." *London Review of Books* 24, no. 15 (August 8, 2002).

Spufford, Francis. *The Child That Books Built*. London: Faber, 2002.

Stafford, William. *The Answers Are Inside the Mountains*. Ann Arbor: University of Michigan Press, 2003.

———. *Crossing Unmarked Snow: Further Views on the Writer's Vocation*. Ann Arbor: University of Michigan Press, 1998.

———. *Writing the Australian Crawl: Views on the Writer's Vocation*. Ann Arbor: University of Michigan Press, 1978.

———. *You Must Revise Your Life*. Ann Arbor: University of Michigan Press, 1986.

Stegner, Wallace. *One Way to Spell Man*. Garden City, New York: Doubleday, 1982.

Stein, Loren. "Huffing Along." *London Review of Books* 24, no. 15 (August 8, 2002).

Steinbeck, John. Letter to Pascal Covici, New York, 1952, which appeared as the final passage of *Journal of a Novel*.

Strunk, William, and E. B. White. *The Elements of Style*, 3rd ed. New York: Macmillan, 1979.

Sturgeon, Theodore. "Slow Sculpture" in *Sturgeon Is Alive and Well*. New York: Putnam, 1971.

Tompkins, Ptolemy. "Recovering a Visionary Geography: Henry Corbin and the Missing Ingredient of Our Culture of Images." Online at: seriousseekers.com/NewsandArticles/article_tompkins_p_recoveringvisionary. htm, accessed 7/28/09.

Twain, Mark. Letter to Emeline Beach, 10 Feb 1868. Online at: twainquotes.com/writing.html, accessed 7/28/09.

Ueland, Brenda. *If You Want to Write: A Book about Art, Independence, and Spirit,* 2nd ed. St. Paul, Minn.: Graywolf Press, 1987.

Watson, Lyall. "The Biology of Being: A Natural History of Consciousness" in David Lorimer, ed., *The Spirit of Science.* New York: Continuum International Publishing Group, 1999.

Wilber, Ken. *A Brief History of Everything.* Boston, Mass.: Shambhala, 1996.

Williams, Mike. *The Hop of the Small-Time Toad.* Denver, Colo.: Bread and Butter Press, 1981.

Wood, Michael. "Let's Cut to the Wail." *London Review of Books* 31, no. 11 (June 11, 2009).

Zelazny, Roger. *Damnation Alley.* New York: Berkeley, 1976, 102.

Zinsser, William. *On Writing Well: The Classic Guide to Writing Nonfiction,* 30th Anniversary Edition. New York: HarperCollins, 2006.

About the Author

Stephen Harrod Buhner is a working writer and has been, full time, since 1995. He is the author of thirteen works of nonfiction and one of poetry. They have been translated into twelve languages and nominated for eleven awards, winning eight. He is most proud of the awards given in recognition of *The Lost Language of Plants*—a Nautilus Award for Best Environmental Book of 2002 and its selection as a BBC Environmental Book of the Month. Stephen lectures and teaches regularly throughout the U.S. and the Western European Isles. His website is www.gaianstudies.org.

ALSO BY STEPHEN HARROD BUHNER

Nonfiction

The Lost Language of Plants • One Spirit Many Peoples • Sacred and Herbal Healing Beers: The Secrets of Ancient Fermentation • Sacred Plant Medicine • The Secret Teachings of Plants

Poetry

The Taste of Wild Water: Poems and Stories Found While Walking in Woods

Ecological Medicine

The Fasting Path • Healing Lyme • Herbal Antibiotics • Herbs for Hepatitis C and the Liver • The Natural Testosterone Plan • Vital Man

Index